# PRAISE FOR ERIC HAMMEL'S
## *ACES AGAINST JAPAN*

"Air combat, as recounted in Eric Hammel's *ACES AGAINST JAPAN,* has the mystic essence of a time warp. The action blazed across the skies nearly half-a-century ago, but is masterfully told with the page-turning speed of today's super-sonic jet fighters."

— Bill D. Ross, author of *Iwo Jima: Legacy of Valor*
and *Peleliu: Tragic Triumph*

"Each account delivers something intensely personal about the Pacific air war. . . . Intriguing. . . ."

— Barrett Tillman,
*American Fighter Aces Association Book Review*

"Eric Hammel brings to life the war in the Pacific and East Asia in *ACES AGAINST JAPAN.* . . . A thoroughly enjoyable foray into the cockpits of the World War II fighter pilots whose skills and bravery gained air superiority for Allied forces in the Pacific and ultimately contributed mightily to the demise of Imperial Japan."

— Major Michael W. Libbee, U.S. Army,
*The Friday Review of Defense Literature*

"*ACES AGAINST JAPAN* is a treat that deftly blends a chronology of the Pacific war . . . with tales of exhilarating escapes and life raft survival. . . . With these former pilots well into their 70s, accounts such as these will only get rarer. Fortunately, they are told here ever so eloquently."

— Peter Donahue, *Providence Sunday Journal*

**Books by Eric Hammel**

CHOSIN: Heroic Ordeal of the Korean War
THE ROOT: The Marines in Beirut, August 1982
GUADALCANAL: Starvation Island
GUADALCANAL: The Carrier Battles
GUADALCANAL: Decision at Sea
KHE SANH: Seige in the Clouds, An Oral History
AMBUSH VALLEY: I Corps, Vietnam 1967
ACES AGAINST JAPAN*
ACES AGAINST GERMANY*

*Published by POCKET BOOKS

# ACES AGAINST JAPAN

## ERIC HAMMEL

**POCKET BOOKS**

New York   London   Toronto   Sydney   Tokyo   Singapore

*This book is dedicated to
all the American airmen
who helped bring about the
great victory in Asia
and the Pacific.*

POCKET BOOKS, a division of Simon & Schuster Inc.
1230 Avenue of the Americas, New York, NY 10020

Copyright © 1992 by Eric Hammel

Published by arrangement with Presido Press

ISBN: 0-671-52908-0

First Pocket Books printing September 1995

10  9  8  7  6  5  4  3  2  1

POCKET and colophon are registered trademarks of
Simon & Schuster Inc.

Cover photo courtesy of Jeffrey Ethell

Printed in the U.S.A.

# CONTENTS

# CONTENTS

CONTENTS

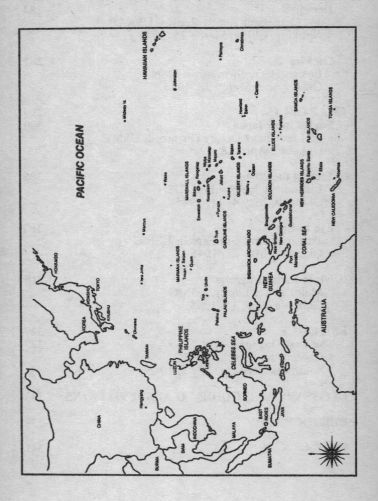

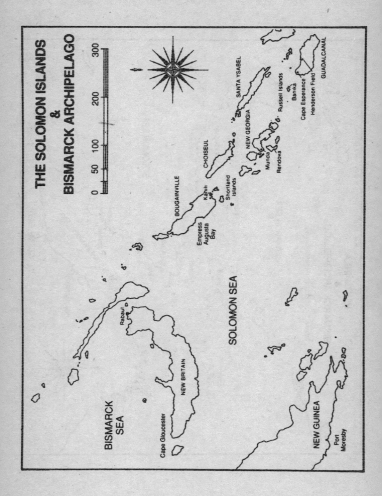

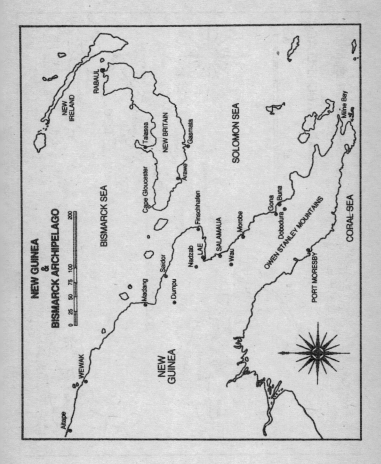

# PROLOGUE

First there were the boys who dreamed of flight. They came by their dreams in a thousand different ways—some on the laps of their fathers, who had flown in the Great War; others from seeing the gypsy barnstormers at carnivals and fairs; others from watching the cropdusters come to spray their fathers' fields; and others merely from reading or building model airplanes. They dreamed the dreams of the sky, and when their nation called upon them to stand fast in a hostile world, they raised their hands and asked to be chosen so that their boyhood dreams of flight—and war among the clouds—might be fulfilled.

That there were bases at which they could train and airplanes for them to fly in the early days was a miracle of political conniving, for as late as 1934 a parsimonious Congress saw to it that the U.S. Army Air Corps was able to field only three permanent fighter squadrons. The U.S. Navy had only five.

Until 1934, all U.S. service officer-pilots were Regular officers, usually West Point or Annapolis graduates. To get around officer-strength ceilings imposed by the Congress, the Navy established a thin corps of enlisted pilots (Naval Aviation Pilots, or NAPs—about 30 percent of all pilots) who were specially selected from the Fleet. Since the U.S. Navy promoted only qualified pilots to command its carriers and carrier task forces, many senior officers, up to the rank of captain, attended flight school throughout the 1920s and 1930s. The Army Air Corps was more restrictive; only those officers who *really* wanted to fly did, because there was no career advantage for doing so. The

1

result was that there was little understanding of the concepts of aerial warfare outside the Army's small brotherhood of aviators.

When the Army, Navy, and Marine Corps began to expand their aviation communities in 1934, the pool of qualified Regular line officers could not fill all the available aviation billets, so the Aviation Cadet Act of 1935 provided for the selection and training of specially qualified Reserve pilots. Recruiting took place mainly among college graduates between the ages of twenty and twenty-eight. Training was extremely rigorous. The Navy's initial AvCad course, for example, consisted of one year of flight school at Pensacola, Florida: 465 classroom hours and 300 flight hours to qualify for wings. Then, once the AvCad earned his coveted Wings of Gold, he spent three years flying with the Fleet. During that time he was ranked somewhere between warrant officer and ensign. The AvCad finally received his commission as a Navy ensign or Marine second lieutenant four years after qualifying for flight school. At the same time he was commissioned, however, the early AvCad was placed on *inactive* status with the U.S. Navy or Marine Corps Reserve. The Army Air Corps maintained a similar program.

The Navy's cadet program was steeply upgraded by the Naval Aviation Reserve Act of 1939. This legislation provided for 6,000 trainees who would receive commissions upon completion of flight training at Pensacola and who would serve a total of seven years on active duty. AvCads who had earned their wings prior to the new act were immediately commissioned, and those who already had gone on Reserve status were given the opportunity to return to active duty. The Army Air Corps establishment was expanded even more precipitously by means of similar legislation.

In 1940, Congress expanded the Naval Aviation Reserve Act in order to train enough pilots to man 15,000 Navy and Marine aircraft of all types. On December 7, 1941, the Navy and Marine Corps had a total of 6,500 active-duty pilots. About half of them were AvCads trained at Pensacola or newer flight schools at Corpus Christi, Texas, and Jacksonville, Florida. In addition, many hundreds of AvCads were in the training pipeline, days or months away from graduation.

As the Reserve aviation-cadet programs expanded alongside flight-training programs for Regular officers and Navy enlisted cadets, the vastly expanded needs of the day resulted in relaxed standards. Earlier, long before the United States faced World War II, only perfect physical specimens were selected (no dental fillings, no broken bones). This was to help reduce the pool of otherwise qualified applicants for a very small program. When more cadets were needed than the perfect-specimen pool could produce, some of the most extreme physical criteria were relaxed, and the educational requirement was rolled back to two years of college. As an added inducement, Army, Navy, and Marine Reserve aviation cadets were offered a bounty of $500 per year for four years, payable when they mustered out. As hoped, many a Depression-poor college sophomore signed up in the hope of earning enough in four years to pay his junior- and senior-year tuition bills.

At the same time that entry qualifications were being relaxed, cadets were required to weather fewer and fewer classroom and flight hours. Ultimately, the Navy's scaled-down twenty-six-week course called for just 207 flight hours prior to commissioning and assignment to advanced specialized training. Even the speeded-up syllabus barely provided enough qualified—which is not to say seasoned—pilots to man the many newly formed air groups.

## THE HAWK

**2d Lieutenant FRANK HOLMES, USAAF**
**47th Pursuit Squadron, 15th Pursuit Group**
**Pearl Harbor, December 7, 1941**

*Besby Frank Holmes was born in San Francisco on December 5, 1917. Up to a point, his story is typical of many of the young American men who volunteered for the Army and Navy flying services before their nation was drawn into World War II.*

I was fishing at the foot of Van Ness Avenue in San Francisco when a bunch of Army Air Corps P-26 fighters went flying by at about 450 feet. The pilots had their helmets and goggles on, and their white scarves were streaming in the wind. The planes screamed by and I said to myself, "I just gotta fly one of those things one of these days." I was fourteen or fifteen years old.

The P-26s were based at Crissy Field in the Presidio of San Francisco and, as I watched those guys fly, I became more enamored of flight all the time. Little did I realize that, in less than ten years, I would fly my first combat mission.

Anyway, that's what I determined I had to do—I had to fly airplanes. So I went to San Francisco Community College, got my minimum requirements, and applied for aviation-cadet training. They accepted me.

I went into the Army in March 1941. I left San Francisco and went to primary training in Oxnard, California; basic training in Bakersfield, California; and then went on to advanced training at Luke Field, in Phoenix, Arizona. We were an experimental class. We had 7½ months total training to become pilots, navigators, and officers and gentlemen. They only did that to two classes. It was just too much to learn in so little time.

Six days after we graduated from Luke Field, we were on our way to Hawaii. We got there late in November 1941. They checked me out in an AT-6, the advanced trainer. Then they checked me out in a P-26, the same type of fighter I had seen over San Francisco eight or nine years earlier. The Boeing P-26 was the Army Air Corps' first all-metal fighter, but it had fixed landing gear and an open cockpit.

Somebody put us on a 24-hour-a-day practice alert from November 30 to Saturday, December 6. Saturday morning, December 6, my squadron commander decided to check me out on a P-36. Oh boy, a Curtiss Hawk! The Hawk, a forerunner of the Curtiss P-40 Warhawk, had retractable landing gear and a closed cockpit, but it was already an outmoded fighter.

We were out at Haleiwa, on Oahu, at gunnery camp. They directed me to take the P-36 off from the little narrow dirt strip; fly up to Wheeler Field, the major base, and shoot three or four landings; and come back to land at Haleiwa.

I checked out that morning and I was flying high. I was on Cloud 19. I had flown a real fighter—a single-seat fighter with a closed canopy. It was a big step. The next step, of course, was the P-40, but I hadn't quite gotten to the P-40.

I was so high and so excited that, as I was talking to my squadron commander, Captain Gordon Austin, I said, "Sir, this alert we've been on, I don't think it was a practice alert."

"Why do you think so?" he asked.

"Well," I said, "I just got over here, but I read the periodicals and I observe. To my way of thinking, the relations between Japan and the U.S. have been very, very strained. I don't think this practice alert was really a practice alert. I think it was the real thing." Then I added, "Are you sure we oughta knock off at noon today, as the schedule calls for?"

Captain Austin admitted, "Well, I don't think we should either." So, he got on the telephone. It was the hand-crank kind; we used the crank to get the amperage to ring the bell at the other end of the line. He called the group commander, and the group commander said, "Well, you know, I'm kind of nervous too." So, the group commander called General Davidson, and the general said, "Well, hang on," and he called General Walter Short, the Army commander in Hawaii. General Short apparently called Admiral Husband Kimmel, the Pacific Fleet commander, and they both conferred and debated. Finally, at 1400 hours, December 6, they called the alert off and we all went to town.

We had been on a seven-day alert, 24 hours a day. Everyone in the military forces had been restricted. Haleiwa was at the extreme north end of Oahu. Wheeler Field, which was right in the middle of Oahu, was our group's main air base. Honolulu was on the other extremity of Oahu, and that's where everybody from the three services—Army, Navy, and Marines—went. We were going to have a fine Saturday night. We'd been restricted for 24 hours a day, but the teacher let the monkeys out.

My tentmate, Lieutenant Johnny Voss, was a cousin of the assistant manager of the Royal Hawaiian Hotel. Johnny had made arrangements to visit his cousin that weekend. He invited me to join him. We went in to the Royal Hawaiian.

5

Second lieutenants in 1941 did not stay at the Royal Hawaiian—our pay was $127 a month—but we were the guests of the assistant manager, in his suite. I had brought a letter of introduction from some friends in San Francisco to their cousin, who welcomed me with open arms and set up a blind date for me.

Nobody had ever warned me about sweet rum drinks. One is fine, two is great, three is murder, and four is death. I don't know how many I had. I woke up the next morning with a horrible headache. I was down. All I could think about was getting up, going to church, getting Mass out of the way, putting my swimming suit on, getting out on the beach, and letting the sun bake the poison out of my body. I was so young that nobody had ever told me about curing a headache with Alka-Seltzer. I got up, got dressed, and went across the street to church. I had on a brown pin-striped suit and a green wool tie made by the Navajo Indians in Arizona.

I was praying to God that my headache would go away when the first bombs fell. The church was open all the way around, for air circulation. I heard this whirring, whooshing noise. I thought, "The stupid Navy! We called the alert off yesterday, and they're still practicing."

The sexton ran out to the altar and whispered in the Irish priest's ear, but the priest didn't say anything to the congregation. He just moved up the tempo of the Mass. I was having trouble following him. I couldn't stay with him in my missal. He didn't say anything about the bombs, but Mass ended real quick. I walked outside and saw all the military trucks roaring up and down Kalakaua Boulevard. I thought, "What's going on?"

I darted across the street to the Royal Hawaiian and got up to the room. Johnny Voss and his cousin, the assistant manager, were so excited they were practically chasing each other around the room. In the middle of the table they had a little portable radio. The radio announcer was saying, "Don't get excited, don't get excited. The Japs have attacked Pearl Harbor, but the Army has the situation well in hand." And I thought, "Oh, dear God, if the rest of the Army feels like me, we're in trouble."

Fortunately, Johnny had had the presence of mind to put his uniform on. I was still in my brown pin-striped suit. We dashed outside, stopped the first car that went by—a little Studebaker Champion—and commandeered it. It was a civilian car. The guy said, "What do you want, kids?" I said, "We gotta get to our air base. We're both pilots." He said, "Great"; moved over to the middle; and said, "You drive." So, I jumped in and drove.

As we passed Pearl Harbor, the battle was in full force. I saw the battleship *Arizona*'s side blow out as we went by, but we still didn't know what was going on. We were in a little fire engine-red car; I don't know why we weren't strafed, because it looked like we were in a fire vehicle or something.

We passed Pearl Harbor and drove up the hill to Wheeler Field, our main base. It was a shambles. There were seventy-five P-40s lined up on the edge of the parking ramp. They were all burning. We drove to my hangar. It was all aflame. As we drove up, the top just melted and crushed in. A big old sergeant saw me and said, "Lieutenant, I got an airplane for you to fly." I said, "Great, where is it?"

Just by the hillside was a biplane with two cockpits. I don't even know what it was. It hadn't moved in the two weeks I'd been in Hawaii. The sergeant said, "There it is, Lieutenant. Let's go." And I said, "Thank you very much, Sergeant, but I don't think I want to fly that thing."

I jumped back in the car and we drove off from Wheeler, back to Haleiwa, which was 8 to 10 miles away. I drove through the gate we had left the afternoon before, but some idiot had put a barbed-wire fence up. Well, I didn't see the barbed-wire fence and drove right through it. I said to this poor guy whose car we'd commandeered, "I'm so sorry. I'll pay for it." He said, "Forget it, Lieutenant. Glad to help."

As I jumped out of the car, a big old line chief saw me. He grabbed me; handed me a parachute and a helmet; and said, "Son, I've got an airplane that's ready to go."

Mind you, I'd only just checked out in this P-36 the day before. I had had one flight in it. He grabbed my shoulders with his big hands and I got my parachute. Someone ran up and handed me a naked .45. No holster; just a .45 pistol.

We were running to the P-36, which was about 150 yards away, when I heard *boom, boom, boom, boom.* I looked around and saw that dust was spreading up around my airplane. I didn't like that at all. I looked over my shoulder and saw that a Val fixed-landing-gear dive-bomber was strafing my Curtiss Hawk. The big line chief was barreling along behind me and showed no sign of stopping. I was thinking, "God, is he helping me carry my parachute or is he making sure I don't run away and hide?" I didn't know. How could I stop him? He was 260 pounds. I was thinking, "I gotta stop him," so I dug both my heels into the dirt. That stopped him.

The Japanese dive-bomber was about 45 yards from me, so I started firing at him with my pistol. One of the kids said, "By God, you got him!" I emptied the pistol. I looked at the empty, smoking thing. I threw it up in the air and said, "Got him, hell! I hit the canopy." I had seen the canopy craze, but I thought, "He's not on fire or going down." I said, "Let's go and hide. I don't want to be out in the open."

We hid behind some bushes, but the Val didn't come back. He dove down over a sandy hummock and disappeared over the Pacific. Maybe he crashed. I don't know.

We picked up my parachute and helmet and went on out to the airplane. The Val hadn't touched it.

I got in the cockpit. The P-36 had a peculiar starting system. It had an 8-gauge shotgun-shell compression starter. The charge was ducted into the bottom three cylinders of the radial engine. If everything was right, it would kick the prop over three revolutions. If you had the primer set, the mixture set, everything set, and your tongue was in the right corner of your cheek, maybe it would fire.

I had six shotgun shells, and I fired five without getting the engine started. I had one left, so I jumped out and handed it to the big line chief. I said, "You start it. I'm all thumbs." It was a cranky starting system. He jumped in and started it. I'm not sure if I said to myself, "Damn him," or "Good for him."

When the engine started, the line chief began to jump out, but I thrust him back into the cockpit. His eyes opened up to the size of saucers, like I was going to make him fly the plane. He could fly. All the old line chiefs could fly the planes they serviced. I had flown with him when they checked me out in the AT-6.

I said, "Sarge, just load the gun. Turn on the switches and turn on the gunsight. I don't know where the hell the

switches are, and I've never loaded the gun in this airplane."
He turned on the gunsight, put the circuit breakers in for the
firing mechanism, and charged the gun. The P-36 was armed
with a .30-caliber machine gun and a .50-caliber machine
gun, which both fired through the prop. However, since we
were at gunnery camp and .50-caliber ammo was considered
too expensive to waste on gunnery training, I had just the
one .30-caliber pop gun firing through the prop for my
second flight in a P-36. That's how I went off to war over
Pearl Harbor on December 7, 1941.

I took off and chased all over the island. It seemed like
everyone on the ground who had a gun fired at me. I flew
over Wheeler Field and Schofield Barracks first, as they were
closest to Haleiwa. They were both a shambles. My next
destination was Pearl Harbor, with Ford Island Naval Air
Station in the middle. The damage was awesome. Huge
ships were sunk and burning, fuel was burning, aircraft were
burning, and hangars were burning. The antiaircraft fire that
was directed at me was pretty intense, but, fortunately, it
was very inaccurate.

I left the vicinity of Pearl quickly when I could find no
enemy aircraft, and I took a quick look at Ewa Marine Corps
Air Station. It was much the same as Wheeler and Ford
Island. Hickham Army Airfield was also beat up. Next, I
flew over the Pali to Kaneohe Naval Air Station, on the
eastern side of Oahu. It was also beat up, but not as badly as
Pearl Harbor and the fighter bases around it. Men on the
ground at Kaneohe fired at me. I thought that it was
ridiculous that everybody on the ground was firing at me
while I never saw a Japanese airplane in the sky. Thank the
Lord I didn't run into a formation of Zeros. They would
have creamed me.

I decided to return to Haleiwa and land. My whole flight
lasted about 30 minutes.

In my absence, some B-17 heavy bombers inbound from
the U.S. had found our tiny little dirt field and had safely
landed. They had no alternative, as all the major airfields
had been put out of commission. We had no tractors to tow
the four-engine bombers, so we manhandled them underneath some tall trees. It was the best camouflage we could
provide.

An extended period of chaos ensued. Rumor after rumor circulated—a new air attack was imminent, it wasn't, a landing was about to occur, a landing was under way at Pearl, a landing wasn't underway at Pearl. I couldn't keep up with the rumors.

Since all Army Air Corps fields on Oahu had been attacked and damaged except Haleiwa—it had been attacked by just that one lone Val I had fired at—all the operable P-36s and P-40s on Oahu came to our little dirt strip. Additionally, numerous pilots who were senior to me—just about all of them—arrived. Naturally, my little P-36 Hawk was taken away from me by one of the senior pilots.

During the rest of the day, there was a lot of scurrying around doing things, and then undoing them. Then all the senior pilots spent that night in the cockpits of their assigned airplanes while the junior pilots were sent to be the beach guards.

Johnny Voss and I were instructed that when—not if— we spotted the Japanese landing craft approaching the beach at Haleiwa we were to fire our weapons—one .45-caliber automatic apiece—at them or into the air (it didn't matter) three times. That was the signal for all the pursuit planes to immediately scramble and take off inland. A late rumor indicated that all the holes in Wheeler's runways had been filled in, so hopefully they would all be able to land safely.

I trudged up and down my mile and a half of beach all that dark and lonely night, passing Johnny Voss every half hour or so. In the tropics and semitropics, the waves take on a luminescence that, to my untrained eye, looked like the bow waves of landing barges. I must have seen a thousand waves I was certain contained troop-filled barges. Fortunately, no one fired a false alarm. If all twenty or so P-40s and P-36s had attempted a takeoff from the tiny dirt strip at night with no runway lights, taxi strips, or a control tower, it would have been awful.

Dawn finally arrived. There had been no further attacks. I cannot remember a more welcome sunrise.

*Following this inauspicious baptism, Frank Holmes went on to survive a breathtaking combat tour in the South Pacific. As* a member of the 67th Pursuit Squadron, he flew utterly outclassed Bell Airacobra P-39 and P-400 fighters against Imperial Navy Zero fighters at Guadalcanal. On the darkest day of the Guadalcanal campaign, Lieutenant Holmes strafed and bombed a Japanese transport that then had to be beached. On another dark day, he located a major Imperial Army supply cache that was subsequently destroyed.

Lieutenant Frank Holmes did not score his first aerial victory until January 5, 1943, by which time he was flying a Lockheed P-38 Lightning fighter with the 339th Fighter Squadron. In all, he destroyed 5 Japanese airplanes and is credited with 4 probables. His last, most memorable, and historically most significant aerial victory came on April 18, 1943, when he was credited with destroying a Zero fighter and a Betty bomber on the famed and controversial mission that resulted in the death of Admiral Isoroku Yamamoto, commander in chief of the Imperial Navy's Combined Fleet.

# CHAPTER 1

The weeks immediately following Japan's virtually simultaneous air attacks against Pearl Harbor and American bases throughout the Philippines were the worst and most humiliating the United States has ever faced. The news was so bad for so many days in a row that the national will could be uplifted only by invoking the memory of the growing thousands of martyred soldiers and sailors.

While most Americans prayed for miracles, the Japanese marched ever forward. From secure bases inside French Indochina, they staged a lightning occupation of neutral Thailand and, at the same time, the outright invasion of Malaya. On December 9, 1941, Saigon-based Imperial Japanese Navy level bombers achieved a sobering historical first: They sank two Royal Navy battleships, the *Prince of Wales* and the *Repulse*, as the British dreadnoughts rushed—without any friendly air cover —to smash the Japanese invasion fleet in the Gulf of Siam.

By then, Clark Field, the mighty U.S. Army Air Corps base near Manila, had been ground to dust; most of the American warplanes based there had been destroyed in a single air raid launched from Formosa on the first day of the war. In the weeks that followed, all but a handful of the very few surviving American fighters and bombers in the Philippines were shot down as they made brave but fruitless efforts to withstand the Japanese tide. In early February, long after General Douglas MacArthur's outnumbered and unsupported ground forces had been bottled up in the Bataan Peninsula, the pathetic aerial remnant was ordered to withdraw to Java to help stem a series of Japanese landings that was falling on ill-prepared Dutch forces throughout the Dutch East Indies.

As the last remaining American warplanes flew south from the Philippines, a band of innocents was sent forward from Australia to meet them.

# JAVA

**2d Lieutenant JIM MOREHEAD, USAAF**
**17th Provisional Pursuit Squadron**
**Malang, Java, February 23, 1942**

*James Bruce Morehead, a native of Washington, Oklahoma, attended the University of Oklahoma and University of California, Los Angeles, before enlisting in the U.S. Army Air Corps in August 1940. He earned his wings at Stockton, California, on April 25, 1941, and was just boarding ship at San Francisco, bound for the Philippines, on Pearl Harbor Day.*

The *President Polk* slipped out of San Francisco on December 19, 1941, and we sailed for Manila. After a few days at sea, our destination was changed and we eventually docked at Brisbane, Australia, after twenty-eight days at sea. We landed 55 pilots, 55 armorers, 55 mechanics—all volunteers—and 55 crated P-40E fighters. Then we simply waited to hear what was to become of us. We had no organization; we were all—planes and men—just replacements.

They took us out to Amberlie Field, near Brisbane. The pilots helped the mechanics assemble the P-40s in a hangar, and we started flight-testing them as they came off the assembly line we had set up.

We were getting very little news about the progress of the

war, and all of it was terrible. There was a huge raid on Darwin, Australia, and many ships were sunk.

We started training with the P-40s until we were ordered to Java in early February. We were to fly in stages across the interior of Australia to Darwin and then continue to Soerabaja. We had a big party in Brisbane the night before we left, and we got to bed late. I was leading a flight of four to our first stop. The sun was beating down warm in the cockpit, and I fell asleep. My P-40 peeled off into a screaming dive, and the three other guys followed me. I woke up going straight down. I grabbed the stick and pulled out okay, but when I landed, all three of the other guys gave me hell for nearly getting them killed.

When we arrived in Darwin, there was a B-17 waiting to lead a flight of eight of us to Java. We heard that the previous flight of P-40s had gotten caught in a storm—it was the stormy season—and most of the fighters and their pilots were lost. The B-17 took off on the leg to Timor, but we were still on the ground when there came the greatest downpour I have ever experienced. The runways were inches deep in water as we took off.

Everything was scary just then, but the *really* scary thing was that we had just gotten into the airplanes after not flying for about six weeks. It takes time to get back in the groove to fly a hot fighter airplane; if you haven't flown for a few months, you lose your hand. I knew I was dangerous and scared, and that I had not rebuilt my confidence. However, I taxied out after the B-17. There was so much rain falling that a foggy halo formed at the tips of my propellers. It was very frightening. I didn't know at the time if the halo was smoke or what. Water was roaring past the cockpit as it was being thrown up by the wheels and the prop. Finally, I got in the air and went up to join the B-17. He was flying around at about 140 miles per hour, which was close to stalling speed for a P-40. It was so frightening to a green pilot. I was trying to fly formation, weaving up and down, pulling the stick way back because of the slow flying speed. The B-17 pilot didn't know about our problems. I tried to get where he could see me so I could signal him to fly faster, but I couldn't get his attention.

We finally got assembled. It was pouring, and we kept

going lower and lower. Soon, we were just off the waves—10 to 15 feet. The B-17 was down there beside us! If anything, the rain increased. The rain was gushing off the cockpit. It was extremely hard to see the other fellows. The black clouds remained above us. It looked like, any minute, the B-17 was going to fly into a cloud and lose us all. But we made it across. We finally landed at Koepang, Timor, where, that night, the Australian Army fed us buffalo meat for supper.

We got up early the next morning—February 5—and went to our planes. As the B-17 was taking off on one of the two intersecting runways, an Australian twin-engine patrol bomber was taking off on the other runway. The two planes came to the intersection at the exact same instant. Fortunately, the Australian had enough flying speed to just about bounce his wheels on the wing of the B-17. It was the closest near-collision I have ever observed.

The rest of the flight was beautiful. It was a beautiful morning. We flew over a couple of islands, lush with groves of banana trees, green hillsides, and rice paddies. We landed at Den Pasar, Bali, but the B-17 went on to our final destination, Soerabaja, Java, which was very close to Den Pasar. We had to pump our fuel with a hand pump from drums of gasoline. It took us hours to finish the job.

While we were on the ground refueling, the flight commander, Captain William Lane, ran over, yelling a warning. We looked into the sky and saw a single plane over us. He yelled, "Everybody who's got gas, jump in!" I was stuck on the ground, but Lane and about four others got into the air. Several Japanese Zero fighters came down in a dive. They shot two or three of our guys down. Meanwhile, a couple more of our P-40s got into the air, where they were chased by the Zeros. One of the pilots bailed out, got hung up in a tree, and suffered a dislocated shoulder. Some islanders got him down.

In the meantime, those of us on the ground started running away from the airport. I had a little .22-caliber rifle and a few rounds of ammunition I had been carrying in my cockpit. We got about a quarter mile away from the runway when thirty Japanese bombers came over and started bombing the base. When they finished, we decided to go back to the airfield. As two of us started back, someone on the base started shooting at us. We jumped in an old brick building. When a handful of the Dutch Javanese soldiers who were guarding the base ran up, we held up our hands to surrender and yelled, "American!" It turned out that they thought we were Japanese because of the yellow Mae West life jackets we had on.

The bombers came back as we were getting back to the runway. I suppose they didn't like the first run they had made. I don't know why, because several of our P-40s were burning. They made another run. There were no Zeros this time, but none of us was in the air either. It was a terrible feeling. I hid behind a palm tree as the bombs started falling in. I was safe from the bomb splinters, but the damn coconuts in the tree were jarred loose by the concussion.

The bombers finally left. Nobody in our crew on the ground had been hurt, but several of the airplanes were burning and there was ammunition cooking off. It sounded like a war. My spare .22 ammunition, which another pilot had been carrying for me, was popping off. It sounded like a ground battle, which is probably why the Dutch Javanese troops had come gunning for me earlier.

My airplane and another one were not hit. We pulled the other one back off the airfield and covered it with palm fronds, but we gassed mine. Then a 5th Air Force administrative airplane arrived on its way to Java, and I was commandeered to escort it to Soerabaja. We landed there, and I was taken to our headquarters in town. The Japanese bombed the airport just after I arrived. My P-40 survived that attack, also, so I flew it out to the little grass strip at Blimbing. I had a very hard time finding Blimbing, which I guess was the reason we were using it: If *American pilots* couldn't find it, maybe the Japanese wouldn't. When I arrived, Captain Lane was already there with the other P-40s that had made it through the fight over Den Pasar. In fact, they had claims in for 4 Zeros. We learned then that we had been attached to the 17th Provisional Pursuit Squadron, whose commander was Major Charles Sprague.

The 17th Pursuit, one of the Air Corps' three between-wars permanent squadrons, had been based in the Philippines. Major Sprague and a few straggling P-40s that had

**17**

made it down to Java were the core of the 17th Provisional Pursuit.

My indoctrination into warfare was with a flight of four airplanes a few days later. It rained nearly every day then. The flight leader, 1st Lieutenant Jack Dale, led us as we taxied out to the end of the runway. As he turned onto the strip, his wheels dug down in the mud, and he couldn't get out. So he motioned to me to take this mission. That was pitiful. I had perhaps 40 hours in a P-40, had never fired the guns, had never fired on an aerial target, had never seen an enemy plane while in the air—and I was the leader.

We took off and started climbing into the vector they gave us on the radio. On the climb out, we got hit by a flight of several Japanese Zeros. They were in a line of flight; they had had plenty of time to drop from formation into a string attack formation. They came at us, and I turned the flight into them. The leader of the Japanese flight did not seem to be very experienced. At least, he had not learned that, at a certain approach angle of a head-on attack of one airplane on another, you can turn to an acute angle and prevent the enemy from getting his nose onto you. You can just fly by, and he cannot reach you. This guy came right over. He did not want to face me head-on, because he didn't have to. At that time the good Zero pilots could shoot down all the P-40s in the world and never get touched. But he was inexperienced, so he pulled up at such an angle as to allow me to pull up in front of him. I was able to fire as he roared over, but there were seven or eight more Zeros coming at me, so I wasn't able to see what happened to the leader. I never knew.

I dropped my nose through the melee that was then taking place and dived away as fast as I could go, jerking the stick and yawing the airplane, creating as poor a target as I could. Fortunately, I had enough altitude to do it. In a brief engagement they could outmaneuver us and get on our tails, but in a dive a P-40 could outrun a Zero. That's the only reason the Japanese didn't win immediate air superiority over Java and northern Australia.

I got away and made it back to Blimbing. That was a sweat job too. It was the first time I had flown off the strip without a leader, and I had a hell of a time finding it before I ran out of gas. I did finally find it. One of my wingmen was shot down. The other P-40 was damaged by enemy fire, but made it back to the field okay. One Zero was reported destroyed, but I didn't claim it because I didn't see the one I shot at go down.

On February 17, Major Sprague led a mission to Palembang, Sumatra. I sure wanted to go on that because I wanted to strafe the bastards. Pearl Harbor had gotten me worked up a little, and I wanted to see some of them jump and spurt blood. But I didn't get to go. They ran into some wheels-down fighters and bagged six fighters and a bomber. Oh man, was I disappointed I didn't make that mission.

We were scrambled from Blimbing at 0940 on February 23. As did most of our air-raid warnings, news of the incoming Japanese raid came through the jungle by way of drumbeats. The warning wasn't meant for us; it was done by the Javanese to warn one another. But we heard it, and we reacted. We usually got a telephone warning 5 to 10 minutes later, but we were scrambling by then.

First Lieutenant George Kiser was the flight leader, and the other pilots in his flight were 1st Lieutenant Nathanial Blanton, 1st Lieutenant Ray Thompson, and 2d Lieutenant William Turner. I also got off, but a little late. I tried to join them as tail-end Charlie, but my airplane was a dog; it couldn't fly fast enough to catch up with the others.

We were climbing in a big circle for about 40 minutes, and I must have been a mile back when the other P-40s finally reached the Japanese bomber formation. I first saw the Japanese bombers at around 22,000 feet over Malang, Java, which was 40 to 50 miles from Blimbing.

A mess of Zeros engaged the rest of the flight. The P-40s had no chance to engage the bombers. As I was closing, I watched the P-40s and Zeros tangling. Before I could get there, however, the P-40s dived away, and the Zeros chased them. That left me clean up there, as the Zeros hadn't seen me.

There were nine Mitsubishi G3M Nell twin-engine medium bombers formed in three vees of three airplanes each. I flew up alongside them on their right. "Holy smoke," I thought, "I'm too close to these guys. They're liable to get me!" I peeled away and flew out a little farther from them. I wanted to get ahead of them and make an attack 130 degrees to their flight path. This was because their guns all shot to the rear, except the nose gun.

I wanted to shoot at the lead bomber. I got a little below their altitude and swept in from the right, 130 degrees to his nose. I put my crosshair gunsight on him and fired from 400 yards with all six of my .50-caliber wing guns. I was trying to hit the leader in the nose and wing root, but my tracers went so far behind the whole lead element that I was embarrassed. I was a good skeet shooter and understood lead real well. But I had no experience in aerial combat. That was the first time I ever saw my tracers go at a target.

I jerked my nose to the right to get in more lead. I had plenty of time at that distance. I got him pretty good and held a good burst into him. Then I dived beneath the lead element, pulled up to the left, and started climbing again. I wanted to make another attack just like the first one.

When I recovered, I saw that one of the bombers was smoking. I saw that it was the lead bomber, so I crossed over from the left of the formation to its right, flew alongside, and started gaining on them so I could pass them and launch another attack. As I was passing the leader, I saw some Zeros coming up. One of them got on my tail, so I eased over in front of the bombers. I decided to make a head-on pass this time.

The Zero was closing on me, but I didn't think he could hit me in the wild maneuvers in which I was about to engage. I was quite a bit ahead of the bombers, so I executed a split-S and pulled back on the stick as hard as I could, so it would black us out—me and the Zero pilot. I knew he couldn't shoot good blacked out.

I pulled around and, when I got level again, I was heading straight for the bombers. I saw that the leader wasn't smoking, so apparently my maneuvering to evade the Zero had brought me in against another one of the three-plane bomber elements. But I didn't realize it then; things were going too fast. I didn't know where the hell my smoking bomber had gone, but I fired at the lead bomber anyway. I fired right smack into his nose, starting at about 250 yards. I was trying to kill the pilot. I had lost a lot of my speed in my maneuvers with the Zero, and the Nell bombers were pretty slow, but I had time for only a short burst before I had to dive beneath the formation.

I dove straight for the ground. The red line on our speed indicators was at 450 miles per hour, but I saw it top 500 in that dive! The Zero was on my tail and he had blood in his eyes, but I left him behind.

I had become disoriented early on in my attack; I had no idea where I was. I circled around for a bit and saw an airfield—Malang. I decided to land there because I was low on fuel. I set down and taxied up to the service area. But there wasn't a soul in sight. Nobody! I continued taxiing up to one of the hangars, and two American ground crewmen raised up from a foxhole and climbed up on my wing. One of them yelled, "What can we do for you, Lieutenant?" I told him I needed some gas and ammunition. One of them mentioned that this was the base the Nells were bombing, which was why everyone was under cover. They had had three waves of bombers already and didn't know how many more were to come. I asked if they had seen any of the action and told them I had attacked the last formation of bombers. In fact, they told me that they had seen two of the bombers start smoking. Both bombers had spun down.

They guided me to a nearby hangar, refueled me quickly with electric pumps, rearmed me, and went back to their foxhole. I took off and returned without incident to Blimbing, where I claimed and was given credit for two Nell bombers destroyed.

*Two days later, all of the U.S. Army Air Corps fighters in Java were destroyed and as many pilots and ground crewmen as could be saved were evacuated aboard a small ship and the last of the heavy bombers. Everyone else surrendered to the Japanese. In the end, Lieutenant Jim Morehead was one of the very few members of his group of fifty-five replacement pilots to survive the Java ordeal. He was flown to Australia aboard a B-17 and soon joined the newly arrived 49th Fighter Group's 8th Fighter Squadron in Canberra.*

*On April 25, 1942, Lieutenant Jim Morehead achieved ace status when he destroyed 3 new G4M Betty twin-engine medium bombers over Darwin, Australia; he destroyed 2 Zeros on August 23, 1942, off the Australian coast. During his second combat tour, as operations officer of the 1st Fighter Group in Italy, Major Jim Morehead destroyed a German Me-109 over Romania on June 6, 1944.*

Everywhere Americans turned, their nation's response to the Japanese juggernaut was, to use Lieutenant Jim Morehead's assessment, pitiful. On February 20, 1942, the U.S. Navy executed a pair of carrier raids deep within Japanese territory —in the Central Pacific and the newly fallen Solomon Islands— but the results made better headlines than strategic sense. Behind the boldly written headlines, the story was as grim as ever. Here and there, the Army Air Corps and U.S. Marines deployed their precious fighter and bomber squadrons in what to even the most sanguine warriors appeared to be futile, sacrificial calls to duty.

One Marine fighter squadron and one Marine dive-bomber squadron, each composed of obsolete or obsolescent aircraft flown mainly by newly graduated AvCads, were sent to defend all of Samoa. Another Marine fighter squadron was sent to Nouméa to fly beside the only squadron of fighters the U.S. Army Air Corps could spare. In Australia, the survivors of the Philippines and East Indies debacles licked their wounds and girded themselves for the expected Japanese invasion of the port of Darwin—a battle that eventually unfolded as merely a few destructive and emotionally crippling air raids.

Only the news from China seemed to have a silver lining. Colonel Claire Chennault's dashing American Volunteer Group —three American-manned fighter squadrons flying under the Nationalist Chinese colors—appeared to be winning any significant victories in the air. But, had the truth behind the headlines been known, America would have gasped anew. For lack of replacement aircraft, Chennault's volunteers—the vaunted Flying Tigers—were on the brink of defeat. After the fall of Rangoon, Burma, in late February, they had been reduced to defensive tactics bolstered by a few daring hit-and-run raids aimed at merely *slowing* the Japanese tide.

# RAID ON CHIENGMAI

**Squadron Leader BOB NEALE**
**1st Squadron, American Volunteer Group**
**Chiengmai Airdrome, Thailand, March 24, 1942**

*Robert Hawthorne Neale, a native of Vancouver, Canada, joined the U.S. Navy in 1938, graduated from Pensacola in 1939, and served with Bombing Squadron 3 aboard USS [Sarato]ga for two years. However, when Ensign Neale was [offered] a Regular commission in July 1941, he signed up for [the A]merican Volunteer Group (AVG) and immediately re-[signed] his commission. He arrived in Burma in August 1941 [and w]as assigned as vice squadron leader of the 1st AVG [squa]dron, which was then flying P-40B fighters.*

*[Con]trary to popular conception, the Flying Tigers did not [fly the]ir first combat mission until December 20, 1941. Bob [Neale] scored his first confirmed aerial victory on January 23, [1942,] by downing an outdated Imperial Army Nakajima [Ki-27] fighter over Rangoon, Burma. During the next two [mont]hs, during which he was promoted to lead the 1st [squa]dron, Neale ran his score up to 11 aerial kills, 2 [proba]bles, and partial credits for 3 airplanes destroyed on the [groun]d.*

Colonel Claire Chennault sent for me at 0800 on March 22, 1942. He told me that, at noon, I was to lead a mission to Chiengmai, Thailand, to strafe the Japanese airport there. It was a hell of a nice mission because Chiengmai was 165 miles inside Japanese lines.

At 1310, I departed from Kunming, China, for Namsang, Burma, via Loiwing, China. I was leading a flight of ten P-40B airplanes. The P-40B was a stable firing platform with four .30-caliber machine guns in the wings and two .50-caliber machine guns firing through the propeller. It offered good protection for the pilot; it had armor plate behind the pilot and self-sealing fuel tanks. The only problems were maneuverability and its slow rate of climb with a full load of gas and ammunition—approximately 1,000 feet per minute.

23

We arrived at Loiwing at 1515, where, due to a delay in refueling, we remained overnight. Loiwing was a wonderful place to stay; we had some *cold* beer from the States. We got up at 0430 on March 23 and I kept the flight on alert until 1505, at which time we departed for Namsang, Burma, via Lashio and Heho. We arrived at Namsang, an RAF satellite field on the Burma-Thailand border, at 1645 (1715 Burma time). It was very hazy, and we had just missed a rainstorm. Upon arrival, we immediately refueled from 50-gallon drums and dispersed the airplanes to facilitate a predawn takeoff. Arrangements were made with the RAF to have about six trucks and several lanterns aligned along the runway. This was accomplished and checked after dark. I then held a conference to discuss the details of the mission.

The following plan was adopted: We would take off at 0545, March 24, and rendezvous immediately at 10,000 feet over the field by flights of six and four airplanes. I was to lead the formation of both flights to Chiengmai, at which time Squadron Leader Jack Newkirk of the 2d Squadron was to leave the formation and lead his flight of four planes on a low-flying attack on the airport at Lambhung, Thailand. I was to attack enemy aircraft at Chiengmai Airport with a flight of four planes, leaving two planes piloted by Flight Leader Ed Rector and Wingman William McGarry as top cover over the target area. Rector was to use his own discretion as to whether he should stay up or come down and aid in the attack, depending upon the nature of the opposition encountered, if any. If Newkirk's flight arrived at Lambhung and found no enemy aircraft there, it was to return to Chiengmai and attack in conjunction with my flight. Upon completion of the mission, Newkirk's flight was to return to Loiwing via Heho while my flight was to return to Loiwing via Namsang.

We got up at 0500. I took off from Namsang at 0545, March 24. Due to the haze from charcoal fires and the flames from our own exhausts, we had to go on instruments as soon as we crossed the end of the runway. Once we got above the haze, however, the sky was clear. By 0610, my flight of six P-40s had rendezvoused at 10,000 feet above the field, but there was no sign of Jack Newkirk's flight of four.

We made several circles over the field, but, by 0630, Newkirk's flight had still failed to join us. I then proceeded to my objective on course 150° True. At no time during the mission was any contact made between the flights.

We had been flying on instruments for about 40 minutes when, roughly at our estimated time of arrival, Vice Squadron Leader Charles Bond pulled up alongside me and motioned that Chiengmai was right below us. He then started his strafing run, and I followed him. Following me was Flight Leader Greg Boyington and Wingman Bill Bartling.

My initial attack was commenced from about 3,000 feet and three to five miles south of the target. By the time we reached the field, we were at treetop level. This attack was made from south to north along a line of fighters and bombers that were parked two- and three-deep on the east side of the field. When I arrived, Japanese pilots were climbing into the airplanes. However, not one of their planes got off the ground. This and all my succeeding attacks were made from low altitude. On completing each one, I turned sharply to evade ground fire. After completion of the run, two enemy planes were on fire.

My second attack was made from west to east along planes parked on the north side of the field. On this run, one plane was set on fire and other planes were badly riddled. After completion of this run, I turned north.

I made my third strafing run from north to south, along the planes strafed on my first run. It was impossible to tell the extent of the damage, as many planes were already burning from our previous attacks. On completion of my third attack, the antiaircraft and machine-gun fire from the ground batteries was so heavy that I rolled my wings in an effort to indicate completion of the attack.

At a point five miles southwest of the field and at 5,000 feet, I circled and waggled my wings in an effort to rendezvous the group, but I maintained radio silence, which had been in effect for the whole attack. However, due to poor visibility, the rendezvous was not accomplished. While circling, I observed eight or nine fires burning on the field, two of which seemed very big. There had been thirty to forty planes on the ground when we arrived, and I know that we destroyed at least half of them. I'm sure we also killed a lot of people.

At 0725, seeing no other planes in the area, I set course for Namsang. En route, Bartling joined me, and Rector, Boyington, and Bond arrived shortly after we did. Bond reported that McGarry had had to bail out about 30 miles inside the Burma-Thailand border. We thought he had a good chance to evade the Japanese, but he was captured four weeks later.

We found three of the planes from Jack Newkirk's flight at Namsang when we arrived. It was then that I learned that they had strafed Chiengmai's depot roads and facilities ahead of us. This explained why the Japanese pilots had been manning their fighters when we arrived. Newkirk had been killed. His plane failed to pull out after he made a strafing run on an armored car.

When I inspected my airplane, I found just one bullet hole in it. We refueled at Namsang and flew back to Loiwing without incident.

I believe that the raid on Chiengmai was the most effective mission I flew in my year in China and Burma. This is because the Japanese air strikes in south China were minimal for a period of two to three months after the raid.

*By July 4, 1942, the day the AVG was officially merged into the U.S. 14th Air Force, Bob Neale had been credited with 13 aerial victories and 6 probables, plus all or part of 6 Japanese planes destroyed on the ground. Neale volunteered to remain in the combat zone to help smooth the transition, though he already had hostile feelings toward a number of the Air Corps staff officers he had met. For this reason he turned down a major's commission in the Air Corps. Along with many similarly disenchanted AVG veterans, Neale returned to the United States to take a civilian flying job.*

Strategy for the Pacific War was based upon the ranges of land-based fighter aircraft. A ground-combat effort with any hope of success had to be supported by adequate numbers of fighters and bombers operating from secure bases to which they could return to rearm and refuel between sorties. Land bases could not survive if they were vulnerable to attacking aircraft. The tool of air superiority was the fighter.

The best overall range of any Allied fighter in the spring of 1942—when neither side was yet employing auxiliary fuel tanks—was under 1,000 miles. Most American fighters could fly only about 800 miles in a single hop, however, so Allied air bases had to be within about 300 miles of one another to be mutually supporting.

The best overall range of the Japanese Zero fighter in the spring of 1942 was about 1,400 miles; Japanese bases could be as far apart as 600 miles and still be mutually supporting. Put another way, at less extreme ranges, Japanese fighters could remain aloft over a friendly base or an enemy target many minutes longer than could Allied fighters sent from a similar distance to attack that base or defend that target.

Due to the constraints imposed upon both sides by the ranges of their fighters, from late February until early May 1942, the only consistent points of friction were where Japanese and American land-based aircraft could reach one another's bases —on the mainland of China and in eastern New Guinea.

The learning curve for Allied pilots in eastern New Guinea was as steep as the precipitous Owen Stanley Mountains that both hemmed in and protected the landward side of the Allied bastion around Port Moresby. Few Royal Australian Air Force or U.S. Army Air Corps pilots of the day reached the curve's summit alive. Many who did owe far more to luck than skill.

# THE NOVICE

## 2d Lieutenant DON McGEE, USAAF
## 36th Pursuit Squadron, 8th Pursuit Group
## Port Moresby, May 1, 1942

*Donald Charles McGee graduated from high school in his native Staten Island, New York, in January 1938. Eagerly desiring a career as an Army Air Corps pilot, he tried to secure an appointment to the United States Military Academy at West Point. Failing that, he enlisted in the infantry for one year in order to compete for a place in the Army's West Point Prep School, which could lead to an Academy appointment from the ranks. That effort also failed, but, persisting in his ambition to become a pilot, McGee continued to study on his own in preparation for testing to enter the Air Corps Flying Cadet program. After taking the test, he was advised that his grade was not high enough. However, shortly thereafter, he was notified that he had indeed passed the exam. Following an enormous hassle, he was reinstated in the cadet program and finally began flight training on May 1, 1941. Exactly one year later, after earning his wings at Craig Field, in Selma, Alabama, 2d Lieutenant Don McGee scored his first aerial victory.*

I was assigned to the 49th Pursuit Group's 9th Pursuit Squadron when we sailed from San Francisco on January 6, 1942. Our unescorted convoy consisted of the SS *Mariposa* and the SS *President Coolidge*. After we arrived in Melbourne, Australia, on January 31, the 9th Squadron was sent to the Williamtown RAAF station, near Newcastle, where we waited for our planes to arrive. None of us had yet flown fighter aircraft, so we tried to snatch a few flying hours in a Wirraway loaned to us by the RAAF. Also, I jumped into a wrecked P-40E as often as possible to "cockpit-check" myself—when our P-40s started to arrive, I wanted to be one of the first to check out. After being designated to fly "that one over there," I grabbed the bit and ran. But the exuberance of youth wasn't all that was required to do the job right and, in less than an hour, I found myself in pretty much the same state as the guy who had wrecked that other P-40.

Not long after this, the 49th Group started receiving pilots who had had combat experience in the Philippines and Java, so most of us were transferred to the 8th Pursuit Group, which was then arriving in Brisbane. When the experienced combat pilots had trained my fellow novices who remained with the unit, the 49th moved up to Darwin. Meantime, my contemporaries and I from the 9th Squadron were assigned to the 8th Group's 36th Squadron when we reached Lowood Station, near Brisbane. We began checking out in P-39Ds. Then we moved to Antil Plains, a grass strip near Townsville. Most of us had 10 to 15 hours of fighter transition but no high-performance or gunnery training when we were ordered to proceed to Port Moresby, New Guinea.

The 36th Pursuit Squadron left Townsville for Port Moresby on April 26, 1942, stopping that night at Cairns. Both the 35th Squadron, from Woodstock, and the 36th Squadron, from Antil Plains, made this move together. We stayed at Cairns on April 27, probably to patch up a few broken birds. I logged a 40-minute local flight there in the afternoon. This was probably to check out work on my prop, since I was flying an F-model P-39 whose prop spattered oil all over the windshield and took out any forward vision.

On April 28, we moved on to Horn Island, arriving there just after a raid by the Japanese. Their leavings were a burned-up B-25 and a couple of wrecked Aussie aircraft. We flew a field-cover mission right after arrival, and I logged two hours and 30 minutes.

Next day, on April 30, we took off for Port Moresby, timing our arrival to be after noon because we expected that any raids by the Japanese would be over by then. We were told that the runway at 7-Mile Strip was very narrow and that we should clear straight ahead after landing and then taxi back on the dirt track at our right. By the time we arrived, ol' Lucky Pierre here had a windshield full of dust and prop oil again, so another blind landing was necessary. That was no big deal except that Izzy Toubman, our operations officer, was taxiing back on the runway as I came in. I couldn't see his plane until just before we hit wingtips —my left to his left. This wouldn't have been a big deal, because the damage was slight, but it kept me off our first attack on Lae. This attack was cooked up and led by Lieutenant Colonel Boyd "Buzz" Wagner, from V Fighter Command, that same afternoon. I stopped my bitching about this turn of events by extracting a promise from 1st Lieutenant Bill Meng, our acting CO, that I'd be on the first field-cover patrol the next day. That promise was kept, and it resulted in my shooting down the 36th's first Zero.

That day, May 1, we were out of bed at about 0400; had a breakfast of bread, Australian canned jam, and tea; and got to the flight line before daylight. Leading the field-cover patrol was 1st Lieutenant Don Mainwaring. On his wing was 2d Lieutenant Patrick "Army" Armstrong. I led the second element, but my wingman never got airborne. The three of us climbed to about 8,000 feet and covered an area north and northwest of the field, expecting to meet any raids coming in from Lae.

After two hours or so we were supposed to be relieved, so Don started back toward the field and set us up in trail formation for landing. We peeled normally and took our distance for landing, but, as I broke, I could see that the near half of the runway was covered in ground fog. Don continued his pattern and tried to land through the fog, but he hit hard and wiped out his landing gear. He called on the radio and told us not to try to land, that the runway was blocked.

Army and I pulled up and broke out of the traffic pattern. Army chose to stay down low because he was low on gas, but I told him I was going to get some altitude. I was low on gas, too, but I didn't want to get caught down there if a raid came in. Also, if I ran out of fuel before the runway was cleared, I wanted to be able to pick a soft spot to dead-stick it in.

I had just reached 3,500 feet when our controller started yelling, "Zeros attacking the field!" I looked back and started a turn toward the field, but I didn't see any Zeros. Then I gulped and checked my gas. The gauges registered just under 20 gallons, which, in combat, would last about 9 minutes.

I was heading in a northerly direction when I saw a single Zero making a run from south to north across our revetment area. I had a debate with myself here, the gist of which was, "It's not smart to jump into a fight with no gas. I'm down low at low airspeed. I can't outturn a Zero. They left me off the mission yesterday. . . . Piss on it, I'm goin'!"

I rolled in on the Zero and pushed over. To conserve fuel, I did not push it to full power. The pilot of the Zero hadn't seen me, and I didn't see several other Zeros above. As I closed in—too slowly—I tried to figure out which crossbar in the gunsight I was supposed to use. Giving up, I simply worked the whole sight out in front of the enemy plane and fired a burst at about 40 degrees deflection. The tracers flew by the Zero on the right side. I adjusted my lead and fired another burst. The tracers flew by just under my target. Adjusting again, I pulled the sight farther out in front, raised it some, and fired at about 15 degrees deflection. This time, the tracers covered an area in front of and all around the enemy plane. There was no fire or smoke, but the Zero rolled slowly to the left as if to start a split-S.

I followed the Zero, but, suddenly, I realized that we were only about 150 feet off the ground! I pulled out at just about the level of the trees and saw the explosion over my right shoulder as the Zero hit the ground. I assume my bullets had hit the pilot.

Then all hell broke loose. A mess of red balls surrounded me, coming from my left, so I automatically broke hard left, pulled too hard, snap-stalled as I tightened the turn, popped the stick [quickly pushed it forward to break the stall], and recovered. Then I was surrounded by red balls coming from my right, so I yanked the airplane around to the right. Suddenly realizing that I had given one of my pursuers a neat, no-deflection shot, I thought, "I got me one, but I'm not gonna be around to tell anybody about it." As I racked the plane around to the right, I snap-stalled again, spun, and recovered just about at treetop level. I was now headed toward Port Moresby and the sea, so I hugged the treetops and started jinking violently so I could keep those other guys from getting a good shot at me. That I had the good sense to do the jinking, I attribute to Captain Ajax Baumler, who had shot down 8 planes while flying for the Loyalists in the Spanish Civil War and had been our tactics instructor at Selma.

I looked back and saw that I had three Zeros lined up in back of me. The closest one was getting a burst in now and then. He missed me on my right, on my left, and over the top, so I knew the jinking was working well, but it still made me flinch when I saw the guns blinking at me. I wondered what it was going to feel like when I got hit. But, one by one, they gave up the chase. Then I only had to think about how far I'd have to swim home if my gas gave out before I reached land again. As soon as the last Zero left, I turned around immediately, staying down on the water. I practically followed the last Zero in as he climbed out to the north. Then, as I crossed the south end of 7-Mile Strip, still at treetop level, I dropped the gear, made a left pattern, and landed. As I turned off the runway, I saw that several of the ground crewmen were pointing at my airplane, so, with pride in my victory, I stuck my arm out of the window and held up one finger. Then the engine quit—out of gas.

The pointing, I learned, was at the damage to my aircraft. It had taken two 20mm hits in the tail, one on each side of the rudderpost, with plenty of little shrapnel holes in the horizontal stabilizer and elevators. There were five 7.7mm holes in the left wing root, four in the right wing root, and one in the top of my canopy. That one had taken my sunglasses off my head without even scratching me (the glasses were a mess, though). The shooter's cowl guns had apparently straddled me.

The Zero I shot down was the first confirmed victory for the 36th Pursuit Squadron. Confirmation was easy since the Zero had gone down only about a mile from the field. Later confirmations were a lot more difficult to come by, and several were lost entirely.

*The next day, May 2, 1942, Don McGee scored a Zero probable near Port Moresby. On May 29, he downed 2 more Zeros, about 50 miles southeast of Port Moresby. After transferring to the 8th Fighter Group's 80th Fighter Squadron, a P-38 unit, in March 1943, 1st Lieutenant McGee downed a Mitsubishi G4M Betty medium bomber near Port*

*Moresby on April 12, 1943. He downed a Kawasaki Ki-61 Tony fighter over Wewak on September 15, 1943.*

*After flying 154 combat missions, Captain McGee returned to the States in November 1943. He was assigned as a P-47 instructor in a replacement training unit at Hillsgrove, Rhode Island, and to piloting target fighters for B-24 gunners at Charleston, South Carolina. He arrived in England as a volunteer replacement pilot in September 1944 and eventually wangled an assignment to the 357th Fighter Group, a crack P-51 Mustang unit. His sixth and final air-to-air kill of the war, an Me-109, was scored near Magdeburg, Germany, on March 2, 1945.*

# CHAPTER 2

Aircraft carriers were the wild cards in the far-flung Pacific war zone, for they could bring fighters and bombers quite close to enemy bases or to friendly bases under enemy attack. On December 7, 1941, six Japanese carriers actually continued sailing at high speed *toward* Pearl Harbor after launching air strikes; the ruse gave the attacking aircraft a shorter leg home than they had had going in, so more time could be spent over the target area.

In the spring of 1942, the Japanese had more carriers than the Americans, and they had many more, better, and longer-ranged carrier fighters, dive-bombers, and torpedo bombers. But the carriers of both sides were equally vulnerable to attack by aircraft and submarines, and both sides determined early in the war to use these precious capital ships with caution, only when the outcome really mattered.

The first time in the entire Pacific War a U.S. battle force was able to prevail over a Japanese battle force—on land or on the water—was in the Coral Sea. From December 7, 1941, until May 4, 1942, the U.S. Navy didn't even try. It had the will, to be sure, but it did not have the strength or, most important, the proper objective on which to risk a major defeat in pursuit of a major strategic victory.

From Pearl Harbor through May 4, 1942, U.S. Navy pilots and aerial gunners accounted for only 24 Japanese aircraft destroyed and another 3 probably destroyed. The U.S. Navy had only one ace on its roles, an aggressive young fighter pilot named Butch O'Hare. On a single mission on February 20, during the American carrier raid in the northern Solomon Islands, O'Hare destroyed five Imperial Navy Betty twin-engine bombers that were attacking the U.S. battle group.

The "proper" objective in the first week of May 1942 was thwarting the virtually inevitable Japanese invasion attempt against Port Moresby—a complex operation whose land-based aerial precursor Air Corps Lieutenant Don McGee barely survived on May 1. In addition to standing up to the Japanese in the Coral Sea, the American carrier air groups attempted to blunt the simultaneous Japanese occupation of Tulagi, site of a strategically important fleet anchorage in the nearby eastern Solomon Islands.

At the price of one of America's six fleet carriers—the *Lexington*—the U.S. Navy turned back the Port Moresby invasion force and sank a Japanese light carrier. However, the Japanese completed their occupation of Tulagi. By midsummer, that would result in the first U.S. offensive of the war—the offensive at nearby Guadalcanal. But the outcome of the carrier battle to keep the Japanese from Port Moresby was the first authentic American strategic victory in the five-month old war.

While the air campaigns in eastern New Guinea and China persisted, the second and strategically most important carrier-versus-carrier battle in history was shaping up in the eastern Central Pacific, at tiny, out-of-the-way Midway.

# HIGH NOON AT MIDWAY

**Lieutenant (jg) SCOTT McCUSKEY, USN**
**VF-3 (USS *Yorktown*)**
**Midway, June 4, 1942**

*After failing to get an appointment to Annapolis, Elbert Scott McCuskey, of Stuttgart, Arkansas, attended the universities of Alabama and Arkansas and entered law school at Arkan-*

sas in 1937. Halfway through his first semester, his boyhood dream of becoming a pilot was rekindled through a chance meeting while he was working at a bus station lunch counter. There he met a young man who was on his way to undergo Navy elimination flight training in Kansas City, Kansas. In a letter he wrote that very evening to the commander of the Kansas City Naval Reserve Air Base, McCuskey indicated his desire to fly for the Navy. In due course he was accepted, and he began flight training at Pensacola in September 1938. He earned his gold wings and was commissioned as an ensign in the Navy Reserve in October 1939.

Ensign McCuskey initially flew dive-bombers from the USS Ranger until, in February 1941, his squadron was equipped with the Navy's newest fighter, the Grumman F4F-3 Wildcat, and redesignated Fighting Squadron (VF) 42. Throughout the latter half of 1941, while embarked aboard the USS Yorktown, F-42 participated in neutrality patrols in the Central Atlantic and high-priority convoy-escort missions in the North Atlantic. The ship had just returned to Norfolk when Pearl Harbor was attacked. Within a few days, with VF-42 embarked, the Yorktown sailed for the Pacific.

On February 1, 1942, in the Marshall Islands during the U.S. Navy's first series of offensive air strikes in the war, Ensign McCuskey and his wingman became the first fighter pilots operating from the Yorktown to shoot down a Japanese airplane—an Imperial Navy Kawanishi H6K Mavis four-engine reconnaissance bomber that penetrated to within sight of the carrier. Following a brief stopover at Pearl Harbor, Yorktown embarked on a 101-day cruise in the South Pacific war zone that culminated in the Battle of the Coral Sea. On May 1, 1942, after strafing several Japanese ships near Tulagi, in the Eastern Solomons, Ensign McCuskey and his wingman crash-landed their aircraft on the beach at Guadalcanal when they ran low on fuel. Both were rescued by the destroyer Hammann late that evening. On May 8, while escorting torpedo bombers over the Japanese fleet, McCuskey chalked up his first full aerial victory, a hard-won Mitsubishi A6M Zero fighter.

After Coral Sea, the damaged Yorktown was ordered back to Pearl Harbor at her best speed. During the ship's brief layover in dry dock, VF-42 enlisted personnel and pilots, with *the exception of the commanding and executive officers, were merged into VF-3 under command of Lieutenant Commander John S. "Jimmy" Thach. McCuskey's group received a full complement of the brand-new F4F-4 folding-wing Wildcat fighters. Then, as soon as Yorktown's Coral Sea damage was repaired, she was dispatched to join the U.S. carrier task force consisting of the* Enterprise *and the* Hornet, *which was by then closing a carefully prepared trap to the northeast of America's base at Midway.*

VF-3 got off to a bad start. On our flight out from the beach to land aboard the *Yorktown,* our new executive officer, Lieutenant Commander Don Lovelace, was killed when one of the new pilots bounced over the barrier and landed on his fighter. The tragedy hung over us all the way out to Midway.

As soon as we lost our exec, we immediately had to reorganize the entire squadron. I wound up as gunnery officer and became involved in getting our new fighters ready to fight the upcoming battle.

It wasn't until we got aboard that we found that our fighters didn't have their guns mounted. The six .50-caliber machine guns were stowed in the wing wells, in preservative. The guns had to be cleaned, mounted, and boresighted. Thank goodness for our wonderful Fighting-42 ordnance personnel! They cleaned the guns and mounted them in short order but were then faced with the problem of having to improvise a template on the deck because, of course, we couldn't fire-in the guns as we would have on a range. We didn't get those aircraft ready until the day before the battle was joined. The ordnancemen worked around the clock.

The switch to the new folding-wing F4F-4s had allowed us to embark twenty-seven instead of the usual eighteen fighters, but we also learned that the F4F-4's six .50-caliber machine guns provided only approximately 22 seconds of fire, whereas the old F4F-3's four guns had given us 40-plus seconds. This factor was not taken into consideration, but it should have been—as I was to learn quite soon.

We knew Something Big was in the making and, after our executive officer was killed, I had a profound feeling of doom. This whole situation looked desperate. Admiral Nimitz was throwing everything he had against the superior

Japanese force approaching Midway Island—including the battle-damaged *Yorktown!* However, we were busy preparing and didn't get to think too much about the coming action. We had the information that the Japanese were planning to attack and seize Midway Island, and we knew the approximate date. I did not know at that time that we had broken their code.

We took position, along with the *Enterprise* and the *Hornet,* to the northeast of Midway and waited in ambush. We were hoping the Japanese wouldn't find us before they had launched their air attack against Midway. The idea was to wait until Midway was hit—poor Marines!—and then we would launch our air strike against their carriers. Surprise was the major key to victory at Midway, and catching their strike aircraft on their decks sealed their doom.

On the morning of June 4, I had the early CAP [Combat Air Patrol]. When I landed aboard, I found that I was on the schedule for the attack against the Japanese carrier strike force as a member of the fighter escort for the torpedo planes. That upset me because of my experience fighting the Zeros over the Japanese fleet during the Battle of the Coral Sea. Our squadron's fighter doctrine was to provide close support by flying above the torpedo planes at an altitude of 800 to 1,200 feet during their attack and retirement. If I could help it, I didn't want to fight the Zeros again without an altitude advantage. I also thought that undesirable duty should have been spread around among other members of the squadron. There were to be eight of us, and I was to be leading the fourth section. My wingman would be one of the new pilots, and I had never flown with him. And being the tail-end Charlie was a hot spot I didn't relish.

I had been shocked by the performance of the Zeros in the Coral Sea. They had flown around me like a swarm of bees. With that in mind, while we waited, I told my inexperienced new wingman, Ensign Mark Bright, "We will fly abeam of each other and I'll shoot them off you and you shoot them off me." It was the only tactic I could think of. There was no way to outmaneuver the Zero, one on one—especially without the altitude advantage.

Escorting the Douglas TBD Devastator torpedo planes was a tough assignment for the Wildcats. The TBDs approached their targets low over the water at 105 to 110 knots and slowed to 80 knots to drop the unreliable torpedoes. In the Coral Sea Battle, no TBDs were lost. This was primarily because the early arrival of our dive-bombers brought the majority of the Japanese CAP up to the altitude of the bombers, and the remaining CAP engaged the fighter escorts. However, in the Battle of Midway, the early arrival of our torpedo squadrons brought the Japanese CAP down to the water while the three squadrons of American dive-bombers made their attacks relatively free of any harassment. As a result of the cool and deliberate dive-bombing attacks on the Japanese carriers, we won the Battle of Midway. But over 90 percent of the TBDs were shot down and VT-8 lost all its aircraft, with Ensign George Gay being the sole survivor. It wasn't intended, but the early arrival of the torpedo planes made the victory of Midway possible.

I missed the action over the Japanese carriers. At the last minute, after sitting in the ready room for over two hours, waiting for the order to launch the air strike, my section of two F4Fs was reassigned to the air-defense mission as part of a twelve-plane relief CAP on standby. That left only six F4Fs to escort the torpedo planes of VT-3. Our squadron commander, Jimmy Thach, was greatly disturbed, but I felt I had received a last-minute reprieve.

At about 1150, while I was in my aircraft on the flight deck waiting to be launched, I switched to the fighter-control circuit. The controller was very excited. Our radar had picked up some bogies 30 to 35 miles away. They were coming straight in.

The replacement CAP of twelve aircraft was directed to rendezvous off the port bow of the *Yorktown* at an altitude of 1,000 feet. But the bogies were too close for that. When I took off, I immediately turned to starboard to fly down the intercept line while climbing at max power. The bogies were approaching from back aft on our starboard quarter.

Ahead of me, but lower, I could see Lieutenant Bill Woollen with Lieutenant Bill Barnes on the same intercept course. Unbeknown to me, Ensign Harry Gibbs was following me, trying to catch up. I was climbing at a faster rate than Woollen and Barnes.

Looking ahead I saw the Japanese bombers—eighteen

Aichi D3A Val dive-bombers—at an altitude of 7,000 to 8,000 feet. They were above me and coming straight on. Woollen and Barnes were about 1,000 feet below me but still ahead. Suddenly, Woollen and Barnes pulled up into a steep zooming attack from directly beneath the Vals. They fired at extreme range. Our six guns were boresighted so that two guns each converged at 800, 1,000, and 1,200 feet—sort of a spray effect. I saw Woollen's and Barnes's tracers rise toward the Vals, but they were widely dispersed. The Vals bobbed up and down; I guess the Japanese pilots must have seen the tracers going through their formation. Woollen and Barnes pulled off to the starboard side of the Japanese formation. No aircraft were shot down or appeared damaged.

Now it was my turn. They were all mine.

I had reached the altitude of the Vals. They were flying in two vee-of-vee formations—nine airplanes in each division arranged in three shallow vees of three. The rear division was slightly higher than the lead division and there was separation enough for me to fly between them—if I did it right.

I thought, "My God! What an opportunity!" It was a dream. There is a hell of a lot of difference between attacking bombers and fighting fighters.

The bombers were within eight miles of the *Yorktown* before I was able to lay my gunsight on the nearest Val to my left—the outside man on the left-hand section of the first division. I closed to within 100 yards of him before I fired. To avoid colliding with the planes in the second Val division, I closed to within one plane length of him. Sliding over, I raked the wingman on the starboard side of the same three-plane vee. In a continuous motion, I swung across and concentrated momentarily on the inside man of the right vee, and then raked the outside man of the same vee. All this time, because of my flat angle of attack, my fire was going ahead into the rest of the lead-division aircraft. With my six .50-caliber wing guns blazing, I literally sawed my way through the lead division.

I wanted to shoot them all down at once, but I had to concentrate, momentarily, on one at a time. So, as I moved across the rear of the first division of Vals, I kept dipping my left wing sharply so I could hang briefly. This gave me a second or two of concentrated fire from my six guns. To avoid colliding with Vals in the second division of nine aircraft, I closed to within one plane length. I didn't use my sight; it was all done at point-blank range.

By going between the Val divisions, I avoided the concentrated fire of the entire formation. Also, they were so close to the ship that I felt I would be more effective if I hit the lead division of nine aircraft. The rear gunners of the lead division didn't concern me; my six .50s didn't leave them a chance. Besides, those Vals were getting ready to attack my ship, and I couldn't let that happen.

I had a great sense of loyalty to the crew of the *Yorktown* and the men in my squadron, as did the other pilots. The ship had been our home for about a year. The men in her were depending on us. We were all highly motivated, especially from the time the ship's air officer was heard to say over the PA system, "Fighter pilots, man your aircraft," together with the plane captains' last words as they helped us into our parachutes: "Get one for me."

As I crossed behind the lead division of nine aircraft, two Vals from the lead vee pulled up into a chandelle to the right, back toward the rear of the formation. One of these may have been the Japanese squadron leader. I pulled up to the right and fired on the trailing wingman. This move brought me on a collision course with the second division of nine aircraft. At the moment I turned—1202, according to the *Yorktown* radar operators—the air seemed to explode with Vals going in all directions. I was told later that there was a big flare-up on the radar—a big blip on the scope.

All I could see were aircraft flashing across in front of me, maybe as close as a few plane lengths away. I was in the middle of it, firing one- or two-second bursts, one right after another. It was shooting from the hip.

I had made a mistake. I should have used only four of my guns and saved the remaining two in reserve. I could have done that, but I hadn't. I fired at four or five Vals in quick succession, and suddenly my guns stopped.

At almost the same second my guns quit, I heard something hit my left wing. I was in a right turn and, as I looked over my left shoulder, I saw two Vals on my tail. The leader—he may have been the Val squadron commander coming back around to engage me in a dogfight—was firing his cowl-mounted 7.7mm machine guns at me. I instantly put my aircraft in a nose dive and a hard-rolling right-hand turn. I easily broke away from my attackers. There was no plane in the sky that could outrun a diving Wildcat.

As I pulled out of my dive, I looked at the water underneath the formation. I could see numerous circular and irregular patterns on the surface. The regular patterns indicated that some of the Vals had jettisoned their bombs in order to engage me in the dogfight. I believe that the irregular patterns were aircraft I had shot down, but I have no idea how many Vals I destroyed. I claimed 3 victories and 3 probables. Ensign Gibbs, who was following me in, later stated in his written report that they were "falling like flies."

Immediately after eluding my attackers, I called the *Yorktown* for permission to land aboard. Just before I had attacked the Vals, I had seen what I thought was a second attack group. I wanted to get down on the deck and be rearmed so I could get back up to attack this second group. It turned out that the second formation was fighters that were supposed to have been escorting the Vals but had fallen behind when they neglected their primary mission and engaged members of our strike group returning from their attack against the Japanese carriers. Both attack groups, Japanese and American, were naturally using the same route, which promoted some interesting situations.

Anyway, when I made my approach to land aboard—about 15 minutes after being launched—the landing signal officer [LSO] waved me off. As I pulled off to the port side of the *Yorktown,* I noticed a Val that was circling at about 400 feet, observing the *Yorktown.* The Val's rear-seat occupant was standing up and I thought that he might be taking pictures, but it has since been revealed that this Val might have been the flight leader directing the attack after he had attempted to shoot me down.

I pulled up behind the circling Val and recharged my guns—hoping I had enough ammunition for one more burst. I pressed the trigger, but nothing happened. Jimmy Thach, our new squadron commander, had told us, "If you run out of ammunition, cut off their tails with your prop." This was a tactic we hadn't practiced, so I started figuring out a way to use it and also ensure my survival. I thought, if I could slide across, I could cut off his elevator and rudder with my prop, but I would be a dead duck if the rear-seat man stopped looking at the *Yorktown* and manned his gun. We were at only 300 to 400 feet. At that altitude, I couldn't bail out. Besides, he wasn't attacking the ship, so I turned chicken and decided to let him go.

*As soon as the Japanese attack was over, Scott McCuskey landed aboard the* Enterprise *and attached himself to VF-6. Within 2 hours, while fending off a second attack group, he shot down 2 Zeros, thus ending the day with official credit for 3 confirmed Vals and the 2 fighters—an overall official score of 6½. In fact, because VF-42 was scattered in the immediate wake of* Yorktown's *loss and neither McCuskey nor Ensign Harry Gibbs, the best witness to his attack, were ever officially debriefed, no one knows precisely how many Vals McCuskey destroyed or damaged at high noon on June 4, 1942. It could have been as many as 6. One way or another, McCuskey certainly prevented or helped prevent as many as 11 of the 18 Vals he encountered from delivering their attacks on Yorktown and thus undoubtedly saved the lives of hundreds of sailors aboard that ultimately ill-starred carrier. He was awarded a Navy Cross for doing so.*

*After returning home following the loss of* Yorktown *at Midway, McCuskey served as a flight instructor with an operational training unit and helped develop advanced fighter tactics. Late in 1942, as an adjunct to fighter-tactics development, he tested prototype gee suits for the Navy. Though the gee suits were initially rejected by the Navy, McCuskey obtained permission to personally contact the developer and manufacturer, and the F6F Hellcats of VF-8 were specially equipped with them for a 1944 deployment aboard fleet carrier* Bunker Hill.

*Though Lieutenant Commander Scott McCuskey specialized in low-level photo reconnaissance—he flew forty-nine such missions—he managed to add 7 Japanese aircraft to his score and ended the war with credit for 13½ confirmed victories. The single 7.7mm bullet the Val leader put into the wing of McCuskey's Wildcat at Midway was the only bullet from a Japanese aircraft ever to hit a plane he was flying.*

# CHAPTER 3

The U.S. Navy's back-to-back carrier victories aside, the only persistent points of contact between Japanese and Allied forces through the first week of August 1942 remained in mainland China and eastern New Guinea. And the gradient of the learning curve remained remarkably steep as new fodder was fed into the maws of the great killing machine, Total Modern Warfare.

## THE SAMURAI

**1st Lieutenant JACK JONES, USAAF**
**39th Pursuit Squadron, 35th Pursuit Group**
**Cape Ward Hunt, New Guinea, June 9, 1942**

*Curran Littleton Jones, a native of Columbia, South Carolina, quit Clemson A&M College in his senior year, as soon as he turned twenty-one, to fulfill his lifelong dream of becoming a fighter pilot. Already a trained Civil Air Patrol pilot, he entered flight school in October 1940 and earned his wings on May 29, 1941.*

*Lieutenant Jones's first assignment was to the 39th Pursuit Squadron, a P-39 Airacobra unit then serving with the 31st Pursuit Group. In February 1942, the 39th Pursuit was reassigned to the 35th Pursuit Group and shipped out to Brisbane, Australia. There the squadron of fledglings discovered that the crated fighters waiting for them were both 37mm-cannon–equipped P-39s and 20mm-cannon–equipped P-400s, the export version of the P-39 redesigned for the RAF. By U.S. Army Air Corps standards, the reinstrumented P-400 was a strange plane to fly. But the pilots, including Lieutenant Jones, preferred its reliable, straight-shooting 20mm cannon to the balky, bulky, inaccurate 37mm cannon mounted in the P-39. After assembling and testing their airplanes, the tyro fighter pilots flew them to 12-Mile (Laloki) Airdrome, outside Port Moresby, New Guinea. At the time, Port Moresby was still the focus of ongoing bitter land battles between the Japanese Imperial Army and Australian Imperial Forces.*

On June 9, 1942, eight of us volunteered to escort a strike of twelve B-26 Marauder medium bombers home after they made a low-level bombing attack against the big Japanese air base at Lae, New Guinea. At that time there were a lot of requests for volunteers. Our squadron leader on that mission was 1st Lieutenant Joe Green, who had been up toward Lae once or twice before. I was leading the second flight of four. My wingman was Lieutenant Bob McMahon, my element leader was Lieutenant George Bartlett, and my number-4 man was Lieutenant John Price. We were a mixed bag of P-39s and P-400s. I asked for and got assigned a P-400 that I had flown several times before.

We took off at about 0900 and flew northeast across the Owen Stanley Mountain Range to rendezvous with the B-26s, which would be outbound from Lae. Their usual method was to bomb the target; dive for the deck; and come out at full throttle, hugging the water. After we had crossed the mountains and gotten over the Solomon Sea, heading toward Lae, Joe Green climbed to about 13,000 feet. As we were crossing the mountains, we could hear the bombers calling for Charlie, our call sign. "Come on, Charlie," they were calling, "We need help, Charlie."

Luckily, I spotted a glint in the general direction I expected the bombers to be coming from. We hardly ever saw an individual airplane at such a distance, just a small glint of the sun reflecting off metal or glass. It was very lucky I saw him all the way down where he was. I called to Joe Green, "The bombers are at ten o'clock low," but Joe kept droning on straight ahead. The bombers were calling, but Joe didn't respond to me or them. I waited a moment and finally said, "Joe, I'm going down." He replied, "Okay, Jonesy, you go ahead. I'll cover your tail."

I started down with my flight. I was hoping the other flight would come along after us, but I had pretty good confidence in my own flight.

I was in a fair—not too steep—dive. As I got down closer, I could see a lot of Zeros—between eight and twelve. They were out over the water, just like flies around what was left of our bombers. Just then, I heard Joe Green announce over the radio that his prop was out and that he was going home. I pressed on.

I picked one of the Zeros out as my target. In fact, there were two together. They attracted my attention first because they were the biggest target up there. Sure enough, the guy I was zeroing in on pulled straight up, hanging on his prop. It was their best evasion tactic.

All four of us fired at him, but he didn't start smoking or catch fire. I had not fired at an aerial target since being assigned to the 39th Pursuit Squadron in 1941. We had only fired at ground targets in Michigan, and I'm sure some of us hadn't even done that. If I hadn't grown up hunting doves, ducks, and quail, I wouldn't have had any idea what to do. Those of us who had grown up with guns and hunting had an advantage.

We came around gently to the right in trail formation, one of us right behind the other, and pretty well strung out. As we pulled around, I heard my number-4 man, John Price, say, "Is that you behind me, Bartlett?"—referring to my number-3 man and element leader. Bartlett came back in the negative, and Price said, "Uh oh!"

I looked back and saw, sure enough, that there were *five* of us in our flight. I made an extremely tight right-hand 180-degree turn and, at full throttle, went straight back down the string toward the fifth fighter. The turn was so tight that I passed my numbers 2, 3, and 4 on the way. They were going one way and I was going back in the opposite direction, somewhat downhill, to engage the Zero, which was stalking Price back there. The other planes in my flight were surprised by my violent 180, so I was alone then, on my own.

The Zero started up in that typical vertical-climb business—hanging on his prop, up and up, expecting me to stall out. If I had stalled, he would have come right back and shot me to pieces. I had a good bit of speed. I guess he didn't realize we had just come down from altitude and that we had a good bit of speed built up. I was going full out—full throttle. He was 12 o'clock to me—straight ahead—and high. I was able to follow him up much farther than he ever expected, firing all my guns—the 20mm in the prop spinner, the four wing-mounted .30 calibers, and the two cowl-mounted .50 calibers—in real short bursts. I had modified my gunsight; I had scratched an additional elevation line on the reticle mirror. That was the bird-hunter instinct.

I'm sure I started firing too early. As I fired those short bursts, I realized I had to be careful I didn't stall, but I tried to hang in after the Zero. Luckily, he turned out to the left, broadside to me. Right then, I was sure I saw just one of my 20mm shells explode just forward of the front end of his cockpit.

The Zero flattened out and I saw movement inside the cockpit, which was beginning to smoke. Sure enough, it was the pilot. He was climbing out of the cockpit, on the left side. I tried to pull in my lead a little tighter to shoot him off the wing, but I sensed that I would probably stall out before then. I was way down below 140 miles per hour. The Zero's nose was just beginning to drop. As I passed behind it, the pilot was holding on to the cockpit, looking back at me. He was standing on the trailing edge of the wing, clutching the rim of the cockpit. He had no parachute on. The wind was blowing his scarf and billowing his flight suit.

I passed the Zero in a tight turn to the left and saw that there were two red diagonal stripes just aft of the cockpit, on the fuselage. I looked at the pilot and he looked at me. He was looking at me like I was the last man he was going to see alive. I cleared my tail and followed the Zero as it dove into the Solomon Sea, off Cape Ward Hunt. It was only smoking lightly when it plunged into the water.

It was my first air-to-air combat. I got on the radio and shouted, "Hey, Joe, did you see that one go in?" I thought maybe Joe Green was circling overhead or that somebody would have seen it. But I got no answer—from anybody. I looked for friendlies or enemies, but I was totally alone in that sky. It was my first experience with how lonely the sky can get after you've finished fighting.

My plane was pretty low. I knew roughly which direction the bombers were heading, so I searched the sky and saw five of them. They were heading back toward Port Moresby. I looked higher up out to sea and saw what I thought were five fighters in loose formation. I thought they might be my guys, but then I thought not. In that direction, they were more likely a bunch of Zeros, so I charged off to overtake the B-26s. They were already over land and climbing to cross the mountains. There were no fighters around them.

I called on the radio to say I was joining up on them. I had heard about fighters being shot at by friendly bombers. Who could blame the gunners; everyone was trigger-happy in those days. We were all just greenhorns. But the bombers recognized me; I heard one of them call on the radio, "Here comes ol' Charlie."

I joined on the left side of the five bombers. They were all shot to pieces. I did a slow roll to the left and heard one of them say, "Oh boy, look at ol' Charlie dance." Then he said, "Hey, Charlie, come on underneath us. We'll protect you." I replied, "Ah, Big Friend, you go on ahead. Ol' Charlie's here now. I'll protect *you*." But I had every intention, if any Zeros showed up, of getting under those five bombers and letting them help me out. We flew on over the mountains and landed.

I learned many years later that the pilot of the burning Zero was Warrant Officer Satoshi Yoshino, of the Imperial Navy's Tainan Fighter Group, the best fighter unit in the Pacific at that time. Yoshino was a very experienced combat pilot flying an airplane far superior to our P-39s and P-400s. He was a 15-kill ace. If we had one advantage over him and his mates, it was that we had radio contact with one another at practically all times. On the other hand, the Japanese pilots we met that day had removed their radios, which didn't work reliably anyway, in order to save weight. Having good radios saved at least one of us that day, and not having any radio helped get Yoshino killed. The other thing that got Yoshino killed was that samurai warriors considered it beneath their dignity to wear parachutes.

One of the other Zero pilots on that mission was Naval Aviation Pilot 1st Class Saburo Sakai, the highest-scoring Japanese ace to survive the war. Another point of interest is that a U.S. congressman named Lyndon Johnson, who was also a U.S. Navy Reserve lieutenant commander, was flying as an observer for President Roosevelt aboard one of the B-26s, but his B-26 aborted before reaching Lae because of an engine problem.

*The official records credit five 39th Pursuit Squadron pilots with 1 kill apiece on June 9, 1942. These were the first confirmed aerial victories scored by the unit.*

*Lieutenant Jack Jones waited nearly six months, until January 6, 1943, to score his second and third kills, a pair of Imperial Army Ki-43 Oscar fighters. By then, the 39th Fighter Squadron was equipped with P-38s, an eminently more suitable combat airplane than the lamentable, high-risk P-39 and its P-400 variant. Captain Jones achieved ace status on March 3, 1943, when he downed a pair of Zeros in two separate missions. He returned to the States in June 1943 and, for the rest of the war, was director of operations for a Florida-based fighter replacement training unit.*

*Major Jones stayed in the Air Force and completed his degree at Clemson in 1949. He commanded a C-54 transport squadron on the Berlin Airlift and a jet training group in Texas. He retired as a lieutenant colonel in 1961.*

One inevitable outcome of the steep learning curve was the early natural selection of survivors for leadership positions within recently blooded fighter squadrons, groups, and even the new V Fighter Command. Until fighter pilots tried and died, however, most fresh units were fairly uniform in their inexperience, for most were composed mainly of lieutenants who had earned their wings within mere months of one another. Even flight leaders and squadron commanders were relatively new to the business of flying fighters, and only the very few of them who had survived the Philippines and Java had ever flown in combat. As a result, all but the obvious losers received early opportunities to lead their fellows into combat—an unexpectedly democratic and often exciting outcome of universal ignorance and woefully incomplete training.

## LEADERSHIP 101

2d Lieutenant CHARLIE KING, USAAF
39th Pursuit Squadron, 35th Pursuit Group
Port Moresby, June 17, 1942

*Charles William King's three years in the Xavier University ROTC program in Ohio and his completion of the Civilian Pilot Training program naturally led to his induction into the Army Air Corps as an aviation cadet in October 1940. Immediately upon earning his wings in May 1941, Lieutenant King was assigned to the 39th Pursuit Squadron, which was then a part of the 31st Pursuit Group.*

The 39th Pursuit was the first squadron in our group to get the new Bell P-39 Airacobra fighter. After very brief training in the P-39, I went on maneuvers in September 1941 with fifteen other pilots from my class—41-D—who were also assigned to the 39th Pursuit. We participated in maneuvers in Louisiana, New York, Georgia, and the Carolinas. We flew from all kinds of fields and under poor conditions, so it is remarkable that the group suffered only one fatality during the whole three months we were on maneuvers.

The P-39 had a lot of deficiencies, but it was not a dangerous airplane, as many people believe. It was a good, honest airplane. The Allison engine was reliable if it was properly maintained and the pilot followed a few simple guidelines. The main problem I encountered with the P-39 was that it had no supercharger and thus began to lose power above 12,000 feet. Also, the armament was poorly selected. The three different calibers of the weapons—four .30-caliber wing guns, two cowl-mounted .50-caliber machine guns, and one 37mm cannon that fired through the propeller hub—all had different trajectories.

We returned to the group, which was then based at Fort Wayne, Indiana, on December 6, 1941. On Sunday, December 7, the group was ordered to proceed west to a new base. We flew the southern route, but were held up by orders at Luke Field, Arizona. On December 12, we were diverted to Washington State to guard the coast. In mid January 1942, the three squadrons were ordered to San Francisco for overseas shipment, but the 31st Pursuit Group headquarters stayed in the States to form three new squadrons. They retained two-thirds of the pilots and about one-third of the enlisted men.

We left the United States in late January and arrived in Brisbane three weeks later. There was a great amount of confusion in those days. No one seemed to know what group we belonged to. All we knew was that we were no longer part of the 31st Group. Eventually, the 35th Pursuit Group was formed in Australia from the three squadrons and some headquarters people who happened to be there.

The 8th Pursuit Group arrived in Australia aboard our convoy. It also had been equipped with P-39s in the States. When we landed, we found that we had approximately seventy-five P-400 fighters and seventy-five P-39E and P-39F fighters, all in crates. The difference between the P-39E and the P-39F was that the P-39E had an electric prop and the P-39F had a hydraulic prop. The P-400 was the British export model of the P-39. The P-39s went to the 8th Group and the P-400s went to the 35th Group. However, it soon became our practice to keep the planes in the war zone when the squadrons rotated, so both groups soon had mixes of P-39s and P-400s. I preferred the P-400 because its 20mm nose cannon was far more reliable than the P-39's 37mm nose cannon, which usually failed after firing only two or three rounds.

Prior to the arrival of any U.S. fighter squadrons in New Guinea, the Royal Australian Air Force's 75 Squadron went. The Aussies had considerable success, but they were badly outnumbered. What's more, the P-40s they flew had the same deficiencies as the P-39s against the Zero fighters, which were flown by much more experienced Japanese pilots. When the Aussies realized that, they had only a few pilots and planes remaining.

The Australians were replaced by the 8th Group's 35th and 36th Pursuit Squadrons. Their losses were not as great as the Aussies had suffered, but casualties were still excessive in terms of both aircraft and pilots. Before the squadrons were withdrawn on June 1, 1942, they had to be reinforced by five pilots each from the 35th Group's 39th and 40th Pursuit squadrons, the two squadrons that eventually replaced them. So, when we arrived on June 1, there were some "blooded" pilots to give us guidance in addition to what we had already picked up from 75 Squadron survivors. We benefited also from the experience of Lieutenant Colonel Boyd "Buzz" Wagner, the Army Air Corps' first World War II ace. Wagner was a twenty-six-year-old veteran of combat in the Philippines who had led missions for the 8th Group and who was the chief representative of what would eventually become the 5th Air Force's V Fighter Command.

The 40th Pursuit Squadron went to 5-Mile Strip, from which both the 35th and 36th had operated, but the 39th was split in half and sent to the new 12-Mile and 14-Mile dirt strips. I was assigned to 14-Mile. (It was named that because it fell on a circle 14 miles from downtown Port Moresby. Later, it would be named Laloki, after the river that lay on one end of it, between the strip and our rather distant living area. Even later, it became Schwimmer Field, named for an American pilot who fell victim to the Japanese.) To get there from our camp, we had to take a primitive ferry across the Laloki River. At one time, the bridge was washed away and we had to be flown in and out each day.

When the Allies started to base aircraft around Port Moresby, the Japanese made regular—almost daily—raids. Early on, there were at times two raids a day. By June, however, there was usually only one. We had little weather information, and it was not until later that we figured out that we did not get raids on some days because of bad weather over the Japanese bases or between their bases and Port Moresby.

The majority of our flying was defensive. We were scrambled on advance notice from an Aussie who was in the hills from which he could see the Japanese taking off from their bases in Lae and Salamaua. Our scrambles were usually a single flight of four or, at most, two flights together. We would try to get off sixteen aircraft from each squadron, but, often, that many aircraft were not in commission. Because we were seldom scrambled with sufficient notice and because of the poor climbing ability of our P-39s and P-400s, we tended to lose formation integrity and were often directed to climb. As a result we ended up underneath the Japanese bombers—at an initial disadvantage.

We were all green. However, even though I was one of the greenest of the second lieutenants, on June 17, 1942, I was leading Charlie Blue Flight in my first opportunity to show my stuff as a combat-formation leader. Our scramble was from 14-Mile Strip. On the climb, I had six other P-400 Airacobras behind me because Charlie White leader aborted. The instructions from control had us climbing right over the port area.

One of the men behind me was Lieutenant Dick Suehr, a brash fellow in whom I then had little confidence. Dick had arrived in Australia even before the 39th had arrived in mid February. He had been one of the contingent of pilots thrust into P-40s and ordered north on the way to the island of Java. He had never even gotten to their jumping-off place, Darwin. Engine trouble forced him down into a swampy area, and a week of hardship ensued. His only food was a few slimy reptiles he killed. I mistook his tales of hardship for fear and marked him as one of the least likely to be a success under combat conditions. We had been warned that we would find a certain percentage of pilots unfit for combat, and we were cautioned to identify them quickly and get them out of the squadron to someplace where they would not endanger the lives of those who would fight. How wrong I was! Dick turned out to be not only the most tenacious wingman I ever had, but he beat me to that coveted magic number of five victories. In addition, we discovered he had the most valuable asset of all: eyesight that could see enemy aircraft miles farther away and minutes sooner than anyone else. I was to discover this latter asset on this very mission.

Ground Control was telling us to climb along the coast when one of the other pilots started calling out, "Bogies at 3 o'clock." I looked out over the water, but I saw nothing. As I continued my turn, the pilot's call changed to "Bogies at 9 o'clock!" I still saw nothing, but he repeated his warning at least once more.

Finally, during one of my turns between 21,000 and 23,000 feet—a terrible combat altitude for the unsupercharged P-400s—I found myself in the center of a formation of eighteen Japanese bombers that had just dropped their bombs after a long, sweeping approach over the sea south of Port Moresby. I was so much in the middle of them and still climbing at such a slow speed that my first opportunity to shoot at a bomber was lost in a mushing turn that carried me past the formation before I was close enough to any bomber to fire.

At almost the same moment, I became aware that the bombers were not alone. Dead ahead and about 2,500 feet higher was something to shoot at. Three Zeros were diving at me in a vee formation. To bring my guns to bear, I had to pull my nose even higher and hope that I didn't stall out before they were in my range—and, of course, I was in their range. All of the guns of the P-400 were on one trigger and, although it didn't happen often in those early days, all of mine fired. My burst was that of a tyro. It was long enough that all 60 rounds in the drum of the 20mm cannon were used up. Of course the 20mm barrel was ruined. However, I saw some of my bullets stream into the fuselage of the number-3 Zero.

I knew that I was about to stall and that I was no longer a threat to either the bombers or the three Zeros. I had heard enough from the Aussies and pilots from the two U.S.

squadrons who had preceded us at Port Moresby and suffered 30- to 80-percent losses that, unless I did something quick, I was going to have a couple Zeros on my tail.

After passing them and going into a virtual stall, I pushed over as hard as I could and was soon going down vertically in a screaming dive to avoid my three attackers. My cockpit was immediately filled with debris. Had I been too late? Was what I saw Japanese bullets and their results flying through the cockpit? My fears seemed confirmed when I felt a warm liquid—blood?—flowing across my face.

I was able to level out at much lower altitude, still in control. As I cleared my tail, I realized that the warm liquid on my face was not blood. The small high-pressure oxygen masks we used back then tended to collect moisture, and the gee forces of my dive had forced water from under the mask and across my face. The debris was not Japanese lead, but the collected dirt of New Guinea that the same gee forces had spread around the cockpit.

What I didn't know until after I landed was that, by the time we made contact with the enemy, my formation of seven had dwindled to two. All the radio calls had been from Dick Suehr as he had spotted the formation of bombers as it circled to the south of Port Moresby and came in off the ocean. As Dick had called them out to me, I had done as I had been taught: I searched for them above the horizon and below the horizon. But I had seen nothing. Yes, I missed the fact that Dick had not said "three o'clock high" or "three o'clock low." The reason for that was they were at our altitude and right *on* the horizon. This was just one of the multitude of the lessons that some of us had to learn the hard way before we acquired the skills that were needed to match the experience the Japanese had acquired in their fighting over China, the Philippines, and elsewhere. Hopefully, we would get them before some Zero pilot got us too firmly in his gunsight.

Dick had gotten some fleeting but not fatal shots at a couple of the bombers before he had to evade some other covering Zeros that chased him off. As things turned out, he landed before I did. In his brash manner Dick reported to Major Jack Berry, our squadron commander, that Charlie King, with only his wingman along, had torn into a formation of eighteen bombers and a bevy of covering Zeros. He added that he was glad to be alive after such a daring attack. Dick being Dick, he made *me* out to be the hero of the day.

So, Major Berry was not quite prepared for my tale of how badly I had screwed up. I could have kept quiet and won an early medal, but I was so glad to be alive after my foolish mistakes that I anxiously shared my hairy experiences with one and all. I confessed that I wasn't aware that my formation had gone from seven to two and, worse, that I never saw the bombers until I was right in the middle of them. Of course, I also mentioned my firing head-on at the three Zeros and that I had seen my bullets strike at least one of them.

I was still very much alive and was going to have the opportunity to fight another day—many other days, as it turned out. But I was much humbled and a lot wiser. I also discovered how near to impossible it is to determine who will turn out to be combat pilots to be relied upon. Dick Suehr went on to chalk up one victory on the P-400 and four in P-38s. My victories all came in the wonderful P-38— after I learned the knack of leadership from a master of the game, a twenty-victory leader named Tommy Lynch.

What I remember Tommy Lynch for most was not his victories but his great skill as a squadron commander and his ability to get our squadron to fight, dominate the fight, and get home with a very minimum of losses. After he trained many of us and got a chance to go home for a short time, he turned the 39th Fighter Squadron over to me. That gave me the opportunity to command the only squadron I had ever been in.

*Between March 20 and November 5, 1943, Major Charlie King shot down 4 Imperial Army Ki-43 Oscar fighters and 1 Imperial Navy Zero fighter. He also claimed 3 more fighters as probables and damaged another 4 Japanese fighters.*

*When Major King returned to the United States in December 1943, he was assigned to command a squadron of America's first jet air group, the 412th, while it was service-testing the Bell P-59 jet fighter. He was one of the first combat pilots to fly the XP-80 jet fighter. King served a brief second tour in the Pacific at the end of the war and flew sixty-six combat sorties in Korea as deputy commander and commander of the 4th Fighter-Interceptor Wing. He is credited with damaging 2 MiG-15 jet fighters in air-to-air combat. Colonel Charlie King retired from the Air Force in 1970.*

Fortunately, while future combat leaders like Lieutenant Charlie King were testing their wings and, by the way, surviving the rigors of the attritional air battles over eastern New Guinea, a new regime was moving in to conduct America's end-of-the-line air war in south China. As Claire Chennault struggled to build the fledgling 14th Air Force into as aggressive a combat organization as his old Flying Tigers had become, he was aided immeasurably by the arrival of one particular professional fighter pilot. Colonel Bob Scott was a West Point graduate whose lifelong ambition was to close in the air with enemy fighters at any cost, a trait that made him a key player in Chennault's new organization. In little more than a year, Colonel Bob Scott would, through his own writings, personify the air war in China.

## "OUR HEARTS FLY WITH YOU"

**Colonel BOB SCOTT, USAAF**
**23d Pursuit Group**
**Leiyang, China, July 31, 1942**

*Though Robert Lee Scott, Jr., of Macon, Georgia, graduated from West Point with the Class of 1932, his career at the Military Academy was only a stepping-stone to his real ambition; becoming a fighter pilot. He earned his wings at Kelly Field in 1933, flew the U.S. mail in the winter of 1934, and trained hard in pursuit planes for the next seven years.*
*Colonel Scott was training young pilots at Cal-Aero Academy, in Ontario, California, when the Japanese attacked Pearl*

Harbor. On that very day, he was informed that, at age thirty-three, he was too old to fly fighters in combat. Then, though Scott had never flown four-engine airplanes in his life, he immediately volunteered for a secret mission, code-named Operation Aquila, which was set to bomb Tokyo from B-17s. The fact that Aquila was most likely to be a one-way mission meant nothing to him. To qualify for the elite group, however, he had to lie about his prowess as a heavy-bomber pilot. Luckily, the raid never came off, but it did help Scott escape from Training Command and landed him in the Far East. There he met Claire Chennault just as the American Volunteer Group was about to be inducted into the U.S. Army Air Corps. The result of the meeting was Colonel Scott's appointment as commander of the newly formed 23d Pursuit Group. Besides Scott, the unit had neither planes nor pilots until a nucleus of six AVG pilots was inducted and a crop of fresh pilots arrived from the States.

After the induction of the Flying Tigers into U.S. Army Air Corps on July 4, 1942, I found myself busy at Kunming, which was the headquarters of the China Air Task Force. General Chennault had me fly with almost every pilot from the new cadre arriving from the States. Those I missed, the squadron commanders didn't miss, for Chennault had long ago discovered that, no matter what a pilot's record showed on paper, he could best be evaluated in the cockpit of the type of aircraft he was going to fly in combat. And he was right, as usual.

Most of the pilots were qualified, but a few didn't make the grade and were sent back to India and even the Zone of the Interior—home. By the end of July, I had four squadrons. Two of the three that made up the 23d Pursuit Group were led by Flying Tigers. The third squadron, the 75th, was commanded by a Regular Air Corps major, John Alison, who was every bit as good as though he'd been flying with the Flying Tigers all the time. The extra squadron, the 16th, which belonged to the 51st Pursuit Group, had recently come into India and now was attached to us.

So, as the last days of the month came, Chennault finally said I'd been at Kunming long enough and suggested I fly over to the east about 500 miles and do some combat flying with one of my squadrons at Leiyang and Hengyang. Then he said, "You'll come to know all your men and what's more, they'll come to know you."

The press had given me a lot of publicity as a one-man air force. From that coverage I had developed the bad habit of flying alone. The general was trying to drill that habit out of me. So, that morning, July 31, 1942, I considered asking somebody to fly my wing, but the training squadron was busy with a dozen new arrivals. And, besides, I was merely flying toward the combat area, not crossing enemy territory.

Combat zones were divided into grid squares, including that part of the terrain that adjoins the combat zone. That part of China was in a grid marked off with a latitude every 20 miles or so. The latitude was measured in letters and the longitude marked off in numerals. With a grid chart clipped to my leg, I was soon climbing out of the deep valley where Kunming nestled at the foot of Shi-Shan Mountain. I was flying through the clouds because there was an overcast sky. And I was all alone. On top, I set course almost due east, which, with the strong crosswind from the south, would drift my true course just about right.

My destination was the middle one of the three fields out there to the east toward Canton and Hong Kong. Kweilin sat in the middle, with Hengyang to the north and Leiyang to the south. With about 60 miles to play with, I figured that even with our crude navigation of that day I couldn't miss—even above the clouds.

Two hours passed. I estimated I'd covered 450 miles. Down below, through some breaks, I could intermittently see a river and some unmistakable topographical features. I knew I was fairly close to a true course. I pressed my mike button on the top of the throttle and reported in the clear—but in our code—my estimated position.

"Roger, Tiger Leader," a familiar voice called out. I recognized the voice of Sasser, who I knew was at Leiyang. That started me thinking about renewing my friendships with those radio operators, who were so important in the kind of guerrilla operations we'd have to continue. Luckily, over half of them had signed up to remain with us.

Besides Sasser there was Richardson at Hengyang and Mehalko down at Kweilin. I was a little surprised when

Richardson's voice broke in. "How much juice you got, Skipper?"

With a quick glance at my fuel gauges on the cockpit floor, I pressed the button again. "Estimate thirty minutes' worth."

"What position by checkerboard, Skipper?" I told him as closely as I could and said I was about ready to start letting down.

Then Richardson said, "Warning net reports unidentified engine noise above clouds, sector northwest your checkerboard position. Filter center has you established but is negative on other aircraft. Can you investigate checker H-nine? Roger."

I heard myself call back, already searching on the map for the square where H and 9 intersected. It was close, very close.

I looked down again at the fuel gauges. I was almost to my reserve. "The hell with it," I heard myself say out loud to nobody. I reached up and checked the gun toggles and put them on. I armed all six guns with one pull. Then I turned on the lighted gunsight.

"Just to give you the picture, Tiger Leader, there's a flight of Sharks [P-40s] just landing Dallas [Hengyang]."

I replied, "They're getting juiced up at Waco [Leiyang]." The squadron hadn't landed yet following a trip against the Japanese base at San Antone—Kweilin. They were too far to matter. "Read you loud and clear. It's up to me, Dallas. I'm looking."

By that time, I was right on top of the clouds, squinting into the brilliance of the sunlight, trying to see the enemy before he saw me. I turned to my reserve. I had 18 minutes left if I didn't run into trouble and have to use full power.

Then I saw it—a Ki-21 twin-engine Sally bomber—silhouetted against the top of a white mountain of cloud. He was crossing my course, flying just about north.

I let the nose of my fighter settle down into a cauldron of clouds. He hadn't seen me. I was safe. In the peaks of the cumulus, while my speed closed the range, I checked my gun switches again. How long to close a half mile? I counted, "One hundred and one, one hundred and two. . . ." I couldn't stand it. Ever so carefully, I eased back on the stick and came out of the clouds like a swimmer coming up for air. The Japanese bomber was so close, I thought it was a different plane.

I moved my aiming point ahead of him for deflection. And only at that moment did I remember one of the warnings that General Chennault had pounded into my head. Wasn't this too easy? Shouldn't there be a fighter escort?

I jerked my eyes away from the target that was sitting out there big as a barn door. And there they were—two escorting Zero fighters—waiting for me. But they had waited too long.

When I turned back to the business at hand, the target was still positioned perfectly. I felt the recoil of my guns slowing the ship and the pungent odor of cordite being sucked into the cockpit. The bomber seemed to tremble all over and stumble like a person startled. Then it nosed up rather gently before swinging away fast, as in terror. It hung there in my gunsight and I could see that I was hitting near the wing root. And all the time, the P-40 was closing the gap so fast I thought its prop would chew right into the tail of the stricken ship.

I continued to climb until flames streamed double the length of the bomber. And then it disappeared in one of those clouds of cumulus. As I closed against the stained place and the brilliant white where the burning enemy had been swallowed up, I thought I saw my own tracers arching into the clouds.

I jerked my hand away from the top of my stick. Only when those lines of tracers continued burning across the sky did it come through to me that my guns were silent. The enemy fighters! I'd ignored them too long. I shoved back against the armor of my seat, squeezing my body into the smallest possible space. No need to look behind. I could tell where they were by the orange lines of the pungent tracers.

With all my strength, I pulled with the stick and shoved the rudder into a vertical turn right into the fighters. I blacked out momentarily in that last-ditch defensive action, even though I yelled to tighten my stomach muscles so I'd keep some blood up high enough to let my brain work and give me enough vision to see my new targets.

The blackout changed to red, and then myriads of indistinguishable objects raced back at me—the first glimmers of returning light. I saw both ships. I tried to concentrate on both airplanes. They were flying so close together. I think the first indication I had of hitting an enemy plane with my fire was when I flew into debris there in the sky.

I heard and felt something slapping against my plane as though I'd flown into a cloudburst, but it was only the oil from the crankcase of one of the enemy planes. After that, I found myself flying as blind as I had been during my blackout. The dirty goo had covered my windshield. And, by then, I was spinning crazily into the clouds myself.

Recovering from that required a defensive, screaming dive. And all the time I wasn't even able to see the clouds through which I was plunging because of my oil-smeared windshield. As I dropped out of the base of the clouds, I got the ship under control and then swung the nose of the fighter in the direction I thought Hengyang had to be.

Anxiously, I stared down at that sinking gasoline gauge. I was at 8,000 feet. My course followed that of a small river with a dirt road running beside it. Ahead, I caught the glint of a large river as the sun found a break in the clouds. If I was lucky, Hengyang would be where those two rivers met. But, for the first time, I remembered about the radio. I called Hengyang over and over. And then, when I finally heard Richardson, I could tell he had been calling me.

I broke in on his transmission. I had to find out where I was. "Listen close, Rich. Check my volume increase. I think I'm coming toward Dallas, but I'm mighty low on juice."

"You're inbound all right, Skipper. Have you two ways. Chinese net has a single plane just north of us on track three-five-zero. We'll have lunch ready."

What luck! I told him what had happened and that the evidence was all over my shark. By that time, I could see the red clay field beside the Siang Kiang River. And across the river in the green paddy was the old walled capital of Hunan Province. My fuel gauge read empty, but I still had 3,000 feet of altitude and full cruising speed. I knew I could dead-stick it in from there.

I had been a cautious pilot since I'd first went into those clouds. But with my goal in sight, I relapsed again into that happy fighter pilot; I shoved everything to the fire wall and dove the length of the runway to muscle that P-40 through two victory rolls.

Later, as hard as Captain Wong drove his jeep, it was nearly dark before I reached the area of Leiyang, where the Chinese warning net reported two enemy planes had crashed. It was simple to find the first wreck. We began to pass villagers carrying bits of metal, obviously parts of the plane.

Some had pieces of clothing. Soon, we came to the stripped body of a Japanese. Wong stopped and questioned one of the passersby. But all the man said was that the barbarian had died of wounds, which wasn't helpful to Captain Wong, who was the squadron intelligence officer.

At the wreck of the bomber, we found nothing of value in the way of military intelligence. What the fire and crash had failed to destroy, the villagers had carried away. Wong was disappointed, but he said he understood. The Chinese near Hengyang had been bombed and strafed for years and hadn't been able to do anything about it. This was the first airplane they'd been close enough to touch. All Wong did was make some notes about the type of bomber—and that it had been evidently carrying important passengers, maybe VIPs, and no bombs. After he questioned a few more people about the number of bodies, we drove away to find the Zero.

We'd never have found it except for the old Chinese who led us there, to the rice he worked every second day. The fighter had dived at an angle into the mud and water of a rice paddy two miles from the bomber. His tail stuck almost straight up from the new fringes of green rice shoots.

When I first saw it, the aluminum empennage reminded me of a gray cross sticking out of the water. If it had been up to me, I'd have left the whole thing undisturbed forever. But Wong had a job to do. And I followed him through the shallow water.

Out there, I watched while he directed some coolies to help remove the broken body of the pilot from the debris. Somehow, I felt no triumph. I didn't even feel it when a prize samurai sword was found with the pilot. And that was the epitome of souvenirs during those days. In the dim glow of the jeep headlights, Wong methodically searched the clothing of the Japanese, pocket by pocket. Every scrap of paper was placed in a waterproof envelope.

Wong found a little green book, which was sodden with rice and paddy water. He wiped the book carefully with his handkerchief before he began to turn the pages. "This is the same thing as your ID card." Then he passed it to me so I could look at the photo page. And there I saw the man I'd shot down. It had his name and birthday and where he'd been from in Japan. It had his serial number, Wong said. I thought it strange that a Japanese number was the same as ours—all numerals.

Then Wong read something else and suddenly looked at me. "He's a colonel, same as you. Commanded an air regiment, like you." I passed the sodden book back to him, happy to get rid of it. But, in the exchange, something slipped out and fell to the roadway. Wong picked it up and, as I moved in to see what he was holding, in the dim yellow light I could see a small photograph. It showed a family group—a man, a woman, and a child. Of course, the man was the broken body of the pilot we had just recovered from the bullet-riddled plane. I could make allowances for that. This was war. Seeing the child shook me. She was a little girl. She stood between the mother and father, and each of her hands held on to one of theirs. I had taken the picture from Wong and, as I turned it over and saw some Japanese writing on the back, I hurriedly gave the thing back and turned away so I could wait in the jeep.

I tossed the samurai sword in back without concern, thus scarring the beautiful sharkskin hasp. Almost absent-mindedly, I reached into my pocket and took out my own ID card. Underneath the glassine cover of my card was a snapshot of my own wife, the one she had sent me recently. I saw Catherine holding Robin's hand. Robin was just about the age that Japanese pilot's little girl seemed to be. Then I looked at the handwriting on the other side. Two lines I had read so many times that I had memorized it long ago: "Our hearts fly with you. Our love awaits your landing."

In the dim splash of light ahead, I could see that Wong had collected all the evidence he needed. As he slipped underneath the steering wheel, he said the body would be buried by two old Chinese.

*In all, the U.S. Army Air Forces officially credited Bob Scott with 13 victories and 9 probables during his tour as commander of the 23d Fighter Group. However, Scott later learned that Chinese sources confirmed all 9 of the probables.*

*After Scott returned to the United States in 1943, he served as deputy for operations at the Army's School of Applied Tactics. He also wrote the immortal and inspirational book,* God Is My Co-Pilot, *the first of his thirteen book-writing credits. He wangled a second assignment to China late in the war and ended his World War II combat service in the air over Okinawa. Brigadier General Robert Lee Scott, Jr., retired from the U.S. Air Force in 1957.*

# CHAPTER 4

The decision to take the offensive against Japan—an extremely brave and optimistic decision, made by courageous admirals and generals—was taken at the tail end of June 1942, only three weeks after the Combined Fleet had been turned back at Midway. The first objective that was seriously contemplated by America's Pacific War leaders was Tulagi, the important fleet anchorage in the Eastern Solomons that had been seized by Japan in early May in the only successful offensive phase of the Coral Sea Battle.

As a mighty Allied invasion fleet was being assembled in New Zealand to escort the 1st U.S. Marine Division to Tulagi, word arrived from Allied "coastwatchers" left behind in the Solomons that the Japanese were building an airfield on the north coast of Guadalcanal, a largish island immediately to the south of Tulagi. Plans were altered on the fly, and the Japanese airfield was made the prime target of the invasion scheme. With luck, in a matter of weeks, Marine engineers could make the Japanese runway operational, and then several U.S. Marine fighter and dive-bomber squadrons based in Hawaii could be flown in to help defend the area from a Japanese counterinvasion.

To help cover the Marine landings at Guadalcanal, Tulagi, and several other local objectives, the U.S. Pacific Fleet assembled three of America's four remaining fleet aircraft carriers—*Enterprise, Wasp,* and *Saratoga.* Thus, it fell to the pilots and aircrewmen of the three carrier air groups to guard and support both the mighty invasion fleet of transports and warships and the 1st Marine Division.

The nearest Japanese air base to Guadalcanal and Tulagi was 600 miles away at Rabaul. Rabaul, the former British seat of government, was located at the eastern tip of New Britain. Though the operational range of U.S. Navy fighters of the day was barely 300 miles, the Imperial Navy Zeros were capable of flying in excess of 1,300 miles—just enough to get them from Rabaul to Guadalcanal and back with some time left over for action against the Allied invasion fleet and its guardian U.S. Navy fighters.

The carrier air groups were indispensable to the success of the Guadalcanal landings, but they were unable to prohibit a determined force of Japanese cruisers from penetrating the Allied surface screen on the night of August 8, 1942. Four Allied heavy cruisers were sunk and the entire Allied armada withdrew from Guadalcanal the next morning, leaving the Marines stranded on the beaches without any form of naval support.

Daily, from August 9 onward, Japanese aircraft attacked the Marines with impunity, as did unchallenged Japanese surface warships. Even otherwise vulnerable Japanese submarines surfaced in plain sight of the Marines' Lunga Perimeter beach-defense line and lobbed shells at the invaders-turned-defenders.

By the end of the first week, the pattern of air battles over Guadalcanal had been set in stone. At around noon every day—weather permitting—a group of twenty-seven Betty bombers escorted by at least one squadron of Zeros appeared over Guadalcanal to attack shipping in the channel or the Marine engineers struggling to complete the captured runway at Lunga.

For three weeks, the Japanese bombers and fighters faced no opposition in the air. Nevertheless, despite the extreme vulnerability of the beachhead and the psychological trauma the flight of the fleet inflicted upon the Marines, the engineers managed to make advances in their work on Henderson Field (named for a Marine dive-bomber pilot killed at Midway). A PBY-5A that carried several casualties to Espiritu Santo on August 12 was the first airplane ever to use the new and not-quite-ready runway. (It was also the first medical-evacuation flight from a war zone undertaken by an American airplane in World War II.)

The first warplanes to land at Henderson Field—a squadron each of Marine Wildcat fighters and Douglas SBD Dauntless dive-bombers—arrived on August 20, 1942, following the daily raid from Rabaul. At dawn the very next day, the Marine fighters helped beat back the first large-scale ground assault on the Lunga Perimeter and, that noon hour, the Wildcats challenged the daily Japanese bomber strike. Thereafter, every air strike the Japanese mounted against Guadalcanal was challenged by American fighters, but the cost was prohibitive. Part of a U.S. Army Air Corps P-400 squadron arrived on August 24, but the export-model Airacobras lacked oxygen and were thus unable to reach the high-flying Bettys. A second Marine Wildcat squadron flew in on August 30, but the Japanese massively reinforced their air groups based in Rabaul and continued to plug away at the continuously outnumbered defenders.

On August 24, the Japanese attempted to send a large troop convoy straight to Guadalcanal by way of New Georgia Sound, the distinctive double column of islands known to all who fought there as The Slot. While the transports made their slow dash, an intricate subsidiary plan brought Japanese carriers into play in an effort to defeat a smaller force of U.S. carriers. In history's third carrier-versus-carrier battle—the Battle of the Eastern Solomons—one Japanese light carrier was sunk, but the *Enterprise* was severely damaged. More important, the Japanese invasion fleet was smashed and many thousands of Japanese soldiers were drowned in the wake of air strikes launched from or staged through Henderson Field.

By the end of August 1942, the two Marine fighter squadrons at Guadalcanal needed to be reinforced, or they might lose the battle of attrition. By then, two fleet carriers—*Saratoga* and *Wasp*—were more or less permanently stationed several hundred miles east of Guadalcanal, but the carrier-fleet commander's will to employ them in strikes against Rabaul had been dissipated by the steady attrition of America's limited carrier strength. As August turned to September—as the fate of Guadalcanal hung by a gossamer thread—the carriers bided their time.

# SNAP SHOT

**Ensign JOHN WESOLOWSKI, USN**
**VF-5**
**Guadalcanal, September 27, 1942**

*John Maxwell Wesolowski, of Detroit, enlisted in the Army
Air Corps in 1939 because a buddy did. He was rejected
because of a deviated septum, and the Army refused to retest
him even after he had corrective surgery. In January 1940,
Wesolowski was accepted for Navy flight training, and he
dropped out of his senior year at Wayne State University to
begin. Ensign Wesolowski was commissioned at Pensacola
on September 6, 1941. After learning to fly fighters at
Opa-Locka, Florida, he was posted to VF-5 in November
1941.*

*Ensign Wesolowski's first victory, a Mitsubishi G4M Betty
medium bomber, was tallied over Guadalcanal on September
12, 1942. He downed a pair of Aichi E13A Jake reconnaissance seaplanes near Savo Island in the early evening of
September 14.*

In early August 1942, during the initial air battles to secure
the beachhead and the airfield at Guadalcanal, my fighter
squadron, Fighting-5, was based aboard the aircraft carrier
*Saratoga*. On September 2, 1942, that ship was torpedoed
and extensively damaged. Since the Marines on Guadalcanal at the time were in dire need of reinforcements, our
squadron of twenty-four F4F-4 Wildcats was launched from
*Saratoga* while she was under tow, and we were sent ashore
to augment the Marine air group at Henderson Field—two
Marine fighter squadrons and two Marine dive-bomber
squadrons. VF-5, with an abbreviated maintenance crew,
arrived at Henderson Field on September 11, 1942, and
became an integral part of the so-called Cactus Air Force
(Cactus was the radio call sign for Guadalcanal).

Our function was to repel the Japanese air and sea attacks
on the beachhead and to provide air cover for our own land
and sea forces. Every day from the time of our arrival, VF-5

stood alert in a tent about 50 yards down the hill from the Pagoda, a Japanese-built structure that was used by the flight-operations people. At first, we had one pilot per plane, so all of us were always on duty. There was nothing else to do anyway. When we got the signal to scramble—a siren or shotgun blast—we all ran or were driven by jeep to our planes, which were parked randomly within a few hundred yards of that tent. As the aircraft attrition went up, we took turns being on alert for a given period, because we then had more pilots than planes. That gave us a chance to take a swim in the Lunga River, wander around within the confines of the beachhead, or play poker. One of our guys, Ensign Foster Blair, even did needlepoint.

Our tactics were adopted from the Marines and were both simple and straightforward: When enemy aircraft were either spotted by coastwatchers or detected on our own crude radar, we would scramble. Typically, as soon as we scrambled, we all made a slow climbing turn around the field so that we could join up and the flight leader could get to the front of the pack. Insofar as possible, we formed into four-plane divisions and made a near–full-power climb to altitude. If we had enough time, we could get to our maximum altitude of about 30,000 feet. We were in radio contact with guys at the base, who gave us whatever information they had on the incoming raid. If there were bombers, they always came in from the same direction and were always in one or more very shallow vee-of-vee formations, flying abreast. They were at 23,000 to 25,000 feet; their escorts were always well above them, at about 31,000 feet. We tried to get into position for an overhead or high-side run, usually on the left side of the bomber formation. The escorts generally didn't make their presence known until almost all the F4Fs had peeled off into their runs on the bombers. Once we had peeled off, we were on our own. Rejoining was very haphazard.

Some days, there were no bombers, just fighters. Whenever we made contact with Zeros, it was every man for himself as soon as the melee started. It seemed that formation flying was forsaken in the heat of the moment, even though we tried to keep track of things. Some days, we were in combat before we had even joined up. Those were some of the more exciting days.

Shortly after 1300 on September 27, 1942, we were alerted and scrambled as usual. Marine F4Fs from VMF-223 and VMF-224 also took off. I was the wingman of my squadron commander, Lieutenant Commander Leroy Simpler, and I joined up on him. Behind me was our second section and a couple of other four-plane divisions of the squadron. The skipper then proceeded to climb at maximum power, but my plane and several others simply couldn't keep up, even at full power. Believe me, we had the best mechanics in the world, working in almost unbelievable conditions, but some planes just did not perform as well as others. Spark-plug age might have had an effect because we weren't able to perform the routine 30-hour checks on the planes and were scavenging parts here and there. No doubt, Lieutenant Commander Simpler's plane was better tended to than many of the others.

Eventually, I lost sight of the skipper and the rest of the squadron in the clouds, but I knew their altitude and general location by way of my radio, so I kept trying to catch up. There were other stragglers, and we stragglers were loosely joined up a few thousand feet below and behind the main body of the squadron. I soon got ahead of the other stragglers and lost sight of them, too. I was completely alone.

When I was somewhere in the neighborhood of 21,000 feet in an all-out climb at about 105 knots airspeed, I swear I heard machine-gun fire. I looked back in my rearview mirror and saw two Zekes diving on me and firing. Of course, it is not possible to hear machine guns in those circumstances, but I thought I did. More likely, I felt bullets impacting on my plane. By the time I looked back, the two Zekes had already flattened out from their high-side pass at me and were essentially at my altitude. They both were firing; I could see the muzzle flashes.

I immediately nosed over to get some airspeed and, when I did, I saw a third Zeke. I believe he had overshot me while making a pass on me. When I saw him, he was below, ahead, and pretty close. He was in the process of pulling up, probably to get a new altitude advantage. He was dead in front of me and in my sights, so I fired at him—almost reflexively. My pipper must have been at least 50 mils or so in front of him because he was starting up and I was starting down. This was really a snap shot from someone whose main purpose was to get out of a nasty situation. I had all six of my guns charged and the ammo mix was one tracer every fourth round in each gun. We also had a mix of standard and armor-piercing ammo. I can't say how long a burst I fired, but I think it was quite short. I don't know where I hit him; he just seemed to break apart with little or no fire associated. He was only there for an instant; I may have overshot him before smoke and flames occurred.

I was thinking of the two Zekes that were still on my tail, so I continued to nose down almost vertically. As my speed went up, I did an aileron roll onto my back and started to pull through. That is, I dove away vertically and then, as the speed built up, executed what amounted to a half slow roll, except that I was vertical. When my orientation was 180 degrees from where I had started, I intended to pull out as fast as I could so that my ending direction was the reverse of my starting heading. We had often discussed doing this evasive maneuver; we felt that the Zero was not rugged enough to follow it without suffering structural damage. However, I was having a pretty difficult time myself. I couldn't seem to pull out, because I was going so fast by then. I don't know what the airspeed was since the needle was on its third time around the dial, which was only calibrated for two turns. I was reluctant to use trim tab for fear of pulling too many gees and breaking up my own plane. I also discarded the idea of bailing out, because I knew that if I opened the canopy the airstream probably would tear the plane apart. So I kept pulling back on the stick and very slowly got my fighter under control. I had long since lost track of the two Zekes.

When I finally got pulled out at about 600 feet, I was going way over 400 knots. I then started to climb back up to join the squadron, whose chatter I could hear on the radio. By the time I got to 16,000 feet, however, the squadron was ordered back to base, so I followed it in.

After landing, I heard the skipper yelling loudly, "Take Wesolowski off my wing; I don't want him there anymore!" He was really angry because I had not stayed with him during the climb, but I was not the only straggler, and the others helped me convince him that I was not at fault. He agreed to keep me as his wingman. He then congratulated me for having survived a brush with three Zekes—which we were all kind of afraid of—and bringing back the airplane with minimum damage.

*When John Wesolowski was evacuated from Guadalcanal because of malaria on October 16, 1942, he was a five-victory ace. (His fifth, a Betty, was downed on September 28.) By that time Fighting-5 had run out of airplanes, and the remainder of the squadron was evacuated the next day.*

*Following home leave and recuperation, Wesolowski served with an operational training unit at Jacksonville, Florida, teaching recent Opa-Locka graduates about survival in the war. He trained and led a replacement fighter division to the Pacific in mid 1944 but was separated from it when he injured his knee in a softball game in Hawaii. Eventually, he joined Fighter-Bomber Squadron 9 (VBF-9) on Manus and went aboard the* Lexington *with Air Group 9. As an F6F fighter-bomber division leader, Lieutenant Wesolowski participated in the Tokyo raids in February 1945. He destroyed his sixth Japanese plane, a Kawanishi N1K George fighter, at sea on April 11, 1945, and bagged his seventh and last victory, a Nakajima Ki-43 Oscar fighter, in the Ryukyus on May 28, 1945.*

*John Wesolowski left the Navy after the war, but he was recalled during the Berlin Airlift crisis and remained on active duty until he retired with rank of commander in 1963.*

And so it went. Through September and into October, the adversaries traded airplanes and lives over Guadalcanal in almost daily engagements. On the ground, as long as Henderson Field remained operational, the Japanese infantry—eventually amounting to well over a division—remained unable to breach the Marine lines, and Japanese ships, including transports and supply vessels, were restricted to nighttime operations. Neither side was able to struggle free of the stalemate.

On September 15, *Wasp* was sunk by a submarine while she

was on patrol east of Guadalcanal. Her loss left America with just two operational fleet carriers.

Finally, at the end of October, the Japanese put everything on the line. The crack Imperial Army division on Guadalcanal was massively reinforced and turned loose to overwhelm the Lunga Perimeter and seize Henderson Field. The Imperial Navy offered massive support in the form of an overwhelming, days-long bombardment by surface warships, including battleships. The attack shut down Henderson Field and its satellite fighter strip. At the same time, the Imperial Navy launched a massive foray by four carriers. Their goal was to at least neutralize and hopefully destroy the two American carriers that were still roving the area east of Guadalcanal.

The Japanese ground assault went off piecemeal, and the Imperial Navy was delayed. The miscoordination resulted in the collapse of the land offensive, but the Combined Fleet commander, Admiral Isoroku Yamamoto, sent his carriers in nonetheless. The result, on October 26, 1942, was history's fourth carrier-versus-carrier confrontation, the Battle of the Santa Cruz Islands.

## BUCK FEVER

**Ensign DON GORDON, USN**
**VF-10 (USS _Enterprise_)**
**Santa Cruz Islands, October 26, 1942**

_Donald Gordon, a native of Fort Scott, Kansas, graduated from Fort Scott Junior College in June 1941 and immediately enlisted in the Navy flight program. By then, he had flown 60 hours as a member of the Civilian Pilot Training program. Gordon was called up in October 1941; earned his Navy wings at Jacksonville, Florida, in March 1942; completed advanced_

*carrier training at San Diego; and, in July 1942, was assigned
to VF-10, a brand-new F4F-4 squadron that was preparing to
depart to the Pacific as part of newly formed Air Group 10.*

*By the morning of October 26, 1942, Ensign Gordon had
about 500 flight hours to his credit, more than twice as many
as most Navy ensigns and Marine second lieutenants who
had preceded him into first combat during the ten-month-old
war.*

I was one of about a dozen VF-10 pilots who were carrier
night-qualified—I had thirteen night landings by then—so
I was assigned to the predawn launch on October 26. We
flew a three-hour CAP mission over the fleet. When we
recovered aboard the *Enterprise,* our attack group had just
departed to hit the Japanese fleet.

By the time I landed, the Japanese attack was already on
the way in, but I was not aware of that. I quickly refueled
and immediately took off at 0940 with Ensign Gerry Davis
on my wing—just the two of us. Everything was pretty
expedited, but this was not an all-out scramble.

Gerry and I were vectored to the north-northwest. On the
way, I could see the *Hornet* to my right; she was about 20
miles northeast of the *Enterprise,* and both ships were
heading south. I ran into a rain squall and flew northwest for
about five miles. At that point, the *Enterprise* fighter director
told me that there were bogies at my 1 o'clock. I looked over
there and spotted five Nakajima B5N Kate torpedo bombers. They were flying in a very open, almost line-abreast vee
formation, about 200 feet apart. They were not more than
two miles from us, flying right above the horizon, and letting
down to commence their attack on the *Hornet.*

Gerry and I were between 12,000 and 15,000 feet. I
dropped my nose to the right and started down in what
would eventually amount to a nearly full 180-degree turn.

As I came out of the turn, I took a bead on the leader, who
was the nearest Kate to me—the airplane on the extreme
right side of their formation. I realized then that they were
just above the water and had spread farther apart, as
torpedo planes normally did, to get optimum angles of
attack on the carrier.

I was at 10,000 feet, so I held my fire for what seemed like ages. I was executing a low-side run, coming in at the Kate from the 4- or 5-o'clock position from about 10 degrees above the beam. When I opened fire, I was still about two miles away. Of course, I didn't hit anything.

When I got down to about 5,000 feet, I fired again. But, of course, I was still out of range. I felt really stupid; we had been drilled and drilled to fire only when we were right on top of our target, when it was impossible to miss with six guns. Man, I was *way* out! I was excited; I wanted to kill. I was more concerned with that than with saving my ammo.

I finally realized that my gunsight pipper was covering the entire Kate I was trying to hit. I suddenly woke up to what I was doing. I knew that the red meatball on the side of the Kate was 2 mils wide and that my pipper was 2 mils wide. The pipper would have just covered the meatball from 1,000 feet away, which was the proper range. But the pipper was covering the whole airplane! It finally dawned on me that I was way out of range, so I decided to hold my fire.

When I finally got all the way down to where the Kates were in range, I continued my low-side run on the nearest one. I was well within 700 feet of him, coming in from 4 or 5 o'clock from his tail. My gunsight pipper was ahead of his nose, and I was drawing a 50- to 75-mil lead to account for my angle of approach and the difference in our speeds. I was trying to hit him in the engine, but he caught fire at the right wing root forward of the cockpit. I'm sure I got him, but I didn't see the airplane crash.

I rocked a bit to the left, recovered above and astern of the first Kate, rocked a bit to the right, and dropped down on the second-nearest Kate. This brought me to the same position from which I had fired on the first Kate—well within 700 feet, 4 or 5 o'clock to the plane's tail, and slightly above the beam. I drew the same lead and fired again, and the Kate immediately started pouring smoke and flame from the right wing root forward of the cockpit. As I broke off astern of him, the rear gunner appeared to be dead; his gun was straight up in the air. I didn't see the second Kate actually hit the water either.

I pulled out to the southeast—three miles north-northwest of the *Hornet*—and started looking around for the other three Kates. I don't know what happened to them.

I never saw them again, but I am sure they didn't hit the *Hornet;* if they had, they'd had to have hit her on her port side, and she was not hit by any torpedoes on that side.

I led Gerry Davis south two or three miles abeam the east side of the *Hornet.* By that time, she was under attack by Val dive-bombers. There were antiaircraft bursts all around her, but I saw a Val dive-bomber come down beside her stack and ram her down to the flight deck. That pretty well put her out of the action. In fact, she had to be scuttled that evening.

I led Davis past the *Hornet* and headed back to the *Enterprise,* which was also under attack but in a rain squall. I thought I better get back into action.

We started to climb and had made it to about 3,000 feet when I saw another F4F, which had the numeral "12" painted on its side. As I prepared to join him, I looked up and saw a Zero just as it made an overhead run on the F4F. The Zero fired, and one of the F4F's landing gear dropped. Then I saw the F4F's canopy explode, and then the other wheel dropped. The F4F spiraled into the water. I don't even know if it was an *Enterprise* airplane or a *Hornet* airplane.

I was only 500 feet off when the Zero started its run, so I took a bead on it and pulled my trigger. One round went out. I had used over 1,600 rounds getting the two Kates—mostly firing from out of range.

Since I didn't have ammo and the *Enterprise* was not being attacked at that moment, I led Gerry down to get in the traffic pattern. Without ammo, we were no good in the air. As we came around in the groove, the F4F in front of me went into the starboard catwalk and messed up the flight deck for several minutes. As I took my wave-off to the right, another pack of Japanese was coming in and a destroyer on my 3-o'clock position took a bomb hit on the bow. I got my gear up in a hurry and pulled away, but Gerry Davis never came out of the AA. I later heard that the AA gunners on the stern of the destroyer that got hit shot down an F4F.

I retired out to the west, where we had a holding pattern to which all the aircraft were being directed. I was joined there by Ensign Chip Redding, the only survivor of one of the two four-plane VF-10 divisions that had gone out with our attack mission against the Japanese carriers. Chip joined up on me, but his radio had been shot up so he signaled to ask how much ammo I had. I signaled that I had no ammo. He then pointed to the aft end of his aircraft and I checked it out. He was really shot up bad.

Chip and I went out about five miles and circled back when I saw a Kate. He was leaving the *Enterprise* and heading west low on the water. I was afraid he would try to shoot me down and my only escape was to head right for him. I got down on the water and aimed my airplane right at him. I wasn't going to run into him, but I figured I could get past him. Apparently, the pilot wasn't paying attention to what was in front of him. I thought I saw him looking back over his left shoulder at the *Enterprise*. He must have been startled by me when he turned back to face the front. All of a sudden, he dropped his left wing to avoid me and cartwheeled into the water. I got credit for that one!

Chip Redding and I circled out there until around 1100, by which time the attack was over. The *Hornet* was dead in the water and burning; the *Enterprise* was taking aircraft from both air groups aboard even though she had taken three bomb hits and had sustained serious damage, including the loss of her forward elevator.

As I landed, the flight deck was so full that the midships elevator was down. That was unheard of, but that's what it was taking to leave enough space to recover as many aircraft as possible. I no sooner landed than they taxied me onto that elevator and struck me below to the hangar deck. By then, another airplane was landing. Fortunately, I got off the elevator before someone piled into me. If the next airplane had jumped the deck barrier, that's exactly what would have happened. I taxied forward on the hangar deck, folded the wings, and shut the engine down. But they refueled me and I was quickly launched again. I had to give up my place to make room for *Enterprise* and *Hornet* dive-bombers and torpedo bombers that had come back from the strike mission and been held in the air while the fighters and crippled bombers were taken aboard before they ran out of fuel. I was up for only a half hour, and then they landed me again. During that time the bombers that ran out of fuel were landing in the water; the crews were being pulled out by the destroyers.

When I got to my stateroom that night, I found that a mess cook who had been killed by one of the bombs had been put in my bunk. He was still there when I returned.

*Don Gordon was given credit for just one of the two Kates he flamed on his first firing pass and for the Kate he scared into the water. The third Kate was scored a probable. During VF-10's second combat tour, also aboard the Enterprise, Lieutenant (jg) Gordon, to whom bombers were the target of choice, downed a Zero fighter over Taroa on January 29, 1944. He downed another Zero during the Truk Raid, on February 17, 1944. Gordon's fifth and last officially credited confirmed victory was a Yokosuka D4Y Judy dive-bomber he destroyed during the Marianas Turkey Shoot, on June 19, 1944.*

*When Don Gordon returned home with VF-10 in mid 1944, he was a full lieutenant. He remained in the Navy, flew with that service's first all-jet squadron, and retired as a captain.*

By the beginning of November 1942, the Japanese had been defeated every time they had attempted a major effort against the Lunga Perimeter or the American carriers. It is true that the *Enterprise* had been damaged again and the *Hornet* had been sunk during the Santa Cruz carrier battle, but the Japanese carriers had withdrawn without achieving their strategic objectives, and that counts as an American victory. Nevertheless, the Japanese commanders decided to try one last time to take Henderson Field. The bulk of a fresh division of Imperial Army infantry was embarked in a flotilla of slow transports and a truly formidable surface battle force was gathered to escort the transports and bombard the Lunga Perimeter into submission.

As luck would have it, the 1st Marine Division—which had already been reinforced by a Marine regiment and a U.S. Army regiment—was in the midst of an even larger troop buildup at just the time the Japanese were preparing their new blow. As always, Imperial Navy air units based at Rabaul were sent in first to clear the way for the transports and surface warships. The first support strike went off on November 11, 1942, and it caught a flotilla of U.S. Navy transports and surface escorts unloading fresh U.S. Army troops just off Lunga. As always, Marine fighters rose to meet the incoming Japanese warplanes. Even by mid November, not much had changed.

## SO FAR . . . A PILOT'S DREAM

### 2d Lieutenant TOM MANN, USMC
### VMF-121
### Guadalcanal, November 11, 1942

*Thomas Henry Mann, Jr., was born on February 6, 1919, in Sullivan, Indiana. He attended Purdue University and Indiana State Teachers College before joining the Navy in May 1941, and he opted for a commission in the Marine Corps when he graduated from flight school on March 14, 1942. Lieutenant Mann was initially assigned to Marine Fighting Squadron (VMF) 122, but he was transferred to VMF-121 four days before that squadron sailed to New Caledonia in August 1942. He gained initial combat experience in September 1942 while he was attached with several other VMF-121 pilots to Major Robert Galer's VMF-224 at Guadalcanal.*

*Tom Mann scored his first victories while flying with VMF-224. He was credited with a ½ Betty on September 28, 2 confirmed Bettys of his own on October 11, and a Zero on October 13. Then, as one of newly arrived VMF-121's most experienced pilots, Mann got a ½ Zero on October 18 and achieved ace status with a full credit on a Betty bomber on October 23.*

Our fighters were operating from a dirt runway—Fighter-1—with absolutely no maintenance facilities. The maintenance crews can only be praised for the outstanding job they did keeping us flying. Living conditions were horrible—shellings, air raids, snipers, and horrible food.

Few of us peons had any knowledge or realized how precarious our tactical situation was. Flight operations on The Canal were primitive. Pilots generally sat on benches or around picnic tables at the edge of the jungle, waiting for a scramble. The alert came from coastwatchers hiding out in the Solomons north of us. We took off when they saw Japanese planes heading down The Slot toward us. It was always a mad scramble—with the hope and prayer that we could get into a decent position to launch our attacks. Briefing and debriefing were nonexistent. It just happened that an alert from the coastwatchers usually gave us just enough time to get up to 20,000 feet by the time the Japanese arrived.

VMF-121 could not be considered a well-organized, cohesive flying unit. I had no squadron duties during my tour on Guadalcanal. The pilots and enlisted personnel found their way to The Canal in increments from September on. The last increment landed from a transport on November 11. However, we had excellent leaders—Major John Smith, Major Bob Galer, Major Duke Davis, Captain Joe Foss, Lieutenant Colonel Joe Bauer, and others—who were able to train us on the job and set wonderful examples for us kids to follow.

On November 11, 1942, I was scrambled at 0905 for an interception of dive-bombers attacking the resupply ships anchored off Lunga Point. I was in a flight of eight F4Fs led by our squadron commander, Major Leonard "Duke" Davis. The weather was CAVU. We had climbed to approximately 18,000 feet and were heading north when I spotted a flight of twelve D3A Val dive-bombers at approximately 12,000 feet, heading east. They were at 11 o'clock down, and they had already started their run on the ships. I alerted the flight and started right down after the Vals.

As I left the flight, I picked up the dive-bombers in a rough right-echelon vee. I dove down on them from west to east and rolled left into their north-south run-recovery path. As I did, I saw one or two of them roll into their runs on the ships. My first run was a tail shot at about a 30-degree dive, directly up the echelon of six or eight Vals. As soon as I started firing, the entire squadron started its dive-bombing run. I easily shot down the last plane in line with a short burst. He puffed smoke and flames and fell into the water. I continued up the echelon and shot down either the lead or second plane in their formation, also with a short burst. He exploded.

I rolled to my left and down and picked up another Val between 1,500 and 1,000 feet. I shot at him from 500 yards. His bomb dropped when my bullets hit the plane. I stayed right on this plane's tail and fired another burst when we were passing down through 500 feet. The bomb landed just short of a small destroyer, and the Val crashed on the north side of the ship. I am sure the ship was firing like the blazes, but I never really saw any of its AA.

As I pulled out of my dive, I saw another Val at water level. The pilot was heading north after completing his run. As I closed on his tail, he started fishtailing, apparently trying to give his rear-seat gunner some shots at me. We were four to five miles north of the ships when I fired a short burst at 100 yards. The plane exploded.

So far, it had been a pilot's dream—all tail shots.

I noticed a fifth Val. It was heading north after recovery. It was directly in front of me. Closing on this Val took longer than the two previous closings; we were going about the same speed. As I closed into firing range, I noticed that the Val was leaving propwash on the water. The pilot was really hugging the deck! I pulled up to between 50 and 100 feet so I could get a good shot. As I did, I glanced to my left and saw that another Val was making a shallow right turn just a few yards from me. I had not seen him until that moment. My flight path was directly in his line of fire. I made an instinctive flipper turn to the right, away from him. As I did, he hit me with his cowl-mounted machine guns.

His 7.7mm bullets hit my oil cooler, in my left wing, and along the left side of my cockpit. The throttle was useless.

When I crashed into the water about halfway between Savo and Florida, I hit my head on the gunsight and lost seven teeth. We did not have shoulder belts yet. I also had shrapnel wounds on the whole left side of my body.

I could not inflate my rubber raft, so I swam in my Mae

West from approximately 0930 until dusk. I had heard that there were Japanese on Savo Island, so I headed for the Florida group even though it was farther from where I had crashed. I did not feel a current, but there must have been one flowing west. I was no weakling, but it took all my strength to get to the nearest island. I finally reached one of the small islands—200 or 300 yards in diameter—in the northern part of the Florida group. We had been warned about sharks, but I did not see any. I just collapsed on the beach. I was lying partially out of the water on the beach when two Melanesians approached me. One of them said, "We watch. Me see." I accompanied them in their dugout canoe to a larger island, where I discovered that one of the islanders, who had been the houseboy for a missionary, spoke broken English—enough so that we could converse to a degree.

I remained with the islanders for seven days. My wounds were treated by a preadolescent under the supervision of the chief's wife. The treatment consisted of leaves and roots from the jungle boiled in water and placed on the wounds. I also rinsed out my mouth with the solution, which tasted awful. However, it must have been effective because there was never any sign of infection. I also had two small boys, ages five and seven, who were with me 24 hours a day. I couldn't move without them trying to help.

The islanders were sincere Christians. Each evening at dusk they had a prayer service that was attended by every member of the village. The village consisted of eighteen living huts and a large central hut. In view of the lack of food at Guadalcanal, the fruits, baked fish, and meats they fed me were like gourmet foods—even without my teeth.

On November 18, I was returned to our base at Tulagi in a large dugout canoe rowed by twenty-two islanders. The entire trip was approximately 45 miles and was made in eight hours without a stop. The islanders chanted or sang religious songs for the entire trip. I returned to Tulagi wearing a Japanese dungaree uniform that the islanders gave me in exchange for my flight suit. They told me that the uniform was from one of three Japanese they had killed on their island.

The doctors at the base removed six or eight pieces of

shrapnel, up to ½ inch in size, from my left hand, left arm, and left leg.

My wife was never notified that I was Missing in Action. The first she heard was when a letter she sent to me was returned with "MIA" stamped on the envelope.

*After recovering from his injuries in New Caledonia, Lieutenant Tom Mann rejoined the rest of the original VMF-121 pilots, who were then recuperating in Samoa. (The squadron itself was never actually rotated, just the original pilots.) When a number of the original VMF-121 pilots returned to Guadalcanal in early 1943, Mann was transferred to VMF-111, and he remained in Samoa until August 1943, when he was sent to the States to recover from malaria. Thereafter, he served with Marine Operational Training Unit 4 in Jacksonville, Florida.*

*Captain Mann returned to the Pacific with VMF-223 and arrived on Okinawa in July 1945. He served with the occupation forces in Japan for a year and remained in the Marine Corps until 1961, when he retired as a lieutenant colonel.*

# CHAPTER 5

The Naval Battle of Guadalcanal was the pivotal naval engagement of the Pacific War. Though the Japanese had been stung at the Coral Sea in May and utterly defeated at Midway in June, it took a major defeat of their *surface* forces—especially the loss of two old battleships—off Guadalcanal in mid November 1942 to convince the Japanese admirals that they might lose the war. At the same time the admirals were glimpsing the future, and taking note for the first time of what they saw, the Japanese generals were finally prepared to concede that the land campaign on Guadalcanal had been going awry. The Imperial Army had won no victories on land there, and they had frittered away more than a crack infantry division in the attempt. Even more telling, by mid November the Imperial Navy had sacrificed for no lasting gain whatsoever a staggering 600 first-line combat aircraft and nearly that many crack pilots and aircrews. The attempt to outduel the numerically weaker, underequipped Cactus Air Force had been futile.

For the mixed bag of combat-aviation units that composed the Cactus Air Force, the outcome of the epic November land, sea, and air battles provided the first respite of the three-month-old campaign. During this break the entire Cactus air establishment was reorganized, modestly reinforced and upgraded, and partially replaced. However, in mid December, even during the needed respite, the Solomons air war began to heat up again.

The reason for the rise in activity was the discovery on December 17, 1942, that the Japanese had finally come to their senses sufficiently to begin work on the first all-weather bomber-capable runway to be constructed between Rabaul and Guadalcanal. The new strip, which would be fielding a small contingent of Zero fighters within a week of its discovery, was at Munda Point, on New Georgia, only 150 miles from Henderson Field. Though the Cactus Air Force commanders could have used and would have liked more time to build up the strength of the largely American air establishment on Guadalcanal, they ordered that an immediate effort be mounted to interdict the building program at Munda.

The Cactus Air Force, now directly overseen by the joint-services command known as Aircraft, Solomons (AirSols), answered the call by immediately mounting limited fighter-escorted bomber strikes against Munda. The strikes against Munda and Japanese observation posts in the Russell Islands were hardly more than probes; they were restricted both by Guadalcanal's limited aviation resources and by a lack of range imposed upon the American fighters by the complete absence of auxiliary fuel tanks in the South Pacific Area.

## THE CHRISTMAS PRESENT

Major PAUL BECHTEL, USAAF
12th Fighter Squadron, 18th Fighter Group
Munda, December 24, 1942

*Paul Sarachon Bechtel graduated from the University of Wyoming with an engineering degree in 1939 and immediately entered the Army Air Corps to learn how to fly. He earned his wings on March 23, 1940, and went on to Selfridge Field to learn to fly fighters. Thereafter, he served with the 31st Pursuit and 50th Pursuit groups until he was assigned to the 12th Fighter Squadron, a Bell P-39 Airacobra unit, in January 1942. By December 19, 1942, when the 12th Fighter*

*Squadron's pilots were shipped to Guadalcanal from Espiritu Santo, Major Bechtel was commanding them.*

On the morning of December 24, 1942, two four-plane flights of my squadron were assigned to provide high cover at 16,000 feet and intermediate cover at 12,000 feet for a contingent of nine Marine SBDs that were going to dive-bomb Munda Field, on New Georgia. The Japanese had built most of Munda underneath the palm trees, and it was only in the past week or so that they had taken the palm trees out to complete work on the runway and operate fighters. It thus became one of the prime targets of the Cactus Air Force, which was just beginning offensive operations north of Guadalcanal.

Along with the nine SBDs and my eight P-39s were four Marine F4Fs, which were being led by Major Don Yost of VMF-121. None of us enjoyed escorting SBDs very much because they flew pretty slow—about 125 miles per hour—as they climbed to altitude with their bomb loads. The fighters were doing 175 miles per hour even when we were throttled back, so we had to weave around an awful lot all over the place, yet keep the bombers in sight and stay with them. We didn't have any fixed position we had to hold with respect to the SBDs; our job was just to cover them. We stayed above them and close enough to them so we would be there if anyone came in to attack, so we could get between attackers and bombers.

The weather was good. We had gone into snowstorms escorting some B-17s to Munda the day before, but, on this particular mission, we didn't run into any weather.

When we came in toward Munda from the east at about 0800, we discovered that Zero fighters were taking off from the airfield. I believe they were taking off toward the west. They kicked up quite a cloud of dust.

The SBDs immediately went into their dives from about 10,000 feet and raised Cain with those taking off and those that were around the field, starting their engines. The four F4Fs followed them down and had a field day shooting down Zeros, mainly in the traffic pattern. I could not see the individual planes from up high, where I was, but I could see flamers as the Marines went around the traffic pattern with the Zeros, which were in their takeoff and gathering pattern. They were burning up, one right after another. My second flight was shooting Zeros off the tails of the F4Fs.

Meanwhile, my flight of four was up around 13,000 feet when we spotted a group of about six Zeros in an echelon formation off to the west. We were up-sun from them. These guys had apparently taken off before we arrived over Munda and were just circling, probably waiting for the SBDs to get away from the AA on the field so they could pounce.

I turned toward the Zeros to attack, but they apparently thought we were another bunch of Zeros. As we approached them, they turned away gently to the left so we could join on to the tail end of their formation. This was very accommodating.

I pulled up behind the rear Zero and followed it into a gentle one-needle–width turn to the left. When I was between 200 and 300 yards from the enemy plane, I took what I thought was an adequate lead. In those days, we used what we called the Christmas tree sight, which was a vertical line with three lines running across it, decreasing in size from top to bottom. The middle one was for a zero-deflection shot, but I never was sure what deflection or lead the other two lines provided.

I fired a long burst with the four wing .30s and the two cowl .50s. (I never fired my 37mm at another plane.) It was the first time I had ever fired at another airplane, and nothing happened. Obviously, I was shooting behind him. If I had hit him or fired any tracers in front of him, he would have realized I was back there and was not friendly. I then doubled the deflection and fired a second burst. I'd have kept trying in methodical increments until I hit him, but this time I was more fortunate. I did not see any strikes, but he promptly began to smoke and lost his power. My wingman later said that he broke into flames.

By then, I was pulling up and had just started firing at the next guy in line, but the rest of the Zero pilots apparently discovered that we were there and they all broke formation. They all tightened their turns, pulled up to the left, and scattered like a flock of ducks. I tried to follow them, but it was hopeless. They turned inside of us. Very shortly after that, I got a call from my wingman, 2d Lieutenant Everett

Anglin: "Paul, you've got a Zero on your tail." I was turning to the right and, when I looked back over my right shoulder, I saw that I sure did have a Zero on my tail.

His guns were blinking and the tracers were creeping up toward me. The tracers came at me in a sort of a spiral—they corkscrewed toward me. I promptly went into a tighter turn to my right to try to get away from that guy. I kept my eye peeled behind me as his tracers crept closer and closer.

About this time the inevitable happened. My P-39 stalled and spun to the right. I guess that's probably what saved me, because the guy who had been shooting at me apparently figured he'd gotten me. He went after somebody else. However, Anglin shot him down.

When I recovered from my spin, I ran into one of those things that seemed to happen quite frequently in air-to-air combat; I looked around and I couldn't see an airplane anywhere. One minute in combat, you've got airplanes everywhere you look, but, a minute later, you look around and can't see any. I think it had something to do with the way fighter pilots focus their eyes. At high altitude, there's nothing to focus on.

Over Rendova Island I recovered from my spin. Then I flew around trying to latch on to somebody to go home with. As I did, I saw a single airplane about 1,000 feet higher than I was and four to five miles off to my left. I thought he might be one of my lads, so I turned and climbed to join up with him. As I got closer, I could see that the plane was a Zero. Like the first bunch we'd run into, he turned out to be very accommodating. He apparently thought I was another Zero. As I got closer, he turned gently to the left so that I could join on his tail.

This time, I was a little luckier than I had been the first time. I had about the same sight picture as I had had on the first Zero, but I had a much better idea about how much lead to put on him. I closed to within 300 yards and fired. I got him on the first burst. As before, I did not see any strikes, but he started smoking, lost power, leveled off, and turned to the right. As he turned, I overran him and turned off to the left to clear my tail. I was alone this time; I didn't have any wingman to warn me or get a Zero off my tail. I had to take care of myself. When I looked back, I never saw him again. Somebody down below me, however, did see a Zero burst into flames at about that time. As a result, I was able to confirm that victory.

I started home then because I figured it was time to get out of there. I was sure I had used up most of my ammunition, and I was a little worried about fuel. Otherwise, as far as I knew, I was in okay shape.

On the way home I found one of my lads, and the two of us joined up. A little later, I looked at my altimeter. It was at 6,000 feet, so I took off my oxygen mask. Then, when I looked over at the lad on my wing, I saw that he still had his mask on. I called over and said, "What're you wearing your oxygen mask for?" He looked at me kind of funny, looked at his altimeter, looked back at me, shrugged his shoulders, and took off his oxygen mask. We descended on our way until I got down to 2,000 feet. But when I looked over the side, it didn't look anything like 2,000 feet. So then I really checked my altimeter. It wasn't 2,000 feet; it was 12,000 feet! I think this was a good indication of how shook up you get when you're in combat. I put my mask back on until I got lower, and we returned to Fighter-2 all right.

The raid turned out to be quite effective. The four F4Fs shot down 10 Zeros, the SBDs figured they did about as well as that with their bombs against the Zeros on the ground, and my two P-39 flights got 4 confirmed victories and 2 probables. It was a pretty doggone nice Christmas present for our little Cactus Air Force.

*In addition to the 2 Zeros and 1 Zero probable he scored on December 24, 1942, Major Paul Bechtel was credited with a Zeke over the Russell Islands on April 1, 1943, and another Zeke over the Russell Islands on April 7, 1943. He was flying P-38s on both of those missions. His fifth and final victory came on September 2, 1943, when he was flying a VMF-124 F4U Corsair fighter on a bomber-escort mission over Kahili Airfield, in southern Bougainville. By then, Major Bechtel had turned over command of the 12th Fighter Squadron and was serving as the XIII Fighter Command's operations officer. Colonel Paul Bechtel retired from the Air Force in 1963.*

The aerial interdiction of Munda continued apace—the Japanese were never able to make effective use of the air base—and the war in the Solomons slowed down. On Guadalcanal, two U.S. Army infantry divisions and a U.S. Marine division conducted a three-month campaign to throw the waning Japanese infantry force from the island. At the very end, in late January, the Imperial Navy laid on a major effort, accomplished entirely at night, to evacuate thousands of Imperial Army veterans from Cape Esperance, Guadalcanal's western tip. Though the effort was accomplished largely without Allied aircraft or coastwatchers discovering that it was underway, there were several clashes between the AirSols combat aircraft and Japanese air and naval sorties charged with covering the evacuation. One such, undertaken only ten days before Guadalcanal was declared secure by the Allied area command, provided America and the U.S. Marine Corps with an indisputable new hero.

## POINT OF NO RETURN

**1st Lieutenant JEFF De BLANC, USMC**
**VMF-112**
**The Slot, January 31, 1943**

*Jefferson Joseph De Blanc, scion of one of Louisiana's oldest French families, was born in Lockport, Louisiana, on February 15, 1921, and raised in St. Martinville, the family seat. De Blanc dropped out of college before beginning his senior year and, with his older brother, Frank, enlisted in the Navy flight program on July 29, 1941. Frank De Blanc opted for a Navy commission, but Jeff was sworn in as a Marine second lieutenant as soon as he earned his wings at Corpus Christi on May 4, 1942. In early October 1942, with less than 250 flying hours to his credit, Lieutenant Jeff De Blanc joined VMF-112 as it was preparing to sail to the South Pacific.*

*VMF-112 arrived at Guadalcanal on November 10, 1942. Though De Blanc had only 10 hours' experience in F4Fs, he scored his first victories—2 Betty bombers destroyed and 1 Betty probable—over Ironbottom Sound on November 12. He added a Mitsubishi F1M Pete float biplane to his tally on December 18.*

*Before dawn on January 29, 1943, 1st Lieutenant De Blanc was forced to ditch a faulty Wildcat fighter in the luminous wake of a friendly destroyer that was fleeing across Ironbottom Sound during a Japanese air raid. He was rescued by the destroyer following the raid and returned to Fighter-2, where he immediately resumed flight duties.*

On the afternoon of January 31, 1943, the coastwatchers on Vella Lavella sent word to Fighter Command that a Japanese fleet was entering the Kolombangara area, escorting cargo ships. The watchers requested immediate dive-bombing action for a sitting-duck attack. This action led our leaders to believe that another attempt to regain control of Guadalcanal was in the making, but the reverse was true. The Japanese planned to evacuate their troops from Guadalcanal and chose this date to commence the action.

Twelve SBD dive-bombers were ordered to strike the Japanese fleet, which was 250 miles away from Guadalcanal. Eight fighter pilots were on standby alert. We were playing acey-deucey when word came down that an escort mission had been handed to Fighter Command. We scrambled for the flight line and, with parachutes strapped on, headed for the assigned Wildcat fighters. This type of mission was not usually lucrative and was usually shunned, if one could get out of it. However, we had no choice because we were on call.

The briefing was short and precise. Takeoff time was 1500; the targets were 250 miles out; and there would be instrument conditions for the return trip, since the moon was down and the weather was closing in rapidly up The Slot.

The operational range of the Wildcat fighter was about

200 miles without external tanks, provided the engine was functioning properly. External tanks were in the experimental phase and were not too reliable. However, emergencies in the war had priority over safety, and the Wildcat was the only fighter we had to oppose the Japanese. So, we would be fighting away from our field and over enemy waters with the added burden of belly tanks. Before engaging in combat, we would have to jettison our belly tanks for two reasons: The added weight would hinder maneuvers and, if the external tank was hit by bullets, it would explode because it was not self-sealing.

I was assigned a fighter that had a blonde bombshell painted on the cowling with the title "Impatient Virgin" lettered underneath. The plane captain handed the yellow sheet to me for my signature of acceptance, and I signed. We made small talk as he helped me strap in, and he said he hoped I would get my first kill that day. I mentioned that I already had a few planes to my credit and this aircraft was not the one I usually flew.

It was after 1500 by the time we got airborne, because the slower bombers took off first. All eight fighters took off, and soon we pilots switched to belly tanks. We wanted to use all the petrol in them so we could release them and have "clean" fighters and lots of petrol remaining in the internal tanks for the coming fight.

Twenty minutes into the flight, one of the Wildcat pilots called in with a rough engine and aborted. Two minutes later, another fighter pilot called over the radio to say that his fuel-pressure gauge was acting up. I wanted to suggest to him that he smash the gauge and not worry about it, because we needed all the guns we could get for the escort mission, but I decided not to. He aborted and returned to base, leaving six fighters to do the job. I resented this a little, since almost every fighter we flew in combat had something wrong with it. I venture to say that out of every twenty planes we flew in combat only two would meet flight standards if we had been Stateside and in training. Some pilots are aggressive; others are not.

The two who had left were members of VMF-112, as were five of the remaining six. The five were Lieutenant Tom Hughes, Lieutenant Joe Lynch, Lieutenant Jack Maas,

Lieutenant James Secrest, and me. Staff Sergeant Jim Feliton, who was flying on my wing, was a member of VMF-121. It was decided that Jack Maas and Tom Hughes would fly the high cover and the rest of us would wing it right over the bombers for the dive on the Japanese fleet. It was never clear in my mind how this decision was reached, but the die was cast. After this decision, we leaned out the gas mixture as much as possible to conserve fuel.

I settled down to a cruising speed, drawing fuel from the belly tank and scanning the area for enemy planes. We were now deep in enemy territory. I was also keeping an eye on the instrument panel. Fighter pilots are able to check the main instruments in the cockpit by simply looking across the panel briefly, watching for any vibrating gauge needles. Movements of any gauge needle mean trouble. It was during such a panel scan that I noticed the gas-gauge needle starting to fluctuate. I quickly threw the emergency fuel-pump switch and started working the wobble hand pump to build the fuel pressure back to normal. The gas selector was switched to the external tank setting, as we were all using our belly tanks first. The needle continued to drop regardless of my efforts, and I quickly switched my selector valve to the main internal gasoline tank. The pressure needle jumped back to normal, and my engine picked up the added revolutions. I could not have used up the 50 gallons in the belly tank so soon—or had I? Either the tank had run dry because of a gas-guzzling airplane or suction had been lost through the external connecting feed lines. The latter was a common occurrence in the experimental phases of auxiliary-tank connections. I quickly got out the plotting board and did some fast figuring with the circular slide rule in the lower quadrant of the board. I could make the run if I leaned out the fuel mixture to the aircraft's engine even more.

We were past the point of no return, and I could see the island of Kolombangara sliding below my wing 14,000 feet below. The Japanese airfield at Vila looked empty. Where were the Zero fighters? We crossed the islands, and I checked my fuel gauge again. It was dropping rapidly despite my efforts to lean out the engine. I now knew I had drawn a gas guzzler or had a gas leak somewhere. I leaned the fuel mixture out until the engine began to drop RPMs. That was the signal to quit this procedure. It was going to be a close one getting back. I notified the others of my situation.

By this time we were over the target; the fleet was below us. All hell broke loose as the dive-bombers went into action and the AA fire started reaching for us. Secrest and Lynch commenced a strafing run against a cargo ship below, and Feliton and I were in a position to protect the dive-bombers against attacks by fighters. It was a lousy run for the dive-bombers. All 12 succeeded in getting near-misses, but no hits.

I picked up a call for assistance. The bombers had come under attack by Pete float biplane fighters while regrouping at 1,000 feet for the trip home. I saw the floatplanes racing in to clobber the dive-bombers after they started to join up. I was well experienced in this type of action and had the altitude advantage. Two of the Japanese floatplanes were closing in for the kill, one following the other about 1,000 feet apart in tail-chase pattern. With luck, I could nail them both. I called Jim Feliton to follow me down and cover my tail in case I missed and overshot. In this way, he could nail the rear floatplane and I could go after the next one.

I had the feeling of perfect control as I pulled the little Grumman fighter flat on the trailing floatplane for a no-deflection shot using only four guns. The rear gunner opened up on me, so I quickly dropped below his flight path at the 6-o'clock position and opened up with four of my guns when his plane filled my sights. The Pete flamed immediately and dropped off in a slow, graveyard spiral, burning furiously. The plane exploded as I flew over and settled on the tail of the second one, the leader.

Evidently, there was no communication between this rear gunner and his pilot because no evasive action was taken. Regardless, I settled onto the Pete's tail below the sight of the gunner, at 6 o'clock to him. When the plane filled my gunsight—when the crosshair of my gunsight was dead center on both cockpits—I opened fire and watched as the plane flamed immediately. The floatplane started a slow climbing turn to the right from an easterly direction to a westerly one. Upon reaching the westerly heading, the plane exploded in a flash that matched the setting sun.

For a moment, I was mesmerized by the sun and the flash of the explosion. It all seemed unreal. The flash of fire and the setting sun appeared to have the same intensity. What appeared to be a slow-motion bit of action had taken only a matter of seconds. All the other floatplanes cleared the area. I pulled up in a climbing right bank to verify Feliton's position and clear my tail. As I raced for altitude with Feliton on my wing, somebody yelled over the radio, "Zeros!"

About ten Zeros were heading straight for us, holding a fixed altitude. They failed to see Feliton and me because we were about 500 feet below them in a climbing attack approach. I pulled up into a smooth gunnery run on the leader. It was like shooting at a fixed target sleeve I had fired on during advanced cadet training. I placed my gunsight in direct line with his flight path and a few mil rings above the nose of his oncoming aircraft. I squeezed the trigger when I was within range. There was no way I could miss. The leader never knew where the fire was coming from. With a jerking motion of such violence that it almost tore the wing off the Zero, he rolled out of my sights in a tumbling flip to the left. I either killed him instantly or his last reflex resulted in this motion or he was the fastest evader I had ever seen. I never saw him again and could not claim him.

The leader's wingman started upward in a slow left spiral climb. As he looked around, trying to figure out what was happening, I locked onto his tail. The following action was witnessed by Lieutenant Joe Lynch, who reported it upon his return that night. The Zero pilot started a slow roll upward and I followed the roll with him. As he came out of the roll, I fired. He never knew what hit him, because his plane exploded violently.

This started one of the wildest dogfights I have ever been in. To this day, I cannot say how many more Zeros came down on us. Targets were everywhere. Staff Sergeant Feliton and I flew a defensive scissor weave to cover each other's tail. On one turn, he pulled too wide. In the first few seconds, which seemed like a lifetime, I watched his fighter take a hit in the engine cooler as he banked across the nose of my fighter. He left the fight streaming a huge trail of black smoke. The Zero broke off his firing on Feliton and cleared out when he spotted my fighter. Feliton would be safe from further fighter action. Crippled aircraft are usually left alone in dogfights until all the action is over. Then they are shot down. By that time, Staff Sergeant Feliton would have bailed out safely.

During the next 10 seconds, the air was clear of fighters. I had taken a few arrows in my fighter during the dogfight and remembered seeing a Zero plunging in flames from above. It was a kill by Lieutenant Jack Maas, who was up on the high cover. The bombers had all assembled for the return trip and were preparing to take a heading back to home base.

As I started a climb toward a position that would take me above our bombers, which were fast disappearing in the distance, I noticed two Zeros closing in from behind me. A glance at my fuel gauge shocked me. I had used up quite a bit of fuel during the dogfight. I could easily join the bombers and fly wing on them as added protection for the return trip; my mission as fighter escort was completed with the safe retirement of the bombers from the immediate combat area. The rear gunners on the bombers could handle the Zeros along with my contributions—if I could reach them in time. If I stopped to engage other Zeros, my chances of returning safely would be in question. I would probably run out of gas. Facing total darkness for the return trip, I kept thinking about the night water landing I had gotten away with two days earlier, an experience I did not want to repeat so soon. I decided to challenge the Zeros and take my chances and, at the same time, draw the Zeros away from the bombers. But I knew I could not outrun the Zeros and would thus have to accept combat. If I ran out of gas returning home after this fight, I would bail out. There would be no more water landings for me.

I switched on the last set of guns, the ones I usually kept for the return flight home as added insurance. Now I had all six .50s ready for action. I have always maintained that if you can't hit them with four guns, you certainly won't hit them with six. But this time I was in an all-or-nothing position.

These Japanese pilots were aggressive. Both fighters came at me as I turned head-on into them. Again, I was in the better firing position. A climbing head-on run is better than a diving head-on run. The Zero pilot had a trim problem diving on me as he picked up speed, but I was slowing down as I climbed toward him. My fighter became more stable as I slowed in the climb. I had six .50s against his two 7.7mm machine guns and two 20mm cannon. I assumed my bullets would reach him before he could hit me. Besides, he couldn't use his slow, low-muzzle-velocity cannons until he had me boresighted.

The Japanese pilot started shooting out of range. Coming at me, the tracers looked like Roman candles on a pair of railroad tracks. In less than a heartbeat, we closed and I fired. His Zero caught fire immediately, but it kept coming straight at me. He was going to ram! The firing had slowed my fighter by about 15 knots or more—Newton's Third Law—and my controls became sluggish. I really became frightened. Could I maneuver out of the way? I held the trigger down and the Zero blew up in a flash of fire. Pieces flew everywhere. Some struck my fighter as I struggled to regain control from an almost-stalled position after flying through the debris.

I banked sharply to get on the tail of the other Zero as he flashed by, but he had already pulled up high above me and completed his turn. He was coming down on me in a high-side run.

While serving as the Cactus Air Force's first fighter commander, Lieutenant Colonel Joe Bauer, one of our most experienced fighter pilots, had always maintained that, if ever a Zero gets on your tail, don't worry. The Zero pilot, Bauer said, will open fire with the twin 7.7mm machine guns to line you up, then cease firing and open up with his twin 20mm slow-firing cannons. You will have plenty of time to skid out of the way. Besides, even if the 7.7s did hit you, the armored plate in the back of your seat will take the shock. Bauer had convinced us long ago that the Zero was *not* invincible but could be dealt with head-on or on your tail. "Dogfight them, for they are paper kites," he had said.

The Zero pilot coming down on me was too eager for the kill and did not judge my speed correctly. With his altitude advantage and his closing rate of speed too great and increasing in his diving run, he stood a great chance of overshooting me—a factor he realized too late. I chopped the throttle, skidded, and dropped my flaps. I was down to a few knots above stalling speed. The Zero, which was closing too fast, sailed by me and overshot me, at the same time fishtailing to stay on my tail. This he failed to do. To this day, I can see his face as we locked eyes for that instant. He froze on the controls and flew straight ahead of me without making any attempt to get away. I shot him down with one short burst.

I have often wondered if this Zero pilot knew that other Zeros were on my tail and, by his flying straight, they would shoot me down after I got him. I had made the almost-fatal error of not clearing my tail before I shot this Zero down. Unknown to me, there were others behind me, already in firing position and making a run on me.

I quickly glanced at the watch strapped on the inside of my wrist and noticed that the time was approaching 1800. Night was rising fast from the earth below. In the next instant, I felt the watch fly off my wrist and saw the instrument panel erupt in flames caused by a 20mm shell coming in over my left shoulder. The gasoline from the ruptured primer on the instrument panel had a good fire going in the cockpit, aided by the floor auxiliary tank. In the next second, I caught another burst in the engine, and it flamed and lost power. In my frantic effort to get out of the line of fire, I caught a glimpse of the Zero banking for another run on me. In the meantime, the damaged canopy worked loose from its railings and, with a loud bang, was lost in the slipstream.

With the aircraft falling apart, I unbuckled my safety belt and jumped for the trailing edge of the left wing. Feeling a jerk on my neck, I realized I had forgotten to disconnect my throat-mike cord.

How peaceful it felt to be free of noise and watching the waters far below as I slowly tumbled through the air. What a sensational feeling! I felt free as a bird and got a beautiful view of Earth from space. I had a feeling I could land without getting hurt. I often wonder how many others who have parachuted felt on the first jump. I don't even remember pulling the D ring of my parachute, but, the next moment, the canopy of silk was above me and I was on the way down.

The Japanese pilot who had shot up my Wildcat had seen me shoot his buddies down, and some Japanese pilots shot at Americans in parachutes, so I was anxious about getting down. Upon parachuting out of the stricken fighter, I had reacted too quickly. Instead of free-falling at least 1,000 feet—clear of the dogfight arena—I found myself floating down in the same sky as the Zeros. I decided to play dead in the chute. As the Zero circled me twice, I let myself go limp, with my head sagging. He even pulled his canopy back on the second pass and gave me the once over. Then he sped off back to Kahili Field, on Bougainville.

The sun was setting as I floated down. The water below looked calm and glassy. I would not have to fight choppy waves, but I would have trouble judging when to release my chute before hitting the water below. I concentrated on the glassy ocean and had to wait an eternity because I had left the fighter at about 2,000 feet. Finally, I knew I was close and said to myself, "What a piece of cake," as I unstrapped my chute harness and sat comfortably in the seat pack, ready for my feet to touch water. However, the instructions I was following were for choppy water, not a glassy sea. Maintaining depth perception over glassy water requires a great deal of concentration. If the waves below are choppy, the pilot can see 3-D immediately and can probably judge the proper parachute height. Height above a glassy ocean cannot be readily judged. This fact flashed through my mind as I was coming down. I knew that, because there was little wind, the chute would collapse on top of me as I hit the water. Therefore, I decided to release my harness about 10 feet above the water and avoid this danger. I thought I had excellent eyesight, but I misjudged this distance—an understandable error. What I thought was 10 feet turned out to be over 40 feet. It seemed an eternity before I hit the water as my chute collapsed and I fell clear of the shroud lines.

My plunge into the ocean was a deep one. I was so far under that I had to pop my Mae West life jacket to help me reach the surface. I could see the reflection of the sunlight on the surface of the ocean, but it seemed ages before I broke clear and gasped for air. Only half of my Mae West was inflated. The other half had been cut by shrapnel. The adrenaline was flowing, and I didn't realize yet I had been wounded in the arms, legs, and side. My .45-caliber pistol, canteen of water, and extra shells had been ripped off my waist when I bailed out. Had I worn my shoulder holster, this would not have happened. Regardless, the back pack of my parachute harness, which was still attached to my body, contained survival equipment. All aviators flying over water carried chlorine pills in their shirt pockets. We were told to break these in the water every 15 minutes to ward off sharks.

After landing in Vella Gulf between Kolombangara and Vella Lavella, I started to swim toward Kolombangara. I wished to get ashore and possibly steal a Zero from the new Japanese airfield at Vila, which I had spotted as we flew over it earlier. This may sound farfetched, but I knew of no other way to get home. I figured stealing a Zero was my only option unless I elected to hide in the jungles for the duration of the Solomons action. I knew I could survive in the jungles with no problems.

*It took six hours for Jeff De Blanc to swim to the nearest beach, and he spent two days subsisting on coconuts before a party of friendly islanders ran across him. The islanders hid him and cared for his wounds while the local coastwatcher arranged for a rescue mission. A PBY flying boat finally arrived on February 15, and De Blanc was flown to Guadalcanal and hospitalized.*

*Promoted to captain in June 1943, De Blanc flew with VMF-122 for about six weeks and then returned to the States. In November 1944, Captain De Blanc departed for the Pacific again and joined VMF-422 in the Marshalls. He shot down an Aichi D3A Val dive-bomber off Okinawa on May 28, 1945, his ninth and last victory.*

*Jeff De Blanc received credit for 5 victories on the mission of January 31, 1943—2 Pete float biplanes and 3 Zeros. Under normal circumstances, this would have earned him an automatic Navy Cross. However, in consideration of his knowledge that his fuel supply was critical and his decision to defend the bombers despite the jeopardy he faced, 1st Lieutenant Jefferson Joseph De Blanc was recommended for a Congressional Medal of Honor. In December 1946, Captain Jeff De Blanc was recalled to active duty and, on December 6, President Harry Truman awarded him the nation's highest military honor at a White House ceremony. Colonel Jeff De Blanc retired from the Marine Corps Reserve in 1972.*

The fighter pilots' war in the South Pacific Area all but petered out during the first three months of 1943. Efforts like 1st Lieutenant Jeff De Blanc's were by far the exception because the Japanese were keeping a low profile. They simply did not rise to the many challenges inherent in the ambitious schedule of fighter-escorted bombing raids conducted within range of the burgeoning Guadalcanal air-base complex.

In all of January 1943, Marine Corps fighter pilots claimed 63 Japanese aircraft destroyed, Army Air Forces pilots operating from Guadalcanal bagged 37, and U.S. Navy fighters claimed 11 kills—all during the naval battle of Rennell Island.

The U.S. Navy's newly deployed and only land-based squadron of the period claimed 20 victories in the Central Solomons in February, none in March, and 8 during a big Japanese raid against Guadalcanal on April 1, 1943. Similarly, the Army Air Forces squadrons working from Guadalcanal scored 18 victories in the Solomons in February, 8 in March, and 2 during the raid of April 1. The Marines, who had many more squadrons in place and a reasonably active bombing program to support, turned in claims for 26 victories in February 1943, none in March, and 11 during the raid of April 1. Thus, between New Year's Day 1943 and the evening of April 1, 1943, the many fighter squadrons of all three American combat-aviation services based in the Solomons brought down a grand total of 204 Japanese aircraft.

The low tally was not for lack of trying; it was for lack of opportunity. The Imperial Navy air groups that had been decisively battered during the battles of attrition over Guadalcanal from August through November 1942 had been withdrawn to regroup and absorb many hundreds of new pilots and aircrewmen. The result, by early April, was that a new and quite large Japanese air component had been built to undertake future battles in the Solomons. But, as quickly became evident, the new force was nowhere close to the quality of the Imperial Navy air establishment that had already been decisively shattered.

The next big contest came on April 7, 1943. The Japanese mounted what for them was a maximum effort.

## SEVEN AND DOWN

**1st Lieutenant JIM SWETT, USMC
VMF-221
Tulagi, April 7, 1943**

*James Elms Swett of San Mateo, California, learned to fly with the Civilian Pilot Training program while attending San Mateo Junior College between September 1939 and June 1941. He earned a pilot's license and completed about 240 hours of flight time. It had been Swett's intention to fly for the Coast Guard after graduating, but he learned that he had to attend U.S. Navy flight training first. He enlisted and qualified for the Naval Aviation Cadet program in August 1941 and shipped out to Corpus Christi, Texas, as a member of that new training center's third class. While at Corpus Christi, Swett was approached by a senior Marine officer and talked into opting for a Marine Corps commission. He earned his wings and a commission as a Marine second lieutenant on April 16, 1942, and, after completing advanced fighter training, was sent to Quantico, Virginia, for a communications course.*

*First Lieutenant Swett shipped out to Hawaii as a replacement pilot in November 1942 and was assigned upon arrival to VMF-221. By virtue of his rank, he was further assigned to lead a four-plane division of the squadron's F4F-4 Wildcats. Following some additional squadron training, VMF-221 arrived in the New Hebrides in January 1943 and, late in the month, flew to Guadalcanal, where the squadron worked out of the hard-topped satellite strip known as Fighter-2. For the next two months, Jim Swett and his comrades worked hard, escorting bombers on strikes against the Japanese air bases at Munda and Rekata Bay, but VMF-221—whose only other Pacific War action had been at Midway—remained scoreless and virtually untested in the Solomons.*

We had no auxiliary gas tanks at the time. We could escort bombers to Munda or Rekata Bay, but that was about it. Those missions were unopposed except for antiaircraft fire. The first time I ever actually saw any Japanese planes was on April 1, 1943, when they put a heavy raid in over the Guadalcanal area. However, VMF-221 was ordered to circle Henderson Field. I saw the fight way off in the distance and heard a lot of the action on the radio, but we didn't get into it at all. It was boring.

On April 7, I led off an early-morning flight of seven other F4Fs from VMF-221. We took off at 0430 or 0500 and flew up to circle over the new airfield our engineers were building in the Russell Islands. I made contact with the fighter director there—Knucklehead. We flew around in the clouds the whole time, and we couldn't see a thing. As we were leaving, Knucklehead mentioned that he had word that there appeared to be a lot of activity going on at the Japanese field at Kahili, in southern Bougainville. I didn't pay too much attention. If they were coming, they were hours away.

We got back to Fighter-2 around 0800, refueled, and took off again around 0900 to circle around up at Cape Esperance, the western tip of Guadalcanal. By the time we landed again a few hours later, word was arriving through the coastwatcher channels that there was a big raid on the way toward us from Kahili. Rear Admiral Pete Mitscher, who was the AirSols commander at the time, put everybody on alert for the intercept. My flight no sooner landed than we topped off our fuel and ammunition and got airborne again.

The Japanese were coming in toward Guadalcanal from the northwest, but they then turned almost due east to head for Tulagi. There were a couple of tankers, a couple of corvettes, and a U.S. Navy destroyer in the harbor. So, as my flight of two divisions was forming up, the fighter director vectored us out north to guard Tulagi, the fleet anchorage about 40 miles from Henderson Field. We were to orbit there to defend the ships.

I no sooner got off Fighter-2 and up over toward Tulagi than the Japanese strike—67 Vals escorted by 110 Zeros—was already in sight. The dive-bombers were already starting to peel off to go down into their dives. The weather was crystal clear. The usual cumulus clouds were in the sky, down low.

I was going along almost at full throttle and the rest of my division was going at full throttle and then some to catch up to me. We were strung out for over a half a mile somewhere between 15,000 and 20,000 feet.

The rest of the guys got jumped by Zeros, but I was unaware of that. I was far ahead. The sky in front of me was full of Vals, so I just sidled in behind a half dozen of them—two vees. They were already into their dives. They still had their bombs aboard.

I was going an awful lot faster than they were. They were just damned slow airplanes. When I intercepted them—the first bunch I could get to—they were pretty strung out, about 50 yards apart from one another. I just made a right turn and got into their formation. There was a dive-bomber behind me and a good half dozen or more up ahead of me. We were all diving.

I was right square on the tail of the first Val in front of me, dead astern. All six of my guns were boresighted at 150 yards, but I was way closer than that—probably more like 50 yards behind him.

I decided to try to kill the pilot, so I opened fire and walked my bullets from the tail forward. My bursts were only two or three rounds per gun. That was all it took. I'm sure I killed the rear gunner, but I'm not sure I killed the pilot. I killed the dive-bomber first and the pilot went with it.

The first Val caught on fire, so I moved up to the next one in front of it and did the same thing. It caught on fire too, so I proceeded up the column and fired at the next one. All three caught on fire. It surprised me that they burned so easily.

The rear gunners had been shooting at me, but I never saw a round hit my airplane. The firing didn't really last long at all. Just one burst from each of them, and they were gone. By the time the third one caught on fire, I was a lot less scared than I'd been when I first opened fire.

I could see bombs from other dive-bombers hitting the ships in the harbor. I saw a tanker get hit, and the destroyer. I'd have kept going after the dive-bombers that were still in front of me, but I was getting too low and going too fast. I was so low, in fact, that I never saw the planes I'd flamed hit the water. That had to be confirmed by way of reports from the ships and people on the beach around Tulagi Harbor.

I began pulling out of my dive at around 1,000 feet and came all the way out of it at around 500. Just as I came out of the dive, I was hit in the port wing—just in the outboard gun—by a 40mm antiaircraft round fired by one of the ships. I felt the hit and looked over. It had left a hole about a foot in diameter in the wing and destroyed my landing flaps. The gun barrel was actually sticking straight up out of the hole in the wing.

I got out of there.

I was by then north of Tulagi, but the heavy clouds were in the way, lying right down on top of Florida Island. I turned east through a break in the cover, between the clouds and the land. I had to stay fairly low to get through.

As I got over the other side of Florida, I saw that a whole bunch of dive-bombers were trying to get together. They were scattered all over the sky! There must have been at least a dozen of them.

I was still around 500 to 600 feet as I approached the dive-bombers, and I was going an awful lot faster than they were. I'd guess they were doing around 120 miles per hour, and I must have been doing 150 to 160.

The nearest dive-bomber was making a slight left turn. I did a little turn to my left to match him, and I suddenly found myself right square behind him; I was coming straight up his tail. He was still in a mild turn when I opened fire, but he was right in front of me at exactly the same altitude. I got him with another short burst, just like I had the first three over Tulagi.

I made a right turn after the first one—my fourth

kill—caught on fire. I went over to the next plane, turning left to come up on his tail. The pilot saw me coming, but he couldn't evade. By the time he tried, he was on fire.

The same thing happened to the next Val pilot. I zig-zagged onto his tail and shot him down from straight back before he saw me coming. And then the same thing happened with the next one.

I was really sweating. I was soaking wet!

I tried for one more, but I got too damn close. I was only 25 to 30 feet behind him when the rear gunner knocked the living hell out of my windshield and oil cooler—and me. I used up the last few rounds in my Wildcat on him. I killed the rear gunner and got the airplane smoking. He wasn't actually on fire, but he was smoking like the dickens.

I was totally out of ammunition, so I made a right turn and headed back toward Tulagi. I was hoping to get home to Guadalcanal, but my oil pressure was zero.

I did get back over Florida Island, but, just as I came across Tulagi Harbor, the engine froze. That was the end of that; one blade of the propeller was standing straight up in front of me: the big finger.

I was still quite low, only a couple of hundred feet. As I went across Tulagi Harbor, I noticed that there was a shore-based machine gun shooting at me. One of our Marines!

I didn't have any flaps because of that 40mm antiaircraft round that had gone through my left wing. So, the airplane literally bounced and dove into the water. I was down 15 to 20 feet in the water right off the bat.

I undid my seat belt and shoulder straps and kicked out, but my parachute harness got caught on a double-ended hook on the raft compartment just back of the cockpit. The water was getting dark and cold! It took a couple of good struggles to get free.

When I finally got to the surface, I inflated my Mae West and managed to get half of my seat raft inflated. That held me up. My face was mashed up from hitting the gunsight. Even though I'd had a shoulder harness on, the straps had been fairly loose. My nose was broken, and I had scratches all over my face from where slivers of my windshield had been shot off by the rear gunner of the last Val I'd shot up. Fortunately, there were no bullet holes in me.

I saw a Coast Guard picketboat off in the distance. My .45-caliber pistol was loaded with tracer rounds. I drained the water out of the barrel and fired the tracers up in the air, and the boat came over. I had been in the water only about 15 minutes by the time it reached me. The men on deck had rifles at the ready and one of them asked, "You an American?"

I shouted, "You're goddamn right I am!"

"Okay," the skipper said, "it's one of them smart-assed Marines. Pick him up."

*Wheels—big wheels—started turning as soon as 1st Lieutenant Jim Swett was put ashore at Gavutu, a small island on one side of Tulagi Harbor. After being shot up with morphine and throwing up a glass of whiskey provided by the Marine base commander, Swett was reunited with another member of his division who had been shot down and recovered in the wild air battle that resulted in the loss of 12 Vals, 17 Zeros, and 7 Wildcats. The two Marine pilots were ferried to Henderson Field the next morning aboard a Navy patrol bomber—a 10-minute flight—and Swett was hospitalized so his broken nose and many facial abrasions could be treated. No doubt, he had sustained a concussion as well.*

*Jim Swett's tally, which was confirmed in short order, apparently included an Imperial Army lieutenant colonel who appears to have been directing the entire attack from aboard one of the Imperial Navy Vals. This senior Japanese officer reached Florida alive, but he was later killed by islanders. His papers, including operational codes, eventually made their way to Guadalcanal.*

*While Lieutenant Swett was still recuperating in the hospital, Admiral Mitscher cabled his superiors with news of the Marine pilot's unprecedented seven-victory mission. Mitscher recommended that Swett be awarded a Medal of Honor, and that was done in very short order. (Only one American pilot, Commander Dave McCampbell, surpassed Jim Swett's one-mission score—with 9 kills in a single mission.)*

Amidst all the hoopla that naturally surrounded his stupendous feat, Jim Swett was offered an early return to the States, but he was only a little over a year out of flight school and wanted to continue to put his hard-won skills to use. He refused the special treatment.

After VMF-221 transitioned to new Vought F4U Corsair fighters in May 1943, Captain Jim Swett destroyed 2 Betty bombers and shared credit for a downed Zero on June 30, 1943, while covering the Rendova invasion. He destroyed another Betty and another Zero over Kula Gulf on July 11. During his second combat tour with VMF-221, he bagged a Zero over Kahili on October 18, 1943, and downed 2 more Vals over the U.S. invasion fleet in Empress Augusta Bay on November 2. Swett returned to the States with VMF-221 in 1944 and redeployed with the unit in 1945. He earned his last victory, a Nakajima B6N Jill torpedo bomber, near Okinawa on May 11, 1945. Overall, Jim Swett's official tally was 15½ confirmed victories and 4 probables.

Major Jim Swett was demobilized at the end of the war and went to work for his father as a manufacturer's representative. He remained in the Marine Corps Reserve and retired as a colonel in 1970.

# CHAPTER 6

The air war in the Solomons remained at a low ebb throughout the spring of 1943. In all of May, Marine fighters tangled with Japanese warplanes only once—on May 13, when 15 Zeros were downed out of a large nuisance raid that penetrated all the way to Guadalcanal. Things picked up a bit for the Marines in the first half of June, when Guadalcanal- and Russells-based Marine squadrons, by then all newly equipped with F4U Corsairs, downed a total of 26 Japanese airplanes in one offensive and two defensive actions.

The land-based Navy Wildcat squadrons operating in the Solomons earned no victory credits in May and only 14 in just two actions during the first half of June. Army Air Forces pilots did a little better. On April 18, a flight of Guadalcanal-based Lockheed P-38 Lightning twin-engine fighters knocked down 6 Japanese planes over southwest Bougainville. One of the 6 was a Betty bomber copiloted by Admiral Isoroku Yamamoto, commander in chief of the Combined Fleet. Yamamoto was killed in the singular ambush, and that more than made up for an otherwise desultory spring. In all of May, Army fighters in the Solomons accounted for 5 Japanese planes and, in the first half of June, another 22.

The Japanese threw in an immense raid on June 16 to disrupt the shipping, troops, and supplies being readied around Guadalcanal for the impending invasion of Rendova Island—the gateway to Munda Field. That day, Army, Navy, and Marine fighters destroyed 73 of the Imperial Navy bombers and their Zero escorts—by far the best one-day tally in the ten-month-old South Pacific air war. Between June 16 and June 29, however, only 2 Japanese aircraft were downed in the entire region, both in out-of-the-way places by Navy Wildcat fighters on long-range patrols.

The Americans invaded Rendova on June 30, and the air war escalated precipitously as the Japanese reacted. Of course, the violent reaction had been factored into the plan, so hundreds of Allied fighters based at Guadalcanal or the Russell Islands were arrayed over or on call in proximity to the new beachhead. On June 30 alone, responses to Japanese attacks against Allied shipping in the Central Solomons accounted for 66 victory claims by Marine pilots, 34 by Navy fighter pilots, and 11 by Army pilots—another one-day record.

And so it went. The Zero-escorted Japanese bombers or Zeros alone sallied from their Northern Solomons and Rabaul-area bases on ten days between July 1 and 13, and they suffered at least one loss—and as many as 21—every time they did. These Japanese forays were, for the most part, nuisance raids aimed at pecking away at the Allied fighters or ships supporting the Rendova and subsequent New Georgia landings. During those first two weeks of July, the Imperial Navy air groups to the north of New Georgia were engaged mainly in mustering what their commanders thought would be a hideous new all-out blow. When it fell on July 15, the Americans were ready.

## TAIL CHASE

**Captain JIM CUPP, USMC**
**VMF-213**
**Vella Gulf, July 15, 1943**

*Eager to satisfy the minimum two-year educational require-*
*ments for the Navy V-5 flight program, James Norman Cupp,*
*a native of Corning, Iowa, took his University of Iowa*

*sophomore finals two months early and enlisted in May 1941,
shortly after his twentieth birthday. He earned his wings and
a commission as a Marine second lieutenant on February 27,
1942, and joined VMF-213 in Hawaii in September 1942. He
trained with the squadron in F4F Wildcats in Hawaii before
proceeding to Espiritu Santo, where the squadron transitioned into F4U-1 Corsair fighters. By mid July 1943,
Captain Cupp was the squadron flight officer and typically led
a daily flight composed of two four-plane divisions on routine
patrols over the Rendova and New Georgia beachheads and
frequent bomber-escort missions to Bougainville.*

The F4U Corsair as we knew it then was a relatively light
airplane, but it was still heavier than any fighter we had
flown. The engine had a lot of torque—so much, in fact,
that if you stood on the runway and gave it full throttle
suddenly, rapidly, it was likely to flip you over on your back.
You had to ease on down the runway until the speed allowed
the rudder to take hold and you could control it.

There was a 500-gallon tank in the fuselage between the
engine and the cockpit. It was rubberized and fireproofed a
little bit, but there was no fireproofing in the wing tanks.
There were no frills. There were no bomb racks.

There were six .50-caliber wing guns. The guns could be
individually charged from the cockpit—and recharged. As a
matter of fact, they jammed up a lot in combat. One or two
would often stop firing by the time you finished a pass, so
you'd recharge those particular guns and make another pass.
If you couldn't unjam them, they stayed inoperative. We
didn't run out of bullets very often because of this uneven
gun operation, and we carried a pretty big supply.

VMF-213 had the guns boresighted to center on any
target about 300 feet in front of the plane. That's pretty
close when you're going over 300 miles per hour. Some
squadrons had all six guns boresighted straight ahead, and
some others had them firing in a box. There were different
ways to boresight the guns, but our squadron had them
concentrated at about 100 yards. That made a lot of
difference as to the tactics we used. At boresight range, the
bullets had a devastating effect, but beyond boresight range
the bullets were dispersed and had little effect. Our pre-

ferred attack was a high-side run initiated in front of the target and slightly to the side from about 3,000 feet above.

The normal four-plane division formation was with the wingman to the leader's left and behind (8 o'clock) and the second section to the right and somewhat behind the wingman and the leader (4 o'clock), so each could slide across under the tail in front without jockeying the throttle. If we had time to get ready to attack, the wingman moved to the leader's right side and the leader waggled his wings and peeled off to the left. The rest of the formation followed closely. The leader would make almost a split-S, or a high-gee 90-degree diving turn, and then reverse it as quickly as possible. There were many variations on the theme, however. We came down, preferably, to fire a full-deflection shot at 70 degrees, which was about as straight down as you could get without going over on your back.

All of the maneuvering was done with hand signals. We never had too much radio chatter. Radio silence was both the operating norm and a matter of unit pride. Even in combat, somebody might only say, "You've got one on the tail at six o'clock," or "Bogey at twelve o'clock high"—something like that. Just the gist of it.

By mid July 1943 we didn't have enough airplanes or pilots left to mount a full squadron. We had enough to send a flight of two divisions of four planes each. We had had twenty-four Corsairs—enough for three two-division flights—plus a few spare pilots to start with, but we were down to ten to twelve operating pilots and airplanes. We couldn't get more than eight in the air at the same time.

Our missions were either high, low, or intermediate cover for patrol over Rendova. Low was about 15,000 feet, intermediate was about 20,000 feet, and high was about 25,000 feet. Generally, we took off and went over Rendova and patrolled around in circles or in a Thach-weave pattern for three hours. Then we went home.

The squadron's first kill in the Solomons had been in early April, near Guadalcanal. My flight was never in the right place at the right time until July 15, 1943, when Red—1st Lieutenant Sheldon Hall—and I were leading our divisions to patrol over Rendova. We were part of a staggered relief of the fighters already on station.

We had just passed the Russell Islands—midway between Fighter-1, on Guadalcanal, and Rendova—when, at about 0800, the radio gave us the news that enemy planes were coming down. We kicked our Corsairs into high gear and were over Rendova in time to see a beautiful formation of Betty bombers coming in over Kolombangara Island. There were about twenty-one of them, with about forty Zeros escorting. The Bettys came down in a line-of-vees formation —three Bettys in an element, seven elements stretched out, one behind the other. Other than vivid Rising Suns, all the Bettys were just silver—bare metal.

We were at 10,000 feet and they were at 20,000. It was obvious from the first that there was not time to reach them before they dropped their bombs. We swung left, over into the sun, and started up, hoping to reach them on their way home. In the meantime, the fighters that were already on patrol located the Zeros and started in on them. During the few minutes it took us to reach our altitude, we watched many burning Zeros falling out of the sky like autumn leaves. But the fighting was going on out of sight, thousands of feet above us. Although we wanted badly to be in on the free-for-all, it was to our advantage to have the Zeros drawn away from us and the bombers.

After the lead Bettys dropped their bombs, they had to proceed several miles beyond Rendova to get the whole series of flights over the target. And then they turned south—to their right—away from land. At that time I was about even with them and farther off to the south. As I gained altitude and they kept turning, I crossed 4,000 to 5,000 feet over them. When they were about set on a direct route back to their airfield at Kahili, I was in a position about 5,000 feet above. They were then to my left and behind me, losing altitude to gain airspeed. I had not seen any of the Bettys falling to this point. They had not been disturbed in the bombing run, so they were still in good formation.

It had been a fast race, and my second section had dropped behind. Red's division was still on its way up. They weren't in sight. I moved my wingman, 1st Lieutenant Ted Brown, to my right side. My mind was all cluttered with the things I had to do. I was nervous as a cat. I was so afraid they were going to get away before we had a real good chance at them. When I got my guns charged and I thought everything else was in order, I waggled my wings and executed a left high-side run on the Bettys, which were still in a line of vees.

Ted and I peeled off and headed for the three leading bombers in the formation. We almost made a split-S as we came around hard past a 90-degree turn and then reversed. We came down in almost a vertical dive. I had the lead three Bettys to choose from. I chose the left wingman of the lead plane so that Ted would be able to pick on the leader or the right wingman, without having to cross under me. One or the other would just fall naturally to him.

I had a full deflection shot coming down. Because of the way we boresighted our guns, I had to get 100 yards away to get the optimum shot. My aiming point was the Japanese pilot's left engine. I had to put the pipper in my sight ahead of the Betty. The cowling of my engine was about on the Betty, and the pipper was straight out in space about as far as it could go. I was hoping to barely miss his tail while diving past him. In that situation barely missing the tail was better than staying in back of him, because the tail gunner would have less time to fire on me. When the bomber filled my gunsight, I opened up.

I saw my tracers going all over the place, but no pieces were falling off the Japanese plane. And the pilot didn't evade; he didn't have time to. When I had been climbing up at full bore to prepare for the attack, I had cranked over the tabs to take care of the full-power climb. When I waggled my wings and came down, it was at full power, but the trim of the airplane was drastically different from the climb and the dive. I had not reset my tabs. My pipper was on the right place and the high-side attack was perfect, but I was going sideways through the air. That's why my shots were spewing like buckshot. I kept going in at him until I thought for sure I had a hit. At the last moment, I shoved the stick forward and barely missed the Betty's tail.

After I passed the Betty, I pulled out to the left and out of the dive. Ted and I went down under full power because we expected Zeros to attack us. None showed up, so we headed our Corsairs for altitude to make another pass. I saw then that the leader had broken formation and was steepening his dive to get more speed. We could not tell what damage we had caused, but it was obvious that Ted's firing on the leader had caused that flight of three Bettys to detach themselves from the rest of the formation, which was still composed of twenty-one Bettys. When the lead three separated, they went to the left, veering slightly south. The rest of the Bettys kept going straight back toward Kahili.

I suppose we were between 10,000 and 15,000 feet. I pulled up to make a right high-side pass. I got my altitude back, and Ted was still with me. That's when I saw the Zero on Ted. The Zero was doing a right high-side on us. I called Ted up and told him, but I was not in position to help him. Ted dove away, and the Zero followed him. I lost track of Ted from there on.

The Betty leader was gaining speed because he was still steepening his dive. I had been losing speed because I had not had as much altitude advantage after recovering from my firing pass as I had had before the pass. The result was that I wound up sitting squarely behind my target—the left-hand wingman again—and his 20mm stinger was blowing balls of fire in my face. I was so surprised that it must have taken me two or three seconds to realize what was going on.

Fortunately, the tail gunner's aim was poor. Perhaps the fact that I was still flying somewhat sideways threw his aim off. I had time to line up on him. As soon as I opened fire, the entire blister seemed to blow out of the tail, and sparkling bits of glass went sailing over my canopy.

I was coming straight up on the target. Pretty soon, I was in danger of running right up his tail. I eased back on my throttle to fly formation on him and then go above him. As I did, the leader decided to cross over on top of his wingman. I could not pull up and get away. I was pinned between the two bombers long enough to be very thankful that they could neither shoot straight up nor straight down.

After an eternity of two or three seconds, I managed to slip out of there by applying left rudder and right aileron. I used my tabs and got my airplane in balance. Then I suddenly realized that, though we had lost a lot of altitude, I still had my plane in high blower and I was still wearing my oxygen mask. After getting my wits together and these matters taken care of, I looked up and found that our cozy little corner of the sky was empty except for me and the Betty I had shot at twice already.

The tail gunner was gone and the Betty didn't have a dorsal fuselage gunner, so I just chased back and forth from behind. I could not understand why he wouldn't go down. The only effect my bullets seemed to have was to make the bomber go like hell. Also, I was down to just three of my six guns. I wasn't paying too much attention to anything else. I don't know how many passes I made. Probably not too many, as a matter of fact, because we were heading down pretty hard and ended up just on top of the water not far from the Shortland Islands, which were between Kolombangara and Bougainville.

I was still firing at him, chasing him, and charging my jammed guns when a sound like a riveting machine came from the armor plate that was the back of my seat. A ramrod might have been shoved down my spine, what with the way I came to attention and started to look around.

I don't know where the Zero came from. I didn't even know where it was. Look as I might, I could not see it. The Zero's pilot had just peppered the inch-thick armor plate behind my seat. I decided that, if he stayed directly behind me and kept hitting the armor plate and didn't open up with his 20mm cannon, I could concentrate on the bomber. I gave up on the Zero because I couldn't see him. If I had pulled around, he would have caught me. I didn't ignore the Zero; there just wasn't much I could do about his being there.

I went straight ahead at the Betty and kept the Zero behind me. Another one of my guns stopped firing as I squared away for what I was pretty sure would have to be my last pass. I was feeling bad about the bad luck I was having.

The Betty had been an obstinate critter, but I finally got it. I must have hit the pilot or a control cable. It seemed that the big plane gave up. The left wing dipped and hit the water. The Betty kind of cartwheeled and went in.

With the Betty gone, the full impact of my situation hit home. I still had a Zero behind me, and he was filling my tail with arrows. There was water very close beneath me. Suddenly, there was a rending of metal to my left. He had finally fired his 20mm cannon, and one of the large rounds had ripped a large hole in my left wing. The drag created by the hole was slowing me down.

I was in a tough spot. Home was over 200 miles behind me, and turning would give the Zero even more of an advantage than he already had. I had used up a lot of gas running at combat power, and I had only one gun firing when the Betty had gone in.

I started about a half-needle–width turn to the left. That worked, so I started very gradually turning farther and farther to the left. I was feeling my way through the turn, but I didn't panic because I thought that my engine was better than his and that my airplane would outrun his. My biggest fear was that he would cross the turn and cut me off. I still had a good engine running, so I just stayed in a gradual turn.

Finally, I saw the Zero behind me. He was cutting across my turn, but he was a long way back. I tightened the turn and straightened out in the direction of home. He gained on me at the end of the turn, but our speed was about equal. He finally pulled off in a chandelle. He'd done his best.

I was still pretty far out. I don't know how many times I charged my guns. Confidence in my prowess started to return, and I began to feel better about myself. I had shot down my first Japanese airplane. I had done it miserably, but—hey—I had done it. Well, I was going along, just minding my own business, when, as I climbed toward 1,000 feet, I came across a Zero. The pilot was circling over the burning remains of another plane, and he didn't see me. He happened to have his tail to me when I arrived. I had a zero-deflection shot at his tail, and I just opened up from about 300 feet. I had better luck with my one remaining gun than I had had before with all six. I saw two of my tracers enter the engine cowling, and then he went in burning.

I continued home. As I passed Munda, 1st Lieutenant Milt Vedder joined up on me. Milt had been in Red Hall's division during the scrap. We took turns looking one another over and, finding each Corsair airworthy, we headed home.

The eight Corsairs from VMF-213 scored 9 Bettys and 7 Zeros. Seven of us, including Ted, made it back, but one of the young lieutenants was never seen again.

*After destroying the Betty and the Zero on July 15, 1943, Captain Jim Cupp settled into a splendid combat career. Before he was shot down and badly burned near Kolombangara on September 20, 1943, Cupp destroyed or took part in the destruction of a total of 13 Japanese planes—1 Betty medium bomber, 4 Val dive-bombers (all in one fight on September 18), a Ki-61 Tony fighter, 5 full Zeros, and two ½ Zeros. He was also credited with 2 Zero probables.*

*Following an 18-month stay in the hospital, Major Jim Cupp returned to flight duty. However, he did not get back to the war zone before the Pacific War ended.*

*In December 1950, while serving as the 1st Marine Division Air Officer, Lieutenant Colonel Jim Cupp planned or directed countless Marine Corsair strikes against Communist Chinese forces that were threatening to overwhelm the division at the Chosin Reservoir in North Korea. Alongside the thousands of Marines he helped save, Cupp walked out of the "Frozen Chosin" in minus-thirty-degree weather.*

On July 15, Marine, Army, and Navy fighters downed 48 Japanese fighters and bombers. That seemed to knock the stuffing out of the Japanese air effort over New Georgia. Only two days later, AirSols kicked off an earnest offensive campaign to neutralize the Japanese air bases in southern Bougainville and the Shortland Islands.

# CHAPTER 7

AirSols initiated the first sustained Allied air offensive of the war on July 17, 1943, with a raid against the Japanese air base at Kahili, in southwestern Bougainville. Thereafter, until the tail end of October, in almost daily attacks by fighter-escorted single- and multiengine bombers of all types, hundreds of Japanese aircraft were downed in defense of the Japanese bases in the Shortlands and southern Bougainville.

To support the burgeoning air offensive, a new fighter-staging field was opened at Segi, in eastern New Georgia, on July 11. After Munda fell to U.S. infantrymen on August 5, the former Japanese base was vastly expanded to handle the bulk of the bomber traffic assigned to strikes against Kahili and Ballale. As the summer passed, several former Japanese airfields were converted for Allied use and a half dozen rather crude fighter strips were rapidly constructed by U.S. Navy Seabees in western New Georgia and on surrounding islands, including Kolombangara. Operating on ever-shorter lines, the growing establishment of American and British Commonwealth fighter and bomber groups assigned to the AirSols offensive were able to pound the Japanese bases at will, almost daily.

Though Kahili, Ballale, and other Japanese airfields were subjected to vicious bombing attacks, the air offensive was aimed chiefly at destroying the Japanese fighters sent from Rabaul and northern Bougainville to defend them. This was to soften the way for the next Allied invasion.

Unbeknown to the Japanese, the Allies were about to put into play the bypass strategy that had been dreamed up by Admiral

Ernest King, commander in chief of the U.S. Fleet. Rather than seize every Japanese base, at great cost, King's plan envisaged neutralizing the existing bases and establishing new bases by means of a series of amphibious end runs. The months-long AirSols campaign against Kahili, Ballale, and nearby Japanese bases was the first step in the first application of Admiral King's bypass strategy. The next target was Cape Torokina, a suitable air-base site in west-central Bougainville, roughly halfway between the new Allied air bases in the Central Solomons and the main Japanese air-base complex at Rabaul.

The bypass strategy worked the first time out. The lightly held Cape Torokina area was invaded by the 3d U.S. Marine Division on November 1, 1943, and the Japanese were caught napping. The only immediate response on D-day amounted to a pair of aerial reconnaissance-in-force bombing missions that resulted in the downing of 25 Japanese aircraft by New Zealand and American fighters in the course of the raids.

AirSols fighters based in the Central Solomons patrolled the beachhead and northern Bougainville. Meanwhile, the 5th Air Force, in New Guinea, continued, as it had for several weeks, to stem a potential Japanese aerial counteroffensive at the source: Rabaul.

In a series of amphibious, overland, and parachute assaults beginning at Buna in January 1943, American and British Commonwealth infantry commanded by General Douglas MacArthur had slowly worked northwest along the northeastern coast of far eastern New Guinea, from Milne Bay to the Huon Peninsula. The development of new air bases along the way and the introduction into the Southwest Pacific Area of long-range P-38 fighters had brought Rabaul in range of strikes from New Guinea. It was from eastern New Guinea, then, that the most effective long-range support for the Bougainville invasion could be mustered.

# BLOODY TUESDAY

**1st Lieutenant MARION KIRBY, USAAF**
**431st Fighter Squadron, 475th Fighter Group**
**Rabaul, November 2, 1943**

*Marion Franklin Kirby II earned his wings at Mitchell Field, Long Island, on December 12, 1941, and sailed for Panama on Christmas Eve. He arrived in New Guinea on July 7, 1942, and was immediately assigned to the 80th Fighter Squadron, 8th Fighter Group, to fly the Bell P-400 Export Airacobra, an ill-starred adventure he survived. The squadron was re-equipped with P-38Gs in April 1943. Lieutenant Kirby scored his first probable victory, a Zeke or Oscar, over Wau, New Guinea, on May 21, 1943. In mid July 1943, Kirby was reassigned with about half his fellow 8th Fighter Group pilots to the newly commissioned 431st Fighter Squadron of the newly commissioned 475th Fighter Group. Flying a P-38H, he scored his first confirmed kill, a Val dive-bomber, on October 15, 1943, over Oro Bay, New Guinea. He next downed a Zeke on October 17 near Buna and followed up on October 23 with a Hamp over Rabaul.*

Our next mission over Rabaul was supposed to have taken place on October 31, 1943, but weather would not permit. The weather also kept us down on November 1. I was the operations officer for the 431st Fighter Squadron, and I was to lead our flight from our strip near Dobodura. Usually, we were on duty for two days and off for one. After the two cancellations—our two days on—we were ready to be relieved. But it was not to be. On November 2, we got orders to get the hell to Rabaul. I bet there was not but a handful of men, both bomber and fighter, that got a decent night's sleep for the three nights prior to the mission. We all knew it was going to be rough.

Our orders were to "occupy the Japanese air force over Rabaul." The key word in that order was "occupy." The Marines were making landings at Bougainville and the 13th Air Force could not offer air protection as far north as

Rabaul from Guadalcanal or the Central Solomons, so the answer was that we, the 5th Air Force, were to keep the Japanese at home from our bases in New Guinea—in other words, keep them occupied. P-38 squadrons from the 8th, 49th, and our own 475th Fighter groups were scheduled for the mission. There was going to be a fighter sweep by one of the other groups and then the main force, us included, was to come on in.

My old unit, the 80th Fighter Squadron, was almost always involved in fighter sweeps, and it was involved on November 2. The pilots of the 80th were my closest friends. I always accused them of going in and picking off all the cripples and making the rest of them mad before the fighting forces arrived.

We were to rendezvous with the B-25s around Gasmata, about halfway up the southern coast of New Britain, and maintain radio silence. The bombers would be flying at 200 to 300 feet above the water, and we would be flying escort 200 to 300 feet above them. The idea was to come in under any radar the Japanese might have had to cover our approach. Flying so low was good for the element of surprise; the disadvantage was that, when you arrived at the target, you were pretty damned close to the muzzles of their guns. They had much greater accuracy at 1,500 feet than they did at 25,000 feet.

We had nine planes in commission that day, so nine men flew the mission. Since I was leading the squadron, I was to take off first. Nervousness, whatever—I had difficulty getting my airplane started. Finally, after the other eight planes were airborne, I took off. Then, in order to make up time, I flew straight to the rendezvous instead of circling the field. I did not think the plane was picking up speed fast enough, so I started tapping the airspeed indicator. Another example of my nervousness: With my taps, I knocked the glass completely out of the instrument and messed up the indicator. As a result of this, when I overtook the squadron, I settled in on my wingman's wing and let him—1st Lieutenant Lowell Lutton—lead. Lowell had been only one class behind me in flying school; he was perfectly capable of leading the squadron. In fact, he had done so on many occasions.

After flying the P-400 early in my tour, I felt much safer in the P-38. I felt like somebody cared about me. If we went down at sea, we had our rubber dinghy right under us, and I do mean right under us. There was no way that you could sit on that darn thing without the valve hitting you right in the brown. I think that valve finally created a callus. Later, after my tour was over, one of the men accidentally pulled the string and caused the $CO_2$ cartridges on the dinghy to discharge. Nothing happened. They then tried the same thing on another dinghy. Nothing happened. Then they tried them all. Same result. The cartridge chamber was too large for the cartridges. This was corrected, but throughout 1943, we were flying across shark-infested waters with a very false sense of security. There we were, thinking we had a real lifesaver hitting us in the asshole and *all* it was was a pain in the ass!

After rendezvous, we stayed very close to the bombers. To do that, we flew at about 220 miles per hour on the way to the target. We made wide, sweeping S curves while flying a few hundred feet above them. The S curves were to help absorb additional speed, but, more important, they also aided in our vision. Your eyesight covering an entire area is greater when you are weaving rather than flying in a straight line. You are more vulnerable from the rear, so you want to be able to cover that area visually. Weaving lets you do that. We would be well throttled back so that our S curves would not be too violent while staying with the bombers. At that time, our mixture controls in the P-38s were automatic.

Our two belly tanks—one for each engine—held 165 gallons of fuel. We had approximately the same amount internally, in four 60-gallon tanks, each pair of which was good for about one hour of normal flight. We took off and landed on our main internal tanks and switched them on again when we were in combat. They were the closest to the fuel pump and the engine, so the fuel flow was better. I was always concerned about fuel while flying in the Southwest Pacific. As long as you were contending with weather, jungles, water, and the enemy, you were constantly concerned about fuel. If weather caused you to miss a landmark, generally it was quite a distance to the next landing area, since so much of the area was dense jungle and did not abound in civilization.

It was about 400 miles from Dobodura to Rabaul. We stayed over the water the whole way. There are not as many rocks in the clouds while you are flying over the water as when you get into the mountains of the Southwest Pacific Area.

We flew on past the eastern end of New Britain, almost to New Ireland. When we were about even with the eastern tip of New Britain, the weather cleared up over the water—only over the water. The island was very plainly in sight when the B-25s turned and headed toward the target, Rabaul. The B-25s continued right on the deck, but the P-38s climbed up to a few thousand feet above them.

About halfway in toward the target, we encountered three naval vessels—destroyers, I assume—and they started firing at the B-25s. They shot in front of the bombers, which were right on the deck, creating a plume of water they hoped the B-25s would fly into. Fortunately, the B-25s missed.

About the time of the destroyer incident, Lowell Lutton, the man now leading the squadron, salvoed his two belly tanks. I followed suit and switched to my main internal tanks. In normal flying, each set of 60-gallon tanks—main and reserve—would ordinarily last for an hour's flying time. The only fuel missing from the main tanks when we switched over was what we had used for takeoff. When we went into combat, first we would switch to our main tanks, then push the props and manifold pressure all the way to the fire wall. Within 15 minutes, I had exhausted the first set of internal tanks, which gives an idea of the intense combat I was facing.

We continued on into the harbor area. I looked to my right and saw a large number of phosphorescent clouds lining the shoreline in proximity to the town of Rabaul, which was on the northern shore of the harbor. About the middle of the harbor, as we came across, we had to start diving to get beneath the clouds. All the way from New Ireland to Rabaul had been clear as a bell, but as soon as we hit the shoreline surrounding Rabaul Harbor, the ceiling over the inland area was 1,500 feet. The farther inland we went, the lower the ceiling became.

As we crossed the shoreline, I could see an airstrip off to my right—quite far to the west—where numerous fighters were getting airborne. It was so hazy, I could barely see them. I could not follow their flight path with my eyes, but I strongly suspicioned that they were flying down the coast to pick us up as we left the target area.

The B-25s came across the harbor at little more than masthead height, and they never got any higher, except to climb over a natural obstruction. They remained on the deck.

After crossing the shoreline, we turned left—south. At that point, I became separated from Lutton and the rest of the flight. The only other P-38 in the area was the one flown by Lieutenant Fred Champlin. Very shortly afterward, I noticed a B-25 with its right engine nacelle on fire. Flames were streaming all the way back to the vertical stabilizer. The B-25 was just inland of the shoreline, at the southwest arc of the harbor, and heading due south. Five or six Japanese fighters were trying to finish it off. They were trying to set up a regular traffic pattern, with each fighter taking its shot.

The traffic pattern on the B-25 was counterclockwise. They were attacking from inland toward the water, then they would fly back inland for another approach.

I was heading south along the coastline, or maybe slightly inland. We were all at about 1,500 feet. I do not think they were aware of my presence. I made a slight dive to my left and shot at the first Zeke I saw in front of me. He took no evasive action; I figure he was concentrating too strongly on the crippled B-25. Later, I heard the pilot parachuted, but I did not see that. I also heard that he was one of their leading aces, which scared me to death. I thought that I was fighting their second or third team—that was what they were telling us at the time.

I headed east and continued my dive and immediately started a turn to my right to pick up another Zeke, but my attention was diverted by antiaircraft fire from the nearby extinct volcano, Vulcan. Gun emplacements—machine guns and cannon—were all the way up the side of the volcano, and they were shooting *down* at me. I made one more pass at the fighters that were shooting at the B-25, and I knocked down my second plane, another Zeke.

When I made my turn this time, the B-25 was gone. It had

crashed just west of the Vulcan crater. A Zero came close to my tail and was firing. Lieutenant Fred Champlin knocked him off.

By this time—after only 15 minutes—I had run out of gas in my main tanks. That is about four times the normal rate of consumption. All of the B-25s were clear of the area, and all of the Japanese fighters were gone too, so I headed home. I switched to my internal reserve tanks and left.

The 431st Fighter Squadron lost three planes out of the nine we sent out that day, by far our heaviest losses for one day during my tour. One of the lost pilots was Lowell Lutton, who had scored his fifth kill just before he was shot down.

*In all, in 45 minutes of air combat over Rabaul on November 2, 1943, 5th Air Force fighters claimed 31 Japanese aircraft destroyed, 21 probably destroyed, and 3 damaged. Lieutenant Marion Kirby's 2 confirmed Zekes, his last kills of the war, brought him up to ace status.*

*When Lieutenant Kirby was ordered home on Christmas Day, 1943, he had spent exactly two years overseas—six months in Panama and eighteen months in New Guinea. He went out on 126 combat missions and never got a single bullet hole in any of the P-400s or P-38s he flew. Commenting on his own combat career, Kirby wrote in 1989:*

> *I would seriously sum up my skills best by saying "conservative." I was not a hell-bent-for-leather type. I would attack anything the enemy had to offer, but I always made certain we had the advantage. I absolutely hated to fight when they had the advantage. All of the men enjoyed flying behind me, for they knew their chances of returning were maximum. They were not going to be led down a blind alley. I am most proud that I never lost a man flying behind me.*

The months-long battle of attrition over Kahili and Ballale, the ambitious program of New Guinea–based raids against Rabaul, and the shock of the Cape Torokina end run prevented the Japanese from responding to the new invasion with any confidence. Almost by knee-jerk reaction, a small Japanese naval surface battle force attempted to attack the American invasion fleet in Empress Augusta Bay, but it was turned back by an American naval surface force in the wee hours of November 2. Hours later, a Japanese bomber strike hit the retiring U.S. surface battle force and inflicted some damage. But, in the only air action of the day, 9 of the bombers and their escorts were destroyed by U.S. Navy and Marine fighters. On the other hand, 5th Air Force fighters out of New Guinea downed 31 Japanese aircraft over Rabaul on November 2. With that, the Japanese stopped trying and settled back to defend Rabaul. Hundreds of fresh Imperial Army and Imperial Navy combat aircraft were ordered in from other Pacific and East Asia bases.

On November 5, in only the third major U.S. Navy carrier strike of 1943, the two U.S. Navy fleet carriers comprising Task Force 38 struck Rabaul from 230 miles out in the Solomon Sea with forty-five carrier bombers and fifty-two carrier fighters. The Navy pilots and bomber gunners claimed 28 victories and 19 probables, mostly fighters.

Finally, on November 8, the Imperial Navy's Rabaul-based 11th Air Fleet mounted its first major strike against the Allied invasion fleet in Empress Augusta Bay.

# "THE MOST BEAUTIFUL SIGHT IN ALL THE WORLD"

**1st Lieutenant GEORGE CHANDLER, USAAF**
**339th Fighter Squadron, 347th Fighter Group**
**Empress Augusta Bay, November 8, 1943**

*George Throckmorton Chandler, a native of Wichita, Kansas, dropped out of California Institute of Technology and entered the Army Aviation Cadet program in November 1941. He earned his wings at Luke Field, Arizona, in July 1942 and was assigned to fly P-40s with the 15th Fighter Group in*

*Hawaii. In February 1943, Lieutenant Chandler was trans-
ferred to the 5th Air Force's 49th Fighter Group in Port
Moresby, New Guinea. In March, he returned to Hawaii to
join the 318th Fighter Squadron, but a little over a month
later he was transferred to the 13th Air Force. Chandler joined
the 347th Fighter Group's 339th Fighter Squadron to undergo
P-38 transition training on New Caledonia. He went to
Guadalcanal in June 1943.*

*Lieutenant Chandler scored his first aerial victory in his
first aerial combat, on July 3, 1943, when he shot down a
Hamp fighter northwest of Rendova. After Munda Field fell
in August, the 339th Fighter Squadron remained based at
Guadalcanal, but it began staging through the newly liberated airfield. After helping to soften intermediate Japanese
bases, the 339th Fighter Squadron was drawn into supporting
the 3d Marine Division's Cape Torokina landings.*

Cape Torokina and Empress Augusta Bay were so far from
our staging base at Munda that we could not respond to
attacks the Japanese launched against the invasion fleet and
beachhead from Rabaul. We had to be there, on patrol,
constantly.

The 339th Fighter Squadron was the only unit in the 13th
Air Force equipped with P-38s at the time—P-38Hs. The
other Air Forces squadrons were all equipped with P-39s or
P-40s. So, it was our responsibility to provide the high
cover. The squadron's mission was to maintain eight P-38s
on high cover above the beachhead from the earliest light of
dawn until after it was dark. Both the 70th Fighter Squadron
of the 347th Group and the 44th Fighter Squadron of the
18th Fighter Group—each flying P-40s—were to have eight
of its planes flying middle cover at all times. There were
Marine and Navy squadrons involved, also. We could see
them in the sky, but we did not have good communications
with them, so we were running our show and they were
running theirs. Maybe there was liaison at higher command
levels, but, who was going to be where didn't filter down to
the level of the pilots.

The squadron's code name at the time was Greyhound.
On November 8, 1943, I was leading one of the flights,

Greyhound-2. Major Hank Lawrence, the squadron commander, was Greyhound-1. Together, our two flights were assigned to take the first and third missions of the day.

Our first launches took place out of Munda at 0400, so we had to get up at about 0230. We had to climb out of Munda in the dark to be over the beachhead about 30 minutes before first light. When we got there, we just settled in at about 23,000 feet and flew great big circles with the power pulled way back. We just sipped away at our two 165-gallon belly tanks.

The P-38s didn't have good heaters, and it was bitter cold up there. On the other hand, even at 0400, it was so hot on the ground that we couldn't stand to take off in fleece-lined jackets or fleece-lined flying boots. About the most anyone could stand to put on was a sweater. We took the fleece-lined boots with us in the cockpit, but not the heavy jackets. We'd just shiver and shake while flying those big circles up there over Empress Augusta Bay.

The next rotation of eight P-38s had to be there before the first two flights could leave. It was about 45 minutes from the patrol station to Munda. That added up to very long missions, over five hours apiece. After our early mission stormed back down to Munda, everyone headed for the outhouse and then grabbed something to eat. In the meantime, our airplanes were being refueled and readied for the late-afternoon mission.

The ground crews were doing everything they could to keep us on schedule for the third mission, but something happened during the second morning mission, and our third mission had to depart early. When it came time to go, I hadn't been able to get all four of my airplanes fueled yet. Hank Lawrence's flight was ready to go. Hank and I were standing there, watching the fueling, looking at the clock, and Hank finally said, "I gotta go." I told him, "I'll be up there just as soon as I can get there. I'll come storming up there. I might use extra fuel getting to you, but I'll be there."

Greyhound-1 flight left and I continued to stand over the ground crews. I had all three of my pilots standing on the wings of their P-38s, helping the two fueling trucks by managing extra hoses. We could fuel the tanks in one wing with the pilot handling the nozzle; one of the ground crewmen on the other wing filling those tanks; and the second ground crewman at the truck, managing the controls. The airplanes were not close enough together for talk, and there was a lot of noise, so my standard instruction was that the pilot of a fully fueled airplane was to climb into his cockpit and get his straps on. That way, I'd know he was ready to go.

Finally, from my position on the wing of my P-38, I saw the fuel trucks pull away. I gave my pilots the hand signal—an overhead circular motion—to close their hatches and start their engines.

I went storming off the runway, and my flight was right behind me. I made a real fast 360-degree circuit over the base to let them join up, and then we went out on course. I was bending the throttles pretty hard to catch up to Greyhound-1 flight. About the time we were getting up over Kolombangara Island, I heard the fighter-control destroyer calling, "Greyhound-One, we have a very large plot of bogies coming down from Rabaul." He gave Hank Lawrence a vector and called "Buster," which meant go to maximum continuous power and intercept. He was sending Hank out there with four airplanes to intercept a big strike. At the same time, he was getting the P-40s and any Navy and Marine fighters that were on station set to defend the beachhead.

I pushed the button for my throat mike and told the controller I was coming up there fast. But I couldn't hear any side tone in my headset. I checked all the connections in my headset, and all my leads. Nothing. I turned around to my wingman and rocked my wings to pull him in closer. He could see me talking and pointing to my mouth, but he shook his head—No, he couldn't hear me. I went through the whole thing again and pulled on my oxygen mask to try the nose mike in it. I couldn't make anything talk. I could hear everything, but I couldn't talk.

I wasn't skillful enough to tell my wingman how to communicate for me so I could report. I figured the controller could see me on his radar, that he would work it out and start talking to me, but nothing like that happened.

I figured out where I was and estimated where Hank Lawrence was heading—out over the water to intercept the attack from Rabaul. I didn't have a plotting board like the Navy pilots had; I had nothing but cowboy arithmetic. I figured if I cranked in about 30 degrees left from where I was, I ought to meet Hank's flight about the time it met the Japanese formation.

The guys in my flight could hear what was going on; I knew they knew what the situation was. So, I came right up on my power, not quite to war-emergency power, but way up to full power. The way I did that was go straight up on the throttle so I could pull away from them. We were already up on the power, trying to catch up to Lawrence's flight, so they didn't have much left to catch me with. But I gave them the idea that they had to throttle up to full power. When I knew they had the idea, I throttled back a little so they could catch up and get back in formation.

We were climbing and on oxygen. Everything was going normally. We were by that time getting good altitude. Pretty soon, I could see a big flight of airplanes dead ahead of us. There were *a lot* of airplanes in the sky! I could see we were going to be getting into a big fight.

There were Val dive-bombers, Betty twin-engine medium-level bombers, and a lot of Zeros above the bombers. I later learned there were about 155 airplanes in that strike, and about 50 to 60 of them were Zeros.

I didn't dare get right in there with all those fighters. In a turning dogfight they'd have gotten us. I didn't know enough yet to cut through them at full throttle from a dive and go head-on through the bombers, trying to shoot down the bombers—to do it with so much speed that no Zero could possibly get us. Instead, the tactic I settled on was to get them from above but stay out of a big turning dogfight. As we'd be turning into them, we'd be making a 6-o'clock attack and coming through the Zeros. Part of the idea was to break them up, make the Zeros break off. That way, when they got to the beachhead, the bombers would be relatively unprotected and the Zeros would be separated from them and milling around.

We were going out full bore, too fast to drop our belly

tanks. When we got to the place where I could see what the timing had to be, I had to throttle back . . . throttle back to slow up my whole flight. I couldn't talk to them, but they'd figured that out and were watching me. When they saw my tanks come off, they dropped their tanks. When they saw me test-firing my guns to make sure I had all the switches on, they got the idea, and they all fired their guns. Everybody settled down. Then I came back up on the power to go for position.

We were not quite flying in line-abreast formation, but we were spread out. My wingman, Lieutenant Robert Smith, was about 150 yards to my right and back a bit. On my left side, Lieutenant Carl Squires, my element leader, was also about 150 yards off and a little behind me. His wingman was flying over to his left. This meant that any Zero pilot that wound up in front of us had to break early. If he stayed too long, I could get him. I might not get good deflection on him if he turned tightly, but, if the Zero broke a little late, Smitty or Carl or Carl's wingman would get a shot. Going through the Zeros, we were going to make them turn—we were going to break up their party.

As we were going in, one of the most remarkable things happened. Hank Lawrence still didn't know I was coming. He was out there with four P-38s, intercepting the Japanese formation. He had the altitude advantage and had figured out about the same thing I'd figured out—attack from 6 o'clock high, right on through the Zeros, then pull up and do it again. The first I saw of Hank's flight, they were doing exactly that—what I was going to do. Hank never saw me come in until he had gone through them the first time. He looked back and saw four more P-38s coming through the Zeros. He hadn't even known we were out there.

We made these passes at the Zeros all the way to the beach—three slashing attacks in all. We didn't shoot down any airplanes, but we sure broke up their formation. With our P-38s coming through them all the time, those Zeros couldn't fly straight and level to keep up with the bombers. They were turning all the time, so the bombers got ahead of them. When they got to the beach, the P-40s and Navy F6F Hellcats worked them over good.

We came on down then to get into the big rolling dogfight. It was at this point that I looked down and saw two Zeros headed down at a 60-degree angle. Earlier, I thought the Zeros had had belly tanks on, but I realized they didn't need belly tanks, as close as they were to Rabaul. As I saw the two Zeros diving away, it finally dawned on me that they had bombs.

So, there were two of them going down at a pretty steep angle. The rear fighter was on the left of the leader, back 50 to 70 yards. He looked like he was making an independent bomb run on a ship, not really flying formation on the leader.

I was above them with a lot of speed, in a very fortunate position. I was coming down with quite a bit of overtaking speed. I had maybe 50 miles per hour on them. I thought about that. If I didn't hit the rear fighter, I'd go past him and he'd be shooting at my rear end. I had to be awfully sure I hit him. I knew I wasn't going to have very long from the time I hit gun range until I had to decide to pull up or pass him.

I decided to try to get close and try for his canopy—to get close and, at the last second, give him a good big squirt in the canopy. If I didn't see the canopy come apart, I'd pull up.

That's what happened. I came down on the rear Zero and opened fire at about 200 feet, from the vertical fin to the canopy. I don't think I fired more than a one-second burst. When I saw pieces of canopy go in every direction, I started to pull out to avoid a collision. That set me up on the leading Zero.

I figured the rear Zero's pilot was dead, so I went on after the leader and did the same thing. Canopy pieces flew and I pulled up. Without waiting to see if the lead Zero's pilot was dead, I pulled up at a very steep angle at full power. I still wanted to get into the fight above me. I didn't see any more of either one of those Zeros, but Lieutenant Tom Walker, who was in Hank Lawrence's flight, saw the whole thing. He confirmed that the two of them hit the water.

When I went back up into the fight, I looked around, but I could not see any of the guys from my flight. I checked my fuel gauges and decided that I couldn't stand any more full-throttle operation if I wanted to make it home to Munda. I had been at full throttle since we had dropped our tanks, and that seemed like a long, long time before.

The only thing bad about that mission was that, in that roiling, boiling fight over the beachhead, my flight got separated. When we got back, my element leader, Carl Squires, wasn't there. He was lost. I know Carl was still with us when we left the Zeros and got caught up in that big rolled-up fight with the P-40s and the Navy fighters, but we never found out what happened to him.

After the war, along about 1950 or 1951, I went to the country-club stag party in Pratt, Kansas, where I live. A bunch of guys were sitting around drinking and talking about the war, and Rudy Fisher, the New York Life Insurance agent, was telling us about how he was one of the Marines going ashore on Bougainville on November 8, 1943. He was talking about how there was a big air battle and how he was standing out on the deck of a ship, watching, when he looked up and saw two dive-bombers coming down. He could see those bombs. The planes were heading right square for his ship. He said he just knew the end of the world was there. And then he said, "I saw the most beautiful sight in all the world. I saw a P-38 come *screaming* down. I never saw one come so fast. He shot both of the bombers down into the water and went roaring back up into the fight." When Rudy said, "I sure would like to meet that guy," I stuck out my hand and said, "Rudy, you just met him. I was flying that airplane."

*George Chandler was promoted to captain shortly after the mission of November 8, 1943. He downed a Zero over Rabaul on January 24, 1944, and a final Zero, also over Rabaul, on February 3, 1944. Captain Chandler returned to the United States shortly after scoring his fifth victory and spent the remainder of the war teaching fighter tactics in California. He left the service in January 1946 with the rank of major and went into banking in his native Kansas.*

During the raid of November 8, 1943, Army Air Corps P-40s from the 44th and 70th Fighter squadrons and P-38s from the

339th Fighter Squadron destroyed 15 Japanese dive-bombers and fighters. U.S. Navy F6Fs from VF-33 downed another 8.

The Japanese were on the ropes. After November 8, Rabaul mounted no serious attacks against the American beachhead at Cape Torokina or the invasion fleet in Empress Augusta Bay. Far from it. On November 11, Rabaul was massively attacked for the second time in a week by yet another U.S. Navy carrier task force.

## RAID ON RABAUL

**Lieutenant (jg) MAC McWHORTER, USN
VF-9 (USS *Essex*)
Rabaul, November 11, 1943**

*Hamilton McWhorter III of Athens, Georgia, attended the University of Georgia and Georgia Tech for two years before entering the Navy's flight program in August 1941. He was commissioned at Pensacola on February 9, 1942, and joined VF-9 in Norfolk a month later. Ensign McWhorter's first combat flight was an attack from USS* Ranger *on November 8, 1942, to prevent the Vichy French fleet from leaving Casablanca Harbor. Flying an F4F-4 Wildcat, he strafed a destroyer and burned several Vichy fighters on the ground, but in four days of combat he never saw an enemy fighter in the air.*

*Following the North Africa campaign, VF-9 returned to Norfolk, where it became the first U.S. Navy squadron to be equipped with the new Grumman F6F-3 Hellcat fighter. The squadron joined USS* Essex, *the first of a new breed of fast carriers, for her shakedown cruise in March 1943 and deployed to the Pacific via the Panama Canal in June 1943. Lieutenant (jg) Mac McWhorter participated in strikes against Marcus Island in August 1943, where he saw no Japanese planes, and against Wake Island on October 5, 1943, where he destroyed a Zero and claimed a second Zero as a probable.*

Rear Admiral Charles Pownall's Task Force 50.3—fleet carriers *Essex* and *Bunker Hill* and light carrier *Independence* —had just arrived in the Southwest Pacific Area on November 5, 1943. We immediately began to hear reports about a big raid against Japanese warships in Rabaul Harbor that day. We also began to hear rumors that we had lost a bunch of our planes in the raid, both fighters and bombers, but mostly bombers. So, the announcement a few days later that we were to hit Rabaul on November 11 caused a considerable amount of consternation, particularly to the dive-bomber and torpedo-bomber squadrons.

We were told during the pre-strike intelligence briefings that, since Rabaul was a land base, there were seventy-five to ninety Imperial Army fighters based at the five airfields near the harbor. Those odds, which were about 2:1, didn't seem to be so bad since we knew that strike groups from other carriers would be there both before and after us. What we didn't know at that time was that just about all of the Imperial Navy carrier fighters from Truk—150 or more— had been transferred to Rabaul shortly before our strike. The intelligence information available to us was, at best, minimal, as indicated by the low estimate of Zeros. Also, the photos of the area were not too good because much of the harbor region was obscured by clouds.

Going into Rabaul was certainly a scary, awesome task, since we knew that it was a very formidable and well-defended base. Even so, we were eager to go in and inflict as much damage as possible.

We were launched just after dawn on November 11, 1943, from a point about 165 miles southeast of Rabaul. This late launch was a big plus factor, as it meant we had a daylight instead of a difficult predawn rendezvous. Our mission in VF-9 was to escort a strike force consisting of about every dive-bomber and torpedo plane on board the *Essex*.

I was section leader in the second division, and my wingman was Lieutenant (jg) William "Bud" Gehoe. Lieutenant Mayo "Mike" Hadden was my division leader, and his wingman was Lieutenant (jg) Jack Kitchen. The squadron skipper was Lieutenant Commander Philip Torrey. The F6F assigned to me, the one I flew most of the time, was lucky Number 7. Whenever we escorted a strike force, as going into Rabaul, our division flew cover near the front of the group, right behind the skipper's division.

While en route to the target, we flew over the top of a 10,000-foot overcast. Our strike was the follow-up strike. When we were about halfway to the target, we heard the first strike yakking over the radio.

While we were still about 20 minutes or so away from Rabaul, we picked up an additional escort of a dozen or more Japanese Zeros. They flew alongside 3,000 to 4,000 feet out and above on either side, making numerous feints toward us in attempts to lure us away from our escort positions.

The division leader's two planes were about 1,000 feet above and to one side of the bombers, and the section leader's two planes were on the opposite side of the escort, even with and abreast of the division leader so that we could utilize the Thach Weave. Each time the Zeros would start in toward our bombers, a section on the opposite side of the escort would turn into the incoming Zeros and the other section would weave back across. Each time, the Zeros broke off and turned back. They really didn't make a serious attempt to get into the bombers, but it surely made for some very interesting and uneasy minutes for us and particularly for the pilots and gunners in the bombers. Although I did not see them, there were undoubtedly more Zeros sitting high above us, waiting to pounce down on anybody foolish enough to be lured away from the main strike force. Although it was certainly tempting, I had no desire to be a hero and leave the safety of our group to go after one of the Zeros. To do so would have been *very* fatal.

One thing that our air group had was excellent air discipline. Neither the group nor squadron commanders had to issue any warnings or instructions not to break formation, and no one did. We also had excellent radio discipline, so there were only a few transmissions from our strike group, mostly about the Zeros. It was a good thing that we didn't need any urgent radio calls, because the other strike force was cluttering up the air pretty badly.

We had no difficulty finding the target even though we flew above solid clouds almost all the way in. Fortunately, the cloud cover broke as we reached the Rabaul area. We were still about five minutes or so out of Rabaul when AA fire began coming up out of the overcast and flak began popping all around us. It continued until we reached the target. Most of the flak bursts were below our altitude and off to the sides, with some going above us. They were close enough to cause considerable concern, but I did not see any bursts near enough to cause damage.

As we got in over the target area at Rabaul Harbor, the first things that I could see were the many long white wakes of the Japanese warships leaving the harbor at high speed. As we reached the pushover point, still with no attack by the Zeros on our bombers, the AA fire from the warships increased significantly.

After all the bombers had entered their dives, we pushed over and passed them on the way down so that we could strafe ahead of them. I did not see any of our bombers get hit or go down.

Our attack at Rabaul was made from a northeast direction. The warships were leaving the harbor in a northwest direction, or from our left to our right. As we were covering the torpedo planes making their long, low, straight-in runs, I selected a Japanese heavy cruiser and commenced my strafing run on her starboard beam from 2½ to 3 miles out.

As I closed in on my strafing run, the cruiser opened up with every gun on board, including her main 8-inch batteries. The entire ship was spewing flame and smoke from all of the guns from stem to stern. I can personally attest to the fact that you can see 8-inch shells coming up at you. They were still smoking and I had time to move over out of their way, hoping that they didn't explode as they passed nearby. Even though I was already going in at full power and at 375 to 400 miles per hour, I think that I probably bent the throttle trying to push it even farther forward to try to go even faster and get out of all that AA fire sooner. I do not know how it was possible for my plane to go through such intense AA fire and receive no hits.

During the last part of the run—from a half mile or so out—I was down to 100 feet or less off the water. I commenced firing at a range of 2,500 feet or so, only having time for a four- to five-second burst, or 300 to 400 rounds.

Since I was jinking—making small direction and altitude changes—on the way in, I did not have to "kick" rudder in order to rake the cruiser from stem to stern. Anyway, if you are not in coordinated flight—not slipping or skidding—when you fire, the bullets do unpredictable things like tumbling and missing the target you are aiming for.

The ammo-belting sequence for our six .50-caliber guns at about that time had an armor-piercing incendiary (API) every fifth round. When the API hit something, it made a very bright flash. Even though I knew that my six guns had a combined rate of fire of about 4,000 rounds per minute, I was amazed at the large number of bright flashes as the APIs hit on and around the open AA gun batteries on the Japanese cruiser. As I passed over the cruiser about mast-high, I could see Japanese gunners crouching behind the gun shields on the deck and superstructure below. They were looking up at me. There were also other Japanese sprawled about, not looking up.

The entire run from pushover at about 12,000 feet to passing over the cruiser took maybe 1½ minutes. After completing my strafing run on the heavy cruiser, I looked back and saw a large explosion on or near the starboard side—the side away from me. I do not know whether it was a torpedo or a bomb. I was expecting to find the Zeros waiting to hit us as we recovered from our attack, but fortunately they didn't show up.

Our job was to escort the recovering bombers back to the rendezvous point. As I was passing near the harbor on the way back to the rendezvous point, which was to the east, I saw over the harbor, about a mile or so away, what looked like a World War I–type dogfight in progress—a real melee with planes twisting and turning all over the sky. Many were exploding and going down in flames. I could see five or six big splashes in the harbor where planes had hit, and several fires were burning on shore.

I was back up to 5,000 to 6,000 feet, so, without further thought, I immediately turned and went barreling into the middle of the dogfight at full speed. As I neared the melee, I could see that it involved twelve or so F6Fs and at least thirty or more Zeros.

As an indication of just how many Zeros there were in the melee, even though I had gone barreling in at about 300-plus miles per hour, I found that almost immediately there were at least six Zeros in my airspace—about a 2,000-foot radius, which is the effective range of their 20mm cannons—and two of them were already firing at me at the same time! There were the two ahead of me, two behind me, one or more above, the one right below, and many others farther out.

Almost directly ahead of me was a Zero on the tail of an F6F, hitting him very hard with his 20mm cannon fire. Many large pieces of metal were flying off the F6F, and it was smoking badly. They were at about my 1-o'clock position, going in about the same direction as I was and at a slightly lower altitude. It took only a small turn and, in 10 seconds or so, I was directly astern of the Zero. My closing rate was so fast that I had time for only a very short burst from 600 to 800 feet. I did not see hits, as I had to immediately pull up to avoid colliding. Then, as I flashed 15 to 20 feet over the Zero, I looked down into the cockpit and saw flames coming out from under the instrument panel. I have no recollection of seeing the pilot in the cockpit. The Zero had no armor plate behind the pilot's seat, and that pilot had made the fatal mistake of not keeping a swivel neck going and checking six—looking behind him.

I have wondered many times if I shot the Zero off the tail of the smoking F6F in time to prevent more damage and allow the Hellcat to survive and get back. I can only hope that I did get there soon enough to save a fellow pilot.

I immediately turned and saw that there was another Zero about 2,000 feet ahead and slightly above and to my right. It was going almost directly away from me in a shallow climb. The plane was in my sights almost immediately, and I was only waiting to get into firing range of about 1,000 feet.

Suddenly, there was a noise that a fighter pilot, or any combat pilot, hates to hear. Imagine the sound when someone throws a handful of large rocks against a galvanized tin roof. I reacted rather hastily and threw my plane over and down into a split-S dive—actually more of a half snap roll and a hard pull down—a maneuver commonly referred to as "getting the hell out of there," which I had used successfully before. As I rolled, I looked back and— sure enough—about 300 yards behind me was a pair of Zeros with a stream of red tracers coming toward me from one of the 7.7mm guns in the nose of the lead plane.

When I looked ahead again in my dive, there was another Zero. He was crossing directly ahead of me, already within firing range. Though I had barely enough time to get the proper lead for a full deflection shot, I fired a short burst and he exploded almost instantly. All of this action had occurred in 30 to 45 seconds.

I didn't know just where or how badly my plane had been hit, so I pulled out of my dive at about 1,500 feet and headed for the rendezvous point, which was at 10,000 feet and about 10 miles ahead. I picked up some of our bombers on the way and escorted them. I found Bud Gehoe, my wingman, and the rest of my division already at the rendezvous point. We escorted the strike force back to the carrier.

The two-hour mission I had just flown was by far the most action-filled of all my combat flights; only one of our F6Fs was shot down over the target and one bomber failed to return. VF-9 pilots shot down 14 Zeros.

When I landed back aboard the *Essex* after an uneventful return flight, I found a dozen or so 7.7mm bullet holes in my plane, but all were in a vertical direction, almost straight down through both wings. A Zero that I had never seen had made an overhead run on me and had hit my plane at the same time that the Zero on my tail had opened fire. Their procedure was to range in, get hits with the 7.7mm machine guns, and then open fire with their 20mm cannons. I have always had the desire to thank the Japanese pilot who made that overhead run on me. He most probably saved my neck because I was overconcentrating on the Zero ahead and making the fighter pilot's usually fatal error: not keeping a continuous lookout.

The Japanese attacked our carriers that afternoon. I was up on Combat Air Patrol at the time and knew that the attack was coming in, but the ship's Fighter Direction Officer (FDO) did not vector us out to intercept the raid. I never did find out why. We spent the entire time orbiting on the side of the task force away from the incoming raid. I didn't even see a Japanese plane on that patrol. However, VF-9 pilots shot down 41 Japanese that afternoon.

That evening, aboard the *Essex*, we received the highest compliment that any fighter squadron could ever receive. The dive-bomber and torpedo-bomber pilots and gunners, who had in the past usually given us a bad time for being hot-shot fighter pilots, came trooping into our ready room with signed commendations thanking us for safely escorting them to and from Rabaul without a loss en route. They also brought in a card table stacked to overflowing with cigarettes, cigars, chewing gum, and candy!

*Lieutenant (jg) Mac McWhorter was credited with 2 Zekes destroyed and 1 Zeke probable over Rabaul. On November 18 and 19, 1943, he achieved ace status by destroying a Mitsubishi F1M Pete floatplane scout and a Betty over the Gilbert Islands. In fact, he was the first pure Hellcat ace of the war. Following the Betty kill, it was discovered that McWhorter's guns had fired only 86 rounds, counting his test rounds. This feat earned him the nickname One Slug. On January 29, 1944, he downed 2 Hamp fighters over Roi Island, in the Marshalls. In the Truk raid on February 17, 1944, he scored his last victories with VF-9, a Hamp and 2 Zekes. That made him the first carrier-based double ace of the war.*

*After VF-9 returned to the States in March 1944, McWhorter was assigned to help re-form VF-12 as a Hellcat squadron following its return from its first tour in F4U Corsairs. Working from the USS Randolph, Lieutenant McWhorter was in on the first carrier raid against Tokyo on February 16, 1945, and he downed a Zeke that day. His twelfth and last victory was a Nakajima C6N Myrt reconnaissance plane he destroyed 24,000 feet over Task Force 58 on May 13, 1945.*

*Commander Hamilton McWhorter retired from the Navy in June 1969. In August 1989, he was inducted into the Georgia Aviation Hall of Fame.*

On November 11, in their morning raid against Rabaul, and in the course of defending the carriers against the afternoon counterstrike mounted from Rabaul, U.S. Navy aircraft—including two carrier-equipped land-based Navy fighter squadrons that shuttled out to the carriers from New Georgia—accounted for a confirmed total of 137 Japanese warplanes. The raid against Rabaul thus yielded the best one-day score of the Pacific War to that point.

# CHAPTER 8

Task Force 50.3's carrier raid against Rabaul on November 11 was the beginning of the end for the vast Japanese base complex. Admiral Ernest King's bypass strategy called for a vicious campaign of almost-daily bombing raids and fighter sweeps of the Japanese headquarters and fleet facility, especially its five airfields. The attacks were to be mounted from existing 5th Air Force bases in New Guinea and several new airfields that were yet to be built around Cape Torokina and on New Britain itself.

In the meantime, until the new airfields could be constructed, nothing much happened. The Japanese remained tethered to Rabaul. The AirSols fighters and bombers based in the Central Solomons remained beyond range of doing anything more than patrolling over Cape Torokina; taking out targets of opportunity throughout Bougainville; and harassing Kahili, Ballale, and other bypassed bases. The 5th Air Force continued to sting Rabaul, but the 5th was stretched thin because its primary mission was to support General MacArthur's ongoing offensive along New Guinea's northeastern coast.

Through the end of 1943, except for the U.S. Navy's newly opened Central Pacific Offensive, the air war against Japan just scraped along.

## MEETING ENGAGEMENT

**1st Lieutenant DICK WEST, USAAF**
**35th Fighter Squadron, 8th Fighter Group**
**Ramu Valley, New Guinea, November 15, 1943**

*A native of Chillicothe, Missouri, Richard Lee West gradu-*
*ated from flight school in late 1942 and was assigned as a*
*tactics instructor for six months at the Orlando, Florida,*
*School of Applied Tactics. He was then assigned to overseas*
*duty and sent to eastern New Guinea to join the 35th Fighter*
*Squadron.*

*On his very first encounter with Japanese aircraft—near*
*Finschhafen, New Guinea, on September 22, 1943—2d*
*Lieutenant West shot down two Hap fighters and scored a*
*Hap probable. For some reason, West equated his "beginner's*
*luck" to the fact that he had neglected to get his hair cut,*
*something he then superstitiously refused to do. Though*
*West's hair grew remarkably long and the lieutenant flew at*
*every opportunity, he did not see another Japanese airplane*
*until November 15, 1943.*

In late 1943 we were flying from the fighter strip at Nadzab,
an adequate and well-maintained field about 100 miles west
of Finschhafen, in the Ramu Valley, which is a flat, wide,
and hot place. We regularly patrolled up the Ramu Valley
because Nadzab was a likely target for enemy aircraft flying
from their nearest bases to the west.

At about 1000 on November 15, 1943, eight of us were on
a routine patrol of the Ramu Valley west of Nadzab. The
weather was mostly sunny with some cloud cover to the
west. We were flying P-40N-5 fighters. The N-5 version was
the most improved P-40 model at that time. It had six
.50-caliber machine guns, three in each wing. The P-40
would have been a dandy airplane if it had been super-
charged. It was easy to handle, but it didn't have much range
or altitude capability.

We were only about 75 miles west of Nadzab when I saw a
wave of airplanes in the far distance. I called them in to the

guy leading the patrol, but it was some time before he saw them, which didn't make all that much difference since we were on the right course to intercept them anyway. We were going west up the valley and they were coming down the valley, eastward, apparently en route to Nadzab to bomb the strip there. We went to maximum power which—in a P-40—wasn't much.

We closed on the enemy formation for as long as 10 minutes without getting a reaction. Pretty soon, I could see that it was a formation of twenty-four Mitsubishi Ki-21 Sally twin-engine bombers and thirty to thirty-five Zeke fighters. Soon, they saw us. I guess they decided not to pursue their mission to Nadzab after being detected. They did a 180-degree turn and then everybody was going in the same direction.

What happened next is hard to believe, but true. The Japanese fighters got in *front* of the bombers! The fighters were in front of and above the Sallys.

We weren't very well led either. We were slowly catching up with the whole shebang from below and behind—at about a 25-degree climbing angle, which would have been fine if we had been going 400 to 500 miles per hour, but we were not. I just knew we were going to get a faceful of bullets at any time from all those Japanese gunners on those bombers.

Though I didn't like the way we were going in on the bombers, I had no great sense of fear. I was never really frightened after my first combat on September 22, but that first time I was *very* frightened. Experience in combat is about the most valuable commodity a fighter pilot can have, of course, but he also needs training. Most good combat pilots, I believe, already had the ability to shoot accurately. Then, if they could fly pretty good, they had it made as they put it all together. Truthfully, not too many mastered both—good flying and good shooting. In my case, I had grown up hunting and, when I was in grade school, my friends and I could break marbles in the air with our .22-caliber rifles. So, shooting was a given for me.

The Zekes stayed in front of and above the bombers all that time. It was like they didn't even see us. I have seen some tactical blunders, but that was a dandy! All they had to do was fall back of the bombers and chase us off. But they didn't and we flew right up their asses. Maybe they thought we were not dumb enough to be doing that.

We flew into them from the 25-degree climbing angle and at slow relative speed. I picked a Sally on the right side of the formation and hammered him in the midsection from slightly below and behind. My intent on that pass was to kill people inside the Sally if I could. Six .50-caliber machine guns were a wicked set of weapons. I mean, if you're firing six .50-caliber machine guns from 20 to 30 yards and closing, something is going to happen. Six .50s up close are awesome!

I figured, after I shot up the Sally's midsection, I would move to the right engine and then break right and rake the Sally on its right. This I did. The right engine burned and the plane peeled off and went down. As that bomber left the formation, the Zekes finally turned on us. As I broke off from the first Sally, I pulled my guns through the one on its right. At the debrief after the mission, some guys said the second Sally fell out of the formation, but everyone was too busy with the Zekes to finish it off. I was credited with a kill for the first Sally and a probable for the second one.

The Zekes arrived from above us as my first Sally started down. Our formation was broken up, and understandably so. It was a hell of a fight, and a wonder everyone didn't run into somebody accidentally—which is exactly what happened to my friend, 1st Lieutenant Robert Parker, who collided with a Zeke. The right wing of each fighter was sheared in the collision. Neither pilot got out of his airplane as long as I watched them, which was almost to the ground.

I had a busy time with targets all around me. I flamed two Zekes in frontal attacks and knocked pieces off two more, one from 90 degrees and the other from 40 degrees. The shooting was all close together. There was no time to reason; I shot by instinct.

Pretty soon, I heard a guy say that there was a second wave of Sallys coming up the valley. I looked east and, lo and behold, here comes this second bunch of twin-engine bombers, just like the guy said. They were going west up the valley, behind the formation of Sallys we had just hit.

I was in perfect position for a head-on attack, so I

split-essed, headed in, and picked one out. I was going maybe 400 miles per hour and they were coming on at maybe 200, so we were closing pretty fast. I gave him a short burst and pulled up and through them. There were *stars* on all of them! They were B-25s!

I turned west and watched the guy I had shot at as I outdistanced the B-25s. He held his position in the formation as long as I watched. I thought my marksmanship was pretty poor, but I was mighty thankful that it was.

I still had some ammo left, so I headed back up the valley to rejoin the fight, which was to my west. I was at about 12,000 feet and climbing to gain altitude advantage. I hadn't gone far when I saw a real Sally below me and heading mostly north, toward Wewak, which was 50 to 70 miles away. Wewak was under Japanese control at the time, but it had long since been pretty shot and bombed up.

The Sally was 2,000 to 3,000 feet below me when I caught up with it and made an overhead pass. On an overhead pass at the angle at which I was approaching, which was 90 degrees (I was going straight down and he was straight and level), you put your gunsight ahead of your intended target. I was shooting at his nose and cockpit, and my gun-camera film showed that that was where I hit him. He did a wingover to the right and went in. He was a cripple to start with, no question. It's possible that this Sally was the second one I had shot out of formation on my first pass.

I was joined by two P-40s. The pilots told me on the radio that they had seen me shoot down the Sally. As I headed back up the valley again, back toward the fight, the P-40s turned back for home. They were low on fuel or out of ammo, having been pretty busy themselves. I still had some ammo, so, since the name of the game was kill them when you found them, I tried to find them again.

I saw the bombers and fighters at the same time. The bombers were together on the right and the fighters were together on the left. I was to the left of both formations. I paralleled the Japanese until I spotted some cloud cover. I figured that, if I flew in the cloud cover for 10 minutes or so, I would break out in front of the bombers, which I wanted another shot at.

Well, my judgment was off bad; I broke out of the clouds in front of the *fighters*. The fighters were in front of me and pretty close and the Sallys were too far for me to hit. So, I went through the fighters, which were going every which way. I picked one that was going straight away. I was almost in range when I felt a jolt. It was like maybe a mule had kicked the ass end of my P-40. My P-40 was hit behind the cockpit by a 20mm cannon shell from 90 degrees. My controls and engine functioned, so no problems. But it was time to leave.

I snapped a burst at the fighter I was lined up on as he broke hard left. I saw a hit in front of or right in his cockpit, but that's all. I was quite a distance from it, and the Zeke didn't flame and I didn't kill the pilot. When you kill a guy in a fighter, the plane takes a different attitude immediately, as the pressure he had on the controls is no longer there.

I put my nose down and headed for Nadzab. A P-40 could outrun a Zeke going down, starting even. They didn't chase me.

The cannon shell had hit behind my cockpit. There was no damage to me, but, as I learned later, it had sheared one rudder cable, except for two strands.

When I landed at Nadzab, my CO, Major Emmett "Cyclone" Davis, told me there was a colonel on the phone who wanted to talk to me. It was the CO of the B-25 group. He was very nice, which was quite a surprise, as I figured I was in for a first-class ass chewing for shooting at one of his B-25s. He said he called to tell me that no one was hurt and that the B-25 had crash-landed on the bomber strip at Nadzab because I had shot out the hydraulics and damaged the throttle quadrant some. Then he said the guys in the B-25s had been listening to the fight on the radio and should have turned back—which they did when I started shooting at one of them.

In a few days I went on leave. We spent the first night in Brisbane, and I was drinking whiskey with three or four guys in a bar when one of the guys said, "The damnedest thing happened to me up in the island the other day. This son of a bitch in a P-40 shot the throttle quadrant right out from under my hand!" I asked him if anyone was hurt and he said, "No." I debated about telling him that it was me who had done the shooting. I decided to confess. After I'd explained how it happened, he was okay about it.

*Seven of the eight 35th Squadron pilots engaged in the November 15, 1943, action over the Ramu Valley turned in claims amounting to 7 Zekes and 1 Oscar destroyed (including 2 confirmed Zekes for Lieutenant Robert Parker, who died following his midair collision with one of his victims), 2 Sallys destroyed, and 3 Zekes and 1 Sally probably destroyed or damaged. Two of the confirmed Sallys, 2 of the confirmed Zekes, and one each of the probables were credited to 1st Lieutenant Dick West, making him an ace on his second confrontation ever with Japanese warplanes.*

*Dick West flew P-40s for six months and saw the Japanese only twice—enough to become an ace with 2 Haps, 2 Zekes, and 2 Sallys confirmed, plus 1 Hap, 1 Zeke, and 1 Sally probably destroyed. In a year of flying P-38s, also with the 35th Fighter Squadron, West saw Japanese planes on only six more missions—and scored on all of them. In every one of those contacts, West was the first pilot to see the enemy airplanes, which is proof to the adage that the pilot who sees his enemy first stands the best chance of emerging as the winner. In all, Captain Dick West ended his combat tour in late 1944 with 14 confirmed victories and 3 probables. In addition to destroying so many Japanese aircraft, West shared credit for burning and grounding a Japanese tanker and leaving a gunboat adrift and abandoned off Borneo. On another mission West destroyed a bridge in the Philippines by dropping one 1,000-pound bomb. He made the drop after many bombers had failed to inflict serious damage. Near the end of his tour, West crash-landed in enemy territory on Mindanao and spent two weeks with friendly guerrillas, the exciting finale to a fruitful combat career.*

The fighter strip on Cape Torokina—the first of a three-airfield complex slated for the beachhead area—was declared operational on December 10, 1943. Its first tenants, a Marine Corsair squadron, arrived that day. The AirSols offensive against Rabaul kicked off tentatively a week later, on December 17, when Marine Major Greg Boyington led his squadron of Marine F4Us, a squadron of Navy F6Fs, and forty New Zealand P-40s out of New Georgia—area bases. After a refueling stop at Torokina, the attack force proceeded to the target. All Boyington's fighters found in the air over Rabaul, however, was a lone Rufe floatplane fighter. This was dispatched as forty Zekes scrambled to challenge the Americans and New Zealanders. Two of the newly arrived Zeros were shot down by a member of Boyington's VMF-214 and 5 more Zeros fell before the guns of the New Zealand P-40s. Another thirty Zeros rose to challenge the Allied fighters. They remained as far away from the unfriendly guns as possible; nevertheless, a Navy Hellcat pilot bagged one of them. After 40 minutes over the target, Boyington led all his fighters home via a fuel stop at Torokina.

This rather inauspicious and desultory engagement—a test, really—was the debut of one of the most intense and vicious aerial campaigns of World War II. In addition to planning to send hundreds of AirSols fighters and bombers out of Bougainville, the 5th Air Force was set to mount an unremitting series of raids out of its New Guinea bases. Several divisions of the U.S. Army and Marine Corps even went to the trouble of invading western and central New Britain so additional airfields could be captured or built even closer to Rabaul.

## CRIPPLED

**1st Lieutenant CORKY SMITH, USAAF**
**80th Fighter Squadron, 8th Fighter Group**
**Cape Gloucester, December 26, 1943**

*Cornelius Marcellus Smith of Brooklyn, New York, graduated from Roanoke College, in Salem, Virginia, in June 1940. He worked in industry for over a year, then quit his job to join the Army Air Corps at the outbreak of the war. He earned his wings in September 1942, trained in P-39s in*

**153**

*Florida, and departed for New Guinea to join the 8th Fighter Group in November 1942.*

*It took six months for Lieutenant Smith to hit the charts, but he did so in a big way. On June 21, 1943, he shot down 3 Zeros and claimed 1 Zero probable in action near Lae. Smith got another Zero probable on September 15, over Wewak; a confirmed Tony fighter, also over Wewak, on October 16; and another confirmed Zero over Rabaul on October 24, 1943.*

The 80th Fighter Squadron, also known as the Headhunters, had been engaged in the war since August 1942. Equipped with P-39 and P-400 fighters and initially stationed at Port Moresby, the squadron had moved to Milne Bay, on the southern tip of New Guinea, in early October 1942. While at Port Moresby, the squadron had seen active combat, and its pilots had downed 6 Zeros. Despite the downing of another Zero in January 1943 at Milne Bay, the morale of the pilots was low due to the few recent occasions on which they had seen combat. The P-39 had proved ineffective against the faster and more maneuverable enemy fighters. Its range and altitude limitations were also major drawbacks. Additionally, an epidemic of malaria and dengue fever had rendered many of the pilots and ground-crew personnel *hors de combat*. It was time for a change.

In late January, the unit was withdrawn from New Guinea and moved to Mareeba, Australia. Rest and rehabilitation to recover from malaria and dengue was the primary reason for the move, but more important was the news that our P-39 and P-400 aircraft were to be replaced by highly regarded Lockheed P-38 Lightning twin-engine fighters mounted with four .50-caliber machine guns and a 20mm cannon. Morale soared. The move was completed in early February.

In early April 1943, the Headhunters brought their new P-38s back to Port Moresby. Our camp was Kila Airdrome, more commonly known as 3-Mile Strip. In the following 8½ months, the squadron proved itself an outstanding combat unit. The P-38 was superior in most aspects to the Japanese Zero fighter aircraft we were facing. By the middle of December, we had contributed a total of 136 confirmed kills to the war effort. All but 7 of these had fallen to P-38 guns.

I had joined the Headhunters at Milne Bay in late November 1942. A year later, I was credited with 5 aerial victories, all in the P-38. Morale of both pilots and ground-crew personnel was at an all-time high. We welcomed the increasing opportunities to bring the war to the enemy with our long-legged fighter.

On December 12, 1943, the 80th Fighter Squadron completed a permanent move from Kila to the multibase airdrome complex recently constructed at Dobodura, on the east coast of New Guinea. During October and November 1943, our air strikes against forward Japanese air and sea strongpoints on New Britain and along the more northern shore of eastern New Guinea had critically interfered with the enemy's ability to pose a major threat to our air installations. We had seized control of the New Britain and southern New Guinea airspace and shipping lanes necessary for our logistical support. General MacArthur's leapfrog strategy was moving northward. Lae and Salamaua had fallen to our forces, and we had greatly negated the capability of the Japanese to operate in strength from Rabaul, Wewak, Madang, and Cape Gloucester. We had also seized Finschhafen, an enemy air base on the coast of New Guinea only some 80 miles distant from the western end of New Britain. On New Britain, Cape Gloucester harbored an airfield still held by the Japanese. Finschhafen had been developed as a new air base by our engineers and was fully operational. In short, the stage had been set for our forces to undertake the long-awaited initiative and push the enemy back.

Unbeknown to us when we arrived at Dobodura on December 12 were plans to invade the Japanese bases at Arawe and Cape Gloucester, New Britain, in the immediate future. Cape Gloucester was to be developed for Allied use as a forward air base. Madang and Wewak, on the New Guinea coast, were to be bypassed, and the Japanese bases on Manus Island (some 50 miles off Wewak), Aitape (north of Wewak), and Hollandia (farther to the north) were to be seized and made into advanced U.S. bases. Once this had been accomplished, we would strike at and seize key areas of northern New Guinea; Java and its surrounding waters; and, eventually, the Philippines.

Initial operations against Arawe took place immediately following our arrival at Dobodura. The Headhunters took part in preinvasion missions on December 14 and covered the actual invasion on December 15. On December 18, we took part in covering bombers on a mission to soften up Cape Gloucester in the morning and went back to Arawe in the afternoon. There was no Japanese air activity on either mission. On December 22, I shot down a Zero fighter—my sixth victory—while escorting bombers against Wewak, and I got shot up myself. I made it back on one engine. On December 25, I helped cover a U.S. naval convoy going into Finschhafen.

During the evening of December 25, we were informed by 8th Fighter Group headquarters that we would provide air cover for an amphibious landing at Cape Gloucester the next day. This was good news; we went to bed in high spirits.

On the morning of December 26, we were called to a meeting at our flight-line operations hut and briefed on the mission. We were to provide air cover over the new beachhead, some 200 miles distant, beginning at 1400. Control of all flights over the beachhead would be handled by a team aboard a destroyer. We would contact the ship upon arrival to receive further instructions. Major Edward "Porky" Cragg, our CO, would lead the mission. Major Carl "Freddie" Taylor, our operations officer, would also participate. As it looked like a big operation with the probability of seeing combat, the more-experienced pilots were chosen to fly. Our call sign would be the same as always: Copper. We would fly sixteen P-38s in the usual flight formation. Call signs of Red, White, Blue, and Yellow would be utilized in that order. Major Cragg was Copper Red-1, his wingman Copper Red-2, and so forth. I was to be the element leader in the fourth flight, Copper Yellow-3.

Since we were to start engines at approximately 1145, we were to be in our cockpits or close by the aircraft by 1130. Taxi would be in order of flights. Takeoff would be by two-ship elements. Climb out and assembly would be the usual circular left-hand pattern. We would climb to 12,000 feet and, using the direct route, maintain loose formation to the coast of New Britain. Then the formation would tighten up for the remainder of the distance across the island to Cape Gloucester. Radio silence was to be maintained by all following takeoff. Aborting aircraft, if any, would indicate intentions by rocking their wings before departing from the formation. Unless in extreme difficulty, aborting aircraft would not be escorted back. Following departure from Cape Gloucester, the route home would be determined by remaining fuel. If possible, aborting aircraft would return to Dobodura. If necessary, Finschhafen or Nadzab would be alternates. The weather forecast was CAVU throughout the mission, but scattered low clouds might be encountered in the beachhead area during the afternoon. We were to use our drop tanks and run them dry unless we got into a combat situation.

If we encountered enemy aircraft, they would probably be fighters with dive-bombers, coming from Rabaul. Their most likely approach was from the east to the south of the hilly-to-mountainous terrain running through the center of New Britain from east to west. We were told to be especially alert for aircraft emerging from behind this ridge.

We were to relieve P-38s from another squadron that were already in the area. P-47s from the 348th Fighter Group would also provide cover. No P-40s or P-39s were expected in the vicinity; their mission would be to provide air cover for Finschhafen, our alternate destination. In short, the only friendly single-engine aircraft we would see near the cape would be P-47s. The large size of that type of fighter would be sufficient to identify it as friendly.

All of us pilots were at our aircraft long before 1130. Shortly thereafter, a jeep came by with the word to start engines. Following start-up, the tower gave the word to taxi. We took off in two-ship formations, as planned; we climbed to 12,000 feet; and headed on course at approximately 1215. The weather was perfect en route. Copper Red-1 contacted our ship control at about 1345 hours. We were instructed to maintain our 12,000-foot altitude and patrol the beach area.

We tooled around for about 20 minutes, watching LSTs and other naval craft running to and from the beach. I observed some shelling by various naval vessels and saw some of our Marines and their vehicles on the beach. Everything seemed to be going well, but there was less activity than I had expected.

The calm atmosphere was broken when our control ship advised us that a large blip had appeared on radar 20 to 25 miles out to sea north of the beachhead. We were instructed to climb to 20,000 feet and given an intercept heading. The radar sighting indicated a large force of aircraft at high altitude. We spent about 10 minutes under radar control, following heading and altitude instructions, but we saw nothing. We were then informed that the blip had completely disappeared from radar and that we were to return immediately to the beachhead. We did a quick 180-degree turn and headed back while descending to our original 12,000-foot assigned altitude. We had no more than started our return when the destroyer contact told us that a large force of enemy fighters and dive-bombers had come in from the south—screened by the mountains—and was attacking the beachhead and shipping in the area.

The word was given by Copper Red-1 to drop belly tanks and get in trail formation. When this was accomplished, we were instructed by the controller to split our force. The first two flights—Red and White—were to engage the enemy aircraft by attacking the area at low level. The last two flights—Blue and Yellow—were to remain at 10,000 to 12,000 feet to intercept a second wave of fighters and dive-bombers should any appear. Since I was in Yellow Flight, I would remain with the high group.

In our brief absence from the beachhead, low clouds had formed against the hills and over portions of the beach. Although thin and scattered, these hindered our view of the coast. Several naval vessels were firing at low-flying enemy aircraft, and I observed sundry explosions in the beach area.

Red and White flights had left our altitude and were closing rapidly with the land. When Blue and Yellow flights arrived over the beach at our assigned altitude, we placed ourselves above the ridgeline to serve as a shield against any attacking force. I could not see either Red or White flights due to low clouds. Blue Flight was then directed to support our first two flights at low altitude. Yellow Flight was to hold our patrol altitude.

We had no more than reinitiated our patrol than my radio receiver went dead. All sound ceased. I hit my mike button to call my wingman, but I received no response. He could easily see me in the cockpit, so I informed him of my predicament by pointing to my headset and shaking my head. He got the picture and indicated that he could not hear any transmission from me. I intended to follow the flight from above and to the rear. That accomplished, I checked my headset and various channels on my radio, but to no avail. I was kaput as far as communications were concerned.

This was for the birds. I wanted to join in whatever was going on beneath me, not fly around looking for enemy aircraft that I had no means of reporting should any arrive. I pulled abreast of my flight leader, waggled my wings, and waved good-bye to signify I was going to leave. He grinned and stuck his thumb up to bid me well. I peeled off and started down to find something to shoot at.

When I arrived below the clouds, I found eight or nine P-47 Thunderbolts engaged in a dogfight with four Oscars north and east of the beachhead and about two miles away from my position. No P-38s were in sight. I decided to help out the 47s. As I headed toward the fracas, three of the Oscars broke off and headed southeast—the P-47s already outnumbered them, and the arrival of my P-38 only lessened their chances. However, one of the Oscar pilots decided to stick it out a bit longer and continued to go around with the 47s. When I got to within about 2,000 yards, he decided to leave and took off with three of the Thunderbolts on his tail, some 500 yards back.

I had played around in mock combat with 47s before and knew that they could not outrun a 38. Moreover, I did not believe a 47 could catch an Oscar in a low-altitude chase. Hence, I took out after them even though I was at a greater distance back than I had originally believed. The start of the chase was at about 4,000—possibly 4,500—feet of altitude. The Oscar was about a quarter mile out to sea and running east at a good clip, parallel to the coast, in a slight descent. Its speed surprised me, but I felt that I could catch the Oscar in the long run if it kept on a straight-away course without attempting to turn and engage. I planned to get real close, fill my gunsight, and hit the Oscar full bore with the four .50-cals and 20mm, all at once. Hopefully, the 47s would bring up the rear and provide cover for me should any other Japanese fighters appear. But this was not to be the case. Each 47 peeled off and headed back for the beachhead area as I overtook it. I then realized that I had put 15 to 20 miles between me and the beachhead. Although alone, I felt the urge to continue the chase. My adrenaline was at high pitch!

We were now close to the surface of the sea, and the Oscar had begun to level out. I was hardly overtaking it. I was well aware of my vulnerability to attack from any other Japanese fighter, should any turn back to render assistance. I kept alert, looking for any to appear. My visibility over the water was clear, but the low clouds over land obscured my view in that direction.

My intention was to wait until the Oscar more than filled my gunsight before I opened fire. This would ensure destruction. When I was about 500 yards away, a Zero appeared at 1 o'clock, diving toward us through the clouds. He was coming fast. I knew it was touch and go as to whether I could hold fire long enough to guaranty the kill before the Zero opened fire at me. I knew the pilot would be confronted with a difficult deflection shot, though, so I took the gamble and concentrated on the Oscar.

When the Oscar filled my gunsight, I let go with my .50s and 20mm, hitting it with everything I had from the tail up through the fuselage and cockpit. The Oscar did not blow up, but pieces of the ship, including a large portion of the tail section, flew everywhere. A sure kill!

The Zero was close upon me and firing as I pulled up in a steep right turn to gain altitude and headed 90 degrees from course. I felt my 38 get hit by his fire, apparently in the right-engine area. I flew over the coast in a shallow high-speed climb, trying to put as much distance between me and my attacker as possible and, at the same time, gain some altitude to enhance my maneuverability in case he pressed his attack. My right engine started overheating, which indicated damage and loss of coolant. I leveled out at about 5,000 feet, still going south. I was well over the land when I shut the engine down and feathered the prop. I scanned the skies through all points of the compass, but with nary a sighting of my attacker.

I had no desire to bail out or crash-land over any part of New Britain in the event my good left engine failed or if any attacking Zero downed me. Hostile natives reportedly lopped the heads off the American airmen, and the Japanese were known to do the same. Subjecting myself to capture held no appeal. I headed back toward the coast and the friendlier sea.

There was still no sign of my attacker, so I decided to get four or five miles offshore and then head toward Finschhafen via Cape Gloucester. I climbed back to about 10,000 feet, well over the sea, and set course. The left engine ran okay, flight controls gave no indication of damage, the voltmeter was okay, and I could not see any sign of damage to the aircraft. However, I knew my right engine had taken some hits, and I had no intention of trying to restart it. The P-38 flew well on one engine. I had no doubts as to my ability to reach Finschhafen. I had previously made four one-engine landings in 38s, so I felt quite confident. Fuel posed no problem; I had dropped my two belly tanks at Cape Gloucester, but I had ample gas in my main and reserve tanks.

I passed the cape about four miles out to sea and saw a few P-47s over the beach area. One ship was burning off the coast. It appeared to be a destroyer, but, at my altitude and distance, I could not be sure. Other than those sightings, the area was clear. I never saw my attacker—or any other enemy aircraft—during the course of my flight. Over the sea between New Britain and the New Guinea coast, I saw one flight of P-39s but nothing more.

As I neared Finschhafen, I saw that the strip and adjacent airspace were very active. Many aircraft, mostly P-38s and P-47s, were taking off, flying in the traffic pattern, and maneuvering in the vicinity of the field. It was no place to attempt a single-engine landing without communication. I could not alert anyone to my predicament. If I joined up with another plane to visually indicate my situation so he could talk to the tower, I would have to descend. Loss of altitude held no appeal; I would need all the altitude I could get should my good left engine act up. Also, the strip at Finschhafen ran from the sea to neighboring high jungle growth—landings were made from the sea. In the event I overshot the strip in attempting to land, I would have to go around on one engine. This was not a recommended procedure, especially with a wall of tall trees to contend with at the end of the strip. I elected to continue on to Nadzab and land at one of several strips there. This would lengthen my flight by 50 to 75 miles, but it posed no problems. I headed on course.

About 10 miles past Finschhafen, my left engine started missing—not a good sign. I immediately turned 180 degrees and headed back, checking the cockpit instruments. Fuel pressure was okay, but my RPM was fluctuating noticeably and would not stabilize. I had come back on the throttles first thing and found that the engine ran fairly smoothly at about 15 inches of manifold pressure and about 1,600 RPM. However, any increase in throttle setting or RPM resulted in engine misfires, and increasing the RPM increased the fluctuation. A landing was essential. I was losing altitude and could not fool around. I also noticed that my voltmeter needle was doing a good bit of wavering, which signified an electrical problem. Everything was coming loose at once!

I was close enough to the field to glide and make it. I wondered about the health of the hydraulic system and wondered if I could lower the landing gear. I was not elated over the possibility of a wheels-up landing, especially on the Pierced Steel Planking (PSP) strip. Landing without wheels would enhance the danger of fire and could render the strip inoperative if the planking was torn up. Also, I would have no control of the aircraft if I overshot and slid into the trees at the far end. If my hydraulic system was not operating properly, I planned to bail out.

I had no way to alert the tower other than to come over the strip at a good clip with the wheels down and my landing and fuselage lights on, rocking my wings to get attention. From past experience, I knew that if I came over at 800 to 1,000 feet at 150 miles per hour or more with the gear down, I could execute a widow-maker, a 360-degree circle descent to the approach end of the runway. If I was not too hot, I could utilize flaps to prevent landing too far down the strip.

I turned on my navigation and landing lights and headed down. I dropped my gear at about 2,000 feet. Fortunately, the gear indicator showed "Down and locked." I decided to dead-stick the landing, as I could not depend on my left engine.

Now my only problem was getting the tower's attention so the crew could advise other aircraft to clear the area for my approach. I observed several planes taxiing toward takeoff position, and others were in the traffic pattern. The tower gave no notice of me. I came over the strip at about 1,000 feet, real hot—about 200 miles per hour—and rocked my wings hard. I peeled off about halfway down the runway in a steep turn, climbing a bit to kill some speed and stay fairly close to the field. Leveling off at about 1,200 feet abreast of the approach end of the runway, I hit one-quarter flaps and continued the turn. I was indicating about 120 miles per hour—still hot—so I dumped half flaps. At that moment, I got a green flare and brought the airspeed down to just below 100 miles per hour. I set my glide angle and cut my main ignition switch and fuel mixture off to safeguard against fire in event the gear collapsed. I set it down about 500 feet from the approach end and came to a rolling stop off the right side of the strip. I made a final cockpit check, climbed out with my chute and other gear, and was greeted by a bunch of line personnel.

In the morning, I was informed that a P-38 on the strip needed to be ferried to its home outfit at Dobodura. I volunteered to fly the plane to its home base and was quickly taken up on the offer. I gave it a quick check ride, landed, signed it off as okay, and flew it home. The receiving unit, based at another strip, gave me a ride to the Head-hunters' camp.

Upon arrival, I learned that our CO, Major Porky Cragg, had been shot down at Cape Gloucester along with our operations officer, Major Freddy Taylor. Both were listed as MIA.

During the afternoon of December 28, Freddy Taylor came home, much to everyone's surprise. His return lifted morale tremendously and gave us hope that Porky Cragg might also have survived. Unfortunately, Porky never returned. He was a fine man, a natural leader in every respect. At the time of his loss, he had a total of 15 confirmed aerial victories and was one of the leading American aces.

I considered myself most fortunate, for I had had an engine shot out over Wewak on December 22, just four days prior to losing an engine at Cape Gloucester. Two single-engine return trips in the month! I didn't need any more!

*By the time Captain Corky Smith returned to the United States in May 1944, he had driven his total of confirmed victories to 11, including 2 Zeros destroyed on January 18, 1944, at Wewak; a Mitsubishi Ki-46 Dinah high-speed reconnaissance bomber over Hollandia on March 31; and a Ki-61 Tony fighter over Lake Santani on April 12. He went on a War Bond tour and then served for the rest of the war as a P-38 instructor at Santa Rosa, California. Smith remained in the Air Force after the war and retired as a colonel in December 1968.*

The first land-based light-bomber raid was staged against Rabaul from New Georgia—area bases via Cape Torokina on January 5, 1944. The planes, Marine single-engine TBF torpedo bombers (used as level bombers carrying 2,000-pound bomb loads) and SBD dive-bombers, ran into heavy weather and returned home before reaching the target. Weather hindered the repeat effort of January 7, too. The light bombers aborted, but Marine and Navy fighters pressed on and destroyed a dozen Japanese fighters at the cost of 3 Navy Hellcats. Sixty-two Allied fighters escorted 39 SBDs and TBFs to Rabaul on January 9. Forty Japanese fighters challenged the raid, and 13 were shot down at a cost of 1 Hellcat and 2 New Zealand P-40s.

The bombing raids—conducted by everything from TBFs and SBDs to B-25 and B-26 twin-engine medium bombers to B-17 and B-24 four-engine heavy bombers—were the least important part of the strategy against Rabaul. The results of bombing were impermanent and often negligible. Bluntly, the bombers were sent daily (weather permitting) against Rabaul for the sole purpose of drawing up the Japanese fighters. As the Japanese attacked the bombers, they were in turn attacked by the Allied escort fighters. The sole objective of the air campaign against Rabaul was to bleed the Imperial Army and Imperial Navy air arms to death—to kill the last of the best Japanese pilots and to terrorize or demoralize the others.

Between December 17, 1943, and February 20, 1944, when the last Japanese fighters were permanently withdrawn from Rabaul, Allied pilots and aerial gunners claimed 789 confirmed victories for the loss of 151 friendly fighters and bombers. The Japanese claimed 1,045 victories, including antiaircraft-gunnery kills, for the same period. There are no surviving Imperial Army records to support the Allied victory claims, and the highest Imperial Navy tally admits to only about 250 losses.

No one knows how many Japanese planes fell over Rabaul nor how many Japanese airmen died in the critical two months of the campaign. What is certain is that Rabaul's last aerial defenders were withdrawn, thus effectively concluding the bloody eighteen-month campaign to wrest the Solomons and Bismarcks from Japan. What had not been or could not be captured without inordinate loss was bypassed and cut off— left, in Admiral Ernest King's words, "to rot on the vine."

Long before Rabaul was tamed, however, the U.S. Navy had kicked off its great Central Pacific Offensive.

# CHAPTER 9

On October 26, 1942, at the conclusion of the Battle of the Santa Cruz Islands—as the sea closed over the burning hulk of fleet carrier *Hornet*—the United States Navy had just two fleet carriers left. Both of them, *Saratoga* and *Enterprise*, were damaged.

*Hornet*, which had been commissioned on October 20, 1941, was the last of America's prewar fleet carriers. The next fleet carrier to be commissioned by the U.S. Navy was the *Essex*, on December 31, 1942, two months after *Hornet*'s demise. It would be another six months before *Essex* would be ready to go to sea, and several months after that before any newer *Essex*-class carriers (27,100-ton, 854-foot ships) would be able to join her. As a stopgap, in January 1942, the Navy had hurriedly grabbed nine completed light-cruiser hulls and begun converting them into 11,000-ton, 610-foot light carriers. Both types were designed or updated along the way as thoroughly modern carriers, incorporating many innovative responses to design defects detected in the earlier, prewar *Yorktown*-class ships, of which *Enterprise* was the only survivor.

For decades the U.S. Navy had planned to respond to a challenge from Japan by launching an offensive sweep directly across the Central Pacific—more or less from Guam, in the Marianas—all the way to Tokyo. The plan had envisioned the use of battleships and other surface warships fighting fleet surface actions along the way. Indeed, the notion of a battleship war had prevailed from the start in the Navy's building plans, and that is why it was over a year between the commissioning of the *Hornet* and the *Essex*.

Until the Japanese demonstrated otherwise on December 7, 1941, carriers had been seen as surface-fleet auxiliaries. The Japanese example (which they themselves failed to recognize until over a year later!) and the loss of so many of America's battleships at Pearl Harbor conspired to force the American admirals to fall back on their then-six-ship fleet-carrier component as the strategic mainstay. The American *carrier*-based victories at Coral Sea and Midway (which, again, only the Americans recognized for what they were) sealed the fate of future battleship programs and brought carrier aviation to the fore of the long-term American Pacific War strategy.

In a way, the sidestep into the Solomons and New Guinea was a mixed blessing for the U.S. Fleet. It was a necessary departure from the prewar plan based on a Central Pacific Offensive. While the new, thoroughly modern carrier-centered U.S. Fleet was being built, manned, and trained, the Solomons sidestep ripped the guts out of the Imperial Navy's air arm. Over or around Guadalcanal alone, the Japanese lost 600 airplanes and nearly that many pilots and crewmen. What is more, Allied actions caused the demise or incapacitation of several Japanese carriers in addition to the four fleet carriers and one light carrier the Imperial Navy lost at Coral Sea and Midway. In the first year of the war, the U.S. Navy lost four fleet carriers; the remaining two were damaged, which left the Imperial Navy with a considerable edge. However, by the end of the Santa Cruz battle, the Japanese had lost their *will* to employ their remaining carriers offensively.

Two other, ultimately crucial differences prevailed between the opposing navies. Eventually, American industry could churn out as many new carriers as the U.S. Navy might ever need to win the war. There was no limit, given enough time. Japan never actually replaced all the fleet carriers she lost in the first year of the war, and she never would have been able to surpass America's capacity to produce them. Equally important, the U.S. services built pilots and aircrewmen in a way the Japanese could not even conceive of doing—on an assembly-line basis. In 1942, the prewar Army and Navy AvCad programs doubled, tripled, and grew some more. To man the new carrier air groups (America would ultimately build more carrier-type airplanes alone than Japan built overall!), the U.S. Navy and Marine

Corps established joint preflight training facilities capable of handling a total of 9,350 pilot cadets at any given moment. In the course of 1942, the qualitative edge in pilot training and experience the Japanese air services had enjoyed on December 7, 1941, began to cut in favor of the Americans. The Imperial Navy pilots lost in the contest for Guadalcanal, for example, were irreplaceable. Long before Rabaul was torn asunder, increasingly better-trained American pilots were shooting down increasingly large numbers of increasingly inferior Japanese pilots.

Just having new and better carriers and more pilots was not quite enough, however. The U.S. Navy had to learn to use them in increasingly larger formations. The Japanese had perfected joint carrier operations before Pearl Harbor, but the U.S. Navy had never had the opportunity. Indeed, coordination between just two carriers had been so poor at Santa Cruz as to practically ensure the loss of one of the precious capital ships. So, as the new fleet and light carriers came on line in the course of 1943, the Navy not only had to man them and train the crews and air groups, it had to develop, practice, and perfect an unbelievable number and variety of standard procedures aimed at achieving unity of command and tactics. The task took most of 1943, and it is a good thing for the Allies that the Japanese did not make nearly the trouble they could have had their morale not remained on the ropes throughout that period.

The first test of the new U.S. joint-operation procedures occurred on August 31, 1943. The test consisted of a multicarrier strike against out-of-the-way Marcus Atoll, in the northern Central Pacific. No Japanese planes rose to meet the strike aircraft from the new fleet carriers *Essex* and *Yorktown* and the light carrier *Independence*, but 4 American planes were lost (3 to antiaircraft fire and 1 to a mechanical failure). A literal book's worth of valuable lessons and experience came home from Marcus, and the Navy made sweeping adjustments based on what the officers and crews learned.

The next test was in mid September 1943, in strikes against several Japanese bases in the Gilbert Islands, in the eastern Central Pacific. The Gilberts were slated to be invaded at Tarawa and Makin atolls later in the year so, in addition to the learning experience, the air groups from fleet carrier *Lexington* and light carriers *Princeton* and *Belleau Wood* made a solid contribution to the preinvasion effort. The Americans launched seven strikes on September 18 and 19. The U.S. force destroyed all targets, sustained no losses, and further refined and promulgated tactics.

The last big test was launched on October 5, against Wake Island, an emotionally pleasing but strategically unimportant target far to the north of the Gilbert and Marshall groups. The Wake sortie was the largest ever undertaken to that time by U.S. Navy carriers. In all, air groups from fleet carriers *Essex*, *Yorktown*, and *Lexington* and light carriers *Independence*, *Belleau Wood*, and *Cowpens* took part. Japanese radar picked up the dawn approach of the air groups from four of the carriers, and the Japanese scrambled several dozen Zeros. In what was essentially the combat debut of the carrier-based Grumman F6F Hellcat, the Japanese fighters were scoured from the sky. In all that day, U.S. Navy pilots shot down 27 Imperial Navy Zeros and 4 Betty bombers and, in two days of bombing strikes, leveled everything in sight on the tiny, flat atoll. For 738 sorties flown, the task force lost 13 planes in combat and 14 in operational accidents, an acceptable margin in the overall scheme of things. In exchange, not counting the material damage inflicted on the Japanese, the American carrier crews and air groups came away from Wake with deservedly boundless confidence in their leaders; their ships; their airplanes; their tactics; and, not least, themselves.

From Wake it was on to Rabaul on November 5 and 11 and then back to the Gilberts to support the invasion of Tarawa and Makin atolls on November 20. The force that invaded the atolls consisted of a division each of U.S. Army and U.S. Marine infantry.

## THE HOLLYWOOD WAY

Lieutenant (jg) RALPH HANKS, USN
VF-16 (USS *Lexington*)
Off Tarawa, November 23, 1943

*Eugene Ralph Hanks, a native of Red Bluff, California, attended California Polytechnic Institute from 1939 to 1941. While there, he completed the Civilian Pilot Training secondary course. He entered the Navy flight program in October 1941 and was commissioned at Opa-Locka, Florida, on August 25, 1942. Ensign Hanks reported to VF-16 at Quonset Point, Rhode Island, on January 2, 1943, and trained with the new squadron until the unit deployed from Norfolk, Virginia, aboard Lexington on July 22, 1943. He took part in the September raid against the Gilberts and the October raid against Wake, but he did not engage any Japanese airplanes at Wake.*

We departed Pearl Harbor on November 10, 1943, and headed for the Marshall Islands. The ship was loaded with extra planes and gear, obviously prepared for action. We fully expected to meet the Japanese Fleet this time. We flew routine patrols every day and, on the ship, studied the details and target assignments on Mili.

Our ship was the USS *Lexington*—the *Lexington II*, that is. And our squadron was VF-16, known as the Pistol Packin' Airdales. We celebrated our first birthday on November 16 and hit Mili on November 19, 20, and 22—early each day. We demolished the place. There was little or no aircraft opposition.

This was the routine leading up to our big day: Tuesday, November 23. On that day we were launched from the *Lexington* at about 0930, somewhere north of Tarawa. The action on November 23, 1943, was unscheduled in that we didn't have to study and sweat over target material for a week or so and go through sleepless nights awaiting a predawn launch. We were just flying a routine CAP, as we had been doing for several days prior.

It was a beautiful day over a calm Pacific, with a few scattered cumulus clouds. My division of four Grumman F6F Hellcats joined quickly as we climbed to our assigned CAP station, about 12,000 feet over the ship. Each pilot gave me a thumbs-up signal as he slid into position.

Ensign William Seyfferle was on my right wing, Lieutenant (jg) Frank Fleming was my second-section leader, and number 4 was Ensign Edward "Tiger" Rucinski. Frank had been my close friend since Pensacola. He was a top gunner, and I was glad to have him on the team. He had been my wingman until a few days earlier, when our division leader climaxed a series of poor leadership maneuvers by forgetting to safety his guns before landing. He shot up the flight deck and was confined to his room until he could be transferred from the squadron. Our skipper, Lieutenant Commander Paul Buie, gave the division to a lowly jaygee—me.

On this particular day, I was feeling just great. All the butterflies of earlier carrier operations and being thousands of miles from friendly shores were gone. We'd completed several island raids, been shot at, shot up, and had shot numerous enemy aircraft on the ground, but we had yet to see an enemy aircraft in the air. We were ready. I really felt we could take on the Japanese this time.

The skipper and his division could be seen just several miles ahead of me. He had just received orders from our fighter director on the *Lexington* to take Angels 12, the same CAP station I had been assigned. I crossed the large climbing circle to make a smart join-up with him. The division was now in tight formation, and I was aiming to give the Old Man a good impression. We executed a perfect join-up.

The Airdales were at war, and war was a bowl of cherries. We had enjoyed a truly country-club life in Hawaii. If one had to go to war, this was the way to go. A crazy statement maybe, but that's what I thought at the time.

We were all steady on the skipper's wing, leveling off at our assigned CAP altitude when those thoughts of satisfaction ran through my mind. We had just reported on station to our fighter director on the ship when he transmitted back,

"Red-One, Red-Seven,"—that was me—"and Red-Four. Vector Three-Two-Zero. Angels Twenty. Buster. Many bogies." Paul Buie gave us a big grin, waved his fist at us, and nodded for more power.

We were on our way, perhaps, to see some of those red meatballs in the air—those famous planes that we had thus far seen only on the runways, burning in Wake, Mili, and Tarawa. Other VF-16 fighters had shot down about 16 Zeros in those raids and combat air patrols, but Red-7 had been on the deck in the wrong place at the wrong time each time. We were totally ready for this one, however. I signaled for the division to run a gun test, and we each fired a short burst. Twenty-four .50-caliber guns were checked and ready to go.

The time en route was short, but it seemed hours to me. I throttled way back to keep from passing the skipper. My division was in tight formation now. I noticed Johnny Johnson, the skipper's number-4 man, creeping up underneath the boss's aircraft, where he couldn't be seen.

I was now leading the lead division and wondering if my Hellcat was really that much faster than his or whether the CO was just being the Old Fud, as he frequently referred to himself. A few weeks before, we had been assigned permanent aircraft, which the pilots polished and waxed weekly. Frank Fleming and I had a lot of time on our hands and put in a lot of work on ours. I thought now maybe it was paying off. My Hellcat was Number 37. She had a new engine, new guns, was highly sanded and polished, and flew like a dreamboat.

Someone called, "Tallyho. Many bogies. Eleven o'clock, down." We were at about 23,000 feet, looking down at what was later determined to be twenty Zeros, all in a big loose formation. A dozen or so were in a large vee of vees and several three-plane vees were straggling behind. They were headed about 90 degrees across our path and were several miles ahead. The sun was just about at our backs.

I was biting my tongue to keep from calling the CO to turn right so he could get into the sun and not get sucked behind. Where we were headed, we would surely be sucked behind and screw up the whole run. If we had gone in as soon as we spotted the Zeros, we could have executed a classic high-side gunnery run.

I was still throttling back to stay behind the Old Man when I decided to take a cue from Johnny Johnson, who had by this time gone ahead of the skipper and was still out of his sight below. I dropped down and slid in under the Old Man, who was still confirming the sighting by radio to the ship. I was getting ready for a right turn and that big high-side run when the skipper called out, "Go get 'em, Airdales!"

My throttle went to the fire wall and I believe it stayed there through the entire flight. I passed Johnny Johnson on his right but decided not to go for the big classic gunnery run; I'd have had eight Hellcats right in front of me. I just took a large lead on those Zeros and headed straight in. I was hoping I wouldn't get shot up by the Hellcats behind me.

We'd been diving for some time, and my airspeed had passed 350 knots. I was standing on the left rudder to keep the needle anywhere near the center. I called Frank and said, "I'm taking the straggler on the right." I don't think he heard me; there was so much static and engine noise on the radio. I was now fighting the Hellcat with every ounce of strength just to keep the ball centered at 400 knots. I could see no one ahead except Zeros, and they showed no signs of having spotted us yet. My Number 37 was just flying super terrible now. That was probably to be expected at that speed.

There was no slowing down at this point, even if I'd wanted to. Seventy-two armed .50-caliber guns were in proximity, and sixty-six of them were behind me, about to open fire in the same direction I was heading. I knew the airplane would withstand the speed even though the red line showed a speed of 337 knots. I'd learned that from the Grumman engineers, back at the factory on Long Island, and from the many crazy high-speed dives I had put it through since.

My target was the right wingman in a three-plane vee at the rear of the big formation. My primary problem at that particular moment was to get that Hellcat under enough control to hold the gunsight pipper ahead of the straggling Zero just long enough to burn it. I was determined not to screw up the attack despite the lousy approach I had started.

My dive had now flattened out to 20 to 30 degrees. The nose of the Zero was at 7 o'clock on my sight reticle, with about 40 mils lead, but I was not yet steady enough or close enough to fire.

The enemy pilot still hadn't seen me. The whole group of Zeros was still in formation and on the same course. My speed was determined to put me in a skid, and that would screw up the attack completely, but I was determined to hold my point of aim. With both hands on the stick and both feet on the left rudder pedal, I opened fire. I was still 20 to 30 degrees off the Zero pilot's line of flight, 500 feet above him, and almost exactly 1,000 feet from him. The tracers streaked and sparked just beneath the engine cowling on that Zero. Then the bullets from all six wing guns converged on his wing root, which flashed fire and folded as I passed under him. Both his wings were at the vertical as I passed.

My first thought was to call, "Splash one Zeke," as we had so many times in operational training and simulated combat, but I couldn't take my left hand off the stick to reach for the mike button. I was straining everything I had just to get that machine headed upward to trade some of that speed for altitude. I was blacking out badly. The nose of the plane was coming up toward the horizon, and the airplane was now in a horrible skid. At that speed, the Hellcat was deafening. Flight had never been more uncomfortable.

The throttle was still fire walled, at full combat power. After the nose reached the horizon and the skid subsided, I was able to report "Splash one," but I doubt anyone could hear me. The radio was pandemonium—high static, pilots inadvertently keying mike buttons, warning calls, splash calls, got-'em calls, break calls, and more.

Before I could get my bearings and thoughts focused back on the Japanese formation, a Zeke passed just above me in a diving left turn, almost in range. I was still pulling up and out of the first pass and my nose was just above the horizon. I was still blacking out, too; seeing was like looking through two shotgun barrels. I rolled hard left to keep the Zero in sight, easily cut across his turn, took a big lead on him, and fired a burst. He instantly blew to pieces. Splash two.

As I passed in a steep climbing turn, I spotted another Zeke closing in on a Hellcat and firing out of range, I thought. The Zero's tracers were bending well behind and below. Closing on the Zero's tail was easy. The pilot apparently never saw me. A long burst from his 6 o'clock brought flame and black smoke. I had to roll high to avoid debris and flames. Splash three.

My throttle was still bent over the quadrant. Fighting at full throttle had become a habit that seemed to pay off in combat in our first fighter sweeps. Old Number 37 was now trimmed up and running smooth and loud. I was flying upside down above the fight and looking "up" through the top of the canopy for another target when I saw a sight below that was something to behold: burning airplanes and detached wings, brightly flashing, falling, tumbling, showing their red meatballs in the sun; fires on the water, white splashes in the water, deep red balls of fire and black smoke—all against beautiful, puffy white clouds along the distant horizon, over a dark blue ocean below. It was a colorful, beautiful sight, particularly from well above it, looking down.

I thought I saw a remnant of the Japanese formation flying straight and level in a northwesterly direction. Could it be that they didn't even know what had been going on behind them? All we heard about their poor eyesight must be true. Those Airdales had chewed up a bunch of Japanese fighters, but there were more to be splashed. My wingman was nowhere in sight. I thought, "What the hell. Who cares if you don't have a wingman to watch your tail, get back in there. Speed can be your wingman."

I was wringing wet with sweat, and my neck was cramping from high gees. I was about to chase the Zeros headed west when I saw a Hellcat just below me, way out of range but firing—and missing—far behind a Zeke. I rolled over and dove almost straight down in an overhead run, hoping to blow the Zeke away from above. I was vertical about 90 degrees to his flight path and really too close to get a good shot. He tightened his turn to the left and I missed.

As I pulled out, I could see another Zero just ahead. He was weaving and jinking as if someone were on his tail. So as not to disappoint him, I latched on his tail and got him with a long burst in the first turn. Splash four.

I pulled out in a left clearing turn. As I looked back,

tracers were arcing behind me, curving off to my right. They were probably from the guy I had just shot at on the overhead. I split-essed and nearly blacked out, and then, as I pulled out, I saw several more Zekes in shallow dives. I was about 2,000 feet above and directly behind the third Zeke, which was trailing white smoke from an oil leak. I was far behind it, but I was closing fast. I was still trying to make sure that the last attacker was not still on my tail. The smoker in my sights never turned. I closed in fast and opened fire slightly out of range. Tracers were passing down both sides of the Zeke's fuselage, but then they converged and produced a ball of black smoke and fire. This was the longest burst I fired that morning. Splash five.

I had only to ease up on the stick to clear the fireball. Looking ahead, I saw that I was 6 o'clock to the two Zeros that had been leading number 4. I had just pulled out of a split-S and I had speed to burn. The two Zeros were in a loose left-echelon formation, and all of us were now down at about 6,000 feet. I held the rear Zeke steady in my sight and pulled up right behind it. But, as I closed fast, the pilot started a slight turn to the left, so I opened fire. I was sure I had him, but no joy. I got only a couple of pops from my guns. I was out of ammo!

I pulled up over him, climbed steeply, and turned, hoping he would not care to follow me back to the skirmish, which he seemed to be leaving. Both Zekes fired at me, and I watched their tracers arcing far behind me and off to my right. I was out of range. I continued to open the distance between us and headed home. They had ammo and I didn't, so I was hauling ass out of there fast. They didn't close on me, and I was glad.

Later, throttling back to slow-cruise speed, I called the ship to report the splash while watching my tail to see if those renegades were behind me. They weren't, so I asked for a vector home. When I reported "Splash five," I could hear cheers in the background and felt like a football player who had just caught the winning touchdown pass.

I had punched my elapsed-time clock when the first tallyho was called, but I completely forgot to check it after the battle. The records confirmed by the fighter-director crew showed that only five minutes elapsed between Paul Buie's "Go get 'em, Airdales" and my last splash call.

Back at the ship, I orbited in silence, wondering where all the fighters were and why the ship wouldn't take me aboard for more ammunition and fuel so I could go back and rejoin the fracas. Hellcats finally started to straggle in by ones and twos, each one joining on me because I was the first airplane to have returned. As each pilot returned with a big grin and holding up two or three fingers, I began to count. I counted 10 to 15 victories. Finally, the Old Man came on the air to report that he thought we had destroyed every Japanese plane in the air.

Our three divisions shuffled around to their original formation, and the *Lexington* turned into the wind to take us aboard. We still had plenty of fuel, but little or no ammo; there was no need to hurry, because the ship reported that the radar screen was clear. Frank Fleming, my wingman, was missing, but it turned out that he was helping Carl Blome bail out of his Hellcat after it lost its entire stabilizer. We all landed aboard without incident, giving the air intelligence officer a finger count of victories claimed as we taxied past the island.

The ship was still at General Quarters. As I parked, deplaned, and headed for the ready room, Paul Buie was waiting for me to take me to the bridge to meet the captain, Felix Stump. I was introduced as Five-shot Hanks and thereafter always referred to by that name aboard the *Lexington*. It had taken me well over five shots to do the job, but I didn't want to burst the bubble at that point.

Shaking all the hands and taking all the congratulations was flattering and embarrassing enough, but Captain Stump insisted that I get on the ship's public-address system and tell the story to the whole ship's company. While I was on the mike, trying to remember the sequence of the fight, the ship's photographers were popping flashbulbs. The world-renowned photographer Edward Steichen and Frank Morris of *Collier's* magazine were also there. The bridge and catwalks were packed with sailors, and I simply couldn't believe what was going on. Who was watching for submarines and torpedoes? (That was no idle fear. The *Liscome*

*Bay,* an escort carrier in our group, was sunk by a torpedo at 0520 the following morning.) But no matter about that; we were doing it the Hollywood way, and I was getting the full treatment. But at that moment, I'd rather have been home in Red Bluff, showing hogs. My only brush with fame before this was when my pig had won the reserve championship at the South San Francisco Livestock Show. Big stuff for me!

Things finally quieted down, I got into the shower, and the flight surgeon got a couple of brandies into me. I slept for three hours, fully convinced that Americans are crazy.

*Lieutenant (jg) Ralph Hanks became the first Hellcat "ace in a day," and, all told, VF-16 claimed 17 kills and 4 probables.*

*Hanks shot down his sixth and final Japanese plane, another Zero, over Guam on the afternoon of June 19, 1944. When VF-16 returned to the States in late June 1944, Hanks was retained to help re-form the squadron. He was involved in a strike against Kisarazu Airfield, near Hiroshima, when the first atomic bomb was dropped.*

*Captain Ralph Hanks retired from the Navy in October 1969.*

After successfully seizing Tarawa and Makin, the Americans almost instantaneously converted them both into advance airfields that could support the projected invasion of the neighboring Marshall Islands. The carrier fleet returned to Pearl Harbor to regroup while the admirals planned the next foray.

The next target was Kwajalein Atoll, the major Japanese base in the Marshalls. It had been in Japanese hands as a League of Nations–mandated protectorate since the end of World War I. By all standards Kwajalein was a hard target. Vice Admiral Charles Pownall, who had been leading most of 1943's fast-carrier forays, took along two task groups composed in sum of fleet carriers *Yorktown, Essex, Enterprise,* and *Lexington* and light carriers *Cowpens* and *Belleau Wood.* The groups embarked a total of 104 SBD Dauntless dive-bombers, 89 TBF Avenger torpedo/level bombers, and 193 F6F Hellcats. For the first time, Pownall, a 1910 Annapolis graduate who had earned his wings in 1923, decided to turn over tactical control of the actual strikes to an airborne strike commander. Using a strike commander was a new wrinkle for the Americans but an important innovation the Japanese had first employed two years earlier, at Pearl Harbor.

The Kwajalein strike of December 4 overwhelmed the Japanese air defenses, but the results of the bombing of shore targets and attacks against shipping were ragged. When returning pilots reported that many Japanese planes still appeared to be operational, Admiral Pownall canceled a follow-on strike and withdrew. The task groups bypassed several secondary targets but did strike Wotje, the northernmost atoll in the Marshalls, on December 5. Sporadic Japanese nocturnal counterstrikes succeeded in getting an aerial torpedo into *Lexington*. This strike was only the second casualty the American carrier fleet suffered from the air in all of 1943 (the *Independence* had been damaged by a bomb on November 20 in the Gilberts).

Another casualty of the disappointing foray was Admiral Pownall, who was deemed too conservative for the job of leading the U.S. Navy fast carriers on to victory. He was replaced before the end of the year by Vice Admiral Marc "Pete" Mitscher. Pownall's replacement was a seasoned carrier pilot, the first skipper of the old *Hornet,* and a former AirSols commander. Mitscher—who was selected by Admiral Chester Nimitz, the Pacific Fleet commander in chief—proved to be an inspired choice.

Pete Mitscher set about reorganizing the fast-carrier task force—redesignated Task Force 58—to his exacting specifications. Meanwhile, the high command ordained a repeat attack against targets in the Marshalls. The new round of strikes was set to go off on January 31, 1944. Before the strikes, however, one squadron of land-based U.S. Army Air Forces fighters had an opportunity to show its prowess. In so doing, the squadron improved the odds for the hundreds of Navy pilots Pete Mitscher would soon be sending into action.

## AMBUSH OVER TAROA

**1st Lieutenant TODD MOORE, USAAF**
**45th Fighter Squadron, 15th Fighter Group**
**Maloelap Atoll, January 26, 1944**

*Robert Wilson Moore was born and raised in the Louisville, Kentucky, area. He attended Duke University for two years. On December 18, 1941, at twenty years of age, Moore entered the Army Air Corps for flight training. He graduated from Moore Field, in Mission, Texas, on August 5, 1942, and was immediately assigned to the 78th Fighter Squadron, which was then guarding Oahu as part of the 7th Air Force's 18th Fighter Group. Lieutenant Moore's squadron was based at Midway from January to April 1943, and he took part in ferrying fighters the 1,300 miles between Hawaii and Midway, at that time the longest over-water single-engine ferry flights attempted. In December 1943, while serving as the gunnery officer and a regular flight leader with the 15th Fighter Group's 45th Fighter Squadron, Moore was transferred to Apamama Atoll, in the newly secured Gilbert Islands.*

The vast expanse of the Central Pacific Ocean was no place for short-ranged, single-engine Army fighter aircraft. The P-38 would have been a much wiser choice and would have given us much greater range and flexibility, but the P-38s were all sent to the Southwest Pacific Area. We were left to do the best we could with our P-40s.

The older P-40s were not very maneuverable, did not have a high rate of climb or altitude capability, and were of limited range. The P-40N however—though still burdened with the Allison engine—did profit from the attention designers had devoted to maneuverability; rate of climb; and, to some extent, range. The improvements were accomplished by stripping the plane down to remove excess weight. Removing the weight involved limiting internal fuel, removing the battery and electrical starting system, and eliminating a lot of metal from the fuselage behind the cockpit. Also, this elimination of metal improved visibility somewhat. The armament—six .50-caliber machine guns— and armor plate were not changed from what had been employed in previous models. Being lighter in weight, the overall altitude capabilities of the P-40N were superior to those of earlier models.

We were deployed in Apamama Atoll, but we staged through Butaritari Island, in Makin Atoll, which was the northernmost of the Gilbert Islands' atolls. Initially, we conducted raids against the southern Marshall Islands— Mili and Jaluit atolls. All of the Marshall Islands were then in Japanese hands, six of the larger atolls were fortified, and five of the fortified atolls had airfields on them.

On January 24, 1944, we flew a low-level cover mission for a PBY patrol bomber. The PBY was picking up a B-25 bomber crew that had gone down in Arno Atoll, which was south of Maloelap Atoll. We were really sticking our necks out by flying low or close cover for a PBY landing so near to a Japanese fighter base. We could have been intercepted at very low altitude by Japanese fighters out of Taroa Airfield, in Maloelap. This would have been a disaster. The Zekes were much more maneuverable than our P-40s, had a much greater rate of climb, and had good offensive armament. However, we had proven a capability to fly as far as their base in Maloelap. If we had to stick our necks out again, I preferred fighting the Japanese on our terms.

After the PBY cover mission had been successfully flown —nothing happened—I talked with my close associate, Captain Jim VandeHey. We decided to suggest an offensive to Colonel S. E. Buckland, who was in charge of all the Army fighters in that area of the Pacific Ocean. Colonel Buckland had been our CO on Oahu; he knew us, and he acted on our suggestion immediately. The result was an ambush-intercept mission to Maloelap. We had to plan carefully to get maximum gas consumption and mileage from our P-40Ns, for this was to be the longest attempted fighter-escort mission yet undertaken by Army fighters in the Central Pacific.

The next day our twelve P-40s took off from Makin at 1117, which was 30 minutes behind the nine B-25s we would be escorting. Our fighter leader was Major Harry Thompson, the 45th Fighter Squadron operations officer.

Our planes climbed on course 340° magnetic at 2,200 RPM and 26 inches of manifold pressure. We reached 10,000 feet at 65 miles out and throttled back to 2,000 RPM, 25 inches, and 160 to 175 miles per hour. We flew on west of Mili and between Majuro and Arno atolls. The schedule was still perfectly coordinated when we approached Tabal Island, the northeast tip of Aur Atoll. We were scheduled to rendezvous with the B-25s at 1530.

This was our first combat mission where we expected an actual encounter with Japanese fighter aircraft. Heretofore, encounters with enemy aircraft were a possibility or probability, but this time we definitely expected the real thing. It is difficult to convey the myriad feelings before such a mission. We all had full knowledge that we would not be able to survive the mission from a fuel-consumption consideration if we became engaged in a running fight with Japanese fighters, which could outperform us at the B-25 escort altitude. Things were fairly normal to start with but, the closer I got to combat, the drier my mouth got. Pretty soon, it felt like my mouth was full of cotton. My primary emotion was that I wanted to do well in front of my comrades—or at least not do anything that would be detrimental or harmful to them.

The flight of four P-40s that I was leading was high cover, but that term was somewhat misleading in that my altitude was only 12,500 feet—which was still considerably higher than the B-25s we were escorting. They were wave-hopping on the deck to keep enemy fighter planes above them and to keep the Zeros from diving on them. Major Thompson's flight was at 8,000 feet and Jim VandeHey's was at 10,000.

As we approached Tabal Island at 1530, I could hear the B-25s call in to us that Zeros were taking off, so we knew we were in for a fight. As soon as we dropped our belly tanks, the two flights of P-40s below my flight spotted the Japanese fighters attacking the B-25s, and they dove to attack the Zeros.

After all of the planes had passed beneath me, I dropped down to pick up stragglers. Between 6,000 and 7,000 feet I spotted a Zero that was attempting to flee from the fight.

The pilot saw me just about the time I saw him, and we turned into each other. Apparently, he decided to change his tactics then; he went into a shallow high-speed dive directly toward Taroa Airfield. I continued my front-quarter run on him and, as he continued his dive, I scored multiple hits in his engine and wing-root area.

I knew better than to try to dogfight a Zeke with a P-40, but I did manage a tight turn onto this Zeke's tail. The pilot tried two or three violent skids to throw off my aim, and then the Zeke did a very strange thing. It just slowly turned over onto its back. It seemed as though the pilot was seriously injured.

I closed to about 700 feet of him and opened fire with a lead slightly below the descending fighter. The Zeke exploded in my face. I will never forget the two red meatballs behind the Zero's cockpit. They reminded me of frog eyes. My two most vivid memories of the experience were the large red roundels and my wingman calling in to me, "Beautiful, Moore! Beautiful!"

After the fight was over, I felt relief amounting to exhilaration. We all had survived a very difficult mission involving precise timing on an 800-mile flight and radio silence all the way to the target. We'd had no mechanical difficulties and no losses to our fighters or bombers. Despite the distance and the fight over Aur Atoll and Taroa, all of our P-40s made it home with at least 35 gallons of fuel left over. Together, eleven out of the twelve of us had destroyed 9 Zero fighters and 1 Kate torpedo bomber and probably destroyed another Zeke and another Kate. It is little wonder that I look back on this mission as my most outstanding mission flown in thirty-seven months overseas in the Pacific.

*In that thirty-seven months, Todd Moore became the 7th Air Force's high-scoring ace. In a far-flung theater in a time when encounters with Japanese fighters were few and far between, Todd Moore hit every Japanese plane he ever shot at. In the end, he came home with 12 kills, 1 probable, and 3 damage claims to his credit. He left the service in May 1946.*

# CHAPTER 10

The ascendancy of Pete Mitscher to the command of Task Force 58 marked the crucial war-winning conceptual shift. Mitscher did not use aircraft carriers as defensive weapons; he used carriers as offensive weapons. Where Pownall had retired in the face of stubborn (but inferior) Japanese opposition, Mitscher determined from the outset to drive the enemy down. Of course, as more carriers and air groups came on line and Task Force 58 grew to four separate, individually formidable multicarrier battle groups, the reality of the situation was that the U.S. Navy's strength in the air could overwhelm the aerial defenses of most any Japanese base the Americans decided to strike.

For his late January foray back to the Marshalls, Mitscher had six fleet carriers and five light carriers. The carrier air groups began striking at targets throughout the Marshalls on January 29, 1944, and the invasion of Kwajalein Atoll went off on January 31. It was a walkover. When Task Force 58 was relieved of the prime responsibility for guarding the invasion fleet, the carriers sailed to newly won nearby Majuro Atoll to revictual. One task group remained to support continuing amphibious operations in the Marshalls, but the bulk of Task Force 58 turned west and attacked shipping and airfields in the Combined Fleet's vast fleet anchorage at Truk, in the far eastern Caroline Islands.

Task Force 58 launched a massive air attack against Truk on February 17, 1944, the same day Marines invaded Eniwetok Atoll in the Marshalls. Hopes of catching the Japanese surface fleet in the anchorage did not pan out; the warships were long gone. But the U.S. Navy pilots shot down 94 Japanese airplanes, sunk a number of ships, and pulverized the facilities at Japan's mightiest Central Pacific fleet base. The only serious damage inflicted by the Japanese on the fast carriers was a torpedo hit that severely damaged the new fleet carrier *Intrepid*.

On April 1, U.S. Army Air Forces B-24 heavy bombers began mounting attacks against Truk from a new 8,200-foot all-weather bomber strip on Eniwetok. At that point Navy planners had already decided to bypass Truk and invade the more-distant Marianas. Indeed, Mitscher had begun softening up the Marianas defenses with about half his carriers on February 23, only six days after the massive Truk raid.

Task Force 58 departed Majuro again on March 22. On March 30, the force struck the Palau Islands, in the far western Carolines, to support General Douglas MacArthur's invasion of Hollandia, New Guinea, which was scheduled for April 22. The attack on the Palaus continued relentlessly for two days. Task Force 58 smashed base facilities and blew 109 Japanese warplanes out of the sky. Then, on April 1, Mitscher moved to attack Woleai, Yap, and Ulithi atolls, in the west-central Carolines.

Rear Admiral Alfred Montgomery's Task Group 58.2—fleet carriers *Bunker Hill* and *Hornet* and light carriers *Cabot* and *Monterey*—drew Woleai.

# THE DOOMED ZOOMIE*

Ensign JOHN GALVIN, USN
VF-8 (USS *Bunker Hill*)
Woleai, April 1, 1944

*John Roderick Galvin, a native of Burlington, Iowa, gradu-*
*ated from Northwestern University in June 1942 and went*
*straight into the Navy flight-training program. He earned his*
*wings at Corpus Christi in January 1943 and, in June, joined*
*VF-8, which was preparing to board the new USS* Intrepid *for*
*her shakedown cruise. Following four months of hard train-*
*ing on Maui, VF-8 boarded USS* Bunker Hill *and set sail for*
*the war zone the first week of 1944.*

After breakfast on April 1, 1944, we went up to the ready
room and Lieutenant Commander William Collins, our
squadron's skipper, gave us our briefing. "You're going in to
attack Woleai Atoll, because we're going to be retiring
by this little place." He smiled, intending his remark to
instill some humor into the briefing. After no one cracked
a smile, he abandoned the attempt at being a comic,
cleared his throat, and continued in a more serious vein.
"Actually, it's a stepping-stone between Truk Island and
New Guinea."

I hung on every word he said, and the excitement and
anticipation of my fifth combat mission charged my veins
with adrenaline. The other pilots felt the same way. As eyes
met around the room, there were a few anxious smiles.
Some of the boys squirmed out of nervousness. The briefing
turned into more of a pep talk, and it reminded me of my
high school coach talking to the guys in the locker room
minutes before a football game. After Collins finished the
briefing, we went down to the officers' wardroom for breakfast.

---

*Galvin, John, with Frank Allnutt. *Salvation for a Doomed Zoomie.*
Indian Hills, Colorado: Allnutt Publishing, 1983. Condensed,
quoted, and edited with permission of the author.

"Attention all pilots," droned the squawkbox. "Get the latest poop on the Teletype screen."

The Teletype screen was mounted on a bulkhead in the ready room. It indicated the wind course and speed, ship's course and speed, heading and distance to the target, homing device frequency and call letters, and squadron flight frequency. The final information was the frequency of Falstaff, which was the call sign of the lifeguard submarine.

Next we were given the intelligence briefing on the target. We studied some outdated maps from World War I (the latest available) and were told how many Japanese planes to expect and the estimated number of antiaircraft guns in the vicinity.

Everything we needed to know was communicated before the takeoff, because there could be no use of radios in flight except during actual combat or some other emergency. This was to keep the Japanese from locating us by intercepting our transmissions and eavesdropping on our conversations. But, if I did need to use a radio, the code words were: *Tiger Base* for the carrier and *Tiger 7-1* for my division leader, Gus. In the air we relied on a visual Morse code for communications among pilots. A fist was a "dot" and an open palm was a "dash."

With the briefing out of the way and our mission plotted, all there was left to do was to sit and wait for the squawkbox to announce . . . "Pilots, man your planes!"

Everyone sprang into action. Hearing that command always ran a chill up my spine. What a thrill!

Just outside the ready room was a convenient head for the Nervous Jervis to toss his cookies in before heading up to the flight deck. Not that there was anything disgraceful about it. The excitement and anticipation got to some of the best of pilots.

Stooped over and waddling along in my cumbersome flight gear and too-tight parachute harness, I clambered along the catwalk and up a ladder to the flight deck. The carrier was blacked out so as not to attract any snoopy Japanese scout planes, and finding my assigned plane in the dim predawn wasn't easy.

The flight deck was alive with activity. Our F6Fs, wings folded back, were jammed close together to conserve space.

The planes were already fueled and armed with bombs and belts of .50-caliber ammo for the six machine guns. The deck crews, with different-colored cloth helmets and T-shirts to identify whether they were plane handlers, mechanics, or whatever, were swarming over the planes like ants on a log, tending to last-minute preparations for takeoff.

With the help of a mechanic, I climbed into the snug cockpit and wedged down into the deep bucket seat. I stowed the plotting board, hooked up my detachable harness to the parachute, connected the oxygen line, fastened seatbelts and shoulder straps, and then began the preflight check. Whatever conversation there was with my mechanic was briefly functional and fast forgotten, because my mind was on the mission and nothing else.

No sooner did I complete the preflight check than the squawkbox blared, "Pilots, stand by to start engines. . . . Stand clear of propellers!"

Most of the deck crew cleared the area, leaving only a few plane handlers to assist with the actual launch—and they darted to the designated safe spot under the planes.

"Pilots, start your engines," ordered the squawkbox, with a slightly detectable hint of emotion.

I pressed the starter and the Grumman's engine grudgingly turned over, coughing and belching white smoke from its throaty exhaust pipes. It caught, and I advanced the throttle with my left hand.

All instruments—check.

Set gyro—check.

Then a faint *beep* came over my earphones, which was a signal to indicate the radio was working.

The thundering roar of all those Hellcats was deafening. White, acrid exhaust smoke swirled in the gray dawn. In moments, I smelled the smoke as it blended in with the odor of my engine's hot oil and the rubber scent of my oxygen mask. Airplane exhaust had a bite to it that I always imagined made my nostrils flare like a thoroughbred's. There were other symptoms also—rapid pulse and fast, heavy breathing. What a facade of confidence, sitting at the controls of that Hellcat. It made me feel like a man of steel—like Superman himself. I'm not proud to say that right then I had more faith in Grumman than God.

Up on the bridge, Admiral Montgomery gave the order for the entire fleet to head into the wind so the carriers could launch their planes. As the *Bunker Hill* turned into the wind, a stiff breeze swept across the flight deck. Moments later, the first Hellcat was launched, and I soon lost sight of its faint silhouette in the predawn darkness.

I sat there, awaiting my turn, worried, scared, apprehensive about the catapult, because you never got used to it. This was when my life flashed past in review. Other than reciting the Twenty-third Psalm, it's difficult to remember what my thoughts were. I just concentrated on what I had to do.

Sitting somewhere in front of me, in the pitch black predawn, was Gus's plane. I taxied up and came to within 10 feet of him. Behind me came T.I. and Chris. Four men—Division 7 of VF-8—hopped up and fully charged, ready to dish it out to the Japanese on Woleai.

Gus moved onto the catapult and, seconds later, was shot off into the darkness. Then it was my turn.

Suddenly, the plane lurched forward as the catapult sped toward the bow. The rapid acceleration caused me to sink back into my seat. The plane vibrated so hard that everything was a blur. I felt totally out of control.

Then, only 2.1 seconds and 110 feet later, I was airborne! The vibration stopped and the plane smoothed out at 90 knots. All was well, and I sighed a sigh of relief as I turned to join up with Gus.

I was never a superstitious person, so there was nothing portentous about April Fool's Day so far as I was concerned. It was going to be my third day of combat flying, and I was cocky and felt invincible.

We didn't observe any ack-ack fire at first, and this only bolstered our hopes of catching the Japanese by surprise. But what about tracers? They can't be seen when coming toward you—only after they have sped past. So, I glanced back—and *saw* them! Hundreds of tracers were speeding away behind me.

Miraculously, I was flying through that deadly shower

unscathed. But there wasn't time to think about anything but hitting a target, then hightailing it back up into the clouds, out of sight and range of the Japanese ack-ack guns.

"Hit something," I told myself. "Find a target."

Then I saw the Betty bomber parked on the end of the runway, and that's when I did the most impulsive thing I had ever done in my life. I acted like one big April Fool!

I broke off from my formation and went after that bomber with all my guns blazing, despite what we had been taught and taught again—to stay together as a team.

And that's when the Japanese riddled my Hellcat with exploding shells.

"Falstaff from Tiger Leader," Gus radioed the lifeguard submarine, the *Harder*.

The *Harder*'s radioman answered the call.

"Fighter plane, burning, falling into the drink," Gus frantically called for help. "The pilot chuted out. He is now in the water—about five miles to the north of Taugalap. . . . That's the second island west of Woleai."

The radioman immediately passed the alert on to his skipper, and that's all Commander Sam Dealey needed to hear. He turned the periscope over to his executive officer, Lieutenant Commander Frank Lynch, then slid down the ladder to the main control room, where the navigation charts were spread out on a plotting board.

Dealey hovered over the chart and quickly plotted the shortest course to my location. It would take the sub around the northeast corner of Woleai. He set a new course northward. "Full speed," he called out.

The officer of the deck rang the command down to the engine room. The *Harder* turned to the north and began picking up speed, slicing through high waves in the rough sea, sending rooster tails spraying into the breeze. Lynch periodically cut in, giving Dealey the ship's position by periscope bearings.

The same thought nagged at each man's consciousness: "Will the *Harder* get there in time?"

I was injured and exhausted from being buffeted around by the merciless sea. I was aware of three Hellcats circling overhead and assumed they were piloted by Gus, T.I., and

Chris. By now, I was confident that Gus had reported my position to Falstaff and the *Bunker Hill*. Good ol' Gus!

But there was no submarine in sight. Where was it? "C'mon, you guys, hurry up, before I drown or the sharks get me!"

I had visions of seeing this big, beautiful sub surface only yards away from where I was bobbing around, making a miserable attempt to swim and stay afloat. The crew scrambles onto the deck and someone throws a line to me. I retrieve it, hang on, and get plucked out of the sea. That's how I envisioned my rescue. But I saw nothing. "Where is that sub?"

Then doubts began to gnaw at me again. What if Gus, T.I., and Chris *didn't* see me? What if they thought I went down with my Hellcat? Surely the sub would check out the vicinity, just in case . . . wouldn't it? But what if Gus *didn't* radio the sub? What if the Navy goofed? What if, through some snafu, there wasn't a sub in the area? But it *had* to be there! "My God! I'm desperate!" In order to keep from totally panicking, I *had* to have faith that Falstaff was cruising in the immediate vicinity.

In reality, Falstaff was 50 miles south of Woleai because her captain did not trust friendly airplanes to leave the ship alone if she was spotted. However, she was racing to get to me before I fell victim to the sea, the sharks, or the Japanese. It was going to be close.

As I pondered all this, I was unaware that I was drifting with the wind and tide toward shallow water and dangerous coral reefs.

Unknown to me, at that moment aboard the *Harder*, Sam Dealey hurriedly plotted my rescue, realizing he was in a frantic race against time.

Hours later, after I had miraculously made my way to the beach, I was buzzed out of my siesta on the sand when a TBM torpedo bomber thundered by no more than 10 feet over my head. But I didn't move. The TBM made several more low passes over me, and I finally rolled over and sat up. The plane circled back and buzzed me again. This time, seeing that I was alive, he wagged his wings and dropped what resembled a large beanbag with a red streamer. The bundle hit the sand and bounced a few times, coming to rest only a few yards away. Somehow, I mustered enough strength to crawl over to it.

Inside I found a written message. With shaky hands I unfolded the note and read: "Swim out to sea, Falstaff is coming!"

"What? You gotta be kiddin'," I thought.

After four and a half hours in the water, my arms and legs were like rubber, and I wasn't about to go back into the ocean! Sounds crazy now, but that's truthfully what I thought at the time.

The *Harder* was one mile off the northeast corner of Woleai when the replacement fighters arrived. The planes zoomed the sub and guided it toward my location on the beach.

Sam Dealey scanned the beach through his binoculars, hoping to spot a sheltered cove or anchorage where the deep-draft sub could enter to pick me up. But all he saw was shallow water and a narrow, sandy beach. He was faced with only one alternative; he would have to bring the sub all the way to shore.

According to the *Harder's* log, at 1145 Dealey finally sighted me "on the northwest tip of the second island to the west of Woleai." The log entry went on to give details of the sub's approach: "Battle surface stations were manned, the ship was flooded down and maneuvered into a spot about 1,500 yards off the beach. White water was breaking over the shoals only twenty yards in front of the ship, and the fathometer had ceased to record."

I'll never forget the spectacle of seeing that sub coming directly toward me. What a sight! It looked big enough to be a destroyer. But I couldn't understand it; how could a sub rescue me off the beach?

Still the sub came closer and closer to shore.

"Are they going to drive that up on the beach for me? They're crazy!"

Then I saw something that almost made my heart stop beating. At first, I wasn't sure, but then I knew that *the sub was backing away!*

"Please, God, don't let them leave! I'll swim. I'll get there. Why do they leave me after all this?" And I guess I caved in.

During all of this, I was unaware of another drama unfolding. The *Harder*'s log shows that one of the circling planes advised the sub that, if rescue looked too difficult from its location, a better approach might be made from another direction.

The *Harder*'s skipper looked the situation over and then decided to go for the alternate approach. He proceeded to back off with the intention of coming back in from another angle. He wrote in the log that he had seen me standing on the beach, then fall and lie there outstretched in the sand. My collapse, he speculated, "was undoubtedly due mainly to physical exhaustion, but also to the disappointment in seeing . . . chances of rescue fade away."

He was correct. And how!

Then, in a crazy change of events, one of the search planes reported to Dealey that the first approach was best after all. I saw the sub reverse course and head back at full speed in my direction. They were coming back! A new hope surged through my veins.

The lookouts on the *Harder*'s bridge had plenty to watch. It was like trying to take in a three-ring circus all at once. I was in one "ring," the jungle was in another, and the air attack was in still another.

They were coming to rescue me, but seeing me as I lay deathlike on the beach gave them some cause for concern. Was the person they saw alive or dead? Was he the American flyer they were looking for—or a clever Japanese decoy?

They had every right to be skeptical because of my appearance. By this time, I had no flight helmet and no Mae West, and my dark-green gee-suit looked black because it was dripping wet. My face didn't even look like an American's. It was too dark. How could they know it was from a blistering sunburn covered with dried blood (from being grated over the coral)?

Added to the confusing scenario before them was a *second* man who looked like he might be an island native. Squatting on the beach only a short distance away from where I lay, he was calmly watching all that was going on. His presence made the men of the *Harder* even more wary of a trap. Was he really a native? Or a Japanese in disguise? If he was a native, was he friendly? Did he have friends hiding out at the edge of the jungle, just waiting for the sub to move into a trap? I didn't even know he was there.

Now the sub's lookouts had all the more reason to scan "ring 2"—the dense jungle's edge where it met the sand of the beach. They had to scrutinize every suspect little shadow, straining their eyes to see any possible telltale signs of men in hiding.

In the "third ring" of this unlikely circus was the sensational air attack over Woleai. But the lookouts weren't interested in being mere spectators; they kept a watchful eye in the event a Zero might appear on the scene. As it turned out, not a single Japanese plane got into the air—thanks to my buddies up there in those beautiful Hellcats!

Gus, T.I., and Chris continued circling overhead as the *Harder* eased in closer to shore. I couldn't hear them talking to me, of course, but I sensed they were praying for me not to give up.

Meanwhile, their gas gauges were going down, down, and down! They would soon have to return to the carrier. But, without air cover, what would happen to me? Were the Japanese just waiting for the planes to leave so they could safely come after me? And what would happen to the *Harder* without air cover? It would also be at the mercy of the Japanese. Was the risk in trying to rescue me too great? Maybe the *Harder* should abort the attempt!

Those were the considerations Sam Dealey had to deal with. To this indomitable sub skipper there was only one thing to do; he sent an urgent message to the 5th Fleet commander, Admiral Raymond Spruance. It read: "Prolong the attack and provide air cover and we will effect the rescue."

My groggy, confused mind heard the drone of several more planes overhead. I looked up, and, squinting into the brilliant tropical sun, made out the silhouettes of a handful of new carrier planes as they joined the formation of planes flown by Gus, T.I., and Chris. I figured they were replacement aircraft sent to keep an eye on me and to ward off any encroaching Japanese. Three of the birds then broke off and headed east. No doubt my wingmates, now low on gas, were returning to their roosting place on the *Bunker Hill*.

Meanwhile, the sub was inching in closer to shore. Brave

men were trying to save my life, and all I was doing was resting on the sand. I didn't know what I could do to help, but I had to do *something!*

Though my battered body was numb all over, I struggled to my feet and tried to wade out into the surf to meet the incoming sub. I was knee-deep in the boiling surf when a breaker hit me, causing my wobbly legs to buckle. The powerful wave tumbled and rolled me across the bottom. Caught in a flood of sandy seawater foam, I was washed back up onto the beach.

A new surge of pain gripped my body, and I passed out. Moments later, I opened my eyes and lay on the beach, panted for breath, and hoped for a resurgence of strength. I *had* to reach that sub! But my muscles were as useless as wet noodles. I couldn't move.

Groggy as I was, I heard our planes as they swooped over the island and strafed and bombed the airstrip, keeping the antiaircraft batteries busy. Blinking sand and seawater from my burning eyes, my vision was blurry as I strained to focus on the jungle, fully expecting at any moment to see a horde of Japanese run out of the trees, guns ablazin'.

I slowly and painfully turned my head in the direction of the sub. It hardly seemed to be moving, it was going so slowly.

"Can't you guys speed that thing up?"

But the sub was in shallow waters, challenged by a myriad of hardened coral heads that could rip open a boat's hull, and the going had to be slow and cautious. By now, the sub was a sitting duck, no longer in water deep enough to dive for safety.

Sam Dealey was preparing to send a rescue squad for me. He ordered some of the crew to make ready the rubber boat. But, through some snafu, there were no paddles aboard, and the men would have to paddle with their hands.

Dealey called for volunteers and explained the risk involved. "I want you to know," he said, "if you go in there, heavy fire from the shore may force us to cut away and back down—and we may not be able to come back after you."

He paused, searching the men's eyes as his appraisal of the risky mission sunk in. Each man was weighing the possible consequences of volunteering. To step forward would require tremendous courage—far and above the normal call of duty.

"And another thing," Dealey added, breaking the uneasy silence, "the Japs may be setting a trap, just waiting for more men to get farther in."

Then Dealey called for those who wanted to volunteer. Practically the whole crew stepped forward! The slight smile that escaped Dealey's face scarcely betrayed the swelling pride in his heart for his men. He would have to make a selection. He singled out the crew's three best swimmers. Lieutenant Samuel Logan, a brilliant Kentuckian who was number one in his graduating class at Annapolis, was chosen to head the rescue squad. The other two were J. W. Thomason, twenty-four, a ship's cook first class from Danielsville, Georgia, and Francis Ryan, twenty, a motor-machinist's mate first class from Shenandoah, Pennsylvania.

As the three men prepared to board the rubber boat and come after me, Sam Dealey turned his attention to maneuvering the sub into shore as close as possible. Dealey skillfully inched the sub closer and closer to shore, until its bow eventually scraped into the coral bottom. Then he saw to it that the slow-moving screws kept the *Harder*'s nose on the reef and helped prevent the stern from turning the sub parallel to shore. Unless the job was handled with great skill, the sub would drift broadside against the crashing waves, washing the boat helplessly onto the beach.

It was an unnatural spot for a submarine to be in, and no one on board felt easy about it. The sub's bow was riding high on the reef while the stern churned up white water. Each wave raised the sub's stern, sending the bow deeper and causing it to bump and grind on the reef. Every time this happened, the clanging and banging echoed throughout the sub. To the crewmen inside, nervously sweating out the rescue and unable to see what was happening, it sounded as if the sub was about to break up. Several members of the crew later confessed they thought the skipper was a bit too daring, nevertheless they had unwavering confidence in him.

*Harder* was aground!

Just before noon, the three volunteers dove over the side and started pushing and towing their rubber boat toward the beach, which was about 1,200 yards away. A line was played out from the sub to the rubber raft in order to pull it back from the beach.

From my vantage point, I could see every gun on the *Harder* aimed in my direction. They stayed trained on me throughout the course of the rescue, obviously in the event I turned out to be bait for a trap.

While the three men slowly made their way in the rubber boat toward the shore, one of our planes dropped a rubber boat to me. It landed in the water only a few yards away from where I lay, and somehow I found the strength to crawl over to it, though the entire right side of my body was virtually paralyzed and totally useless by now. I yanked the $CO_2$ toggle and the raft quickly inflated. I was in great pain, and it took considerable effort, but I managed to crawl into the surf, dragging the rubber boat with a tether line. I pulled myself over the boat's slippery rubber shoulder and slid into the bottom.

Oh, was I exhausted! But there was no time to rest.

One-man rafts came with no oars since they were not intended for travel, but simply to keep an occupant afloat. Yet I needed to *travel*—all the way out to the waiting sub. I'd just have to lie in the raft and paddle with my hands—and they barely reached the water. It was almost a futile effort, but I hastily started paddling as best I could out to sea in the direction of the sub. I was heading into the wind and going against the current, and several times I spun around in a circle, getting nowhere fast.

What was a bane to me was a blessing to the rescue party. The wind and current were actually helping the three men by floating their rubber boat directly toward me. The line connecting the rescue boat to the sub paid out, fortunately, at a point where they could touch bottom.

Sam Logan took Ryan with him and left Thomason with the rubber boat. The two men waded and swam through the rough surf toward me, cutting their feet and legs on the coral.

My rubber boat kept drifting parallel to the shore, and my

would-be rescuers were gaining little ground. I would have to abandon my raft and wait for them. I slid off into the water and clung onto a coral head.

For about half an hour, I watched as Logan and Ryan struggled through the surf. Finally, they reached me. I was the happiest guy in the world, though the best I could do to show it was manage a weak smile.

My rescuers were almost as exhausted as I was, and their legs and feet were cut and bruised from being scraped over the coral. For them to volunteer to come for me was incredibly self-sacrificing. And for them to reach me took superhuman strength and determination.

Just as their helping hands were getting me into their rubber boat, I heard a *plop* in the water and turned my head to see a splash only a few feet away. Then there were more *plops*. Snipers' bullets! We'd all been so busy we'd forgotten to keep an eye on the beach, and now the Japanese had sneaked up and were taking potshots at us.

Logan waved frantically at the men on the deck of the *Harder,* signaling to them to begin pulling us back with the line. The men on the sub had also seen the bullets strike the water and answered with a burst of machine-gun fire that ripped palm trees to shreds and kicked up sprays of sand. It was enough to send the Japanese scurrying back into the jungle for cover.

Sam Dealey, one to take every precaution, immediately radioed the planes circling overhead to give us some cover. Our airmen were quick to oblige. They came in low over the water and strafed the edge of the jungle, surely killing some snipers and making the rest lay low until we got farther from the beach. When the planes pulled up to circle for another attack, the snipers resumed firing. Bullets whined over our heads and an occasional one plopped in the water near the rubber boat. They were shooting at the men on the bridge of the sub as well, and Dealey almost got a new part in his hair when one bullet, fired from 1,200 yards away, shot through his cap, barely missing his scalp! Fortunately for those of us in the water, strong hands aboard the sub were hauling in the tether line and pulling us to safety. With the current and wind against us, even with paddles, I doubt that the exhausted men could have rowed the boat back. It was a free ride, with 500 yards to go. I lay in the bottom of the boat, totally spent from the ordeal, while the others were in the water, swimming and guiding the boat toward the *Harder*. In a few minutes, I thought, we would be safely aboard the sub. Safety seemed so close, yet so far away.

Then a new problem developed.

One of the cruisers in the task force heard that a flyer was down at sea off the coast of Woleai and she sent a floatplane to make the rescue. The plane arrived and landed on the water, evidently intending to pick me up and take me back to my ship. The plane began taxiing toward us, but the pilot failed to see the vital line that stretched from our rubber boat to the sub.

Dealey and the men on the deck of the *Harder* saw the plane heading toward the line, and, alarmed at what was about to happen, they waved and shouted to the pilot to look out for the line. But the pilot didn't comprehend.

On came the floatplane, and it taxied right over the line, severing it with the sharp edge of its pontoon! Those of us in the rubber boat as well as the men on the sub stared incredulously at the parted line. My heart sank. My hope of rescue was growing dim.

But, as the story was later told to me, Sam Dealey wasted no time in swinging into action. He ordered the severed line hauled in and had one of the crew use a signal light to tell the rescue party what to do. Thomason, the only man in the raft who wasn't too exhausted, was to swim back to the sub. Logan and Ryan were to guide our drifting raft to the reef nearest the *Harder* and hang on until we could be rescued.

In the few minutes since the line had been severed, our rubber boat had drifted until we were 800 yards from the *Harder*. To swim that distance in rough sea and against the strong wind and current was a challenge for the best of swimmers. It would have been foolhardy for anyone less than the Olympic champion to even consider trying it. But, without hesitation, Thomason jumped overboard and started swimming. He battled the thrashing waves and rushing current—and was gaining! Meanwhile, Logan and Ryan paddled our raft to the reef, a distance of 1,200 yards from the *Harder*. All we could do was wait.

Gunner's Mate Freeman Paquet, Jr., volunteered to swim

a new line out to us, but Sam Dealey, exercising sound caution, told him to wait in case Thomason should need help first. There was other reasoning behind Dealey's decision. The *Harder,* like most submarines, did not carry 1,200 yards of line that was strong and light enough for a swimmer to carry and handle in a rough sea.

Agonizing minutes crept slowly by as the men on the sub shouted encouragement to Thomason as he struggled against the tossing waves.

Meanwhile, Dealey had a detail scour the sub for all the line it could find. The lighter-weight line that was originally attached to the rubber raft would be played out first, with the heavier scraps tied to it. Line of every size and description was hauled up to the deck. The last length was tied on as Thomason reached the hull of the sub.

Several of the crew precariously climbed down over the slippery side of the boat, clasping strong hands together to form a human chain. The man farthest down grabbed Thomason's outstretched hand and pulled him out of the water. Other crewmen helped haul him up to the deck.

Paquet's time had come. He dived over the side and began swimming the 1,200 yards to where Logan, Ryan, and I, still in our rubber boat, were clinging to a breaker-washed coral reef. He hastily tied the line to the raft, and all hands on deck started hauling it in by hand, pulling all four of us in the rubber boat through the surf, against the wind and current, and finally alongside the boat.

I looked up at the sub and thought, "Man, that's a big turkey!" What a welcome sight!

Strong hands reached out and pulled me out of the rubber boat and onto the deck. I must have been semiconscious, because I only vaguely remember being carried across the deck and up into the conning tower.

*Ensign Galvin spent thirty-three days aboard* Harder. *His first mission following his return to VF-8 was over Guam on June 14, 1944, but he had to wait until September 21, 1944, to score his first victories, a pair of Zekes over Luzon. Three Ki-44 Tojo fighters fell to Lieutenant (jg) Galvin's guns over Formosa on October 12, 1944; on October 16, 1944, Galvin was credited with 2 Mitsubishi G3M Nell medium bombers.*

*By the time John Galvin reached his full potential as a fighter pilot, Commander Sam Dealey and all the brave men who had rescued Galvin were dead—lost at sea when* Harder *was sunk by depth charges off western Luzon on August 24, 1944.*

Rescue submarines had been involved—at least on station and available, but rarely used—in every fast-carrier raid from 1943 onward, but none had gone to nearly the lengths *Harder* did to rescue John Galvin on April 1, 1944. Doing so was of paramount importance. Once news of Galvin's rescue permeated the carrier air groups, it gave the combat pilots that much more incentive to press home their attacks with a deepening aggressive resolve they now knew would be matched by their countrymen who supported them.

It is also worth noting in this book devoted to the combative spirit that Sam Dealey was the consummate combat submariner. By the time *Harder* took John Galvin aboard, her skipper had been thinking long and hard about how to reduce the effectiveness of the submarine's mortal enemy, the destroyer. While Ensign Galvin was aboard, Dealey turned his thoughts to action and deliberately stalked and sank a Japanese destroyer. Before *Harder*'s luck ran out, Sam Dealey and his gallant crew sank a total of seven Japanese destroyers, an unsurpassed record and a lasting testament to a fighting spirit that would have done any fighter pilot proud. In his unremitting aggressiveness, Sam Dealey earned a Congressional Medal of Honor. More important, he and his brave crew changed the very nature of submarine warfare—a legacy that survives to this day in the form of the U.S. Navy's fleet of *attack* submarines.

On April 22, 1944, the day MacArthur's amphibious forces invaded Hollandia, Task Force 58 returned from a layover in Majuro and directly supported the landings. The fast carriers stayed through April 24, losing only 2 fighters and 2 torpedo bombers in combat and 16 other airplanes in operational accidents. On the last day of the foray, a carrier-based F4U Corsair night fighter shot down a Japanese night intruder, the first such victory of the war to be garnered from a carrier deck.

After the carriers spent two days refueling at sea, Admiral

Nimitz ordered them to "polish off" Truk—to wipe out its base facilities and everything of value that had been missed during or replaced since the raid of February 17.

## MELEE AT TRUK

**Lieutenant (jg) DICK MAY, USN**
**VF-32 (USS *Langley*)**
**Truk, April 29, 1944**

*Richard Hobbs May quit the University of Portland, in his native Portland, Oregon, to join the Navy on October 8, 1941. He completed flight training and was commissioned at Corpus Christi, Texas, on June 15, 1942. Following advanced carrier training, Ensign May served briefly with VF-3 in Maui and then with VF-10 aboard* Enterprise *and land-based at Espiritu Santo and Guadalcanal. After VF-10 was ordered home in May 1943, Lieutenant (jg) May helped form VF-32.*

I was a member of Fighting 32, part of Air Group 32 attached to *Langley,* an *Independence*-class light carrier. *Langley* was fast enough to stay with larger, full-sized carriers and much quicker to build. Task Force 58's three task groups consisted of both fleet carriers (CVs) and light carriers (CVLs).

Air Group 32 consisted of VF-32 (fighters) and VT-32 (torpedo bombers). At that time of the war, our fighter plane was the Grumman F6F-3 Hellcat. This fighter achieved the enviable record of a 19:1 kill ratio against enemy fighters in air-to-air combat. With six lethal .50-caliber machine guns and 2,400 rounds of ammunition, the Hellcat proved to be a top strafer. The Hellcat also proved to be such a good dive-bomber that the Navy did not need to put a VB (dive-bomber squadron) aboard a CVL. This saved valuable space aboard and allowed *Langley* to carry forty-four Hellcats. A CV, having considerably more hangar and flight-deck space, carried all three squadrons.

VF-32 consisted of nine divisions of four planes each. Divisions were led by the commanding and executive officers, both lieutenant commanders, and by senior-grade lieutenants. I was the exception. I was only a jaygee, the most junior in rank of all the division leaders. Prior to the Truk raid, I had two confirmed kills, a Kawanishi H8K Emily four-engine reconnaissance flying boat and a Betty twin-engine medium bomber. Both of these came about from radar-vector intercepts while flying CAP within 100 miles of the fleet. Both vectors were lucky happenstance for me. CAP flying was monotonous. There was little chance to shoot. Fighter sweeps, raids, and interdictions was where the fighter action was. We CVL fighters were handicapped, though, because our ship's captain and the air group commander, a full commander, were junior in date of rank to those of the CV. So, the CVL fighters got assigned to "action" missions only about 35 percent of the time. The rest of the time, we were assigned to CAP to defend and protect the fleet.

In February 1944, the fleet planes attacked Truk, Japan's bastion of the mid Pacific, knocking down some planes and sinking some ships in the harbor. Two months later, submarine intelligence showed that Truk's fighter force had been replenished and that there were over 100 ships in the harbor. Admiral Nimitz ordered Task Force 58 to sail north and east, to attack, sink the ships, and neutralize Truk. He wanted total destruction. The task force operations planning command set the date as April 29, which would be the time the fleet reached a position about 200 miles southwest of Truk. The CVLs were to furnish 35 percent of the fighters and torpedo bombers. Over 100 fighters were to be launched predawn. Bombers and escort fighters were to be launched 20 minutes after the first fighters had launched. Launches were to continue all day until all Japanese capital ships had been sunk in the harbor and all the enemy fighters had been destroyed.

VF-32 was ordered to supply eight fighters to the predawn launch. Twenty minutes later, the squadron supplied eight more fighters and twelve torpedo bombers. Our skipper, Lieutenant Commander Eddie Outlaw, decided not to take his regular division of four. He decided to take his regular wingman, Lieutenant (jg) Donald Reeves, and substitute me and my wingman, Ensign John Pond, as his second section team. He wanted my gun, as he put it. Lieutenant Hollis Hills and his wingman were selected for the third team, and Lieutenant (jg) Harry McClaugherty and his wingman were the fourth team.

Both Hills and McClaugherty were experienced combat pilots, but only Hills was experienced in air-to-air combat. He had downed a German airplane over Dieppe, France, while attached to the Royal Canadian Air Force in Britain. When the U.S. entered the war, Hills transferred to the Navy.

Up to this time, all squadron kills had been single snooper bombers. All our offensive missions had been strafing and bombing against shipping and various Japanese-held islands and airfields. Our combat flying started in January with the Marshall Islands campaign.

On attack day, April 29, 1944, early-morning weather was foul. We manned our planes on the flight deck about 1½ hours before daylight, in a driving rainstorm. The ship was rolling and pitching in moderate seas. The skipper and Reeves's planes were spotted on the two catapults on the bow. My plane was tied down about 40 feet aft of the skipper's. The wings had already been spread from the folded position by the night spotting crew. As I came up the short ladder from the ready room, Benny—my plane captain, who was dressed in foul-weather gear—grabbed my arm and, with his red-lensed flashlight, led me to my plane. He held my plotting board while I scrambled up onto the wing and into the cockpit. Benny reached down behind me and attached the two rugged hooks on the bottom of my parachute harness, which I had put on in the ready room, to the seat parachute pack on which I was sitting. Between my backside and the parachute itself was my survival pack. I slid the plotting board into the rails just under the instrument panel and secured the locks, which prevented it from sliding back into my stomach during launch. On that plotting board was all that I needed to navigate to Truk and return. Over my flight coveralls I wore my .38-caliber revolver in a holster that strapped over my right shoulder and hung under my left armpit. I had a number of rounds interspersed along the leather strap. The revolver was a six-chamber Smith & Wesson that I kept loaded and on safety. Over the holster I had on a Mae West life vest and, worn over all this was the parachute harness. The parachute itself and the survival pack always stayed in the plane.

During catapult procedures, night or day, the VF-32 standard procedure was that the cockpit hatch was always locked open. This was necessary in case of sea ditching. However, due to the heavy rain, I opted to lock the hatch cover closed. I didn't relish getting soaking wet. We would be climbing to 24,000 feet. It is cool at that altitude, and the Hellcat had no heater. I strapped my oxygen mask over my nose and mouth and set the selector on 100 percent oxygen. In case of sea ditching, I could breath under water while extricating myself from the plane. Sucking 100 percent oxygen also helps night vision.

Benny patted me on the shoulder and dropped off the wing. I was ready. Soon I'd know if my favorite plane, Number 9, was ready.

The fleet turned into the wind and the ship settled down in pitch and roll. Now came the command from the *Langley* air officer: "Pilots, start engines." Shortly after start-up, I was sitting in the cockpit, engine idling, watching the catapult officer's illuminated wands signal the skipper to go to full power. Then the wands dropped and the catapult shot the skipper's plane off into the black void of night. All I saw was his exhaust-stack flames as the plane disappeared into blackness. Then the catapult officer signaled me forward onto the catapult. Out of the corner of my eye, I saw wands starting to bring Pond forward on the other catapult. Pond would be launched 10 seconds after me. The two illuminated wands maneuvered me into the correct position. I locked down on the rudder toe brakes. Two catapultmen, one from each side of the plane, crawled under the belly and connected the catapult cable to two burly hooks protruding a few inches below the belly and just to each side of the 150-gallon belly tank. During this hookup, I ran the engine at idle power. Otherwise, I could, with higher power, blow the men down the deck. The marvelous Pratt & Whitney engine idled in a deep, smooth roar. I loved this 2,000-horsepower engine. It helped make the Hellcat the greatest fighter plane. I trusted it with my life.

Quickly, the wands signaled that the connection was complete and that the men were clear of the plane.

Now entered the most critical factors of a catapult launch. I was signaled to bring the engine to full power. I did this firmly and smoothly, with the throttle grasped in my left hand. I went all the way forward to the quadrant stop. I was at maximum power. I tightened down on the friction lock on the side of the throttle quadrant with my gloved right hand. I returned the right hand to the control stick between my legs. I now had only 10 to 15 seconds before launch. I eyeballed the engine instruments for normal reading at full power. The engine roar was smooth to my ears. The cockpit instruments were hooded and illuminated by red light only, which prevented destroying night vision. At idle, I had disengaged the artificial horizon and reset the gyro compass to the ship's launching heading. I locked the fingers of my left hand over the forward edge of the throttle quadrant and straightened out my left arm. This would prevent my left arm from inadvertently pulling back the throttle once the immense impact of the catapult cable unleashed. The huge prop tore at the night air and tugged hard at the brakes and cable. Number 9 was raring to go. I was ready.

At this point, under daylight conditions, the pilot gives the thumbs-up gesture to show he is ready. Under night conditions, of course, nothing in the cockpit can be seen from the outside. The catapult officer crouched forward of and just outside the end of the right wing. My wingtip running lights were on, red for left, green for right. They were set on dim. I flashed the lights, the signal that I was ready to go. My right hand held the control stick in the neutral position. I brought my right elbow in and nestled it against the top of my right thigh, arched my head back against the padded headrest, and concentrated my eyes solely on the artificial horizon instrument. I knew that immediately upon launch I would be flying on that instrument. It was the primary instrument used in night flying or instrument conditions.

During the last few seconds of my eye sweep of the gauges

and readiness check, the catapult officer had to complete the second critical factor of the launch procedure. He had to check with his subordinate who manned the important steam gauge and controls to get final okay that the catapult was fully up to pressure and ready for release. It was. Suddenly, the catapult officer dropped his two lighted wands downward. It was the signal for release.

Wham! The tremendous, slamming pressure of the cable releasing forward knocked my toes off the rudder brakes and slung the Hellcat forward. I riveted my eyes on the artificial horizon. Proper pilot technique was mandatory. I was at gross weight. Number 9 was loaded with 2,400 rounds of .50-caliber ammunition, six guns, full internal gas tanks, and a 150-gallon belly gas tank. Airspeed was low—it read only 10 knots above stall speed. Immediately upon becoming airborne, I initiated landing-gear retraction. As the wheel retracted into the wing wells, the airspeed jumped up. The landing gear on a fighter created 60 percent of the whole drag in the air, so it was critical to retract the gear immediately after a cat shot or a deck launch. I reached flap-retraction speed, and up came the flaps. Number 9 jumped up to rendezvous speed. I was then at 1,000 feet altitude. The plane flew beautifully; all systems read normal. I was past the first step. Next came the rendezvous, and then the flight.

Fleet rendezvous procedure was to continue flying on the same heading as the ship, climb to 1,000 feet, and continue for a predetermined time on heading until you visually picked up your flight leader coming back at the same altitude, off to your port side, on the reciprocal heading of 180 degrees. The skipper, after a predetermined time, made a two-needle–width turn to the left, maintaining altitude, until he had turned to the 180-degree reciprocal heading. He was then flying back toward the ship. In time, I sighted the dim red left wingtip light of his plane. I commenced a left turn to intercept his course. By adjusting my speed, I swung in slightly behind and slightly below the skipper. I clearly saw the red light of his wingman off his starboard side. My wingman, Pond, had been launched right after me, so in a short time he came out of his left turn and joined up on my left side. Each pilot was flying close formation by reference to the wing light and exhaust-stack flame of the plane ahead. The skipper was the exception. He was flying the instruments. We relied totally on his expertise to fly the gauges correctly and to navigate accurately.

By the time we had circled the ship in a large arc, the other four Hellcats had joined up. The skipper turned to a course that would take us toward Truk. At 50 miles from the fleet, we orbited in 360-degree circles, waiting to rendezvous with the fighters from the other carriers. We spotted no other lights at our altitude. We knew we were the first to arrive at the group rendezvous area. Unknown to us, the other fighters had had problems in rendezvousing their teams. Heavy rain clouds had prevented the pilots from spotting running lights. Radar control was trying to cope with the situation. Meantime, the delay was making us anxious, and the orbiting was using up gas. We had passed the mission time for departure from this area. The skipper made his decision. We had to leave now in order to climb to 24,000 feet and arrive at the airspace over Truk at daybreak, when we would have enough light to see the enemy through our illuminated gunsights.

We started to climb on course to Truk. At 4,000 feet, we entered the storm clouds. I had never felt such heavy rain hitting my plane. The water was so concentrated that the cockpit hatch was leaking around the seals. I wondered if enough water could enter the engine cowling to stop the engine. If our engines quit, we were goners. But ours didn't miss a beat.

At 16,000 feet, we broke clear of the storm. No more rain. We reached 24,000 feet. Ahead of us, and far away, dawn was starting to lighten the blackness. The storm was now far behind us. Far below, we could make out white, broken overcast. It was light enough by then to open up our formation distances, drop belly tanks, transfer over to internal gas, and test-fire each gun. I hydraulically charged all six guns and fired all at once. The recoil impacted the plane. It shuddered. It was a familiar feeling to me. I safeteed the two inboard guns. I would fly with four guns only and keep two guns, with 400 rounds each, for emergency use. If I used up the ammo of the four guns, I still had two guns to take me home.

The skipper dropped us down to 22,000 feet to pick up extra speed. I knew that Truk was only a few more minutes ahead, if the navigation had been accurate. We were ready for the fight. My mouth was dry, a sure sign I was apprehensive. I had to concentrate hard on my flying and try to keep all other thoughts out of my mind.

Suddenly, I saw ahead and below us, at about 16,000 feet, a mass of Japanese fighters climbing in formation, turning from south to east a short distance from us. I tallyhoed them over the radio. The enemy was at our 10-o'clock position. We swung toward them, dropping out of 22,000 at full throttle. They had not seen us yet. We were flying out of a blackish sky. A fighter is a small silhouette head-on. The element of surprise would be on our side. I gulped at the surprise. My God! I counted forty-four fighters—eleven divisions of four each. There were only eight of us. Our other Hellcats from the fleet were some 20 minutes behind us. Our fight would be over, one way or the other, before help arrived.

Beginning at the rear of the group, I counted what I took to be sixteen Kawasaki Ki-61 Tony Imperial Army fighters. I could not get a silhouette of other fighters ahead of them. Maybe some Zeros were in the mix. The Tony was the new Imperial Army fighter. We had not had the time in action against it to know of its performance and speed.

We were streaking toward the rearmost group of eight planes. By then, the Japanese had copied the Navy's tactical fighter formation—they were also flying two teams of two each to a division. Each of us was committed to shoot at the enemy plane flying the same team position as we were flying. I lined up on the second-element leader of the second division from the rear. The skipper lined up on the leader of the second division. Both our wingmen lined up on the enemy wingmen.

The number-1 pilot of the rear Tony division spotted us. He fired a burst of rounds up over his group leader's head. I could see the arch of flaming red tracers. I thought at that time, "The enemy fighters do not all have radios."

The Japanese pilot's warning was too late. We were in firing range, at 300 yards. At the tremendous speed we were moving, things happened in microseconds. I squeezed off a one-second burst. I held only a small mil lead on the gunsight. As the Tony blew up, I pulled up over the flaming debris.

The Tonys were coming after us. They had broken up the formation, and the sky was full of them. The skipper was ahead of me. He turned right in a high-gee turn, back into the center of the fight. As the skipper straightened out his right turn, he spotted a Tony crossing his bow from right to left at about 100 yards. He swung back to the left to get on the Tony's tail. Pond and I were on the outside of our right turn; we were still turning toward the skipper when I spotted a Tony swinging in on the skipper's tail. As second team, my job was to keep the skipper's tail clear of the enemy. I went full deflection on my gunsight and fired a one-second burst. Four streams of tracers poured right into the Tony's left wingtip and on into his left gas tank. I had fired from approximately the 9-o'clock position to the Tony. The Tony exploded in my face. Damn! I hated to fly through debris, which could disable my prop or control surfaces. However, I was so close that I couldn't avoid some of the debris even though I pulled up hard and went into a hard controlled turn to the left. I sighted the skipper ahead. His target was falling in a burning mass.

The eight of us were engaged in a violent, deadly dogfight. The Tonys were showing us how elusive and determined they were. There were so many of them! They were under us, over us, diving through us—and they were all firing. Some circled, looking for an opportunity to boresight our tails. We stayed in hard turns, which made it very difficult for the enemy to line up on us. Their random shooting had not hit me or Pond yet, nor Reeves or the skipper. I didn't know how the other four were doing.

The skipper turned in toward two Zeros, which were firing at him from the right. I followed with a hard turn. Suddenly, a Tony roared right over my cockpit from my left. He almost collided with me. Evidently, he didn't see me. He was after Reeves, the skipper's wingman, who was some distance behind the skipper, and to one side. I pulled off all power, boresighted the Tony as he started to fire at Reeves, and squeezed off a one-second burst. The Tony blew into a ball of fire.

I poured on full power. I started a left turn so Pond, below and behind me, could join up. Suddenly, a stream of tracers shot past my nose in a slightly climbing arc. I ducked the nose and turned hard left, toward the source of the shots. Just then, a Tony screamed up and over me, just missing the hatch with his right wingtip. Another near-collision! Pond was off to the side of my tail, on the right side. His job was to protect my tail. He was in position to fire. I saw a stream of tracers drive into the Tony. They tore it in half, and the remains fell in flames. A fine shot.

We were in the center of a hailstorm. Our danger of collision was almost as critical as being shot out of the sky. I kept thinking, "How in hell are we going to fight our way through such overwhelming odds? Where are the other Hellcats?" I lost track of time. Sweat was running into my eyes. I pulled my goggles up and wiped the sweat away. My flight suit was soaked through with sweat. My neck ached from constant twisting of my head, to see all areas around us. My right arm ached from the hard effort of constantly manhandling the Hellcat in high-gee turns.

I looked ahead. I swept the sky. No skipper. He evidently had turned around 180 degrees instead of coming back to the heading we were on when the last Tonys attacked us. It was a bad tactic. There was no way I could follow such a maneuver while I was involved in a fight myself.

Pond rejoined me as we eased out of a 180-degree turn. I looked up. There were four Tonys bearing down upon us. They were not firing at us. The angle told me why. They had misjudged the distance of our turn and were too close to get proper mil lead on us in order to shoot. We had the advantage in that we were slower in speed from the turn and we could pull our noses up and get in a shot. Three of the Tonys were flying in formation off the leader's right side. Pond was on my right side—the *wrong* side. He could not shoot at them. I pulled up, gunsighted the lead Tony, and squeezed off a one-second burst. The burst hit the Tony full force in the nose, destroyed the prop, and tore part of the engine off. The Tony shuddered, skidded sideways, and fell over my head.

I turned down and hard left. The three other Tonys were zooming down and away from us. The third plane was aft of the other two. I had no time to boresight. There was a chance to hit him, but the odds were long. I was probably past effective range. I fired a snap two-second burst and hit the tail. The Tony tumbled crazily out of control. The other two Tonys flew into the overcast, which was only about 1,000 feet below us. The fight had started at 16,000 feet.

In the last hard turn, to make the shot, Pond had to swing under me and out to the right side. I turned back to a level heading. Just as I did, a stream of tracers flashed past my left wing in a climbing arc. The enemy plane was below me. I flipped the Hellcat on its left side so I could see down better. There, carving a beautiful left wingover, was a trim Zero. Good luck had saved me from being hit. My turn back to level heading had caused him to miss. Evidently, he had popped out of the overcast or had been hiding in one of the open breaks in the cloud cover, had spotted me firing at the four Tonys, climbed up under us, and fired from a nose-high position. His angle and mil lead had been accurate. It was a good shot. But, then, the pilot made a crucial mistake with his wingover, a maneuver in which, from a vertical or near-vertical position, the pilot drops a wing down as he applies rudder to bring the nose around and down. The plane makes a 180-degree reversal of direction and heads vertically downward. The Zero pilot had made a smooth wingover to the left. He should have made it to the right, which would have taken him under and below me. This would have made it impossible for me to get on his tail for a shot.

The overcast was too close to us. I pulled off all power, rolled over on my back, and pulled back hard on the control stick to bring the nose of the plane through vertical. I was dropping fast, straight down. As I pulled through vertical, I looked through the glass section at the top of the hatch. The Zero had completed the wingover and was dropping straight away from me toward the overcast. I could see that I was still 20 degrees or so below the Zero's angle of flight. I pulled the elevators harder. I had to get the nose up another 20 degrees. My vision started to tunnel—that's where excessively high gee forces pull blood from the eyes. If the pilot sustains such control-stick pressure, the eyes can black out. It was a fact of life fighter pilots learned to live with and to handle in the hundreds of hours of training to dogfight and do aerobatics. I eased off a little back pressure on the stick and my vision returned.

I was on the same angle of descent, about 70 degrees, that the Zero was flying. I had no more time. I centered the enemy cockpit in the gunsight and simultaneously squeezed off a one-second burst. Four tracer streams headed right for the enemy cockpit. As I fired, the Zero turned hard left. At that second, my burst missed the cockpit but tore off half of the vertical stabilizer and part of the horizontal stabilizer. The Zero cartwheeled into the overcast. Could the enemy have bailed out below the overcast? That was possible, I suppose. He was an experienced pilot. He had to have been watching me in his rearview mirror. When he saw my four guns blazing, he had started a hard turn to the left. It saved his life at that point.

I leveled off and Pond zoomed into formation. We commenced easy S turns and scanned the sky, but there were no enemy to be seen. The sky was empty. We throttled back to cruise power settings, to save gas and our engines. My gas supply was okay.

The radio came alive. The torpedo planes and the Hellcat escorts were coordinating their order of sequence of dives. Finally, we spotted them above and to the west of us. Planes were diving down through a large open area in the overcast while a bunch of strung-out flights were circling, waiting for their turn to dive. The bombers were to bomb or torpedo the ships anchored in huge Truk Lagoon. Teams of Hellcats dove down ahead of the bombers. Their mission was to strafe and destroy as many of the ships' antiaircraft batteries as possible.

It was hard to believe that the dogfight was over. What a relief! It had been a hellish fight. It all involved frantic radio hollering, explosions, burning and broken planes, sweat, fears, and determination. There had even been a couple of parachutes—all Japanese. I wondered how many kills the eight of us had scored, and if we had lost anybody. I wondered, also, where all the remaining Tonys and Zeros had gone, and what lay down below the overcast. There was time to find out, so down we went.

We broke out of the overcast at 8,000 feet, about one-half

mile south and slightly east of the atoll. All hell had broken loose. Very heavy AA fire was pouring up from the heavily defended ridges and land areas rimming the land side of the atoll. Intelligence had briefed us that over 100 large ships were anchored inside the atoll. The sky was pocked with exploding 20mm and 37mm shells. Ships exploded, burned, and sank as the marksmanship of the bombers proved excellent. It was Pearl Harbor in reverse!

A mile or so northeast of our position lay the Japanese airfield, backed by a long, sweeping high ridge covered with heavy vegetation. It was alive with gun crews. The guns pumped accurate fire at the base of the large cloud break the bombers were diving through. The bombers that got through unscathed dropped their bombs or torpedoes and zoomed toward the western rendezvous area outside the reef. This was a safe area. Escort Hellcats circled above, and, a quarter mile west of the reef, a rescue submarine lay below the surface. As soon as the attacks were over, it would surface and pick up downed pilots and crewmen. Too many bombers and fighters were being hit by the accurate and deadly AA fire. Planes were exploding, burning, and falling out of control. Pilots and crewmen were parachuting out of the stricken planes. The AA gunners were shooting purposely at the men coming down in the chutes. All of the parachutes were falling into the lagoon. If the men survived, they would be captured. There was no way the sub could rescue them.

Fury overtook me. The dogfight had tired me, but Pond and I were now aroused. We would strafe and destroy as many gun batteries as our ammunition and fuel allowed. I leveled off at 3,000 feet and headed east. I wanted to attack the easternmost gun emplacement. We would recover 90 degrees to the east, over the sea. We would then attack successive emplacements to the west of the previous one. Thus, we would reduce the number of guns that could hit us in the attack dive or the escape. I signaled Pond. He positioned himself in a loose left formation, slightly behind me and level with me. He would take the battery emplacement next to the one I lined up on. Down we headed.

I fired from 1,500 feet. The Hellcat shuddered from the recoil of the four guns. The gunsight pipper was on a twin-37mm gun. A lot of men were working around the battery. At nearly 600 miles per hour and in the steep dive, the .50-caliber bullets hit with terrific impact, blasting the twin guns into debris. Many of the gunners were killed diving over the sandbags surrounding the emplacement. I squeezed off three one-second bursts before I pulled out of the dive and zoomed right over the emplacement. I dropped on down over the east side of the ridge, turned hard left, executed a climbing turn to the right, and then a descending turn back to the left. I wanted to keep those gunners guessing. Guns were firing at us, but the exploding shells were way off line. The shells exploded where we had been, not where we were. Pond joined up. We were out of their range. We went back for two more complete strafing runs. We destroyed a total of six batteries of guns.

After the final run, Pond joined up at 1,500 feet. I throttled back. I was about out of ammo. It was time to think of going home. I swept the sky and the sea, a constant habit. Suddenly, my eyes picked out a faint shadow, just over the surface of the sea, headed east. Without taking my eyes off the shadow, I turned toward it and headed down at full throttle. I didn't want to lose the shadow against the backdrop of a dark sea. As all carrier pilots learn, I had to fly to the same level to change a shadow into a silhouette against the sky. Dropping out of 1,500 feet at full throttle, we were moving fast. When I got close enough for identification, I saw that the shadow was made by a fast-moving Tony. I figured its pilot was inexperienced and had been scrambled during the attack. He must have been orbiting off the water, just east of the ridge and the beach below it.

The enemy pilot finally spotted me. He turned hard to a heading directly away from me. I was now positioned directly behind him. A deadly chase commenced. Unfortunately for this pilot, the Tony was not swift enough to run away from the fast Hellcat.

We were gaining nicely at full power. I needed only a little more time to catch and kill it. I reached down and turned off the safety switches of the two inside guns. They were now hot, with a full 400 rounds each. I doubted that I had enough rounds left in the other four guns. I couldn't chance that one or more of them might quit firing. The resultant uneven recoil would kick the plane off the target line.

The gunsight told me I was out of range. I had started the chase about one mile behind. Shortly, I would be 300 yards behind the Tony, ready to fire a burst. It would be an easy shot, a straight-on shot with the gunsight pipper resting on the Tony's cockpit hatch. Our guns were boresighted to converge in a vertical pattern of rounds at 300 yards. One burst should kill the pilot and destroy the cockpit. Pond was off my right wing, wide enough away to have the kill if the enemy turned right. If the Tony continued straight or turned left, he would be mine.

Suddenly, I saw six lines of tracers arcing down from above me—toward the Tony. I looked up in surprise. One hundred feet or so above me was a Hellcat, firing its guns. Ejected shell casings fell between me and Pond. I checked the Hellcat identification as he flew past. Hell, it was the skipper! Off to his left, directly above me, was Reeves, his wingman. Luckily for me, Reeves did not fire, or shell casings would have fallen into my plane and hatch cover. Bad things would have happened if the prop had caught a shell casing. Later, back on the *Langley,* Reeves told me he was surprised the skipper had fired. He thought they had come down to watch us get the kill and then to rendezvous.

The skipper's tracers slammed into the ocean with a splash, short of the Tony. He realized he was out of range, stopped firing, and came off of water injection. His plane no longer pulled away from us. Water injection gives the engine at full power about 5 percent more speed. It also overboosts the engine by about 10 percent. Squadron procedure allowed it to be used only under emergency conditions—if an enemy plane is on your tail.

I was upset over this whole development. Was I to shoot or not? The skipper was above me, slightly ahead, and off to my right about 50 feet or so. I was still holding a heading directly behind the Tony. All of a sudden, that was no longer a question. The enemy pilot finally panicked, made a hard turn to the left, failed to hold level altitude, caught his left wingtip in a wave, and cartwheeled into the sea. In seconds, we were over the spot. Only the end of the tail showed after the huge shower of spray settled. Then the tail slipped slowly below the surface. The pilot went down with the plane.

The skipper circled. I brought Pond into formation with

him and Reeves. We all had a fuel check. Pond had 20 gallons less than I did. We were within 15 minutes of the scheduled return time from Truk. This last fruitless chase at full power had gulped the gas. It takes a lot of gas to feed a 2,000-horsepower engine, especially at full throttle. The skipper indicated that he had plenty of fuel to stay until our scheduled departure time. He had not done our three strafing runs. I asked permission to return at once to the ship, and he okayed it. Pond and I peeled out of formation and headed home.

*In all, the two VF-32 flights were credited with 19 victories over Truk. Dick May was credited with 3 confirmed kills and 3 probables. On September 21, 1944, he destroyed another Imperial Army Tony fighter over Manila Harbor, thus raising his official total to 6.*

*The end of the war found Lieutenant Dick May serving as an experimental test pilot at Patuxent, Maryland. He was separated from active duty in October 1945; graduated from the University of Portland in June 1946; and remained active in the Navy Reserve until 1964, when he retired with the rank of commander.*

# CHAPTER 11

After the second Truk raid, the fast carriers laid low. The Pacific high command was marshaling its forces for the next big jump to the west: the invasion of the Marianas. There, the Japanese were expected to react with an enormous naval counterattack. Task Force 58 spent the month of May 1944 readying itself for what many thought might be the decisive confrontation of the Pacific War, the long-anticipated grand-fleet action.

The fifteen American fleet and light carriers sortied from Majuro on June 6, 1944. The first softening-up raids were run against targets on Saipan, which was to be the first island invaded in Admiral Nimitz's new Operation Forager, by far the largest naval operation yet undertaken in the Pacific War.

Japanese land-based fighters and bombers stoutly resisted the 5th Fleet's initial incursion into a region that, except for Guam, had been a Japanese mandate from the end of World War I. The result, however, was a slaughter. In the afternoon action of June 11 alone, American carrier fighters destroyed 97 Japanese warplanes while the carrier bombers bombed Saipan and adjacent Tinian with virtual impunity.

The carriers hit Guam on June 12, but the Japanese responded lightly. Only 22 Imperial Navy warplanes were destroyed in the air. June 13 and 14 were light days; only 8 Japanese planes were downed as the bulk of the U.S. fleet sailed up to the Bonin Islands to neutralize the airfield on Iwo Jima. On June 15, the day those fields were hit, the Japanese lost 53 airplanes. June 16 and 17 were transit days; action was light and only 12 planes were claimed. Continuing action in the Marianas claimed 31 airplanes on June 18.

The big day was to be June 19, 1944. A large Japanese carrier fleet had sallied from anchorages in the East Indies. Though the Combined Fleet's Operation A-GO looked good on paper, it was in fact a paper tiger. The Japanese battle fleet was large and many new carrier air groups were being committed, but the level of training among the Japanese pilots was execrable. It is why the air action of June 19, 1944—officially styled the Battle of the Philippine Sea—is known in history as the Marianas Turkey Shoot.

Despite aircraft contact and sighting reports from several morning search teams, Task Force 58—the Fast Carrier Task Force—carried on with the day's plan, which had begun with a massive morning strike against targets throughout Guam. There was some action in the air as Japanese Zero-type fighters scrambled to intercept the inbound carrier strike groups, but the escorting fighters handled them with ease.

Then, at about 1015, the battle was joined from another quarter. Task Force 58 itself became the target of the all-out Japanese carrier strike. The three Hellcat squadrons of Rear Admiral William Harrill's Task Group 58.4—fleet carrier *Essex* and light carriers *Cowpens* and *Langley*—were effectively part of the Task Force 58 fighter reserve when hundreds of inbound Japanese carrier-based warplanes were spotted by U.S. Navy scouts. As the Task Force 58 fighter direction officer yelled "Hey, Rubel" to alert all the fighters his squadrons could muster, the Combat Air Patrol and fighters returning from missions over nearby Guam rushed to take on the incoming Japanese air groups as far from the friendly carriers as possible. Scores of Japanese carrier bombers and fighters were shot down, but scores more pressed on.

### "HEY, RUBE!"

**Lieutenant (jg) DON McKINLEY, USN**
**VF-25 (USS *Cowpens*)**
**Philippine Sea, June 19, 1944**

*Donald Joseph McKinley learned to fly in the Civilian Pilot Training program while attending Iowa State College. He earned his private license in the fall of 1940 and completed the secondary program during the fall quarter of his junior year, on December 5, 1941. At the conclusion of the fall quarter, he enlisted in the Navy, and, in February 1942, the same month as his twenty-first birthday, Don McKinley left his native St. Ansgar, Iowa, and reported to the Navy's aviation elimination base in Kansas City. He earned his wings at Jacksonville in November 1942 and was assigned to fighters. After qualifying for carrier landings, he reported to VF-25, which was forming at Willow Grove, Pennsylvania, and remained with the new unit through all subsequent training ashore and aboard light carrier* Cowpens.*

*Lieutenant (jg) Don McKinley scored his first victory, a Jake reconnaissance floatplane, northwest of Truk on February 17, 1944. His next two victories were over Betty medium bombers (one each on February 22 and April 21, 1944), and, on June 11, 1944, he was awarded a shared credit for a Nakajima Ki-43 Oscar Imperial Army fighter over Saipan.*

Shortly after our squadron, VF-25, returned to *Cowpens* from a morning strafing mission against the partly completed airstrip at Rota, we knew that an enemy attack was imminent. We were in the squadron ready room, ready to go. We were receiving intermittent reports from our CIC [Combat Information Center] on action throughout the fleet. The ready-room climate was like a locker room before a big football game—butterflies and little conversation.

Shortly after 1000, VF-25 was scrambled to intercept and destroy incoming Japanese planes. We were advised not to take time to join up as a squadron or even a division, but to start climbing and head in a westerly direction immediately after launch. If any vectors were given, I did not hear them. We did not have planes assigned, so it was a matter of getting up to the flight deck and into the first Hellcat that was available. The planes were spotted for flyaway, not catapult. We were off within a few minutes of getting "Man your planes." I was the third plane off the flight deck.

Shortly, another F6F joined up on me. After it took position on my left wing, I was able to identify the pilot visually. It turned out to be one of my roommates, Lieutenant (jg) Fred Stieglitz.

The sky was full of planes at all altitudes, some burning and falling. I thought that this was the ultimate in air battles. In my area, there were planes from several of our carriers involved.

We were about 50 miles southwest of Task Group 58.4 and climbing through 7,500 feet when I saw a three-plane section of Japanese Nakajima B6N Jill torpedo planes with torpedoes attached. They were painted a brownish gray with red meatballs on their wings and fuselages. They were flying a tight vee formation, probably 1,500 feet below us and headed toward the U.S. fleet.

The radio traffic was unbelievable. There was so much garbage on the radio that no transmission was possible; there was no way I could communicate by radio with Stieglitz, who was flying close formation on my port side. When I spotted the Jills, I got his attention and pointed to them. He nodded to let me know he also saw them.

We did a kind of a wingover–split-S and got behind them. After we reversed course, we closed rapidly on the Jills for three to four minutes. At that point, the Japanese pilots surely saw us. As we came up from behind, they split up. The left Jill veered and dived away to the left and the other two dived away to the right. I followed the two and Stieglitz broke off and went left, after the single.

The Japanese had split up when we were almost in firing range. I continued to close on my two Jills. When I was within firing distance—within about 100 yards—I targeted the lead Jill and fired slightly above and to the left of it. I led it a little when I opened fire. After three or four short bursts, the Jill started smoking. We were going down in a fairly shallow dive, probably between 250 and 300 miles per hour. The two Jill pilots took little evasive action; by this time in the war, the well-trained Japanese pilots were gone.

The lead Jill burned and lost altitude. I throttled down and made S turns until I was sure it was gone. By then, the second Jill had gained some ground. When I caught up and was in firing range, the B6N pilot was down to between 300 and 250 feet. Then he leveled out at about 50 feet over the water. I was directly behind him, and his gunner was firing at me. I noticed splashes in the water at that time, but I did not equate them with my going after the Jill. I was so intent on this plane that I did not see that we were approaching the American task force and that the splashes were coming from friendly AA guns trying to get the Jill before it launched its torpedo.

Apparently, my fire hit the pilot. The plane began to smoke, and then it nosed over and hit the water.

After the second Jill burned and crashed, I looked up and saw, directly ahead of me, an *Essex*-class carrier, about a mile away. It was not Task Group 58.4; I don't know which task group it was. The antiaircraft fire was extremely heavy, so I pulled up steeply and turned to port. The AA fire ceased almost immediately. I presume they recognized my F6F.

I turned away from the task force and started to climb. Another F6F joined on me and we climbed to 10,000 feet. I think it was from VF-15, off the *Essex*. We flew CAP over several task groups until the carriers began to recover planes.

My roommate, Fred Stieglitz, did not return from the mission, but, based on my account at the time, he was awarded a probable for the Jill he chased. This was in addition to a Judy dive-bomber he had shot down the day before, June 18, and a confirmed Oscar and a probable Oscar he had claimed earlier. In all that day, VF-25 had 8 confirmed kills and 3 probables.

*By the time VF-25 returned to the United States in July 1944, it had racked up 34 solid victories, 5 probables, and 2 damaged. Don McKinley went on to help form VF-36. In August 1945, VF-36 was outbound toward Pearl Harbor when the end of the Pacific War was announced. Lieutenant Don McKinley was released from active duty in September 1945, but he remained in the inactive Reserves until 1956.*

Even with their fleet under attack, entire American carrier air groups continued to ply the day's "routine" business. Guam was scheduled for mass destruction, and that's what happened. And while they were at it, the relatively nerveless fighter pilots on escort duty added immensely to the day's total.

## THE RESCUE

**Ensign WENDELL TWELVES, USN**
**VF-15 (USS *Essex*)**
**Rota Point, Guam, June 19, 1944**

*Wendell Van Twelves, of Spanish Fork, Utah, completed his sophomore year at Brigham Young University and enlisted in the Navy as an aviation cadet on July 6, 1942. He earned his wings at Corpus Christi on June 16, 1943, and joined VF-15, then training at Atlantic City, New Jersey, in August 1943.*

After flying a four-hour morning CAP mission over the carriers, my division, which was led by Lieutenant Commander George Duncan, the VF-15 exec, landed back aboard the *Essex* when the morning strike group returned from its first bombing mission of the day. Though we had been able to see the air battle over the carriers, we had been kept off to guard against intruders from the other direction.

The refueling operation was completed quickly, and we were launched again. This time, we drew a fighter sweep. We formed up on Duncan and headed for Orote Field, on Guam. We hoped we would be able to catch some of the Japanese carrier planes at the airfield.

Duncan climbed the division to 6,000 feet for the flight. That altitude kept us below the base of the clouds and above any small-arms fire that we might encounter over the islands. Cruising at 260 knots, we were pushing the airplanes somewhat. We wanted to keep our speed up so we would have enough energy to maneuver if we encountered enemy aircraft. We also just wanted to get there in a hurry. We had missed out on everything while we were flying CAP. We didn't want to miss out again.

The islands were coming up. Even though I'd never been there before, I recognized everything. In preparation for this strike, I'd committed the charts of the islands to memory. I knew exactly where I was, where Orote Field was on Guam, where Marpi Field was on Saipan, and where the other targets were.

We never made it to Orote Field. As we approached Cabras Island, southeast of Guam, we spotted two Zeros flying above our altitude. Duncan sent the section leader, Lieutenant (jg) William Henning, and his wingman, Lieutenant (jg) Carlton White, up to engage them.

At the same time, Duncan and I heard a distress call on the combat frequency. The pilot of an SOC Seagull, a rescue seaplane, called out his position just off Rota Point on Guam. He and another SOC were on the water a thousand yards off the beach. They were being strafed by two Zeros. He wanted immediate help from any fighters in the area. The man was scared. I could hear the desperation in his voice.

At that moment, a couple of Zeros jumped Duncan and me from 2 o'clock high. They came out of the cloud cover from nowhere. We jinked out of their line of fire and Duncan radioed me to go help the Seagulls while he tangled with the Zeros.

Rota Point was eight miles from my position. That was at least two minutes away. I rolled into a left turn, pushed the throttle to the stop, and took up a heading for the Seagulls. I leaned forward against the straps to urge a little more speed out of my airplane. If I was going to do anything for the rescue planes, I had to get there quickly. They were like sitting ducks for the Zeros.

Even though my focus was on getting to Rota Point, I kept up my scan of the sky. Getting shot down on the way to help the Seagulls wouldn't do them or me any good. Things had become very busy. The sky was a turmoil of battle. I could see a dozen or more planes turning and twisting in combat. Several were trailing smoke. The combat frequency was full of chatter.

Nothing I could see presented a direct threat. Rota Point was coming up. I could see the brilliant white parachutes floating in the water. There were three or four of them. They belonged to the pilots the Seagulls were picking up.

As I got closer, I could see the Seagulls. They were under way, taxiing away from the beach. The Seagulls rode high above the water on a single pontoon below the fuselage. I could see the men they'd rescued in the water holding on to the pontoons. I picked up a Zero on my next scan. It was ahead of and below me. Its dark wings glinted in the sun. The Zero was turning to line up for a pass on the seaplanes. A sinking feeling hit me as I realized that I couldn't get into a firing position before he strafed them. I was just too far away.

The Zero was only a few hundred feet off the deck. I was at 4,000 feet. Our headings were converging on the seaplanes. The Zero's course would cross mine from the right. I pushed the nose down and went after it.

My guns were armed, my gunsight was on, and my airspeed was building up. I was closing the distance between us. The airspeed indicator was showing 360 knots. I made a quick scan for the second Zero, but I couldn't pick it out. I returned my attention to the one ahead of me.

The Zero had opened up on the lead Seagull. I could clearly see the 7.7mm smoke tracers fly from his guns to the seaplane. The men who were hanging on to the pontoon dove underwater for protection. The pilot of the Seagull gunned his engine and turned his aircraft in a circle to make it harder for the Zero to hit it. The water all around the Seagull turned white as the bullets impacted. I knew that the Zero pilot would use the 7.7mm guns to get on target before he opened up with the two 20mm cannons mounted in his wings. The cannons would wreak havoc. I was still out of range. The boiling water around the Seagull erupted into a fountain of white spray. The Zero pilot was using his cannons. I just couldn't catch him quickly enough to stop his run.

I was concentrating solely on the Zero. Its pilot stopped firing. I was closer. The Seagulls flashed past as he flew directly over the top of them. He started a shallow bank to the left. My guns were set to converge at 1,200 feet. My position called for a 45-degree deflection shot. I had to pull three gees to bring my guns to bear. I had the Zero in my gunsight. The sight was an illuminated reticle consisting of a central dot surrounded by three concentric rings. The enemy plane was out about 500 yards. I led it by 100 mils. That put its nose just touching the second circle.

At 400 yards, the Japanese pilot spotted me. He tightened his bank, but he was too late. I was already squeezing the trigger. I fired a good burst, a full three seconds. The glowing tracers appeared to curve toward the Zero as they streaked out ahead of me. Watching carefully, I saw that my lead was on the money. I could see the hits on the Zero.

Our courses crossed and the Zero passed below me. I rolled to the left to get into another firing position. The Zero was still below me. It was only 200 feet above the water. I didn't need to make another pass. The Zero had started to flame. Its nose pitched down and, in a matter of seconds, it dropped into the ocean. The plane hit at a shallow angle. It skipped and cartwheeled endlessly, leaving a brilliant trail of fire on the water.

I bent my Hellcat around to see how the Seagull was faring. Halfway through my turn, I spotted the other Zero at 12 o'clock. It was high, maybe 5,000 to 6,000 feet up, and two miles out. Its heading was crossing mine from right to left at almost 90 degrees. Its wings were banked in a shallow turn to bring him around for a run on the Seagulls.

I still had a lot of speed from my dive on the first Zero. The airspeed indicator showed nearly 340 knots. I pulled up and traded the speed I had gained in the dive for altitude. The Hellcat literally leaped skyward. Things looked better this time. I'd be able to nail this one before the pilot could hit the Seagulls.

The Zero pilot was concentrating on the Seagulls. He hadn't seen me yet. He continued his wide turn to line up on the seaplanes.

I had a clear picture in my mind of the quickest intercept course to put myself in a firing position. A depressed wingover would bring me in behind the diving Zero for a high-side deflection shot from above and behind him.

I flew it just like I saw it in my mind. The world turned upside down around me. I kept my nose ahead of the Zero as I turned. The plane slipped nicely into my gunsight. The deflection angle was large. One hundred and fifty mils lead in the gunsight would be about right. I retarded the throttle slightly to keep from overrunning.

I fired several short bursts while sliding through to a stern position. I could see debris coming off the Zero as my bullets struck home. Heavy black smoke poured out of the stricken aircraft. The plane rolled away to the right and spiraled down into the sea. It hit the water hard. Then it was gone.

I had just started to look around for other aircraft when I found myself in a hail of 7.7mm smoke tracers! They were streaking past my cockpit like a blizzard. A Zero had jumped me from behind.

I rolled left and pulled a six-gee turn. I needed to break the Zero pilot's aim before he opened up with his 20mm cannons. He had a good bead on me. I could feel the impact of 7.7mm bullets all over my airplane. I was in deep trouble. The Zero could easily turn inside my Hellcat. I was buffeting on the edge of a high-speed stall. I couldn't turn it any harder. I threw the plane right, then left again with all my strength. I'd be torn to pieces by his cannons if I couldn't break his aim. My options weren't good. I didn't have enough altitude to dive away from him. There were no clouds close enough to use for cover.

The smoke tracers stopped momentarily. I twisted my head around to get a fix on the Zero. To my absolute relief and delight, I could see another F6F firing on the Zero! All right! Good timing!

I righted my machine and quickly scanned everywhere for

enemy aircraft. A breath of air that I didn't know I was holding escaped my lungs. What a relief! The Zero that had been firing on me was smoking and headed down. The unidentified Hellcat had left the area. Except for Duncan's F6F far above me, the sky was empty and quiet. I double-checked everywhere. All the Zeros were gone. Perhaps two minutes had elapsed since I first arrived on the scene.

I checked the gauges and looked my plane over for damage. I could see numerous holes in my wings, but everything seemed to be in working order. Thank you, Leroy Grumman, for that nice slab of armor plate behind my back and the self-sealing fuel tanks.

It was a little unreal how quickly everything had returned to normal.

I let down to check on the seaplanes. I was happy and more than a little amazed to see that both of the Seagulls were still underway. Both of them were severely damaged. I could see a lot of daylight through their wings and fuselages. Blue smoke from a damaged oil line was swirling in the prop wash of the lead Seagull. They would taxi out to a point where a rescue submarine was stationed. The submarine would have to take all of them aboard. The flying days of those two airplanes were definitely over. Circling low, I could see the survivors sitting on the wings. Everyone on and in the airplanes was waving and cheering. I felt like cheering myself. I rocked my wings in answer. I knew just how they felt. I'd sure like to have shaken the hand of the pilot who had shot that last Zero off my tail.

Duncan called for the division to regroup. I rogered the call and heard Henning and White acknowledge. I was glad to hear their voices. As we rendezvoused, Duncan reported that he had shot down 3. Henning got 2, and White got 1. With mine, that made 8 Zeros. Not bad for a bunch of beginners.

The wild excitement of the battle slowly drained away on the flight back to the *Essex*. This had been my first engagement with enemy fighters. My feelings were kind of jumbled. I was elated to have knocked down the Zeros that were strafing the seaplanes. I felt terrific about being able to save the men down on the water. All the work I'd put in to sharpening my skills had paid off. I was also sobered by the close call I had had with the third Zero. I can only thank the good Lord and an unknown Hellcat pilot for pulling me out of that fix.

I was in the pattern for landing on the carrier. I'd pretty much settled down. I was glad to be alive. I was ready to refuel, rearm, and get back into it again. I was a whole lot smarter. I'd be keeping a close eye on my tail from then on.

My approach to the carrier was rock solid. When the LSO gave me the cut, I chopped the throttle, and planted the Hellcat on the deck. The tail hook snagged the number-3 wire. I was home.

The day after the battle, I learned from the ship's Combat Information Center that the two Seagull rescue planes had successfully rendezvoused with a submarine. All hands were safely taken aboard, and the submarine sank the Seagulls with gunfire. They were damaged beyond any hope of salvage.

I never did learn who shot the third Zero off my tail. The brief glimpse I had of the Hellcat was nearly head-on. I wasn't able to pick out the tail markings or any other identifying features. He was there when I needed him, and then he was gone. I would still like to shake his hand. I definitely owe him one.

*Lieutenant (jg) Wendell Van Twelves followed his first 2 Zeros with a string of 11 more confirmed victories before the amazing, high-scoring VF-15 completed its combat tour in November 1944. Before returning to civilian life, Lieutenant Twelves spent three tours of duty in Korea. His combat medals include a Navy Cross and a Silver Star.*

Wendell Van Twelves earned his victories at 1615 on June 19. Less than an hour later, in a separate strike in the day-long rotation against Guam, fighter pilots from the *Hornet* added a large chunk to the day's vast and growing score of victory credits.

## "I HAVE FORTY JAP PLANES SURROUNDED"

Ensign SPIDER WEBB, USN
VF-2 (USS *Hornet*)
Orote Field, Guam, June 19, 1944

*Wilbur Butcher Webb, a native of Ardmore, Oklahoma, joined the Navy in October 1938, several months after his eighteenth birthday. He served in the gunnery and radio divisions aboard battleship* Colorado, *and eventually was assigned to the aviation division as a radioman-gunner flying aboard OS2U scout planes. His persistent requests for flight training were finally acted on in June 1942, and he earned his pilot's wings as an aviation pilot first class in July 1943. Shortly thereafter, he was temporarily commissioned as an ensign.*

*Spider Webb joined VF-2 in Hawaii in December 1943 and sailed with it aboard* Hornet *for the March 1944 strike against the Japanese fleet anchorage in the Palaus. Thereafter, through the first half of June, VF-2, with Ensign Webb along, participated in one far-ranging strike after another.*

June 19, 1944, was not like any other morning we had been at sea, because General Quarters was sounded at 0300. Daylight broke to reveal an ominously placid sea. The night had passed peacefully enough, but the morning dispatches carried with them forebodings of busy and hectic hours ahead. The message from one of our subs was cheerful, indeed. It told of six torpedo hits on a *Shokaku*-class carrier.

At 0715, intercept fighters and the Combat Air Patrol were launched, and fighters from all parts of Task Force 58 intercepted several hundred Japanese torpedo planes, dive-bombers, and fighters at distances up to 150 miles from the carriers. Our fighters stopped them cold.

I took off on a strike to Guam at 1030. Our targets were the airfields, to prevent enemy planes from landing and refueling. I returned from this hop about noon, and things settled down a bit. Radar reported nothing. We were all tired, and we thought our flying was over for the day, except for the Combat Air Patrol and searches for the Japanese fleet. However, our division was not scheduled for this duty.

At about 1300, June 19, a special strike group was put together to silence AA at Agana, on Guam, and to destroy some ammo dumps that Air Combat Intelligence had reported. This was a volunteer hop because everyone had flown at least one hop during the day, and all of us were very tired. I normally flew with Lieutenant (jg) Tex Vineyard, who was the division leader for Ginger-12 (our radio call sign). I asked Tex if he wanted to go, but he replied in the negative because he had already flown two hops. I advised the squadron operations officer that I would go. We were assigned to the fighter escort for the strike group. I was flying on the wing of Lieutenant (jg) Conrad Elliott and was the escort flight's tail-end Charlie. We were given our targets, plotted our course information, and waited for the word to go. Flight quarters had already sounded.

About 1440, the word was passed, "Pilots, man your planes." My assigned aircraft was Number 31. Takeoff and rendezvous were normal, and we proceeded to our assigned targets, climbing on course to 28,000 feet. On approaching the target, our division remained high cover for the torpedo planes and dive-bombers, and then we headed down to drop our 500-pound bombs and strafe our assigned targets around Agana. After the strike on our assigned targets, we proceeded to make a running rendezvous across Guam to just off Orote Peninsula, which was on the west side of the island. We completed our join-up at 3,000 to 4,000 feet, and the entire strike group turned back toward the *Hornet*.

As our strike group passed over Orote Peninsula, I looked down at the water; 200 to 300 yards off the tip of the peninsula, I spotted a life raft. It was a one-man American raft, and it had a pilot in it. He had spilled out one of his dye markers to attract attention. Just a few minutes before, I had observed one of our OS2U Kingfisher floatplanes down on the water several miles ahead, picking up another pilot. I felt that the pilot in the raft would have a better chance if a fighter went down and stood by him until the OS2U could pick him up.

I called Elliott by his code nickname and suggested that

he obtain permission from the strike-group leader (Commander Jackson Arnold, who was Ginger-1) so he could go after the OS2U while I circled the downed pilot. Ginger-1 gave Elliott permission and Elliott gave the signal for us to break from the formation. I rocked my wings and headed for the downed pilot while Elliott headed for the floatplane.

I arrived over the life raft and lowered my speed by throttling back and lowering my wheels and flaps, so I could fly a tight circle around the man. My first thought was to throw him some more dye markers in the event he was not picked up before dark, and also to give him another life raft. I opened my canopy, took my knife out, cut two of the dye markers loose from my Mae West, and threw the markers to the pilot in the water. I was circling him at about 100 feet. After throwing out the dye markers, I proceeded to remove my life raft from under my parachute.

While I was wiggling around trying to get my life raft loose, I glanced backward toward Guam. There was a high ridge of mountains right down the center of the island, with some saddles in them. On my second glance back at the ridges, I saw a long line of airplanes. It stretched as far as I could see. They were in the saddles and along the ridges, apparently heading for Orote Airfield. My first thought was, "What in the dickens are our planes doing that low over the island with their landing gear down?"

The first planes of the group were heading for me, and they got to within less than 100 yards of me before I realized that they were Val dive-bombers, with fixed landing gear, flying in divisions of three. The aircraft above the Vals were Zeros. When they began to reach the landing pattern for the field, they banked away from me, and I could see the large red meatballs on their sides. I estimated that there were thirty to forty planes in all.

I was not very concerned about my position at the time. I just thought, "Boy, this is it. Make it good and get as many as you can before they know you're here." I picked up my microphone, told Elliott of my situation, asked him to come help me, and told him that I was going on in alone. I retracted my landing gear; closed my canopy; tightened my seatbelt, which I had loosened in order to remove my raft; flipped on my gun-camera and gun switches; and hit my gun chargers. I had not been detected so far, so I decided not to gain altitude, but to just slide into their traffic pattern and get as many as I could before I was detected.

As I started to slide in, I again picked up my microphone and made a blanket broadcast: "Any American fighter, I have forty Jap planes surrounded at Orote Airfield. I need some help!" By the time I had dropped my microphone, I was less than 20 yards behind the first group of three Val dive-bombers. I started overrunning them, so I lowered my landing gear and flaps.

The first plane on the left of the three was the first in my gunsight. I squeezed my gun trigger, and my six .50-caliber machine guns tore into the aircraft, which exploded instantly. I eased over to the middle plane and again squeezed my trigger. The top of the Val's vertical stabilizer disintegrated, and several bullets hit the rear-seat gunner in the chest. Then the starboard wing of the aircraft came off, and the plane exploded.

By the time I eased in behind the third plane, my speed had built up; I started overrunning it. The rear-seat gunner was firing directly at me, but he did not hit my aircraft. I was holding down the trigger, but this plane did not seem to want to burn. I kept saying, "Burn, you bastard," over and over until it finally did explode. If this plane had not exploded, I would have collided with it, I guess. When it did explode, I flew through and sustained several holes in my F6F from pieces of it.

After these first three, I slipped in behind another group of three Vals, and again I started by firing on the plane on the left. The rear-seat gunner of this aircraft was firing directly at me from no farther than 30 yards. I could see the colors of his flight suit, helmet, and skin. Then he seemed to kind of give up. He put his hands up before his face—maybe he thought I was going to run into him—just before several .50-caliber slugs hit him in the chest and face. The aircraft started burning, and the pilot bailed out over the side. We were at no more than 200 feet, so I doubt if he made it.

The next plane, which was in the middle, got away, but I managed to get behind the one on the right. When I fired, it started shedding pieces and smoking badly. Then his tail disintegrated, and he just fell.

There was considerable fire coming up from around Orote Peninsula; I could see tracers continually coming up in front of me. I guess they had never seen an F6F Hellcat flying so slow. At the time, I did not realize that my plane had been hit.

By this time, there were planes all over the sky. Many other American fighters had arrived and, no matter where I looked, I could see either a parachute or a burning plane. It seemed like a mad flying circus, only this was real.

After the fifth Val had fallen, my guns had stopped firing, so I headed out, away from the fight, and pushed my gun chargers until I got two guns working, one on each side. Then I headed back into the fight.

Almost immediately, I saw a Val coming toward me from above. It was at about 1,000 feet. I got it into my sights and squeezed the trigger. As my guns fired, a third gun started working. This Val seemed to explode in half just behind the pilot, but the pilot bailed out.

My guns quit again. Again I headed out of the fight until I managed to get two on one side and one on the other working. Then I headed back into the fight again.

I saw another Val low on the water, so I nosed over to intercept it and started firing. I killed the rear-seat man, and the plane started smoking. We were heading toward the cliff edge of Orote Peninsula. I had to pull up to avoid the cliff, so I did not see whether this plane crashed or not.

My guns quit again, and again I headed out of the fight until I managed to get one of them working. At that moment, I spotted one of our Hellcats, which was only about 200 feet over the water, with a Zero on its tail. The Hellcat was in a bad way. I had only one gun working, but I managed to shoot a few pieces off the Zero and run him off of the Hellcat, which, it turned out, was flown by Lieutenant (jg) Bill Levering, a night-fighter pilot from my ship.

After that, I fired at many more Val dive-bombers and Zero fighters. I knocked pieces from some and caused others to burn, but none of them was seen to crash. When all my guns became permanently inoperative, I headed out of the fight and toward the open sea. I then realized that my canopy was shot up, there were several holes in my wings from both ground fire and from the Val that exploded, my goggles were gone, my radio was out, the cylinder-head temperature was high, and oil was all over my cowling and windshield. I found out later that there were over 100 holes in my aircraft.

I was beginning to wonder how—or if—I was going to get back to my carrier when a VF-2 Hellcat joined up on me. I quickly gave him the lead and, by hand code, told him to lead me home. The pilot was Ensign Jack Vaughan, and I was never happier to see anyone than I was to see him at that time.

When I returned to the carrier, Lieutenant (jg) Elliott had already arrived, so the crew knew what had happened. Elliott had seen most of the action and had already made his official report. My gun-camera pictures confirmed four of my victories before the camera jammed. For this action, I was recommended for the Congressional Medal of Honor by Admiral Mitscher, but I was awarded the Navy Cross.

*Spider Webb was given credit for 6 Vals destroyed and 2 Vals probably destroyed on June 19, 1944. On September 22, 1944, he destroyed an Imperial Army Ki-61 Tony fighter over Corregidor, for a grand total of 7 air-to-air victories and 2 probables. He is also credited with 2 assists and the single-handed destruction of a Japanese 500-ton cargo ship.*

*In 1946, Lieutenant Spider Webb voluntarily resigned his commission and reverted to his permanent enlisted rate, chief aviation pilot. He retired from the Navy in November 1958 as a lieutenant, his highest commissioned rank.*

# A VERY FINE DAY FOR FLYING

Lieutenant (jg) BUCK DUNGAN, USN
VF(N)-76 (USS *Hornet*)
Orote Field, Guam, June 19, 1944

*After being turned away repeatedly by the Navy flight program—even though he had been licensed to fly by the Civilian Pilot Training program—Fred LeRoy Dungan, a native of Pasadena, California, and a mechanical-engineering student at Pasadena Junior College, was instantly signed up on December 8, 1941. He was ordered to active duty on February 12, 1942. Ensign Dungan was commissioned at Corpus Christi on November 13, 1942, and assigned directly to night-fighter training at Quonset Point, Rhode Island, where he worked at developing operational radar and night-fighter tactics.*

*Dungan was an original member of VF(N)-76, the Navy's first Hellcat-equipped night-fighter squadron, and he trained with the new unit until it was ordered to the war zone. Once in the Pacific, in January 1944, VF(N)-76 was broken up into four five-man four-plane flights and assigned out to four fleet carriers. Dungan's flight went aboard Captain Joseph "Jocko" Clark's* Yorktown *and was transferred to the* Hornet *with Clark when Clark was promoted to rear admiral and given command of Task Group 58.1. At the time, Clark was virtually the only carrier admiral who supported the night-fighter program, and he made certain that his night-detachment pilots were given ample opportunity to cut their teeth on day as well as night missions.*

*Lieutenant (jg) Buck Dungan's first aerial victory was a Betty bomber. He destroyed it on April 23, 1944, while the* Hornet *night-fighter detachment was calibrating its radar during a daylight check flight off the coast of New Guinea.*

On the afternoon of June 19, 1944, Air Group 2 was assigned to conduct a strike against Orote Field, Guam. Thanks to Admiral Clark's support, the night detachment was assigned to man a four-plane day-fighter division attached to the VF-2 strike escort. At the last moment, one of our fighters would not start, so we went out as a threesome. Lieutenant Russ Reiserer was leading, and Lieutenant (jg) Bill Levering and I were on his wings.

The airplane to which I had been assigned for that mission was a brand-new Hellcat that belonged to the commander of Air Group 2. It was painted Navy blue and lacquered, and it had camera gear in the belly. All you had to do to operate the camera was point the left wing at the target and press the trigger on the throttle.

The flying conditions that afternoon were perfect. It was warm and clear with puffy, broken clouds at around 7,000 feet. It was a very fine day for flying.

After the dive-bombers and torpedo bombers made their runs on the field and flew off to rendezvous for the return flight, the VF-2 fighters went in to strafe. During my last recovery, as I pulled up low over the runway, I noticed many Japanese airplanes in revetments under the trees. In the hangars, there appeared to be many 55-gallon drums, which I assumed to be aviation gasoline. I wasn't in position to take pictures just then so, while we were re-forming, I told Russ Reiserer that I had cameras in my airplane and asked if I could make another run on the field to take some reconnaissance pictures. Russ said, "Okay," and Bill Levering said, "I'll stay with him."

Bill and I climbed up to about 10,000 feet and positioned ourselves over the northeast end of the runway. That would place the revetments I had seen to my port side, the side to which the cameras were aimed.

We dove straight down to build up as much speed as we could. I wanted to flash down the runway, downwind, and take my pictures as quickly as possible. On the way down, I was hit in the starboard guns by what appeared to be 37mm AA fire. But I kept going and pulled out only inches over the runway.

On my way down the runway, I strafed the AA battery that had hit my Hellcat. It was on the starboard side, toward the water. Then I pressed the camera trigger and hoped that I was taking pictures of the airplanes in the revetments.

At the end of the runway was a cliff overlooking the water.

Instead of pulling up, I led Bill down over the cliff and recovered over the water a couple of miles out. As we were climbing out, I could see where my track had been during the dive; it was just two long strings of black AA puffs.

As I was climbing back through around 6,500 feet to set up for another camera run, I looked back down at the field. There was no more AA coming up at us, but that wasn't because we had knocked it out. It was because a Japanese carrier air group was breaking up in the landing pattern. The whole formation was circling counterclockwise into the wind, and several flights of bombers were peeling off and going in to land.

I got on the radio and yelled and screamed that a whole Japanese air group was landing on the field we had just hit. I said "Orote Field," but someone radioed back, "Understand Rota Field," which was another island base that bombers from other air groups were striking at around the same time. I radioed back, "No! O-ro-te Field! Guam."

While the exchange on the radio was going on, I had turned to Bill and pointed down. He had already seen what I had seen, so we just dove down into the landing pattern. I wanted to break up their formation by flying head-on into them.

As we approached the bombers, I looked back over my shoulder. Bill was beside me and, behind him, it looked like hundreds of Zeros were coming down right on us. Luckily, the Zeros did not go down through their own bomber formation, so they didn't get through to Bill and me.

Only three of my port guns were working smoothly, and one of the starboard three, which had been hit during the photo run by the AA, was working intermittently. I wasn't too much of a threat to the Japanese bombers, though I suppose I *looked* very threatening.

The first plane I saw was a Kate torpedo bomber. It was on the base leg, just about to final letdown. I led it very slightly from dead ahead and let my tracers trail back toward it, into his wing root. I had some trouble holding my tracers on the Kate because of the uneven recoil caused by the loss of my starboard guns. The Hellcat skewed to the left, but I held it steady by applying quite a bit of right rudder. The Kate blew up just in front of me, and I flew through the explosion. I felt the heat through my canopy.

I was worried about the Zeros I had seen, so I dove down toward the water and zoomed back up, but I never saw a Zero. By the time I recovered, most of the bombers had disappeared. I pulled up and made a run back down the field to be certain no one had landed. If someone had landed, I was going to strafe him. I did see what appeared to be a Zero taxiing out to take off, and I gave him a short burst. I saw the airplane start to smoke. Just as I flashed over the top of the airplane, the pilot jumped out and started running toward the palm trees bordering the runway.

I pulled up and around and went out to sea, where I noticed three Zeros that had a Hellcat pinned to the surface. I guessed it must have been Bill Levering. Every time they made a run on him, he made an evasive move, turning as sharply as he could. But they wouldn't let him climb out. Every time he tried to gain altitude, they bounced him. As I approached, the Zeros broke off and disappeared, but that might have been because other Hellcats had arrived and were coming after them too.

About then, tracers flashed past my cockpit. A Zero was closing in on me, and I made what I consider to be the finest evasion maneuver ever developed—a slow full-power climbing turn to the left. As my speed dropped from an initial 180 miles per hour, the Zero continued to close on me, but the pilot couldn't cut inside my turn to bring his guns to bear ahead of my plane. He fired a lot and I could feel some hits in the tail, but he couldn't lead me enough to get hits into my cockpit or engine.

We made two or three circles on the way up toward 5,000 feet. As I continued to climb and turn as efficiently as possible, I slowed to about 115 miles per hour and faked the Japanese pilot into making a tighter turn than his airplane could manage. He spun out, and I executed a controlled spin to try to come down on top of him. He was about to cross my line of fire about 1,000 feet away, which was perfect for our boresighting pattern. I could see him approaching the optimum point in my gunsight, but I had to apply forward pressure on the stick, which threw me upside down. I had time to give him just one short burst as he passed through the perfect spot. I guess it was perfect. In spite of my Hellcat's tendency to skid to the left from the uneven recoil, every round I fired looked like it was going right into the cockpit. I lost track of him for a second and, when I had him again, his airplane had resumed normal flight—a powered gliding turn toward Orote Field.

The airplane looked like it was traveling without a pilot. It seemed to be rigged for cross-country flying, with the trim tabs set to fly the plane straight and level without pilot intervention. I'm sure my gunfire into the cockpit had killed the pilot, and the Zero was definitely headed down. However, I couldn't claim it as a kill because two other Hellcats jumped on the plane and torched it before it hit the water.

I saw another Zero about a mile ahead. It was pulling up and away from me, so I applied full throttle and went after it. I chased it at full power, but the Zero was still about a mile ahead when it went into a cloud bank. Before I could close into the cloud, the plane came out. It was upside down and firing at me. I could see that the 7.7mm machine guns were blinking rapidly and the 20mm cannon were doing so more slowly, but I didn't see any tracer passing me.

Well, I was so frightened I didn't know whether to pull up or down or what to do. I eased back on my throttle very slightly and dropped my nose a little bit, but I couldn't do anything else. If I'd have pulled up and over the Zero, the pilot would have had a shot at my belly. And, if I'd have tried to dive away from him, he'd have been able to execute a split-S and get on my tail. So, we just maintained our headings toward one another. I thought I'd maybe bluff him out. We passed so closely I could recognize the features on his face. We were just a few feet apart when we passed.

I pulled up into an extremely tight vertical turn and chopped my throttle to kill speed so I could get around quickly. He was going much faster than me, so it took him longer to get back around. As he pulled through a left-hand turn, I got a 90-degree deflection shot on him—it closed to 45 degrees as I turned—and I could see my tracer passing close by his airplane. I eventually got on his tail and threw a fast shot into him. He chopped his throttle and headed for the water in a diving follow-through to his continuing left-hand turn. He kept turning to the left and went all the way down to within a few feet of the surface.

I pulled up alongside of him and closed my throttle off tightly. In fact, I even hit my landing-gear control to trail them to slow me down. We were both in a vertical bank, and I was just about 50 feet from his cockpit. His canopy was open and he was throwing books and maps and what looked like secret papers out of the cockpit. He might have been the air-group commander, getting rid of anything that might be helpful to us. He looked like he might have been wounded by my last burst.

He looked over and saw me and made a motion with his hand that I took to be a salute. Right then, his wingtip caught the water and he plunged in and cartwheeled.

I couldn't claim that Zero, either, because another Hellcat had come up on his tail and was firing at him while I was flying abreast. The other pilot had the Zero's last moments on his gun-camera film.

Alone, I went straight back to the *Hornet* and landed. I then learned how much damage Bill Levering's plane had sustained in his tangle with the three Zeros over the water. His Hellcat was so shot up that he had to land aboard the *Hornet* with wheels and flaps up. Somehow he got his hook down and stopped the plane. As soon as he climbed out, they dropped his Hellcat over the side. A little later, the film I took of Orote Field was developed. It showed that there were indeed many airplanes and war goods stored all around the field. That night, they sent the battleships and cruisers in to shell the area. I heard that the whole place just erupted as a fuel or ammunition dump was hit.

*In the end, Buck Dungan was credited with the Kate and 1 of the 2 Zeros he is certain he shot down. That brought his score to 3 victories. His last direct confrontation with Japanese aircraft was over Chichi Jima, in the Bonin Islands, before dawn on July 4, 1944. On that mission, while flying a F6F-3N Hellcat night fighter, he shot down 4 Nakajima A6M2-N Zero-type Rufe float fighters, bringing his overall score to 7.*

*Due to a slow recovery from wounds he sustained on July 4, Dungan returned to the U.S. in October 1944. He spent some time in the hospital and then trained night-fighter pilots at*

*Quonset Point well into the summer of 1945. He was among the first Navy pilots to be demobilized at the end of the war.*

In all on June 19, 1944, U.S. Navy carrier pilots and gunners were credited with 380 confirmed air-to-air victories. Gunfire from ships destroyed an additional 18 Japanese attackers over the U.S. fleet.

Any hopes the Imperial Navy had harbored of ever again fielding a world-class carrier air arm were dashed irrevocably in just that one day's bloodbath. When Task Force 58 counterattacked the Japanese fleet the next day, July 20, matters went from bad to worse. By the time the day was over, 3 Japanese fleet carriers had been sunk and scores of additional Japanese warplanes had been lost, including 42 destroyed in the air by U.S. carrier warplanes.

# CHAPTER 12

The Japanese fleet had been utterly defeated on June 19 and 20. All targets throughout the Marianas had been so utterly worked over that Vice Admiral Pete Mitscher decided to withdraw three of his four carrier task groups on July 21 for replenishment at Eniwetok. As the plan was being promulgated, Rear Admiral Jocko Clark asked to be released to strike the Bonins again with his Task Group 58.1. Mitscher agreed. He left Task Group 58.4 to guard the fleet in the Marianas and sent the aggressive Clark merrily on his way to the Bonins.

## NIGHT HECKLER

**Lieutenant (jg) JOHN DEAR, USN**
**VF(N)-76 (USS *Hornet*)**
**Chichi Jima, July 4, 1944**

*John William Dear, Jr., quit Mississippi College and enlisted in the Navy V-5 flight program at the end of his sophomore year, soon after he heard of the Japanese attack on Pearl Harbor. Trained at Corpus Christi, Texas, Dear earned his wings and commission on April 10, 1943. After a quick stop at home in Meridian, Mississippi, to marry his childhood sweetheart, he proceeded to operational training in F4Fs at Melbourne, Florida. During Dear's stay at Melbourne, his application for the new night-fighter training program was approved. Upon graduation, he was sent to Quonset Point, Rhode Island, to help form VF(N)-76, the first night-Hellcat squadron to be deployed on carriers in the Pacific.*

*It was while flying a daytime scramble in the Bonins, on June 24, 1944, that Lieutenant (jg) John Dear achieved his first victories: 3 B5N Kate torpedo bombers he shot out of a formation of 18 that was attacking Task Group 58.1.*

Following a four-day stay in Eniwetok while the ships refueled and replenished, we sailed back to the Bonins—the Jocko Jimas, as we called them. We reached the Bonins again on July 3, 1944, and the first strikes were launched against Iwo Jima. One of our night-detachment pilots, Lieutenant (jg) Tom Cunningham, went along with the VF-2 fighter escort. It was a long flight—290 miles—and in the ensuing fracas, Tom got 3 Zekes and a probable. He was our last virgin. But he also got some flak in his left leg. Fortunately, it was not too serious, and he was out of action for only a week or so.

The next morning, the fireworks really began, and rightly so—it was the Fourth of July. Four of us—Lieutenant Russ Reiserer, Lieutenant (jg) Bill Levering, Lieutenant (jg) Buck Dungan, and I—were launched at 0400 on a predawn heckler mission to Chichi Jima. The objective was primarily to badger the enemy and keep the Japanese upset for a few hours before the strike force arrived. We each carried a 500-pound bomb, and our assignment was to harass, draw fire, and determine the extent of Japanese air strength. Also, since our intelligence reports were skimpy at best, we were to determine the size and description of the ships in the harbor.

The latter was particularly important, for the size of the ships would dictate the loads for the bombers and torpedo planes. For example, because of the cost and the complexity of torpedoes, they were used only on merchant vessels of 10,000 tons or more or on certain types of warships. Then there were some ships that required special armor-piercing bombs, and so on.

The task force was about a hundred miles southeast of the island. There were no clouds, but the skies were black and moonless. As usual, after being catapulted from the carrier, we joined up in two two-plane sections and stayed together in tight formation until we reached the island. I was flying on Buck Dungan's wing.

Chichi Jima is a rather dome-shaped volcanic formation with a small teacup-shaped harbor in the northwest side. The harbor had a relatively small entrance and was completely surrounded by sheer and tall cliffs. As we approached the island at 10,000 feet, we could make out its shape and the harbor, but there was no way to tell what was waiting for us.

Russ Reiserer and Bill Levering broke off and headed for what we were told was a seaplane base on the east side of the island. They started their strafing runs on the seaplane base right away, while Buck and I were still headed for the harbor. The enemy started shooting, and I was awed by the antiaircraft fire, which was liberally spaced with tracers and looked like the Fourth of July fireworks at the local park. The tracers came from several directions, but they all converged on a point about 2,000 feet over the island. It looked like a Fourth of July fireworks display forming the shape of an Indian tepee.

The Japanese evidently had no radar aiming devices, so they were firing in patterns when they heard our engines, apparently hoping that we would be picked off as we flew through. I was stunned and amazed at the amount of firepower on display. Streams of multicolored tracer-illuminated ammunition spewed from hundreds of guns of all sizes like from so many fire hoses. I wasn't frightened, but I should have been; they could have gotten a lucky hit.

After making the first run through the antiaircraft fire, Buck and I split up because it was futile to try to get back together in the dark. We just kept in touch by radio, periodically giving our approximate location and describing what we were doing. We would wait to take our turn when we were sure the other Hellcat had cleared the target area. Our runs were made as close to the deck as possible because we felt our chances of having more than one gun trained on us at a time were nil. Our night fighters were equipped with radio altimeters, which gave us an audible warning at 50 feet and again at 25 feet, so flying near the deck in the dark was easy and we were well trained to do so. We couldn't really see anything except the black, starry sky; the black ground; and white and yellow tracers of all sizes. Usually, we fired only the two outer pairs of our .50-caliber machine guns, which did not have tracers. This was to help us maintain our night vision. Only the inboard pair of guns in each night fighter had tracers.

We did not make continuous runs, but spaced them out at about 10-minute intervals. We just wanted to keep them busy, not inflict any damage. In fact, I made a couple of runs without even firing a shot.

We ate up an hour just pestering them. Then things got kind of quiet. Except for occasional ack-ack, it seemed like the whole mission was going to be a piece of cake. We had been told that there was no airfield, so we did not expect any air opposition.

There were a number of ships anchored in the harbor. Even in the darkness, I could see by their luminescent wakes that they were steaming out to sea at flank speed. Most of them were cargo ships and tankers. The cove was too small for large warships, but there were destroyers or destroyer escorts, which I could identify because of our continual training on the subject. I still had my 500-pound bomb, which I had saved until I could find a worthwhile target. When I spotted what I took to be a couple of warships hightailing it out of the cove, I figured I had found my meat.

From my station at 4,000 to 5,000 feet, I pushed over on a destroyer escort and flattened out my dive about 1,000 yards abeam so I could make a masthead run right on the water, from directly astern of her. As I closed in to about 1,000 yards, she began a steep turn away from me, firing everything she had. I sprayed her with all six of my .50-caliber machine guns. I had even switched on my inboard guns, the only ones with tracers. I do not know if any of their shots hit me, but I do know that I sprayed her decks pretty good. I could see my rounds raking her.

I had practiced bombing dozens of times, so when I tried to release my 500-pound bomb from 50 yards, I knew my range was right. Just as I reached the drop point, I pressed the bomb-release thumb switch on my control stick. The bomb did not release. I pressed the thumb switch again, but the two or three additional seconds it took me to spring the bomb caused me to miss the target by a couple of hundred feet. As I pulled up and did a slight wingover, I looked back and saw the bomb explode harmlessly in the water. I was really pissed! I had thought I had myself a Japanese ship all my own.

Before I could get around to make another run on the destroyer, I heard Buck's excited voice on the radio calling for help. He said he had Japanese planes on his tail and he could not shake them. When he told me his approximate location—he was to the east of the harbor—I immediately turned in that direction and told him to head for the harbor. My heart sank a little when he told me he was at 10,000 feet. I was practically on the deck. I knew it would take some time to get up there.

I gave that little Hellcat all she had and, at the same time, I thought, "I wonder where those planes came from?" The light was getting better, but the sun was not yet bright. It was not too long before I spotted Buck making evasive turns and leading a snake dance of at least three little float fighters.

Float fighters! They were Nakajima A6M2-N fighters, floatplane versions of the Mitsubishi Zero we called Rufes. Fortunately, they were hobbled by the floats and could not maneuver as well as regular Zekes. As we found out much later, they didn't carry the armament of regular Zekes, either.

Buck was taking frantic evasive action when I spotted him. He must have seen me at the same time, because he pushed over and headed in my direction. As we passed in opposite directions, I had perfect head-on shots at his pursuers, and they were caught completely by surprise.

They were coming head-on at me but evidently did not see me. I still had all my gun switches on from my run on the can. I just fired, using my reflector gunsight with almost no deflection. With two three- or four-second bursts from my guns, about five seconds apart, two of them exploded in flames right before my eyes. They disintegrated before me. Before I could get my sights on the Rufe, it turned away.

What followed was a classic dogfight, like I had seen as a child in the movies. It was sheer bedlam. Buck and I should have joined up so we could scissor them as we had been trained, but there was no time to think things through. Buck and I had each other in sight most of the time, and we were talking constantly on the radio. The Rufes were no match for us, and we chased them all over the sky—in and out and around clouds, straight up and straight down.

Light scud clouds had formed since we arrived over Chichi, and I watched as Buck chased a Rufe through one. I headed for the other side of the cloud and, when the Rufe popped out, I picked him off just as he broke clear. I think I surprised him; he made no effort to maneuver. I had a nice, easy quarter-deflection shot, and he burst into flames.

One Rufe that I followed in a dive flew through his own antiaircraft from the ground and exploded. In the meantime, Buck had burned four more. I could see a couple of smoke trails from some of his kills.

All of a sudden, things got quiet. We could not find any more planes. We figured we had gotten them all. Dawn was just beginning to break, and in the dim light the harbor became clearer. Ships of every type were steaming out to sea. We decided not to try to join up but, instead, to record those ships and transmit the information back to the fleet. Our UHF radios were too limited in range to carry on any conversation with the carriers, so, as always, we were busy writing down everything we saw on the notepads we had strapped to our legs. Buck told me he was east of the cove and, since I was to the west, we decided to keep that interval by making slow and wide counterclockwise circles.

Suddenly, to my left, I saw a flash of light. I turned to see what it was, but I saw only the sun, which was just breaking over the horizon. I did not think much of it, but, a few seconds later, I looked out in horror as my Hellcat's wings were being ripped to shreds by bullets. I had done a stupid thing; I had let a Japanese fighter slip up behind me, and he was shooting the hell out of me.

Among other things, he punctured my oil line, and hot oil

was spewing over my cowl—and me! Instinctively, I pushed over into a vertical dive. The smell of the hot oil caused me to think that I was on fire—something every pilot dreaded more than anything else.

The only escape from a burning plane was to bail out, so I rolled back the canopy in preparation for a jump. Parachute jumps in themselves are not dangerous, but my chances of ever hitting the ground alive were practically nil because of the enemy planes and antiaircraft fire around.

The air-suction forces in that dive with the canopy open were enormous, and my helmet, which I foolishly had neglected to fasten, was sucked right off my head and into the Chichi Jima sky. Along with it went my headphones and my ability to communicate.

I then realized that I was not on fire, so I closed the hatch and wrestled the plane into a left-turn pullout. I had been told many times that Japanese planes were not as structurally sound as ours, and that they probably could not make a pullout against the fierce engine torque in a dive. As I strained out of that screaming dive, I looked back briefly— in time to see my pursuer breaking up. Although I did not watch him all the way, I am sure he never survived the trip.

Now, I was alone again—and I mean *alone*. I had no way of communicating with Buck or with the fleet. I could not use the radio homing gear to find my way back to the ship. And I was losing oil at an alarming rate.

I pulled out the chartboard tray that was under my instrument panel and stared at it as though I had never seen it before. The fact was, as much as I had worked with it in ground school and during squadron exercises, I had never before had to depend on it in an emergency. I wished that I had put more information on it during the preflight briefing and that I had been more careful marking down the data I had recorded.

I nervously spun the round plastic grid until it gave me a heading to Point X-ray, the spot in the huge Pacific Ocean where the task group was supposed to be. It was nearly 200 miles away, which meant well over 30 minutes of flying that crippled airplane. I did not know if I could make it—even if my heading was right. But I had no choice, so I pointed the nose in the direction I had calculated and I prayed.

I swear that flight seemed longer than the eight-hour butt bruiser I had endured over the fleet in the Marianas. It was one of the very few times I can remember being really uptight and anxious about a situation during the whole time I flew with the Navy. I felt so helpless—questionable navigation, no radio, and a plane that was full of holes, leaking oil, and running like a secondhand school bus.

Then I saw them: little black spots on the horizon a million miles away. Why wouldn't that crate go any faster? What if it was the wrong fleet? What if the wheels and flaps would not come down? What if I did not get there?

As I got closer, I could make out *Hornet, Yorktown, Bataan,* and the other ships in Task Group 58.1. My heart picked up a beat. I was going to make it. Or was I? When I got over *Hornet,* I could tell she was not spotted for landing. Oh, well, I could put it down in the water, although the idea did not appeal to me.

I noticed that the signalman on *Hornet*'s bridge was focused on me with his blinker. He was feverishly sending me a message. Each ship had a code name for communication purposes. As I circled the ship with that blinker winking at me, I again had to brush away the cobwebs to recall cadet school, at which we had read blinker messages until our heads felt like they were exploding.

I made out one word loud and clear: C-O-A-L. I did not need any more. Coal Base was *Yorktown.* She was several hundred yards away, and she was spotted for landing.

I made a tight turn onto *Yorktown*'s downwind leg and dropped wheels and flaps. Thank God they worked! As I turned into the final groove, I saw one of my best buddies waving the flags—Lieutenant Richard "Dog" Tripp. I even thought I saw that devilish smile on Dog's face as he gave me the cut.

Just as I hit the deck and caught the wire, my engine expired. I could not even taxi out of the gear. Up on the bridge, I could see Captain Ralph Jennings flashing a big smile and giving me the thumbs-up sign. When I held up three fingers, the whole bridge burst into applause.

The plane handlers pushed me out of the gear, and I went below to the fighter squadron's ready room. There I found that Buck Dungan had landed shortly before me with a bullet in his shoulder. I immediately went down to the sick bay to check on him. Buck had been sedated, and they were preparing to remove the slug, so I did not have a chance to talk to him. I later learned that the same thing happened to him that had happened to me. Only difference was, when Buck learned he was being followed, he made a sharp turn to the left. As a result, one of the 7.7mm rounds missed his armored seat back and shattered his clavicle.

The next day, July 5, Russ Reiserer flew over to *Yorktown* in a TBM and flew Buck's Hellcat back to *Hornet*. By then, my plane was patched up enough to fly—even though it had over a hundred holes in it—so I flew it back alongside Russ.

About a year later, I was standing officer of the day in the hangar at Vero Beach, Florida, when two replacement Hellcat night trainers were brought in by ferry pilots. The logbooks were turned over for me to sign. When I saw the number of one of the trainers, something clicked. It should have; I had written it on flight plans and yellow sheets many times. While the pilot looked on in dismay, I ran down to the flight line and looked up under the starboard wheel well, where I knew there was a bullet hole. It was still there. The Navy had brought my old Fourth of July plane halfway around the world to use as a trainer.

*Lieutenant (jg) John Dear finished off the Fourth of July heckler mission with 6 confirmed victories. He did not claim the Rufe he chased into Japanese antiaircraft fire or the one that probably fell apart following him into a tight diving turn. In addition to Dear's 3 confirmed Rufes, Lieutenant (jg) Buck Dungan was credited with 4 confirmed Rufes.*

*Through the summer, Dear continued to fly night patrols, night heckler missions, and daytime strikes from Task Force 58.1. On September 22, 1944, on the* Hornet *night detachment's last scheduled combat hop before rotation home, Dear scored his seventh and last victory, a B6N Jill torpedo bomber east of Manila Bay. Ironically, though he got some shots in at several Japanese aircraft at night, all of Dear's kills were scored in daylight.*

*Lieutenant John Dear finished out the war training night-*

*fighter pilots at Vero Beach, Florida, and he left the Navy in January 1946 to complete his education at the University of Texas.*

July and August 1944 were slack months for the U.S. Navy carrier task forces. They pushed the Japanese around beyond the rim of the Marianas, but the Japanese didn't push back.

The end of the Solomons and Bismarcks campaigns left Marine aviation with virtually nothing to do. There was no action in the South Pacific after Rabaul was abandoned, and the Marine squadrons sent to garrison newly liberated island bases in the Central Pacific found slim pickings on the many bypassed bastions nearby. In all of March 1944, Marine fighters accounted for 17 Japanese warplanes in just five incidents. In April 1944, there were only 2 Japanese Bettys destroyed by Marines in one action near Eniwetok, and only 1 Marine night-fighter victory in all of May. This was followed by 1 Marine victory in June; none in July, August, or September; and 1 in October 1944.

The 5th Air Force was moderately busy through the summer of 1944. Since the fall of Hollandia, the main Japanese supply base in New Guinea, MacArthur's leapfrog amphibious advance toward the Philippines was relentless and smooth. The Japanese resisted as well as they could, but they were thoroughly outclassed. By August, the 5th Air Force fighter squadrons had to vie for very few targets. There was action on only five days the whole month, and only 15 Japanese planes were brought down—8 on one day. September 1944 was busier, but in eight action days, 5th Air Force pilots downed only 12 Japanese, and they had to fly all the way to Borneo on September 30 to get 3 of them.

The Navy used the hiatus to reorganize. The end of the Solomons and Bismarcks campaigns had left one of the nation's most aggressive and proven admirals—Bill Halsey—with nothing worthwhile to do. So, Admiral Nimitz established the platoon system for running future fast-carrier campaigns. On September 11 Halsey replaced Raymond Spruance as the fleet commander, changed the designation of the 5th Fleet to the 3d Fleet, and replaced Spruance's top subordinates with his own. The Fast Carrier Task Force became Task Force 38, and so on down the line. All of Mitscher's chief subordinates were replaced. While

Halsey was running the fleet, Spruance, Mitscher, and company would be resting and planning future operations. Eventually, everyone would swap jobs again.

Task Force 38 ranged around MacArthur's objective, the Central Philippines, and found no worthy opposition. Then it traveled farther north, striking Manila Bay and former U.S. bases such as Clark Field. The opposition was stiffer, but there was really no contest.

Ulithi Atoll fell on September 23. Work to turn its perfect lagoon into another advance fleet anchorage soon began. The Palaus were invaded on September 15 to support the upcoming Central Philippines invasion.

Several small islands just off Leyte were to be the initial targets of MacArthur's October 17 amphibious assault in the Central Philippines. Leyte itself was to be invaded on October 20. To help divert Japanese attention, Task Force 38 struck far and wide. On October 10, carrier air hit Okinawa for the first time, and raids against Formosa began on October 12. On that day alone, Task Force 38 pilots destroyed 224 Japanese aircraft in the air, and they downed 37 more on October 13. Though the Japanese attempted to strike back on October 14 with a force of 40 D4Y Judy dive-bombers escorted by Ki-61 Tony fighters, no U.S. warship was damaged and most of the strike aircraft were downed. In all, on October 14, Task Force 38 warplanes downed 92 Japanese aircraft over and around Formosa.

The invasion of Leyte triggered a preplanned Japanese response that crystallized into the Battle of Leyte Gulf. In the opening move, on October 24, 1944, U.S. Navy submarines located one of three Japanese surface battle forces closing on Leyte. Halsey attacked with everything he had.

# ADRIFT

## Commander FRED BAKUTIS, USN
## VF-20 (USS *Enterprise*)
## Sulu Sea, October 24–30, 1944

*Fred Edward Bakutis was born on November 4, 1912, in Brockton, Massachusetts. He graduated from the U.S. Naval Academy with the Class of 1935 and served at sea until 1938, when he was permitted to attend flight school. He graduated from Pensacola in February 1939 and flew dive-bombers for two years aboard the USS* Saratoga. *On December 7, 1941, Lieutenant Bakutis was at Annapolis to begin a postgraduate course in aeronautical engineering. The course was disbanded, and he was assigned with the rest of his classmates to inspect catapults being installed in escort carriers. He served as executive officer of VF-16 for a year. Then he was reassigned to form VF-20 at North Island, San Diego, just before VF-16 shipped out for combat duty.*

*Commander Bakutis's first victories were against a pair of Tojo fighters on October 12, 1944, over Ein Ansho Airfield, Formosa. On October 15, he damaged an Oscar on a morning mission over Manila. That afternoon, he destroyed 2 Jill torpedo bombers, damaged a Zeke fighter, and shared credit for destroying a Dinah reconnaissance bomber over the fleet. Next, on October 18, Bakutis achieved ace status when he destroyed a Tojo fighter and shared credit for destroying an Oscar fighter over Clark Field.*

On the morning of October 24, 1944, two search teams consisting of six SB2C dive-bombers and six F6F fighters were launched from *Enterprise* to locate a formation of Japanese warships reported to be in the Sulu Sea, approaching the Philippines. I was leading the fighters on one of those teams. I was the senior pilot.

We were on a search leg of about 280 degrees from the *Enterprise,* out to 320 nautical miles. We were about to turn back with no sightings when one of the SB2Cs sighted a formation of seven Japanese warships consisting of two *Fuso*-class battleships, one *Mogami*-class heavy cruiser, and four destroyers. The ships were approximately 70 miles southwest of Negros Island, steaming northeast.

We decided to attack, so our two search teams joined up. Our search altitude was about 2,000 feet, so we climbed in circles to about 12,000 feet. While we were doing so, the battleships were firing at us with broadsides of their main batteries. We could see the blasts of nine 14-inch guns from each battleship. Then we waited to see where the rounds would explode. They were using multicolored bursts for identification of their own batteries. We held our breaths and prayed between the blast of the guns until the airbursts detonated nearby. The fireworks were spectacular but not appreciated by us. Fortunately, none of the detonations hit any of our planes.

When we got to about 12,000 feet, we attacked the enemy force in a conventional, coordinated manner, concentrating on the two battleships and the heavy cruiser. The SB2Cs made vertical dives, and we fighters went in at about 45 degrees just ahead of the bombers so we could release rockets from about 2,000 feet. We were using 3.5-inch HVARs—high-velocity aerial rockets—with 5-inch heads. My wingman, Ensign Frank Gallagher, and I made our rocket attack on one of the battleships to neutralize the AA for the bombers. We then pulled out to the southwest of the main body of ships at low altitude.

A destroyer was directly ahead of me on pullout. The ship was shooting at me. I made the decision to shoot at it instead of pulling away. I opened fire at 700 feet with all six of my .50-caliber wing guns. As I passed over the destroyer at about 300 feet, still firing, my engine was hit, probably by 25mm AA.

The engine immediately began to smoke and lose oil. I turned southwest to get as far away from the Japanese ships as possible. As I did, I noticed that the oil gauge registered "0." The engine ran smoothly for another minute, then lost power and soon froze. I broadcast my difficulty and heard Ensign James Shingler reply, "We're all for you,.Skipper," which boosted my morale considerably. There was no wind as I dropped my belly tank and set down, headed south, on a smooth sea at 80 knots with my wheels up and my flaps down. I was between two and three miles from the Japanese force. It was a good landing; the shock was no more severe than in the case of a normal carrier landing, but I was a little surprised at how quickly the cockpit filled with water.

Climbing out of the plane onto the right wing was no problem, even with my back pack and parachute still buckled on. The plane remained afloat for approximately one minute, which allowed me plenty of time to get organized. I was too busy to be panicky, but I neglected to grab my canteen and binoculars.

When I saw that the plane was about to sink, I somewhat reluctantly jumped into the water, unfastened my chest strap and inflated my life jacket. I then unbuckled my parachute, which was still buoyant, but hooked my arm through a strap, knowing that it would soon become water-logged. In trying to inflate my life raft, I had some difficulty with the $CO_2$ bottle, which was threaded the opposite way from what I expected. When the life raft was inflated, I fastened the parachute and back pack to it, took off my life jacket and fastened that to it, and climbed aboard on the second try. During that operation, I could see my F6F spiraling down through the clear water.

The other planes were still circling overhead. One of the SB2Cs dropped a two-man life raft, which broke apart on hitting the water. Some of the gear and a lot of dye marker spilled out. At first I was afraid that the dye marker might reveal my position to the Japanese ships. After the raft was dropped, I wished the circling friendly planes would go away; they were still drawing AA fire from the ships and there was shrapnel falling all around me. Also, I was afraid that they would reveal my position to the ships. However, I was relieved to see the pagoda masts disappearing over the horizon. I learned after the war that several of the ships were busy fighting fires from various hits.

I paddled over to the two-man raft and discovered that the $CO_2$ bottle had sheared off. But I found the pump in the oar compartment, pumped up the raft, and climbed in, tying the smaller raft to it. I gathered a number of articles from other compartments—a can of water, two containers of dye marker, a kneepad, and a map of the Visayan Islands.

I was too exhausted to recover other articles that I saw in the water.

Having satisfied themselves that I was well equipped for the sea voyage, the pilots of the circling planes started for the *Enterprise.* It was suddenly very peaceful and quiet.

Using the sea anchor of the one-man raft as a scoop, I bailed out both rafts and took inventory of my possessions. I found that I had practically everything that I would need to sustain me for quite a period of time.

A half hour later, a B-24 flew overhead from the southeast at high altitude. I fired three star shells and put out some dye marker. The crew answered my signal by dropping two more life rafts then proceeding northwest, toward Palawan. The first of the rafts was too far away to recover. The second one was fairly close, but my one-man raft came unfastened. By the time I had paddled back to pick it up, I was too tired to chase after the other B-24 raft. I decided there was no point being a hog and collecting a whole fleet of rubber rafts.

At this point, it seemed advisable to work out a definite plan of some kind. There appeared to be little hope of an early rescue, so I decided to settle down to a long cruise. According to a rough calculation, my position was 08 degrees 50 minutes North and 122 degrees 05 minutes East. I figured that I would drift in a southwesterly direction at approximately three to five knots. (This estimate of speed proved highly optimistic.) I hoped eventually to reach the islands at the south end of the Sulu Sea, some 150 miles distant.

I did not eat anything the first day, but I drank two swallows of water before going to sleep for the night. After restraining myself for a considerable period, in accordance with survival doctrine, I decided it was not worth the discomfort and urinated. The bailing cup came in handy for that purpose.

The first night was a pleasant one with a first half-moon and no rain. However, the bottom of the raft was too cool for comfort and I slept only spasmodically. I picked up an old coconut covered with barnacles, which I stowed away for possible future use.

I had had no survival training beyond lectures and the usual pamphlets. I had had a little experience in canoes and small rowboats, but that didn't make much difference in using a rubber boat. I was initially discouraged that I was not picked up right away, but I became resigned to making the best of things. I figured I was in for a long haul to Borneo.

### Second Day: Wednesday, October 25, 1944

At 0830—my regular Navy watch continued to run throughout the trip—two B-24s flew by, heading northwest toward Palawan. It was so quiet out there that I could hear them long before I could see them. They returned at approximately 1230, but they were too far away both times to see my signals.

I did not eat until noon, when I took a malted-milk tablet and two hard candies. The sea was very rough, soon causing me to become seasick. I vomited and felt better after that, but I became nauseated every time I attempted to do something in the boat. I found that eating fruit drops and chewing gum helped considerably in fighting off seasickness.

I kept looking for rescue planes all day. Occasionally, I either heard or saw a B-24, but they were all flying too high to see my mirror or flare signals. I slept a good part of the time and sipped water frequently. I opened the coconut, but it was putrid and the smell almost made me sick again. In the evening, I ate half of an apple I had brought along with me and three more hard candies. This, together with two gulps of water—mixed one-half fresh and one-half salt— made up my supper. I fished for a long time with the fishing tackle, but I had no luck. That night, it was colder and damper, with occasional light showers, but there was not enough rain to collect drinking water. Again, I slept spasmodically.

### Third Day: Thursday, October 26, 1944

A warm sun dried me out fairly early. Some more B-24s flew over at about 0930, but I could not attract their attention with dye marker and the mirror. They were at high altitude, so I did not expect much. At noon, they flew back toward Morotai, singly and at high altitude. Since the B-24s were still flying almost directly overhead, it was apparent that my drift was considerably less than I had anticipated.

I noticed that my hands and buttocks were beginning to get sore. The water was still rough and a good bit was shipped from time to time during the day. I took my usual rations for food until suppertime, when I caught a red-footed booby bird that was trying to alight. He landed on my head and I grabbed him by the legs. Then, after a few moments' tussle, I wrung his neck, cut off his head, and drained out nearly a cupful of blood, which I forced myself to drink with no little effort. I promptly vomited. Next, I cut off the breast meat for future use. From its craw I removed a small flying fish, which I ate. I threw the rest of the bird away. It smelled pretty bad. I tried eating part of the breast but could not get it down. I decided to use the rest as fish bait.

As evening drew on, I began watching the direction the birds were flying, having been told that they head for land. They disappeared in all directions.

That night was the same as the night before—occasional rains but not enough for drinking water. I tried cementing two sails together to form better protection from the weather. It stood up under a day of steady rain and then parted. I then used the parachute for a sail and cover.

## Fourth Day: Friday, October 27, 1944

Early on the fourth day, it poured hard for an hour. I collected water in both rafts from which I filled all my water cans and my life jacket, dumping the excess into the one-man raft, which I thereafter used as a water tender. At times, there was too much water in my one-man raft and I considered bailing part of it out to increase my speed of drift.

My hands were now badly soaked and very sore. I found I could do little with them until the sun dried them out some hours later. My buttocks were also sore from heat rash and sitting in water so much. I tried sleeping on my stomach with my rear end exposed to the sun, and I think this helped somewhat.

I tried fishing again, using the booby-bird meat for bait, but I had no luck. That evening, having become thoroughly discouraged with the fishing tackle, I tried scooping up minnows that were under the raft. I used the two-man raft container as a net. This method worked like a charm, for I found that I could catch eight to ten minnows whenever I felt hungry. I swallowed the smaller ones whole, but I cleaned those bigger than 1½ inches. After eight minnows, two small clumps of seaweed for salad, two pieces of candy, and plenty of water, I felt considerably refreshed.

After supper, I tried trolling for fish, but again had no luck. In order to make more room to stretch out in, I cut away the seats, one of which I later fashioned into a crude visor to shield my eyes from the glare. I also managed to lose the Verys star projector overboard.

That night was miserable. It rained almost steadily from 0200 until noon, but, in spite of being thoroughly drenched and cold, I slept through a good bit of the rain. My hands now felt as if they would drop off.

## Fifth Day: Saturday, October 28, 1944

The sun reappeared at noon and, by 1500, my clothes had pretty well dried out. I caught some minnows and seaweed, which I ate along with my usual fare. In my desperation, I rubbed some insect oil on my hands, which helped a little.

The weather remained clear until 0400 the following morning, when the usual downpour began. It lasted until 1000.

I put more insect oil on my hands.

## Sixth Day: Sunday, October 29, 1944

The sun dried me out again. A large tuna jumped three feet out of the water four times as it chased some small flying fish. Six or seven B-24s—mostly singles—flew overhead, but I could not attract their attention. More minnows and seaweed helped to satisfy my hunger, but it was becoming increasingly difficult to get comfortable. It rained slightly that night, but not enough to disturb me particularly.

**Seventh Day: Monday, October 30, 1944**

Monday was a beautiful, hot, and uneventful day. Two more high-altitude B-24s flew over. My hands were a little better, but my buttocks were covered with small white blisters and terribly sore. I rigged a new large white sail and turned in.

It was a peaceful bright moonlit night. I was sleeping soundly when a growl of diesel engines made me start out of my sleep. Peering ahead, I saw what appeared to be a Japanese gunboat bearing down. I fumbled for my knife, slashed the parachute sail down, covered up, and stood by to jump overboard. As the vessel drew closer, I recognized it as a sub, and I was tremendously relieved to hear someone call "Ahoy!"

I called back, "American pilot. How's to pick me up?"

The sub, which turned out to be Commander Francis Greenup's *Hardhead*, came alongside and hauled me aboard about 2200. They had spotted my metal mast on their radar at the same time one of their lookouts spotted my white sail in the moonlight at about 300 yards. I climbed aboard looking like a monk because of my parachute-top bathrobe. They offered me soup, a sandwich, coffee, a shower, some whiskey, two pills, and a bunk. There was no doctor aboard, only a pharmacist's mate. I had no immersion problems, and no special medical attention was required.

It turned out that I had made only 50 miles during my raft trip.

I was aboard the *Hardhead* only one day. The following night, I was transferred off Manila to the *Angler*, which was commanded by my classmate, Commander Frank Hess. I was aboard the *Angler* for seven days, until she docked in Perth, Australia, to take on supplies and give her crew some leave. I proceeded by various airplanes to Pearl Harbor and then back out to rejoin the squadron, which was aboard the *Lexington* when I caught up on December 5, 1944.

*After returning to VF-20, Commander Bakutis destroyed a Kawanishi N1K George fighter on January 15, 1945, and shared credit for a Nakajima C6N Myrt reconnaissance plane on January 20, 1945. He thus ended the war with 7½ confirmed victories. Bakutis spent the last months of the war serving as the Bureau of Aeronautics fighter requirements officer. His duties included flying the Navy's first jet fighters.*

*Rear Admiral Fred Bakutis retired from the Navy in July 1969 following 34 years of service.*

The fast-carrier attack of October 24 amounted to a strike at the center of three Japanese battle forces. The result was the sinking of one Japanese battleship. The Japanese, in response, turned temporarily in their tracks. With that, Halsey moved the entire 3d Fleet to the north to take on another powerful force, which was built around several battleships and four aircraft carriers. Unbeknown to the Americans, however, the ships embarked only 114 warplanes among them. Halsey's new adversary was, in reality, a decoy.

Halsey's turn to the north to take on the decoy force exposed the U.S. Leyte invasion fleet to the wrath of two even stronger surface battle forces, which were driving in from the west and southwest. In the end, all that stood between the Japanese and a stunning victory was a small force of relatively light 7th Fleet surface warships—including PT boats!—that was tasked with guarding the transports. Also on hand was a force of tiny escort, or "jeep," aircraft carriers (CVEs) from which ground-support missions were being run against the invasion beaches.

The Japanese mounted a preliminary air strike from the north, straight in against the transports, at 0830, October 24.

## INSTANT ACE

**Lieutenant KEN HIPPE, USN**
**VC-3 (USS *Kalinin Bay*)**
**Leyte Gulf, October 24, 1944**

*Following his enlistment in the Navy Reserve at age twenty in late 1939, Kenneth George Hippe, a native of Burlington, Iowa, earned a pilot's license at his own expense in the Civilian Pilot Training program. He was called to active duty in November 1940, following his graduation from Bradley College, in Peoria, Illinois. Hippe served as a seaman aboard a Navy transport for several months, until his application for flight school was accepted. His training was accelerated due to his civilian experience, and he earned his wings on September 24, 1941. Ensign Hippe was assigned as a primary-flight instructor, and he served in that capacity until October 1943 at Pensacola; Philadelphia; and Pasco, Washington.*

*When finally ordered to the Fleet, Lieutenant Hippe found himself flying FM-2 fighters—the General Motors contract version of the Grumman F4F Wildcat—from* Kalinin Bay *(CVE-68), one of six jeep carriers composing Task Force 77.4 ("Taffy 1"). As a division leader with VC-3, Lieutenant Hippe flew numerous close-support and general ground-support missions during the Saipan and Peleliu battles, and endless hours on Combat Air Patrol over the Fleet.*

On the morning of October 24, 1944, my division of four FM-2 Wildcat fighters was on Combat Air Patrol at 10,000 feet, standing by for radar vectors in case any enemy aircraft showed up in the area. At about 0830, our radar people vectored us toward Leyte Gulf. They told us that a large flight of enemy aircraft was approaching from the northwest. When we reached Leyte Gulf, they told us to investigate a lone bogey approaching Leyte from the west. It turned out to be an Imperial Army Kawasaki Ki-48 twin-engine Lily light bomber. I made a high-side run on it and shot it down with my four .50-caliber wing guns. It turned out that he was a decoy, meant to draw us off from the main group of attacking planes, which was coming down in a dive over Lungi Point from 20,000 feet.

About the time I shot down the single Lily, Radar called again to say that a large bogey was approaching from the west, high up. We turned west and started to climb. The weather was clear that day, which made it easy to see the approaching Japanese formation. Shortly, we counted twenty-one Lilys flying in a vee-of-vees formation. They were all in a dive, headed for our ships in Leyte Gulf.

Being on a small jeep carrier, our primary mission was providing ground support for the troops ashore. We seldom had a chance to see Japanese planes, let alone get a chance to shoot at any. Being there at that moment made my whole eight months at sea worthwhile!

The Lilys appeared to be kamikaze planes. My wingman, Ensign John Buchanan, and I made one high-side run on their formation. I could see that there wasn't time to make successive runs, so I told Buchanan I was going to stay on their tails and shoot from there. I was so excited that I forgot to drop my wing tanks. I had been waiting a long time to get a few of those bastards. That was the only thing on my mind at the time.

I did not know and did not care if any of my other pilots followed me in. I just got in back of the Lilys and fired my guns until I ran out of ammunition. By then, I had gotten 4 more of them.

We had descended to about 8,000 feet, and the antiaircraft fire was getting heavy. Only one kamikaze had gotten through. I considered trying to come up under him and cutting off his elevator, or ramming him. But our ships were throwing up a lot of flak, so I thought they would get him anyhow. As it turned out, however, he got through and rammed an LST. I have been very sorry ever since that I didn't ram the bastard and bail out.

My problem was that, being in back of the planes I was shooting down, I had gotten oil all over my windshield. That hadn't bothered me when I was firing my guns, but it was a little hard for me to see the landing signal officer to land back aboard *Kalinin Bay*. I had to stick my head out the side of the cockpit to see.

*Altogether that morning, Lieutenant Ken Hippe's FM-2 Wildcat division destroyed 12 Lilys and claimed 2 others as probables. Hippe's wingman, Ensign John Buchanan, scored 3 of the victories. A division of Taffy 3 pilots, also flying FM-2s, took care of all the rest, except for the one that crashed into the LST. (VC-3's other credits in the war were for 2 Zero fighters destroyed around noon on October 24, 2 Val dive-bombers destroyed on October 25, and a Zeke fighter destroyed on October 26—a total of 17 victories and 2 probables.)*

*Lieutenant Ken Hippe was awarded a Navy Cross for the day's action, which, he estimated, amounted to all of five or six minutes. He had never been in a fight with a Japanese plane before, and he was never in one again.*

*Hippe spent the last year of the war in San Diego. He left active duty shortly after VJ Day to fly for TWA, but he remained in the Navy Reserve until his retirement as a captain in 1965.*

In all its phases, the Battle of Leyte Gulf cost the Imperial Navy 4 carriers, 3 battleships, 6 heavy cruisers, 4 light cruisers, 9 destroyers, and 387 aircraft. It marked the unquestionable demise of the Combined Fleet as a world-class fighting force.

The U.S. Navy lost the light carrier *Princeton*, 2 escort carriers, and 3 destroyers.

# CHAPTER 13

For the remainder of 1944, the main attraction was in the Philippines. While Task Force 38 expended most of its energy scouring the northern Philippines, particularly the Manila Bay region, the 5th Air Force concentrated on tactical targets in the region immediately around its new airfields on Leyte. Thanks in large part to the efforts of the many thousands of American aviators, the Philippines became a vast sinkhole for what remained of Japan's war-making might.

## A FIGHTER PILOT'S DREAM

**1st Lieutenant JACK PURDY, USAAF**
**433d Fighter Squadron, 475th Fighter Group**
**Visayan Sea, December 11, 1944**

*John Edgar Purdy was drafted into the U.S. Army from his native Wyandotte, Michigan, on June 21, 1941. He served in the cavalry until, shortly after the outbreak of World War II, he was accepted for pilot training. He graduated from Luke Field, Arizona, in May 1943. After extensive training in fighters, Purdy was sent to New Guinea in December 1943 to join the 475th Fighter Group's 433d Fighter Squadron. Lieutenant Purdy's first aerial victory was over a Ki-43 Oscar Imperial Army fighter near Noemfoor Island on May 16, 1944. He destroyed two Val dive-bombers over Cebu City on December 5, 1944.*

On December 7, our deputy group commander, Lieutenant Colonel Meryl Smith, was shot down over Ormoc Bay, on the Japanese-held west coast of Leyte. A day or two later, in the same area, 1st Lieutenant Perry Dahl, also from our group, collided in midair with a Japanese fighter. On December 11, as part of the ongoing search for Smith and Dahl, my flight was assigned to cover a PBY amphibian search-and-rescue plane to Ormoc Bay. We took off from the satellite strip at Dulag and rendezvoused with the PBY, which was out of Tacloban, our main field.

On that type of mission, the PBY flew as close to the deck as possible, with four fighters flying at about 3,000 feet. To keep the PBY in sight at all times, we had to fly an S pattern back and forth over and above the PBY—to compensate for the PBY's slower speed. So, while the PBY crew checked for the enemy down on the water and along the coasts of islands, the fighter pilots had to keep an eye on the PBY. We figured that the PBY crew would be on the lookout for enemy planes, also.

We had been out for some time when, all of a sudden, at around 0900, we saw a convoy of ten to twelve ships. It was about 15 miles south of Cebu, heading southeast across the Visayan Sea toward Ormoc Bay, on the west side of Leyte. We didn't know whose it was. With the PBY flying toward it, I assumed at first that it was ours. But, then, one of the wingmen called in that there were three or four bogies in the area. I realized then that it was a Japanese convoy, and the doggone PBY had been taking us right into it.

As the flight leader, I was very unhappy that the PBY had been leading us directly into this enemy hornet's nest, so I immediately called the PBY and told the pilot to make a 180-degree turn and get into the cloud cover. The clouds had been above us all along, but we had passed beyond them just about the time we spotted the Japanese convoy. I needed to get him to fly to a safe area so our P-38s could climb for altitude. The moment he was in the clouds, we headed up.

In the meantime, I could see more and more fighters. I estimated overall that there were twenty to thirty Japanese fighters in the area, all between 500 and 7,000 feet. I'm sure they had spotted us, but, strange to say, they were not paying any attention to us. All they did was converge more tightly over the convoy. No doubt, their mission was to cover the convoy at all costs. They didn't want to go up after just four airplanes. I'm sure they figured we were decoys, meant to pull them away from the ships. Their fear probably was that we were decoying for bombers. Four fighters couldn't do much to sink the ships, but low-level bombers could.

After we got up to about 22,000 feet, I looked all around. There was nothing above us. Well below us was the group of fighters. I knew the odds—I wasn't going to tangle with twenty to thirty Japanese fighters—but I figured I could very safely make a pass at the top echelon. If it looked like we were getting into trouble, we could just head for home. Making a pass from above would give us plenty of speed to run. I made sure that everyone understood that we were to keep together and complete the pass in the direction of home.

I told the other pilots to pick out a Japanese plane, continue through, and rendezvous on the other side. I checked the air around us again thoroughly, and then I led the flight in. We made a pass at the top echelon. They split-essed and scattered but made no attempt at all to come after us.

I came down on an Oscar from the 6-o'clock position and fired a short burst. The plane went into a right turn, started smoking, momentarily straightened, and finally split-essed downward. I claimed it only as damaged, because I immediately came up on another Oscar and followed through to go after it. I came up on this Oscar from astern and fired an 80-degree deflection burst from 200 yards, just as it split-essed. I saw many strikes and followed the plane down. It crashed into the ocean several miles from Bantayan Island.

We had been noticing for some time that we were meeting

increasingly inexperienced Japanese fighter pilots. We had discussed it among ourselves. I felt that the enemy pilots flying over the Japanese convoy that day were among the least experienced I had ever met.

After going through the fighters and seeing that we were absolutely safe, I cleared the air and looked down to see if any P-38s were going down or looked to be in trouble. We circled around and climbed again, checking the air around us all the way. When I knew we were totally undamaged, I told my pilots, "Let's do it once more."

On the way down, I found two more Oscars and turned into them. The Japanese element leader broke away before I could get into range, so I closed on his wingman. I got to within 50 yards and fired a short burst at 10 degrees of deflection. I observed many hits and stayed with the Oscar until he crashed about five miles northwest of Bantayan.

We were scoring kills, but none of the Japanese made an attempt to take any offensive action against us. We made the two passes at them, but with absolutely no danger at all. It was a fighter pilot's dream.

We could have stayed forever, but our fuel supply was becoming a concern. I made a decision to turn for home. I had personally witnessed five Japanese airplanes going down into the water with no damage to any of us.

During the early part of the mission, to the point where the PBY departed, we had been flying on our belly tanks. When we had first seen the enemy fighters, we dropped our belly tanks and switched over to our main tanks for the fight. Then, on turning for home, we switched on the outer wing tanks, which should have been enough to get all the way back. Whatever was left in the main fuel tanks was a reserve.

As we pulled away toward home, I saw that the gauges for my outer wing tanks read empty. That put me in a bad situation. I called the other men in the flight, and they all reported that they were in good shape; they all had full outer wing tanks. I remembered that, when our P-38L-5s had first arrived, pilots had reported siphoning from their outer wing tanks. That is, the fuel in those tanks had siphoned into the air through a little hole that was meant to relieve vacuum pressure as the gas was used up. The siphoning was caused when the airflow over the top of the wing sucked the gas through the hole. That's probably what happened to me: My fuel in the outer wing tanks had been siphoned.

I thought I could make it if I employed fuel-conservation measures, but we ran into bad weather on the way back, and I used more fuel than I might have on a clear day. We had to fly by a roundabout way to miss the worst of the weather.

I kept checking my main fuel tanks, figuring and refiguring my options, until the main-tank gauges were all the way down to "Empty." I had to make a decision to bail out or find a good spot to crash-land. I knew doggone well that I was close to our air base at Tacloban, but I did not feel I could risk trying to reach it. I told the rest of the flight that I was going to crash-land.

I spotted a shoal—a sand beach—about 100 yards out from the shore of an island, Cabugan Grande. It looked like it was 300 to 400 yards long, a beautiful place to attempt to crash-land a P-38. I told the others to keep going, that I had found a perfect spot. I did not want them to take chances covering me; I knew that their fuel supplies were too low for that. I just asked them to report my position so a PBY could rescue me.

I made my turn back toward the shoal while the other three P-38s continued on to Dulag. I wanted to land while I still had power on the airplane. If I waited to run out of gas and had to make a dead-stick landing, I'd be in much more trouble than if I was able to land under my own power.

I released the canopy and came in with my flaps down and wheels up. The sand went up in every direction and I slid off the end of the bar into about eight to nine feet of water. The water went up in a big plume, and then the plane came to rest. The cockpit was only partially flooded, so I climbed out and sat on the canopy.

Within minutes, four islanders from Cabugan Grande came out in a canoe to get me. I had no idea who the islanders were or what their sentiments toward us were, so I stayed on the canopy with my .45 out. I thought of swimming away, but I couldn't think of where I could swim to.

The islanders started waving as they set out, so I waved back. They were completely friendly. They took me across to the island and gave me the royal red-carpet treatment—

fed me well and gave me a change of clothes. I told them that a PBY would undoubtedly be coming out to get me and asked that they put spotters out to signal the PBY. The Filipinos told me that they hated the Japanese; to show me their appreciation for the liberation of the Philippines, I was their honored guest.

The islanders wined me and dined me until, sure enough, after about 90 minutes, a PBY started circling over my P-38. The Filipinos waved at him, and I went out to wave too. They looked me over and landed, and the islanders rowed me out to the flying boat.

I got back to Dulag just about the time it was getting dark. There wasn't a scratch on me. The other pilots in my flight and I had a great time telling the rest of the squadron what a great mission we had had. We had been truly outnumbered, but I don't think we had a shot fired at us through the whole thing.

The position of the Japanese convoy had been reported to 5th Air Force headquarters, and a major anti-shipping mission was launched. It turned out that the convoy was carrying troops to Ormoc Bay to reinforce Japanese fighting forces on Leyte.

As far as the reason for our morning search went, we never did find Lieutenant Colonel Meryl Smith, but Lieutenant Perry Dahl returned about two weeks later with a monkey on his shoulder and a great story to tell.

*On December 17, 1944, Lieutenant Jack Purdy destroyed a pair of Zeros over Mindoro Island, bringing his total credits for the war to 7 Japanese airplanes destroyed. The crash-landing he survived on December 11, 1944, was his fourth. On January 9, 1945, Captain Purdy crash-landed once again, this time behind enemy lines near Cavite, Luzon. He spent 16 days with Filipino guerrillas before being picked up by a PBY.*

*Captain Jack Purdy returned to the United States in May 1945, following eighteen months overseas. In that time, he had flown a total of 184 combat missions, all in P-38s. He left the service in January 1946 and settled in Dayton, Ohio.*

Though America's strategic sights were set beyond the Philippines—against the Bonins, the Ryukyus, and the Japanese home islands themselves—the Philippines remained the focal point of American attention through the end of 1944. And, within the vast archipelago, Luzon remained General Douglas MacArthur's prime objective, for it was on Luzon that MacArthur had been defeated by the Japanese in early 1942.

Long before Leyte was fully secured, Task Force 38 strike aircraft were regularly over Clark Field and the many other former American airfields that guarded Manila Bay and the road to the Filipino capital. Then, as January 9 and the invasion of Luzon's Lingayen Gulf neared, the 5th Air Force shifted its attention to offensive strikes against the projected battle arena. The first big 5th Air Force raid went off against Clark Field on December 24, 1944.

## GUERRILLA ODYSSEY

### Captain BOB ASCHENBRENER, USAAF
### 8th Fighter Squadron, 49th Fighter Group
### Luzon, December 25, 1944–January 15, 1945

*Robert Wayne Aschenbrener was born in Fifield, Wisconsin, on November 22, 1920, and raised on the Indian reservation at Lac du Flambeau. He attended Loras College, in Dubuque, Iowa, for two years; enlisted in the Army Air Corps in September 1941; and was called to active duty in December 1941. He earned his wings at Moore Field, Mission, Texas, with Class 42-H. Aschenbrener was training in fighters at Pinellas, Florida, when, with only 40 hours in fighters, he was ordered to the Southwest Pacific.*

*While flying P-40Ns with the 49th Fighter Group's 8th Fighter Squadron, Lieutenant Aschenbrener destroyed 2 Japanese fighters over Dumpu and Gusap, New Guinea, on November 15, 1943. He destroyed a third Japanese fighter over Wewak, New Guinea, on February 15, 1944.*

*After flying 272 combat missions with the 8th Fighter Squadron, Captain Aschenbrener returned to the United States in the late summer of 1944, transitioned to P-51s, and was assigned as an instructor to Pinellas Field, Florida. After only three months as an instructor, however, Aschenbrener wangled a reassignment to the 49th Fighter Group. By then, the group had moved from New Guinea to Tacloban, on the Philippine island of Leyte.*

The B-24 I hitched a ride on for the last leg of the trip arrived at Tacloban at dusk in very bad weather. The pilot missed the metal strip twice on the final approach, but, on the third try, he got it on the ground. I had been reassigned to the 8th Fighter Squadron, which was commanded at the time by Captain William Drier, a former wingman of mine, a steady and untiring combat tactician.

During my brief tour in the States, the 49th Group had been re-equipped with P-38s. I had flown P-40s, P-43s, P-47s, and P-51s, but never the P-38. I took off on my first flight to experiment with the aileron boost—after being advised not to use it on takeoffs or landings. Then I tried the fuel-transfer system. On the first try, I managed to kill the left engine. At just about that time, a Japanese Dinah recon plane escorted by two Zekes passed by about 300 yards to my left and slightly above me. I felt like a sitting duck until I got the left engine started again, but by then I was too late to do anything about the Dinah. I'll never know why the Zekes didn't attack me, but they stayed right on the Dinah's wing.

There was a lot of combat to come. Between November 24 and December 21, 1944, I destroyed 7 Japanese fighters of assorted types. That brought my total to 10 kills, all fighters.

Willie Drier made me the squadron operations officer, and part of the job was scheduling pilots for the various missions assigned to our squadron. On December 24, I tacked up the roster for Christmas Day. Willie and I had flown quite a bit and had gotten quite a bit of action, so I scheduled the next–most-experienced man to lead the squadron. Fifth Air Force had ordered a monstrous raid again on Clark Field. It was explained to us that the Japanese were in the habit of flying everything off the field when an attack was to take place. We were ordered to take off 15 minutes after the main strike, mark time off the east coast of Luzon, and then move in as the Japanese were returning to base.

I left camp to go to the strip along with those who were to fly the mission. Shortly after takeoff, the squadron leader had to abort because of a mechanical malfunction. When he reported the problem, I grabbed my chute, took off, caught up with the formation, and assumed the lead. We headed for the tarrying spot and waited there until the strike was over. We then vectored toward Clark at 10,000 feet. Approaching the south area of the base, we saw very little of returning aircraft. Then I spotted a lone Zeke a couple thousand feet below us and almost directly ahead.

I broke off with the lead flight and directed the other flights to maintain altitude. Then I dove for the enemy.

Just as I was about to fire, the Zeke rolled onto its back in a split-S and lost about 500 feet. I went wide and came back in, firing a short burst. He performed the same maneuver again, also without damage. Then the same thing happened a third time. I got lined up dead astern, but I was then only about 500 feet off the ground and nearing the south edge of Clark. As I fired, I heard and felt a thud as 20mm ground fire tore through my left engine. Tiny bits of aluminum tore into my knees and thigh and left a gash on the front of my skull, but I was relatively unhurt.

In front of me and about 100 feet below was the old concrete strip, crossed by the grass strip the Japanese used most of the time. I hit the feather switch on the left engine and pushed down to make myself as small a target as I could. Then I bent the wings over to escape to the northeast. I knew the P-38 wasn't going to fly long, and I wanted to get as far away as I could. It wasn't far.

The coolant lines in the right engine had been hit; the gauge was in the red. I sunk into a hedge of low trees first and then bellied into the rice paddies. It was not the growing season, so the dikes were like concrete. Flying into one was like flying into a brick wall. As I hit, the right propeller spun completely clear of the plane. The shoulder straps restrained me from flying out of my seat, but the jolt so injured my back that I could barely get out of the plane. That became urgent because fumes in the cockpit ignited. My eyebrows and lashes were singed and my forehead was burned.

I managed to get out of the cockpit, but I couldn't stand or walk. (I later learned that I had fractured the tips of two vertebrae and compressed two spinal disks.) I crawled about 30 feet from the P-38. As I did, some of the remaining ammo began to cook off from the heat of a small fire in the nose of the plane. The flames, which did not spread, eventually died out.

Only as I pondered my plight did it suddenly occur to me for the first time that I wasn't going to get back to base. Our last survival briefing stated that all means of rescue had evaporated, except for a possible submarine rescue off the east coast of Luzon. As this flew through my mind, I noticed a group of Filipinos approaching. As I tried to stand, they shouted, "Don't shoot!" They didn't have to worry because I had left my .45-caliber pistol in my tent.

The Filipinos approached warily, indicating all the while that they were friendly. When they reached me, I tried to get up again, but I couldn't. They helped me to my feet. Seeing that I was in a lot of distress and that I couldn't navigate on my own, one of the men went to fetch a caribou. On his return with the animal, one of the men mounted and the others lifted me up behind him. Then another member of the group mounted behind me. It was only a few hundred yards to their barrio, where one of the villagers tried to treat the visible wounds on my head and legs. They handed me a raw egg with a hole in it and indicated that I was to eat the contents.

They made me understand within a few minutes that I had to be taken elsewhere for fear of Japanese patrols. After they helped me board the caribou in the same fashion as before, we left the barrio for a small guerrilla camp hidden in the brush and trees at the foot of Mount Arayat. The Filipinos helped me into a small hut. They brought me some kind of a potion, which, I learned later, was made from dried and fermented fish. I could hardly get it down. Shortly, they brought the rubber boat from my parachute pack, partially inflated it, and spread it on the ground. I didn't leave it for the next six days. For some reason, I did not have a need to evacuate my bladder or bowels in all that time.

A guerrilla named Doming, who was about my age, was designated to look after me. Later that day, which was still Christmas Day, Doming escorted the commander of the local Hukbalahap guerrillas and his wife to visit me. The commander's name was Acquino, and I believe that Doming was an Acquino, too. I exchanged greetings with the Acquinos, but they did not know much English, and I had no knowledge of Tagalog, the native language. Doming knew a little English, so he acted as some sort of interpreter. He explained that Mrs. Acquino was complimenting me on being a Christmas guest. My mother had given me a tiger's eye ring, which I removed from my finger and gave to her.

The guerrillas had very little food. Once a day, Doming brought me a bowl of rice and, more often, a tea made from the leaves of the guava tree. It was medicinal and had the effect of a pain reliever. We talked about the Japanese and the Huks. Doming kept telling me how much more effective the Huk guerrillas could be if they had had more weapons and ammunition, but they had no recognition from the U.S. armed forces. In fact, the Huks, who were Communists, were virtual enemies of the U.S.-backed USAFFE guerrillas.

After a week had passed, I began to gain my strength and was able to move around a bit, but the pain in my back was excruciating. A few hundred yards north of the camp was a riverbed with a shallow creek flowing through it. There was a chance to wash up there, and we often lay on the edge of the creek, in the sun. Mount Arayat was only a few miles from the east side of Clark Field, and our location was beneath the landing pattern of the Japanese planes. Some of them were close enough while banking into the final approach for me to see the pilots and crewmen. I was getting another lesson in identifying enemy aircraft in very unusual circumstances.

After I had been mending for a week, a small column of guerrillas entered camp. They had with them three Navy airmen who had been shot down a few weeks before. One of them, Lieutenant James Robinson, was a Hellcat pilot who had suffered a nasty gash on his upper arm when he bailed out of his fighter. The other two were enlisted members of an Avenger crew. They told me that we needed to get to the USAFFE guerrillas if we were to escape from Luzon. Kenong Acquino, who seemed to be the senior of the young Huks in the camp, said that we would have to cross the valley and the main highway connecting Manila and the Lingayen Gulf area in order to contact the USAFFE guerrillas in the mountains west of Clark Field. That is what we decided to do.

A couple days later, we left Mount Arayat in the early morning with a band of thirty-five to forty Huks, three or four of whom were women. They were armed with an assortment of weapons, some of them out of commission and many of them without ammunition. I had no weapon of my own, so they gave me a Japanese pistol that looked to be in rough shape and also had no ammunition. I still wore my khaki uniform and had my flight helmet strapped to my belt. A short distance out of camp, we arrived at a narrow-gauge railroad, about the size of a trolley. There was a small flatcar waiting. I imagine it was used to transport bags of rice out of the paddies. The Huks put me on it, but all three of the Navy airmen chose to walk. As the column moved off up the tracks, the Huks pushed me on the flatcar. We proceeded northwest until that direction no longer served to get us to the planned highway-crossing point. Then I was on foot.

We spent the day passing through barrio after barrio, pausing a few minutes in each. The reason for this procedure, I learned, was that Huk runners had to be dispatched to the next barrio to make sure that no Japanese patrols were in the vicinity and that it was safe to proceed. When night came, we remained at the last barrio, sleeping in an elevated hut that accommodated ten to fifteen people besides myself. We slept in our clothes—as I had for the past ten days—with no cover and on the bare sapling floor. That night, a young guerrilla woman slept next to me. She was very light complected and the Huks described her as a "mestizo." No one thought anything of the arrangement, including the Navy trio.

The next day was similar to the first, but the following night brought some real concern. As we ate our rice at dusk, a runner from the next barrio informed us that a Japanese patrol was approaching. I was told that the Japanese often made night excursions into the territory surrounding Clark Field, often confiscating whatever fresh food they could obtain. It was decided that we had to keep moving, so we hiked until early the next morning, always keeping one barrio between us and the Japanese patrol. We came very close to the spot that had been picked for crossing the highway, but we were too exhausted to undertake the delicate operation.

After pausing for a couple hours at the last barrio, we headed for the highway and arrived at a spot I was certain had been selected carefully. There was a deep drainage ditch intersecting the highway. The ditch was covered with a dense growth of canelike grass and young trees. We were to hide in the undergrowth until the opportune moment arrived to cross the road, which was well traveled by processions of Japanese vehicles. The plan was to cross at noon, a natural lull.

While we waited, sporadic traffic traveled north and south along the highway. Then, at just about noon, a truck slowed down and came to a halt just past the ditch. We heard the Japanese talking, but they made no effort to proceed. Kenong decided to investigate. He moved closer to the highway until he could see the vehicle. In a few minutes, he returned and told us that the Japanese were fixing a flat tire. We waited another half hour or so before we heard them start up and leave. The time to cross had arrived, and Kenong hurried the entire column across the highway, staying in the undergrowth until we were well clear of the road.

Farther on, we came to a river. It was wide but had only ankle-deep water flowing in it. We followed it toward the foothills on the opposite side of the valley. As we moved along, we climbed a few hundred feet and soon had a good view of the valley and Clark Field, which was a little to the south of our path.

Late in the afternoon, Kenong explained that a USAFFE camp was ahead and that he wanted to turn us over to them before dark. We went on to a point a hundred yards or so from the USAFFE camp and halted. I didn't really realize until then how much tension there was between the two groups of guerrillas. Kenong sent a runner ahead to explain the purpose of the visit. We watched as he approached the USAFFE camp, walking very slowly. A few words were exchanged and then he returned to the column. Everything was okay, Kenong said; we were to go over. We shook hands there, wished each other well, and I returned the Japanese pistol. Then, at the direction of Kenong, I guess, one of the Huks handed me a scabbarded Japanese samurai sword. I was surprised, honored, and very grateful.

As soon as we joined the USAFFE unit, we were informed that we had to move to another camp, which was higher in the mountains. We left almost immediately, even though it was almost dark. Several water buffalo were brought out, and the four of us got aboard. I had a guerrilla seated in front of me because of my bad back. The skin on the animal was so loose it was difficult to remain aboard. It became dark before we moved very far, so it was difficult to see the landscape. I knew, however, that we were climbing.

I hoped the animal could see better than I could. A short time later it proved its hearing ability. As we approached the mountain camp, a sentry called out "Halt!" He waited a second or two and then worked the bolt in his rifle. That noise spooked the water buffalo I was on, and it broke away to the right; my guerrilla partner and I both fell to the ground. The guerrillas let the animal go. A few minutes later, we were in the camp, which was a half dozen or so thatched huts with the floors raised about three feet off the ground. We turned in right away to get some sleep.

I discovered the next day that we were going to eat a little better than we had with the Huks. In addition to their rice, there was a kettle of some kind of stew simmering on an open fire. It was the Filipino version of *menudo*—the highly seasoned entrails of a water buffalo. In a grassy area near the camp was the flesh of the animal, cut into strips and drying into a jerky. Although I had eaten neither before, it tasted really good. However, there was really very little to go around.

I did a lot of relaxing during the next few days. There was a long grassy slope near the camp and a small stream among trees on the opposite side. I could sleep in the sun and bathe in the stream. I thought a lot about the Huks and their plight. The Huks helped a lot of pilots evade the Japanese, and I began to figure out ways I might help them. I thought about putting guns and ammunition in a belly tank and skip-dropping it near Mount Arayat. The idea, I thought, would likely net me a court-martial. I spent some of my time watching air battles from the Japanese side. There were several attacks on Clark while I watched. As I stood on the grassy slope during one attack, a P-47 flew by at 4,000 to 5,000 feet. I was in a good position to use the signal mirror the Huks had returned to me from my parachute pack. The P-47 pilot saw the flash, winged over, and had a look, but there was no recognition between us. It probably was fortunate. He might have taken me for an enemy soldier and come in shooting.

We were told that a Japanese Zero had crashed some time before on another grassy area a short distance above camp, so the four of us went up to have a look. The Zero lay in the middle of the clearing. As we approached it, a lone aborigine, wearing only a loincloth and carrying a wooden spear, crossed the knoll in front of us. He seemed oblivious to our presence. We went on to the Zero, which was almost intact; only a patch of metal had been ripped from its side. Alongside the plane was a skeleton. It must have been there a long time, and I wondered why the pilot was never sought out by his comrades.

One day, as we were sitting around talking, a small column of USAFFE guerrillas entered camp. With them was Lieutenant Alex Vraciu, a Navy ace with 19 kills. We had been hearing some distant heavy guns, but we didn't know what they were until he gave us the news that an invasion by U.S. forces was underway at Lingayen Gulf. He was on his way there and left the next morning with the small band. The day after, we followed suit, going to Lingayen with another small band of guerrillas.

Heading down for the valley again, we moved to the northeast. In each of several barrios we passed through, we learned that many Japanese contingents were retreating south in disarray. We avoided them and soon were on the main road once again, heading north. Fortunately, the Japanese troops were steering clear.

Our first contact with our own forces was just south of Lingayen, near San Carlos. A jeep with four heavily armed 43d Infantry Division troops approached us. Fortunately, they were quick to recognize friendly Filipinos and the four Americans with them. We were told to proceed on north to their base camp and division headquarters.

We arrived safely and, after interrogation, the four of us airmen were sent on to a landing strip. The Navy airmen were transported to their ships off the coast. Eventually, I was put aboard a C-47 heading for Mindoro, where the 49th Fighter Group was by then located.

On the way back, I began to think about the case of beer I had left under my cot back on Leyte. I had wangled it from some sailors who were unloading supplies at Tacloban a couple of days before Christmas, but I hadn't had a chance to break it open. Upon my return to the squadron, I learned that several of my friends had put it to good use. I hope that one of them toasted me.

*Shortly after his return to the 49th Fighter Group on January 23, 1945, Captain Bob Aschenbrener was given command of the 7th Fighter Squadron. After flying a total of 345 combat missions amounting to 850 combat hours, he left the 49th Group to command the fighter division of the V Fighter Command's Replacement Pilot Center. He married the former Ann Middleton, a Red Cross staff assistant, at Clark Field in August 1945 and returned with her to the States in September 1945 to be mustered out of the service.*

# CHAPTER 14

The campaign in the Philippines was never completed; it was simply overrun by the end of the war. In time, as the drive toward Japan itself was renewed, Spruance's 5th Fleet command establishment replaced Halsey's 3d Fleet organization and oversaw the preparations for and support of the invasion of Iwo Jima on February 19, 1945.

The bloody seizure of Iwo Jima provided the Army Air Corps with an emergency airfield on the B-29 route between air bases in the Marianas and the Japanese home islands, but Iwo was only a way station. The real show—the invasion of Japan—was to begin on April 1 with the invasion of Okinawa. Okinawa was to be the logistical and bomber base from which Kyushu would be beaten to a pulp before American boys set foot on Japanese soil. Decoy and support operations for the Okinawa invasion began early and ranged all around the periphery of the shrinking Empire of Japan.

## DECOY

**1st Lieutenant RANDY REEVES, USAAF**
**530th Fighter Squadron, 311th Fighter Group**
**Nanking, China, March 25, 1945**

*Though accepted to college on a football scholarship in 1940,
Leonard Randolph Reeves of Lancaster, Texas, opted to work
for a year when an injury prevented him from playing for his
college team. In the end, he kept on working and finally
applied for the Army aviation program in February 1942. He
passed the Army Air Corps Equivalency Test, was sworn into
the service in April 1942, and was called to active duty in
October. Reeves was commissioned at Luke Field, Arizona,
on September 30, 1943, and served with an operational
training unit in Florida until flown to Assam, India, in
March 1944. When 2d Lieutenant Reeves and his fellow
replacements arrived in India, they were given only five hours
to check out in 311th Fighter Group P-51As before being sent
out on their first combat mission, escorting B-24 heavy
bombers over Burma.*

*Reeves shot down his first Japanese plane, a Ki-44 Tojo,
over Meiktila, Burma, on May 12, 1944. He destroyed 3
Ki-43 Oscars over Sinsiang airdrome, China, on January 5,
1945.*

In the spring of 1945, before the invasion of Okinawa was to
begin, the 14th Air Force moved several groups into the
forward base at Ankang, to hit airfields on the China coast.
This was to destroy the Japanese aircraft based on the
coastal fields, or keep them busy so they could not reinforce
units on Okinawa, which was going to be invaded at the
beginning of April.

Ankang was a small field with pierced-steel planking for
the runway. It was muddy and raining, and you had better
not stray off the mat or you might be stuck for good. Ankang
was about a three-and-a-half-hour flight east of our regular
base, Chengtu. From there, our P-51Cs had the range to hit
our target, Nanking, if we flew with external tanks. We could

**283**

drop the tanks over Nanking, dogfight for approximately 15 minutes, and still fly the 560 miles back to Ankang.

Major Fritz Coleman was our new squadron CO. He had only flown four or five missions, but he was a West Pointer and gung ho. He was ordered to take 12 of our planes down to Nanking to strafe the planes on the ground, and he wanted me to lead one flight. I told him "No," because Intelligence had reports of as many as 20 Japanese aircraft flying Combat Air Patrols over Nanking. I told him that as soon as we destroyed all the planes in the air, I'd strafe all day with him. I felt the planes in the air needed to be destroyed as well as those on the ground. With the planes in the air gone, the planes on the ground could be destroyed much more easily. However, the order said to have 12 of our planes strafe, and Major Coleman's West Pointer attitude was to follow orders explicitly. I tried to point out that it did not say *when* to strafe, but he insisted he was going down with 12 fighters immediately. In the end, however, he decided to lead his and two other four-plane flights down while I led six additional planes to engage the Combat Air Patrol.

Major Coleman got all 12 of his planes off on schedule, at 0940 hours, but I still had four planes that were not yet fueled. This was because we all had to refuel with 5-gallon cans, straining the fuel through chamois to clean out the contaminants. There were 75 planes based at Ankang at the time, and refueling had been going on continuously since we landed. I took off with my wingman, Lieutenant Maurice "Pete" Beck, and told the other four-plane flight to follow as soon as the aircraft were all fueled. That left Beck and me to take on an estimated 20 or so fighters—Imperial Army Tojos or Oscars. The latest model Navy fighter had also been noted on some of the airfields.

Beck and I broke off from Fritz Coleman's group about 50 miles west of Nanking. Fritz led his fighters down on the deck from 16,000 feet, and I led Beck higher. Beck and I were over Nanking at 1215 hours, arriving from the west at 26,000 feet. The air seemed to be full of Japanese planes. We made a large circle about 15 miles west of Nanking, and I saw four Tojos and a lone Oscar about 1,000 feet below us. The Tojos were in a four-ship flight with the Oscar slightly ahead and at the same altitude. The Oscar appeared to be in trouble, and the pilot did not seem to be paying attention to business. That was always one of the Japanese ploys—to use a plane as a decoy and draw our planes into chasing an apparent cripple for an easy kill. Once you concentrated on the decoy, all the other Japanese planes jumped on you and usually shot you down while you were concentrating on getting your kill.

I made a pass at the flight of four, then, while they were looking at me wondering what I was going to do, I broke off very quickly. Beck and I came in at 20 degrees from behind the Oscar, and I opened fire from about 300 yards. I saw tracers enter the left wing and fuselage, and several small pieces of wing flew off. The Oscar started to split-ess, but he got about halfway over and then settled back to straight-and-level flight. I kept firing until the Oscar let out a belch of black smoke and fire.

As the Oscar started down, I observed four Tojos coming up on our tails, so we turned to our left and climbed to 19,000 feet. We observed eight other Tojos at about 20,000 feet, off to our left. I came in and got on the tail of one of these Tojos and started firing from about 350 yards, dead astern. The Tojos had self-sealing tanks as well as armor plating behind the seat to protect the pilot. The Tojo started turning to his left in a diving spiral and I followed him down, firing all of the time. I fired up to 50-degrees deflection, until I saw the Tojo go into a vertical dive. He was streaming smoke or fire, although I had observed hits in the wings and fuselage behind the cockpit. As the Tojo went into his dive, I led Beck into a climbing turn to the right. I saw the Tojo crash and burn approximately three miles west of Nanking satellite airdrome.

By the time the Tojo crashed, I had lost Beck. I climbed back up to 20,000 feet and made another pass on the same formation of Tojos. All my guns, except one, quit firing, so I broke away and started calling Beck on the radio to join up so we could head for home. Just as I pulled around on course, at approximately 20,000 feet, I saw Beck coming in on me and it looked like he was taking a lead on me. I was yelling "Beck! This is Randy! Don't shoot!" About that time, something hit me and I lost control of my plane. Beck later reported that he had seen three Tojos coming in on my tail and was shooting at them and trying to warn me on the radio. Apparently the lead Tojo hit me.

I was going down at approximately 600 miles per hour with the stick back in my gut and the throttle in idle. Finally, I started rolling the elevator trim all the way back. After a few seconds, the plane started coming out of the dive and eventually, around 6,000 feet, I had it nearly straight and level. I regained complete control at 5,000 feet.

I started looking around to see where I was hit, cussing Beck for shooting me out of the sky. As I surveyed the tail section, I saw that the whole right side of the horizontal stabilizer and elevator was missing. I climbed to get over the mountains and get back to Ankang. Someone joined up with me and I asked who it was, but there was no answer. I asked him to check my plane over, but there was still no answer. He then moved up closer, pointed to his headset, shook his head, and pointed at me. I knew then that my radio was out and probably had been out for some time. He also pointed to my tail section and I nodded my head that I knew.

We got to Ankang and I thought I had it made until I lowered my flaps to full on the final approach and found I had no more elevator control. I managed to get the flaps up and leveled off just as I hit the runway. I hit so hard I didn't even bounce. Then I lowered the flaps back to full to help me slow down on the short 5,000-foot runway. It was scary and became more so when I got out and looked at what was left of my horizontal stabilizer and elevator.

Beck, in the meantime, was having troubles of his own. He became lost in bad weather and was running out of fuel, so he decided to bail out near the Han River. His foot slipped down between the seat and the fuselage as he gathered himself to jump at the trailing edge of the wing. He fell outside with his right foot caught inside. Finally, before the plane started doing any unusual maneuvers, he kicked loose, fracturing his ankle in the process. His chute did open and he landed in friendly Chinese territory. He made it home three days later with the help of Chinese officials.

In all, the raid resulted in the destruction of only five Japanése planes—the two I shot down and three on the ground. One of our pilots was killed, and two pilots—Beck and Major Coleman—had to bail out over friendly territory.

*Randy Reeves finished out the war with the 530th Fighter Squadron and was sent home by boat from Calcutta in September 1945.*

The beginning of 1945 had seen the Fast Carrier Task Force striking virtually everywhere within the shrinking Empire of Japan. There were raids against Hong Kong and Hainan, on the China coast, and Formosa. February 16 and 17 were the dates of the first big carrier raids against airfields and industrial targets around Tokyo Bay. Indeed, raids against mainland Japan persisted, and the naturally violent responses resulted in the steady loss of hundreds of warplanes and fledgling pilots that Japan could ill afford to lose. As the invasion of Okinawa drew nearer, the intensity of the carrier raids increased. For weeks on end, everything in range of the fast carriers that floated, flew, or even breathed heavily was fair game.

## ON FIRE

**Ensign HARRY SWINBURNE, USN**
**VF-45 (USS *San Jacinto*)**
**Off Kyushu, March 28, 1945**

*As a high school graduate from Delhi, Iowa, Harry William Swinburne, Jr., enlisted in the U.S. Navy V-5 flight program on August 15, 1942. Starting with Civilian Pilot Training under the V-5 program, he progressed through flight training and earned his wings on December 8, 1943. Flying F6F-3 and F6F-5 Hellcats off light carrier San Jacinto from late December 1944, Ensign Swinburne scored his first victory, a B6N Jill torpedo bomber, as he was guarding the kamikaze-damaged fleet carrier* Franklin *on March 21, 1945. Later, he sank a freighter during a strike against Takao Harbor, Formosa.*

We were east of Okinawa, working over targets in preparation for the invasion, which was to begin on April 1, 1945. Late in the afternoon of March 28, the pilot of a B-29 bomber at high altitude reported that the Japanese Fleet had been sighted steaming south along the east coast of Kyushu, Japan. Since all but one task group of Task Force 58 were refueling and replenishing in a relatively safe area, immediate-launch orders were issued to all available aircraft of the remaining task group, which was under the command of Rear Admiral Jocko Clark. The mission was to search out, attack, and destroy the enemy surface force.

I was launched in a brand-new F6F-5 Hellcat, fresh from the factory; it had less than five hours of flight time on it. My call sign was Lucky-13, which designated me as leader of the second section of the first division of the eight-plane flight of Hellcats launched from *San Jacinto* (Lucky Base).

The flight leader of our eight Hellcats was Lieutenant Levern Forkner, who was also the air group commander and the VF-45 squadron commander. Forkner's ascension to command of the squadron, much less the air group, was highly unusual in that he was only a lieutenant. However, Commander Gordon Schecter, our original group and squadron commander, had been killed on March 18 and was never replaced during our combat tour.

After launch and rendezvous with aircraft from other carriers—other F6Fs, SB2C Helldiver dive-bombers, and TBM Avenger torpedo bombers—the entire formation proceeded northeast from Okinawa and along the east coast of Kyushu.

Even prior to the launch, it had been obvious to all that the return from the mission and landings would be made after dark. This would be a relatively new experience for most of the pilots, although all had completed two practice night carrier landings before leaving the Hawaii area for combat duty. Well, even though we were supposed to be on strict radio silence, it wasn't too long before someone called in and said his engine was running rough and he was going to return to base. It was obvious he didn't want to make a night landing. A little later, his section leader called in and said he was returning to base too—to escort the first guy home. When that call came in, I heard a few calls of "Chickenshit" and words to that effect over the air.

We flew along in formation, all units heading in the same direction. Our speed was approximately 150 knots, which would give us plenty of range, and we were at about 8,000 feet, which gave us the best visibility for searching. The weather was excellent. If there were any clouds, they were very high.

We were just off the east coast of Kyushu, about 240 miles from our carriers, when the strike group overflew a Japanese destroyer, two destroyer escorts, and a formation of twelve Imperial Navy gunboats. There were some comments about the gunboats, but the strike commander said, "No. We'll proceed on north."

On the way north, between 1630 and 1645, a component of VF-82 F6Fs off the *Bennington,* was assigned by the strike commander to go after four individual Japanese aircraft that we encountered. They got all four airplanes, but they had problems destroying a glider that had been cast off by a Nell twin-engine bomber moments before the bomber was shot down. It was strange listening to the VF-82 pilots trying to figure out how to shoot down the glider. Unless they killed the pilot, there was no way to get it to fall. They worked it over for some time and finally shot it down.

We continued on, almost to the northern tip of Kyushu, but a thorough search failed to locate the fleet of large Imperial Navy warships. It was finally surmised by the strike leaders that the high-flying Air Force heavy bomber had misidentified the small ships we had overflown earlier. We turned back toward our task group, now certain that we would be arriving well after dark.

As the strike group approached the flotilla of light ships we had passed up before, the eight Hellcats in the VF-45 flight were ordered to destroy the twelve gunboats by hitting them with rockets. Each gunboat was only about 60 feet long. The SB2Cs were armed with bombs and any TBMs that were along had torpedoes or bombs, which would best be used against larger ships.

The gunboats were proceeding along in formation when

we arrived. As soon as they saw us, they went off in various directions, maneuvering independently. Our flight broke up and commenced attacking the individual gunboats.

My Hellcat was armed with six .50-caliber machine guns with 400 rounds per gun and six HVAR rockets with 3-inch bodies and 5-inch warheads. The rockets were very inaccurate! I'd fired them on earlier missions and, at times, they hadn't come in sight over the leading edge of the wing. The head was too heavy for the body, so the rocket frequently did not follow the line of sight.

On my first run on a gunboat, I was in about a 30-degree dive, coming almost right up her wake. My aiming point was the middle of the bridge. If the rockets had been accurate, I'd have fired from about 1,000 feet. I decided to get closer, however, to be sure the rockets hit. Though it was dangerous, I stayed in my dive until the Japanese crew must have thought I was going to dive right into the gunboat. I let go a pair. The rockets couldn't miss; no matter what they did, they had to hit.

The two rockets hit almost simultaneously with my pushing the pickle on them. *Zip-BAM!* Debris flew by my plane. I automatically pulled up into a steep climbing turn to the left and looked back over my shoulder. The gunboat was smoking, burning, and sinking.

I came right around and made a run on another gunboat. This one was all by herself and none of the other Hellcats were making runs on her. I used my remaining four rockets on the gunboat, firing from farther out this time so I wouldn't fly through the debris again. I know I got her, as I saw solid hits.

I went around once or twice more, making strafing runs on some of the other gunboats. I got hits, but I don't know how much damage I caused. I didn't sink any of the others.

In a very short time, in a matter of minutes, all but three of the gunboats had been sunk. Japanese sailors were swimming all over the place. Of the remaining three gunboats, all were on fire and two were dead in the water.

Then I heard Lieutenant Forkner call, "Lucky Flight, this is Lucky-One. Rendezvous south of the force." Since I had just completed a strafing attack and happened to be to the north of the remaining gunboats when the call came in, I decided to make one last minimum-altitude strafing run on the only gunboat still underway.

I slowed down as much as possible and began pumping every round I could into her. During the completion of my attack, I was so low I had to pull up to clear the mainmast.

Stupid me! I don't know why in the world I wasn't thinking that an Imperial Navy gunboat would certainly have antiaircraft guns! I hadn't seen any guns firing or enemy tracer on my previous passes, so I didn't give it a thought on my last pass. I saw AA fire that time! In fact, I saw the round coming right at me, smoking all the way.

My new F6F-5 Hellcat was hit in the left wing-root area by what I am sure was a 20mm incendiary shell. It jolted the airplane, and I heard the shell rip through the left wing. It really tore things up when it went through. The wing burst into flames instantaneously, and all six machine guns went on automatic fire. Hydraulic pressure was lost and the gun chargers had no effect when placed on "Safe." The electrical gun switches were also inoperative. In fact, all my electrically powered gauges went out. I manually released the external fuel tank and kept my Hellcat pointed away from other rendezvousing aircraft until the guns stopped firing.

With the wing fire becoming more intense, I decided I'd have to bail out. I opened the canopy and stood up, but I forgot to unfasten my earphone cord and that yanked me back into the seat. Almost simultaneously, I heard the skipper calling me on the radio. My relief was profound. I didn't know I had a radio left until I heard Forkner's voice. He recommended that I immediately land in the water and told me he would drop the five-man emergency life raft that he was carrying on a bomb-rack dispenser. I didn't like this idea for two reasons. In the first place, I was concerned that the weakened wing might collapse close to the water, resulting in a low-altitude spin with no chance of a successful bailout. Secondly, there were numerous Japanese seamen in the water in that area, and I didn't relish sharing the life raft with them. I decided to gain some altitude, fly the plane as far as it would hold together, and then bail out. I left the cockpit open and kept the seatbelt and shoulder harness unfastened in the hope that I'd be blown clear if a fuel tank exploded. I figured I could pull the ripcord when clear of the plane.

I had already dropped my drop tank and shifted to my left fuel tank. Now, we didn't study much engineering in those days, so I visualized my three internal tanks—left, right, and reserve—as being much farther apart than they actually were. I thought the left tank was in the left wing root. In fact, they were all right together near the centerline of the plane. The left tank and right tank were against each other and the reserve tank was behind them. We always took off on right tank because the carburetor overflow returned to the right tank. After takeoff and rendezvous on the right tank, to make room for any overflow, we switched to the 150-gallon drop tank. I had used it all the way up to Kyushu and until we had gone into the attack, when I switched to a full tank.

So, I had immediately jettisoned the drop tank for fear of explosion, as it was not bulletproof or self-sealing. After I dropped it, I switched to my full left tank and put the mixture control on "Full rich." My thought was to use up as much gas in that left tank as I could before the fire reached it.

Once I decided to stay with the airplane, my main concern centered on how long that left wing was going to stay on. I could look right through it at the water. The hole was three to four feet from the cockpit and getting bigger. As the minutes passed, however, I began to feel more confident even though the wing continued to burn and I couldn't hope that I'd make it all the way to the carriers that night. But at least I was indicating 240 knots and was flying in the direction of "home."

It was getting dark. Other aircraft in our flight joined on the flight leader or me, as my aircraft, with its long, trailing sheet of flame, was highly visible in the rapidly darkening sky. I was a great rendezvous point.

As the fire in my left wing continued to burn, my wingman, Ensign Larry Grossman, flew up close to have a look. At length, he said, "I think it's your wheel, Harry. If you drop your gear, maybe it will go out." We had magnesium wheels and I could smell rubber burning. But I hadn't been thinking about the tire; I had thought it was the self-sealing gas tank, which had a rubber liner.

I didn't want to drop my wheels. If I did, they would cause a drag on the airplane and slow me down. At the speed I was going, every minute that plane held together was another four miles toward home. I was willing to risk the fire and make the extra knots. If the fire was going to blow me up, I figured it would have done so by then.

I was praying. I wasn't praying that I'd get back to the carriers that night, because initially I felt I didn't have a chance. I was praying that if I was captured, I'd get back home after the war was over. But, every mile that went by, my fears diminished. I was getting closer to home, 240 nautical miles from where we had attacked the gunboats. I knew that the task group was leaving that night to refuel and replenish, that they weren't going to hang around to locate any downed pilots, but each mile that I flew increased my confidence that I might make it.

Eventually, the fire went out. I guess the wheel finished burning. I couldn't see the hole any longer in the dark, but I knew it was there. I also knew the hydraulics were gone. I was sure the system had been destroyed by the 20mm shell and the fire and that all the hydraulic fluid had leaked out or burned off. I knew the gun chargers were out and was certain I'd have no flaps or regular landing-gear control. If I wanted to get the gear down, I'd have to blow it down with the emergency system. But those concerns were in the future; I had to get to the carriers before I had to worry about how I was going to get the gear down and land without flaps.

We were flying at about 8,000 feet. At that altitude, when I heard the YE/ZB homing beacon in my earphones, I realized I was only 80 miles from the carriers.

Eventually, radio contact was made with the ships of the task group, and my condition was reported. There was a pause and Lucky Base—*San Jacinto*—responded that the ship would not take me aboard. The deck was too small to take a damaged plane without undue risk to the aircraft already there or being recovered.

The other planes in my flight broke off and went into the pattern to land. That left me up there by myself. I was feeling a bit lonely when I received a direct call from a station identifying itself as Bull Durham. I didn't know it at the time, but that was the call sign reserved for the exclusive use of the task-group commander, Jocko Clark. "Lucky-One-Three," he said, "this is Bull Durham. What's your problem?" I told him that I'd been hit and that I had no flaps and no landing gear and that a large portion of my left wing was gone. At that point, I didn't know if my gear would blow down or not when I activated the air bottle. He came right back: "Lucky-One-Three, this is Bull Durham. If you will remain airborne until we get all our airplanes aboard, Arab Base [fleet carrier *Hornet*] will take you aboard."

I kept circling and circling. Night landings never went very fast, and I was due to be about the last plane taken aboard. I could see the ships below and their wakes in the water.

The prospect of landing a badly damaged aircraft at night was not a pleasant one, but it became relatively less pleasant as time passed. Because the electrically operated fuel gauges were inoperative, I didn't know how much fuel the Hellcat had left. The question was becoming critical. Two of the three internal tanks had been run dry, the latter of the two about 40 minutes earlier. The remaining tank, the right one, had been used for takeoff and rendezvous at the beginning of the mission, so it had not been full when I switched over to it, and I had no idea how much fuel had been expended. An accurate estimate as to how long my engine would keep running was impossible to make. I just knew I was running short.

I decided to contact Arab Base to explain my dilemma. My call brought an immediate response. I was directed to enter *Hornet*'s landing pattern by the shortest possible route. Arab Base informed me that only six *Hornet* Helldivers were still airborne and that they would clear the landing pattern when I reported I was on final approach. I was further informed that the landing signal officer (LSO) was aware of my difficulty—that it was probably impossible for me to take a waveoff. I asked how I would know which was Arab Base, and she came back with, "We're showing red truck lights."

I knew I was in the vicinity of *Hornet* and I almost

immediately spotted a set of red truck lights. I thought, "How lucky can you get. Boy, right there!" I blew my landing gear down with the emergency air bottle and commenced a standard approach.

I flew upwind and then turned downwind. However, as I turned in on final approach and started up the groove, I could not see the carrier's dustpan flight-deck lights nor the LSO's luminous paddles. Also, I couldn't see a sign of any other planes in the area, which I would have expected if Helldivers had been waved off so I could make my landing. When I looked again, the wake looked far too narrow. Something was wrong! I decided to discontinue my approach.

I pulled up and away and aimed my Aldis lamp—a trigger-activated signal light—at the ship. As I went by the starboard side, I discovered that I had just made a carrier approach on a destroyer! (I have often wondered what the men on that destroyer thought I was doing.)

"Arab Base, this is Lucky-One-Three. I just made a pass on a destroyer. I don't know where Arab Base is. I'm shining my Aldis lamp vertically in the air. Do you have me in sight?"

There was no hesitation whatsoever. "Lucky-One-Three, this is Arab Base. You are proceeding up our starboard side."

"Arab Base. Lucky-One-Three. Give me a mark when I go by abeam to starboard." I knew the heading into the wind by then, because of the bright, fluorescent wakes I could see.

"Lucky-One-Three. Arab Base. Okay. Stand by." And, almost immediately, "Mark!"

I proceeded for about 10 seconds, made a 90-degree left turn, and asked for another mark when I was directly ahead of Arab Base. I was about a mile out by then, so a very short time later they said, "Mark! You're passing directly ahead of Arab Base."

The problem was solved. I could see *Hornet*'s truck lights; I knew right where she was. I made a slow 90-degree turn into the downwind leg and began a slightly wide, no-flaps approach. I was confident from the exchange only a minute earlier that the LSO knew the kind of trouble I was in and would guide me up the groove accordingly. We both knew I could not take a waveoff, that if I had to pour full power on with no flaps and part of my left wing missing, I might torque-roll to the left and crash.

My airspeed indicator wasn't working; I was flying by feel. Fortunately, the Hellcat was probably the most stable airplane we ever built in America. It was the perfect carrier plane. The way to land her at night was just to bring her down close to the ground, cut the throttle, and slowly ease back on the stick. She'd fall straight through for a three-point landing. I was lucky I was flying a Hellcat that night.

I could not see the outline of the ship, but I could see the truck lights and the dustpan lights shining on the deck. I started my pass to come up the groove, bloody happy to be there but still praying.

The plane was trimmed. But, without flaps and with much of the left wing missing, my left wing would start to drop when I eased the throttle to slow down. The ailerons lost their effectiveness at real low speed. So I had to put in just a little bit of right rudder and, very subtly—to avoid a torque stall—add an inch or two of manifold pressure for extra power. That brought the left wing up. But the whole process happened again, for the same reason and with the same response. It was a very delicate operation each time. That was the way I was riding her in. I didn't have any choice. It all came down to "I gotta get it aboard." If I had gone into the water, they might have gotten me, or they might not.

I slowed the aircraft as much as seemed safe, but I knew I was probably going 10 to 15 knots faster than a normal approach. The LSO was giving me "fast" signals, indicating I was coming up the groove too fast. Next thing I knew, the LSO was giving me agitated "fast" signals—indicating that I was coming in much too fast. He was really pumping his right paddle up and down! I had taken off all the speed I could, so I kept chugging up the groove.

I was still well astern when the LSO gave me my cut signal—left hand dropped to the side and right hand drawn quickly across the throat or face.

There are two LSO signals that are mandatory, that any pilot is obliged to take without question—the waveoff and the cut. But, this time, I *knew* he was premature. I needed extra distance. I didn't exactly disobey him; I just took my time responding.

The Hellcat settled in and met the deck. As she caught the arresting wire, the left wing dropped to the deck. "Oh," I remembered with a start, "No left landing gear!" The stub of the landing-gear strut nearly cut through two cross-deck pendants. It didn't sever them, but it damaged them so they would have to be changed before the SB2Cs could resume their landings.

Before I could leave the cockpit, the LSO was up on the wing beside me. "Why didn't anyone tell me you were damaged?" he bleated.

"What were you told?" I croaked from an extremely dry throat.

"They just said you couldn't take a waveoff. I assumed you were out of gas." This explained the "fast" and agitated "fast" signals he had been giving me.

"Well, I assumed that they told you *why* I couldn't take a waveoff."

As the crash crew jacked the left landing gear onto a dolly, I climbed down from the cockpit and went over to the scuttlebutt to get a drink of water. My mouth and throat were so dry that I couldn't swallow. I had to rinse the water around in my mouth to prime the pump.

The deck crew was unbelievable. I doubt it took those sailors five minutes to remove both of the damaged wires.

I feel that my ability to control my airplane that night was born of many extra hours in the cockpits of F6Fs. I truly loved the Hellcat and—when we were forming the squadron in Atlantic City, New Jersey, and during our stay in Hawaii—I frequently flew after the squadron secured and on weekends. By the time VF-45 embarked aboard *San Jacinto* in December 1944, I had over 500 hours in F6Fs. That extra time paid off in combat, and it certainly paid off the night I had to land my damaged Hellcat aboard *Hornet*.

My flight that night had been five hours, and the F6F-5 had had five hours on it when I took off. Next morning, as I was waiting to transfer to a destroyer to ride back to *San Jacinto*, it was decided that my brand-new Hellcat was unsalvageable, not worth the effort to repair. About 20 square feet of the left wing had been burned away, all the way through the top and bottom surfaces. The clear Plexiglas canopy was still unmarked, so they saved it as a replacement. While they were removing the canopy, I grabbed the clock. Then my Hellcat was jettisoned over the side.

*Within three weeks of his miraculous recovery aboard* Hornet, *newly promoted Lieutenant (jg) Harry Swinburne achieved ace status by shooting down 4 Japanese warplanes—2 Zekes off Ie Shima on April 6, 1945, and a Zeke and a Kate off Okinawa on April 16.*

# CHAPTER **15**

The 10th U.S. Army invaded Okinawa on April 1, 1945. Almost instantly, Japan responded by launching a cloud of aircraft piloted by men determined to die in final plunges into the decks and sides of the hundreds of U.S. Navy transports and warships off Okinawa. This was the divine wind—*kamikaze*.

The tactic of self-immolation was an old one in Japan, and it had been carried to its logical modern derivative off Leyte, when suicide planes had attacked the U.S. invasion fleet there. But the effort in the Philippines had been puny compared to what the Japanese launched from bases in Kyushu almost as soon as the first U.S. infantrymen set foot on Okinawa.

Not all the Japanese pilots and aircrewmen sent to Okinawa were meant to die. Many were too skilled at what they did to be wasted, and the modern fighters and bombers they manned were too precious to be expended in the national suicide gesture. But Japan had thousands of outmoded airplanes and seemingly no end of recruits who wanted to fly them unto death. For the U.S. Navy and Marine pilots who were charged with defending the invasion fleet and their countrymen on the ground, the distinction hardly mattered. Whether a Japanese pilot had his heart set upon crashing into an American ship or simply shooting down an American fighter, the only outcome that mattered for the American pilot was shooting the Japanese plane out of the sky.

And that is what happened. Thousands of times.

## BOGIES FROM JAPAN

**2d Lieutenant DEWEY DURNFORD, USMC**
**VMF-323**
**Okinawa, April 18, 1945**

*In the spring of 1942, at age nineteen, Dewey Foster*
*Durnford, a native of Columbus, Ohio, completed his second*
*quarter in engineering at Ohio State University. He dropped*
*out with the intention of enlisting in the Marine Corps. In a*
*last-minute change of heart, he applied for the Navy's V-5*
*flight program but failed the eye exam due to an astigmatism*
*of the right eye. He soon found that the problem could be*
*corrected sufficiently to pass the exam by exercising the eye,*
*and, on August 12, 1942, he was accepted as an aviation*
*cadet. Durnford was called up in October 1942. On December*
*3, 1943, he graduated as a Marine second lieutenant with*
*orders to Jacksonville, Florida, for operational training.*

In the late summer of 1944, I was part of a group of
replacement pilots sent to Hawaii fresh from operational
training in F4U Corsairs at Jacksonville and El Toro,
California. Major George Axtell's VMF-323 had lost a pilot
in a training exercise being run out of Ewa airfield on Oahu,
and I was selected to be the replacement. The next thing I
knew, we were on an old jeep carrier heading into the South
Pacific. After short stays on Emirau and Espiritu Santo,
we were sent north to the Okinawa invasion staging
area at Ulithi. For a twenty-two-year-old second lieutenant, this massive armada was the most impressive sight of
the war.

By now I was an assistant engineering officer, which, in
reality, meant I was to fly and stay out of the way of our
capable mechanics. By the time we arrived at Okinawa, I
had spent thirty days on an LST—a tank-landing ship. I was
delighted when, at last, the bow ramp was dropped on shore.
Then I was slightly awed when the ship was immediately
strafed by a Zero.

In surprisingly short order, we were operating out of
Kadena airfield. I was on several ground-support missions,

but most of my time in the air was spent on CAPs, day after day. (I believe these CAPs began the phrase about "hours of boredom relieved by seconds of sheer terror.") There was the occasional scramble, when the fleet's radar picked up large groups of bogies heading its way.

The days at this period of the year alternated from clear and sunny to low overcast and rain. The foxholes we used were quite often muddy, especially, during the morning strafing and bombing run, when the howitzer shells greeted us from up in the adjacent hills. It took about two weeks to quiet the howitzer, during which time we would get to our planes by running from foxhole to foxhole.

It is true that the majority of planes we encountered were old one-way types that offered little evasive action. Some of this must have been due to the technique of our approaches —we came in high and out of the sun—and to the caliber of our radar positioning. We quickly learned, however, that if you spent too much time getting in position, someone else would get there first and shoot down the bandit. From the very first encounter, I drove straight in upon sighting the target when it was I who had made the sighting and been given the lead.

It was unwise to be complacent about the caliber of our enemy. On one day of heavy cloud formations, I found myself separated from my wingman and in the company of two Mitsubishi J2M Jack high-altitude interceptors. They flew a highly professional section attack and, when I realized my guns were jammed, I was able to clear out only after forcing them into a head-on attack. Their shots went over the top of my canopy and they broke off first—clearly not willing to die for Hirohito.

I do believe our equipment, the F4U, gave us the edge when we engaged a combat-ready pilot. They were just as aggressive as we, and just as courageous. Our good pilots were at least as good as theirs, but we lost our less-able pilots, as did they.

On April 18, 1945, 1st Lieutenant Jim Feliton, as division leader, and three others of us were scrambled northward to intercept bogies heading in from Japan. Feliton was a gutsy, no-nonsense person, and a very capable fighter pilot. He had a wry sense of humor, little use for the inefficient officer, and he had my respect.

We were vectored northwest of Okinawa to intercept a bogey making bombing runs on one of our picket ships. It was one of those days when visibility was unlimited—no clouds, no haze.

We were about 30 miles north of Ie Shima, still on radar vector, when we were told that we were in the bogey's vicinity. I spotted a Kawasaki Ki-48 Lily light bomber way below us. It was low and alone, south of the destroyer. When I first saw the Lily, it was beginning a turn to the north, back toward the destroyer. The destroyer had already been hit. There was smoke and what appeared to be damage to the superstructure.

When I called out the bogey's position, Feliton replied that he didn't have it and that I should take the lead. We were somewhere between 8,000 and 10,000 feet when I rolled into my dive. We did not have external fuel tanks, so there was no time lost salvoing them.

Without exception I planned my firing approach to come in at either the 4- or 8-o'clock angle and level to the target. For a bomber, these are not the optimum approaches, and I was aware of the increased exposure to turret gunners. My reasoning, faulty or not, centered on my advantage in firepower, range of effective fire, and the increase in accuracy I obtained from that angle. Therefore, as I recovered from my dive toward the Lily, I reduced throttle some to keep from overrunning and closed to about 100 yards before firing my first burst from the 8-o'clock position.

When I started firing, I must have been less than 1,000 feet above the water. Concurrent with this observation was my noticing a large number of little white popcorn puffs appearing just ahead of and also below both me and the Lily. I immediately recognized this as antiaircraft fire from the U.S. ship. I couldn't blame them for shooting, but I wanted to get the heck out of there as soon as I fired.

We were closing rapidly on the destroyer as I fired. I realized the Lily was firing at me. Which gun I do not know, and I was too preoccupied to care. I led the Lily's nose with my pipper, squeezed off a short burst, saw the tracers on target, and followed immediately with a longer burst.

After my second burst, the Lily nosed over and crashed into the sea about 500 yards short of the ship. Maybe less. I can't be sure, for I was in no mood for measurements at that time. I immediately pulled up to the left to leave the scene and the Navy's antiaircraft fire.

I can only assume the Lily was in a bombing run and was not a kamikaze. It apparently had made one hit already, and I thought it was going in for the kill. Whether it was going to drop another bomb or crash into the destroyer is anyone's guess.

The rest of my division had remained above, circling. I rejoined on Feliton's instructions during my climb out. The second section then returned to Kadena because the section leader got oil on his windscreen and asked to return. I resumed my position as Feliton's wingman. We began loitering, waiting for another call.

After reporting the "splash" to control, we were immediately vectored south to intercept another target, which had slipped through our defenses. There was no one else nearer to handle the assignment. We poured on the coal; climbed to about 12,000 feet; and, after 20 minutes, I picked up a bogey heading toward Kerama Retto. It was at 2 o'clock and slightly high on a converging course. I remember thinking at the time that whoever was running the radar intercepts was really sharp.

Feliton picked up the bogey on my call. As we came into position to start our pass, Jim told me to hold my place while he made the first run to feel things out. He instructed me to take a position high on the port side as he went to the starboard side to commence the action. This was the attack position we had been taught to use when engaging bombers. Our target was a Nakajima Ki-49 Helen twin-engine heavy bomber, and it bristled with machine-gun turrets.

I watched Feliton roll into his run, make his reversal as he neared the Helen; and, a second or so later, break off and start in my direction. At the same time, he told me to take the bomber because his Corsair's guns were jammed.

I was surprised. This was totally unexpected. I just knew that when Feliton rolled in on his run that he would shoot down the Helen. I felt bad for him, knowing his disappointment, but, at the same time, I was elated to know that I had a chance for another kill.

The school solution to bomber attacks at that time was to place the attacking elements equally on both sides of the target at, approximately, the 11- and 1-o'clock positions. The attacks were to alternate—one from the starboard, then one from the port, and so on—with recoveries to the opposite side on completion of the run. The process continued until the target was destroyed. Firing was to commence when slightly high at the 4- or 8-o'clock position; break off was at 6 o'clock.

I had learned, when I shot down a Betty on my first engagement, on April 12, to press home the attack while I had the chance. The Japanese bombers were not Flying Fortresses, and a sustained firing pass would take them out. I also believed that a level—rather than a descending—firing angle from the 4- or 8-o'clock *through* rather than *to* the 6-o'clock position increased the target area and chances for sighting accuracy.

I rolled in to my right and flattened out during my reversal, firing a short burst as I closed at 8 o'clock, another burst as I went through 7 o'clock, and a frustrated long burst at 6 o'clock. My gunsight pipper was leading the nose of the Helen during the first burst, and I gradually let it slide back to the nose as my angle decreased and my distance from the Helen closed to where I could see the gunners.

I was frustrated because the Helen was still flying. I was sure I must have hit it, but I couldn't see any results. By the time I broke off, I was about 50 yards away from the enemy plane's stern.

During my pass, as I went in firing from the port side, I noticed a steady stream of tracers over and around me. I knew I was being fired on, but I was determined to press home the attack.

As I pulled up and to the right of the Helen, I realized my cockpit had filled with smoke. Certain that I had been hit and not wanting to go down in a flamer, I undid my seatbelt, opened the canopy, put one leg over the side, and started to climb out. Then I realized that the smoke had cleared! I sat back into the cockpit and checked all the gauges. All was as it should be, so I buckled up again.

The Helen's gunners had not hit me. I guess I was so concentrated on my gunsight that I failed to notice I had hit one of the bomber's engines. It was the enemy's engine smoke that had come into my cockpit.

On my second pass, I rolled in to my left. As soon as I was out of my reversal—high this time—I put the pipper ahead of the nose again and fired a long burst at a downward angle. I was coming in from the Helen's starboard side, and I opened fire from the 4-o'clock position.

Immediately after I commenced firing, a small winged object dropped from the underside of the Helen. I radioed Jim that the Helen was carrying a papoose. It was later identified as a Baka bomb, the first seen, and it carried a pilot for a one-way mission. The Baka just dropped, and I couldn't see if there was a pilot inside. I suspect the pilot of the Helen simply released the Baka to get rid of the increased drag.

During the next sustained burst—it was the same pass—the Helen's right engine seemed to jump out of its housing, along with pieces of the adjacent wing. Then that part of the wing flew off. The Helen rolled immediately on its right side and fell seaward like a bird with a broken wing.

Our work was done. There were no more bogies to chase that day. We were sent straight back to Kadena.

*Lieutenant Dewey Durnford ended his Okinawa tour with 6.333 confirmed victories. His score included 2 ancient Ki-27 Nate fighters on a kamikaze run on April 28; an extremely aggressive Val downed on June 3; and a third Nate, also on June 3. Durnford remained in the Marine Corps and shared credit in a victory over a Chinese Air Force MiG-15 in Korea. He retired as a colonel in 1971, following a tour in Vietnam.*

# TAMING THE 20mm

Lieutenant JOE ROBBINS, USN
VF-85 (USS *Shangri-La*)
Okinawa, May 4–11, 1945

*Joe Draper Robbins, a native of Chester, South Carolina, majored in textile engineering at Clemson College for over three years before entering the Navy flight program in March 1942. He earned his wings at Jacksonville, Florida, in December 1942 and joined VF-6 in March 1943, while that unit was transitioning into the F6F Hellcat.*

*Ensign Robbins's first victory was a Ki-57 Topsy transport, which he downed near Kwajalein on January 29, 1944. On February 16, 1944, he destroyed a Zeke over Truk.*

*When VF-6 returned to the States that spring, Joe Robbins was reassigned to VF-85, a new F4U Corsair squadron that was forming in Atlantic City.*

After the landing-gear bounce problem that had plagued early carrier-based F4U squadrons (VF-17 and VF-12) was corrected and the bubble canopy was installed, the F4U became a good carrier plane.

On August 24, 1944, VF-85 was expanded from thirty-six to fifty-four planes, and VB-85 was reduced from thirty-six to twenty-four SB2C dive-bombers. However, after the Japanese introduced the kamikazes in the Philippines in October 1944, even more fighters were needed on carriers. So, on December 24, 1944, VF-85 was expanded to seventy-two planes, all F4U-1Ds, and VB-85 was decommissioned.

In addition to being a good carrier plane, the F4U was a good dive-bomber. It could carry two 1,000-pound bombs. The pilot simply dropped his landing gear at the top of a dive in order to slow the airplane. Then he pulled the gear up when pulling out of the dive. So, on January 2, 1945, VF-85 was ordered to divide into a thirty-six-plane fighter squadron (VF-85) and a thirty-six-plane fighter-bomber squadron (VBF-85). Both squadrons would fly the F4U-1D.

On February 2, 1945, the *Shangri-La* docked at North

Island, San Diego. On February 3, VF-85's F4U-1Ds were flown ashore and left there. On February 5, new F4U-1Cs were hoisted aboard. We arrived at Pearl Harbor on February 13, and the ship remained there until April 10. This gave VF-85 a chance to get in some training with the new 20mm cannon; VBF-85 had a chance to train with the F4U-1D.

The squadron CO, Lieutenant Commander Warren Ford, had served with the Bureau of Ordnance before taking command of VF-85. The 20mm cannon was a new weapon for fighters. He liked it, and he was in the right place to be able to get it for his squadron. The 20mm cannon was a good gun. When a shell hit a target and exploded, it did a lot more damage than the .50-caliber gun could do. However, VF-85 was not the first squadron to take the 20mm-armed F4U-1C into combat. From USS *Breton* VMF-311 flew its first missions in cannon-equipped F4U-1Cs against ground targets on Okinawa on April 7, 1945. VMF-441 also had the 20mm-equipped planes.

On May 4, 1945, I was the leader of twelve F4U-1Cs assigned to fly target CAP over a picket destroyer located about 12 miles north of Okinawa. We took off from the *Shangri-La* in the early morning and headed toward our station over the destroyer. Once we reported on station to the ground-control unit, we were under its control. My division was assigned an altitude of 20,000 feet, the second division was at 10,000 feet, and the third division was at 5,000 feet. Except for a little haziness, the weather was good.

We had been on station only a short time when, at about 0830, we received a vector to the north. We were told the distance to the bogey and that it was below us. We had fuel in our belly tanks. These flights were about four hours long, so we didn't want to drop the tanks until we spotted a bogey and had to. I had my left hand on the switch to go to the main gas tank and drop the belly tank as soon as I saw the enemy plane.

The vector was ordered at about 0830, and the intercept was at 0838. The distance to the intercept was about 26 miles from our CAP station. We were all looking down when, all of a sudden, about thirty Zekes attacked us from above. When we saw the bogies for the first time, they were

**307**

already diving on my division. We hadn't seen them due to haze and because we had been told they were below us. These Zekes were escort cover for the kamikaze planes below, which the division at 5,000 feet intercepted.

I immediately switched tanks, dropped the belly tank, and made a sharp turn all at the same time. I had to. However, when I did this, the engine was not getting any fuel, so it stopped. It would have taken only a few seconds to switch and get suction again, but I didn't have that few seconds. You don't get suction when you are making sharp turns, and I was really making them.

My first turn was left, into my second section. My wingman was on my starboard side. I dropped my nose to the left and saw one of the Zekes coming up at the 10-o'clock position. It was a 30-degree deflection shot. I pulled the trigger. No guns! I had to keep my nose down because I had no engine.

I was banking right and then left as steeply as I could to keep them from shooting at me. Still no engine. I kept recharging the guns. No guns. I kept banking from one side to the other with the nose down, still losing altitude. I had at least four of the Zekes in my sights, but no guns! I tried to charge my guns at least six times.

Everybody was too busy to say anything on the radio. The first radio message I heard was from my wingman, Ensign Frank Siddall, who said he was hit. The Zekes shot down Frank and my second-section leader, Lieutenant (jg) Sonny Chernoff, and the two of them headed down to make water landings. Fortunately, no bullets had hit my plane.

I was at about 16,000 feet when my engine finally started. I followed Siddall down. He made a good landing in the water, and I stayed over him for about 35 minutes, until a destroyer picked him up. My fourth pilot, Ensign D. E. Meyers, followed Chernoff down and joined up on me after Sonny was picked up.

I soon discovered that, out of the four planes in my division, none could fire the 20mm cannons. Three days later a VF-85 CAP over our own ships was sent to altitude to test the guns. The pilots tested them at different altitudes on the way up and found that none of the 20mm cannons fired above 15,000 feet; the guns were just too cold. We checked with Washington, D.C., and learned that the flights on which the guns were to have been tested at high altitude had been canceled. Our squadron electricians made some heaters, and we got some others from the States in about two weeks. In the meantime, VF-85 was restricted to 12,000 feet until the heaters were installed. We still flew CAPs and target strikes below that altitude, but VBF-85, which was armed with .50-caliber machine guns, flew the higher CAPs. After taking off from the carriers, when in a combat area, everyone always test-fired the cannons. We had done so on May 4, but below 15,000 feet. After May 7, all VF-85 planes that went to high altitude test-fired their 20mm cannons at high altitude.

On May 11, 1945, I was on another early-morning takeoff to fly target CAP over our picket destroyer north of Okinawa. We had sixteen F4U-1Cs. Lieutenant Commander Ted Hubert, our exec, was the mission leader. Ted's division and one other were assigned to 12,000 feet; I was leader of the other two divisions, at 6,000 feet. Ensign Frank Siddall was my wingman again.

After about an hour on station over the picket destroyer, which was 12 miles north of Okinawa, we were given a vector to the north. As we had on May 4, we flew for about five minutes—about 25 miles—before sighting sixteen Zekes directly ahead and a little below.

My altitude was about 5,000 feet when they were sighted. They were at about 4,000 feet. I was leading the two divisions, and the second division was on my starboard. The Zekes were just flying together, in no particular formation. Some were probably kamikazes, but, from above, I did not see any bombs. I would rather have gone after the kamikazes if I could have told which ones they were; they were the ones that went after our ships. I spotted the enemy planes first and made a left turn. During the turn, I broke off to make a run on them. As I started down, they just broke up and went in all directions. The rest of the formation followed me down, each F4U pilot picking out a target.

I picked out one Zeke on the outside. It just took off, heading west, and dove down to about 1,000 feet. I was on its tail, and there were other Zekes and Corsairs going in the same direction. This was not the desired type of attack, but we had to get the Japanese as fast as we could, before they got to our ships. The Zeke and I were going about the same speed. I was in range, about 600 feet behind the Zeke, so I opened fire. No deflection. I aimed at the middle of the fuselage and fired one medium burst. Every third bullet was an explosive round. I could see damage to the tail, but no fire. The Zeke rolled over into a split-S and went down. That's the last I saw of it. Everything happened so fast, I couldn't tell if I hit the pilot. My 20mm cannon should have gotten through to him. I don't think there was any way he could have survived, but I didn't claim him because I didn't really see him crash or burn. The Zeke was listed as damaged. I didn't have the time to look, because there was another Zeke in my sights immediately.

The second Zeke came from my left. The plane just came over and parked in front of me. I probably made a slight left turn, and he was probably trying to make a run on Siddall and me and ended up there. I knew that this plane was not a kamikaze because the pilot was trying to attack me. Kamikazes carried bombs but had no guns, and the pilots did not have parachutes. The Zeke was about 750 feet away, within range, so I fired a medium burst. The plane caught fire. Except for the fire, I saw no damage. My gun camera filmed a parachute leaving the enemy plane, but I never saw the pilot bail out, because I looked left and saw a third Zeke.

The third Zeke was at 10 o'clock and out of range—about 2,000 feet ahead of me. The enemy plane was at about the same altitude as I was, 1,000 feet. I turned left about 20 degrees and started chasing it. Siddall and I chased it for about 10 miles before we came to a little island, Tari Shima, which was about 300 feet wide and two miles long.

I assumed that the Zeke pilot was going around the island, because he made a 30-degree left turn to get there. He was very close to Tari Shima and low—about 100 feet. Sure enough, he started a left turn when he reached the far end of the island. He was taking the only chance he had to shake us: He was trying to trick us into following him low around the island. We could not make tight turns in F4Us at low altitudes; the planes would stall and spin. Zekes could out-turn us and gain distance, then try to pull away and go home.

I pulled up while making a left turn. Then I made a right turn, and that set me up to make a head-on run at the Zeke when the pilot completed his tight turn around Tari Shima. I didn't tell Frank to keep on his tail. I didn't have to. He saw what I was doing and knew that one of us would get him. He had been my wingman for a long time, and a good one. He was always there with me. Most of the time, I didn't have to tell him what to do.

As it was, I had an easy head-on shot. The Zeke pilot was about 800 feet ahead of me when I fired. I was above him. This made an easy shot because I could aim ahead of him a little bit and let the sights move back into him. No deflection, just a high-to-low head-on shot. I gave the Zeke a long burst. I didn't see the bullets strike. I just pulled the trigger and the Zeke blew up. The plane was a big ball of fire. I took a southeast heading in the direction of our station.

It was only a couple of minutes before I saw a fourth Zeke. It was at my 11-o'clock position, headed toward me, but the pilot made a left turn that brought him on a course about the same as mine. I was at about 500 feet and he was lower. I started chasing him. Fortunately, he was going in the direction I wanted to go. He was out of range, and I had my throttle as far forward as possible. I was at only about 200 feet. He dove even lower to pick up speed and got down to between 10 and 25 feet above the water. I went down to about 100 feet. Frank Siddall was on my right wing. I was wide open—going 405 miles per hour—for at least 10 minutes, but I wasn't gaining on the Zeke. I couldn't stay wide open much longer or I would burn up my engine. Frank told me that sparks were coming out of my exhaust. My job was to shoot the *Zeke* down; I didn't want to be the one—with my wingman—to have to land in the water.

I had started out with 230 rounds per gun, but I had used up a lot of ammunition already and I wasn't going to waste any. There could be several more out there we could run into. I thought about how to use my firepower efficiently. If I fixed my sights on the Zeke in level position, my bullets would hit the water behind the plane. So, I raised my nose, and fired. By raising my nose I could send the bullets straight for about 800 to 900 feet. Then they would turn downward due to gravity. As in a deflection shot, I had to aim at the point at which the Zeke would be when the bullets got there.

After I fired the short burst, the Zeke hit the water, bounced back up, and kept going. But I knew I had hit it. The pilot hadn't bounced to throw off my aim; there is no way he could have seen me fire.

I pulled my nose up and fired again. He hit the water again, but he bounced back up. My guns were boresighted to converge between 700 and 750 feet. The Zeke was 1,000 feet ahead, so my cannon rounds were opening up again when they hit him. Only a couple of bullets could hit him each time I fired.

I fired again and, again, the Zeke hit the water and bounced back up. But, the fourth time, it went down to stay. The last Zeke had been the fourth aircraft I had shot at that day, but only the third I claimed.

It had been a long day. I was tired. We reported to our control ship and then Frank and I returned to the *Shangri-La*.

*Following two combat tours off Okinawa, VF-85 was involved in raids against Tokyo and other targets on mainland Japan from July 10 until the armistice, August 15. In fact, on August 15, 1945, Joe Robbins was within sight of the Japanese coast on a bombing raid when his flight was ordered to jettison its bombs at sea and return to the ship.*

*On August 22, 1945, Lieutenant Joe Robbins flew in a 1,000-plane dress formation over the U.S. carrier fleet, and he was in the 1,000-plane parade over Tokyo Bay on September 1, 1945, in honor of the peace treaty that was signed aboard USS* Missouri *that day.*

## EYE TO EYE

**1st Lieutenant BILL FARRELL, USMC**
**VMF-312**
**Okinawa, May 25, 1945**

*William Farrell, of Paterson, New Jersey, graduated from high school in February 1940 and worked for Douglas Aircraft until he was sworn in as a Naval Aviation Cadet in August 1942. He earned his wings and a commission as a Marine second lieutenant on August 1, 1943, and joined VMF-312 in October 1943. The squadron shipped out to the Pacific in February 1944 and served in the Central Pacific until its F4U Corsairs were catapulted from an escort carrier to Kadena Airfield, Okinawa, on April 9, 1945, only nine days after the island was invaded.*

*Bill Farrell's first victory claim came on April 16, 1945, when he and another Marine F4U pilot shared credit for destroying a Val divebomber during a kamikaze attack on the invasion fleet. A few weeks later, when about forty relief pilots arrived, all the veteran pilots were offered reassignment to the States. Farrell was one of only two senior squadron pilots who opted to remain in the war zone and continue flying combat missions.*

Following a predawn launch on May 25, 1945, my division, led by Captain Herb Valentine, flew about 60 miles north of Okinawa for a routine CAP mission. Herb and I were the only two pilots left from the original squadron. I believe our wingmen, 2d Lieutenant Malcolm Birney and 2d Lieutenant John Read, were on their first combat hop that day. Herb and I had shared a kill on April 16, but we had not had any air-to-air action since. We were extremely eager to bump into something.

Nothing happened. We just flew around under radar control for 90 minutes, at 10,000 feet beneath nine-tenths cloud cover. Just after we were relieved by another Corsair division, at about 0730, we made a big final left-hand circle before heading home. As we turned south, I looked up to

**313**

take a better look at something I had seen out of the corner of my eye. About 2,000 feet above me was a formation of a *bunch* of airplanes—a vee of three vees composed of what we later estimated to be eighteen Val dive-bombers escorted by eighteen Tojo and Zeke fighters. They were heading south quite slowly, toward Okinawa.

I called them out and everyone just pulled up toward the rear of the Japanese formation. All the fighter tactics we had ever learned went right out the window. We just pulled up and opened fire at whatever we could hit.

My first encounter was with the Vals flying in the rear vee formation. I am certain that they didn't know we were back there. They took no evasive action and, if there were rear gunners in the Vals, they never opened up on me. When I got to 600 to 800 feet directly behind the rear one, I put the gunsight pipper right on its tail and fired a two- to three-second burst. The Val started flaming and dropped off to the left. Then it blew up. I swung over just a little to my right, and there was another Val. The same thing happened to it. By then, there were planes flaming all around me.

As soon as the second Val blew up, I immediately pulled to the right again, onto the tail of a Zeke that was making a slight turn. I started firing into it and, as it went up in flames, I looked off to the side and saw that another Corsair was also firing into the Zeke. It was Lieutenant Read, with whom I shared credit for the kill.

It sure seemed easy. These airplanes were just catching on fire and blowing up. I had shot down three airplanes from 6 o'clock with single bursts of only two to four seconds each.

The formations—theirs and ours—were pretty well scattered. None of us had wingmen; we were all fighting alone. I had a lull, so I started looking around for more planes to shoot down. After three to four minutes of making sweeping turns, I saw a Corsair. I thought I better close in on it, but as I swung off I found a Tojo at about my 9 o'clock. As I cut over to my right to get to it, the enemy pilot spotted me and started to swing to his left to get on my tail. My turn was a little tighter than his, so I got in close to his tail and nailed him with a 25- to 30-degree deflection shot from very close in. He started burning immediately and went down.

Two to three minutes after I shot down the Tojo, I spotted

a Zeke down below me. It was diving away from the fight. I dived after him and opened fire. I know I knocked some pieces out of it, but I couldn't follow it down, so I did not claim this Zeke as a definite kill.

In the lull that followed, I kept cruising and searching for more targets. Finally, as I looked up off my starboard nose, I saw these two planes scissoring about 2,500 feet above me and off to the side. They were heading toward each other when one of them blew up with a big flash.

It never entered my mind that the survivor was the Japanese plane, so, as it made a turn in front of me, I closed up to join on its wing. As I got closer, within about 3,000 feet, I finally realized that the plane did not have the Corsair's familiar inverted gull wings. It was a Zeke.

I don't think the pilot had seen me, but I fired at him as soon as I realized what he was—even though I was out of range. He reacted by pushing over in a dive toward the water. As I fired my guns each time, I blew off a piece of the plane, but the recoil of my guns slowed me down, and I fell back out of range. The Japanese pilot made some turns and ended up leveling off over the water. I was finally able to pull in closer, and I got a good burst into the Zeke.

The plane started burning and slowing down a bit, so I chopped back on the throttle and pulled up right behind the right wing root, very close. Flames were shooting back over the cockpit, and the pilot started to climb out. As he looked over his shoulder, he saw me. He stared right into my eyes. He had on a leather helmet with fur around the edge, and a white scarf. At that moment his plane hit the water and exploded. I can still see his face.

*When the May 25 claims were tallied, Bill Farrell was credited with 2 Vals, a Tojo, and 1½ Zekes destroyed, plus another Zeke probably destroyed. He not only achieved ace status, he was awarded a Navy Cross for the day's work. Captain Herb Valentine, who scored 5 confirmed victories and a probable, was also awarded a Navy Cross. The Corsair that Bill Farrell saw as it was blown up in midair was piloted by his wingman, 2d Lieutenant Malcolm Birney, who shot down a Zeke before he was killed. In all, Valentine's four-plane Corsair division destroyed 9 Japanese fighters and 4 Val* dive-bombers, probably destroyed 2 additional fighters, and claimed damage on 2 more fighters.

Captain Bill Farrell flew 125 combat missions in F4U night fighters and jets during two Korean War tours. Though he served as commander of the Chu Lai Air Base in Vietnam—a nonflying job—Colonel Bill Farrell managed to fly 184 ground-support missions in jet attack bombers. Farrell retired from the Marine Corps with rank of colonel in June 1974.

## NIGHT RADAR INTERCEPT*

Major BRUCE PORTER, USMC
VMF(N)-542
Okinawa, June 15, 1945

Robert Bruce Porter, of Los Angeles, left the University of Southern California in 1940, at the end of his sophomore year, and was commissioned a Marine second lieutenant in July 1941. He shipped out to American Samoa in March 1942 with the first U.S. fighter squadron to be sent to that threatened front-line area. Following more than a year's rigorous training in Samoa, Captain Porter was transferred in May 1943 to VMF-121 as it was converting to the new F4U-1 Corsair fighter. By then a seasoned senior pilot, 22-year-old Bruce Porter downed three confirmed Zeros—one each on June 12, June 30, and July 17, 1943—and one Zero probable over the Russell Islands and New Georgia.

Porter returned to the United States in September 1943 and

---

*Porter, R. Bruce, with Eric Hammel. Ace!: A Marine Night-Fighter Pilot in World War II. Pacifica, California: Pacifica Press, 1985. Quoted with permission.

*briefly served with an operational training unit before volunteering to fly Marine Hellcat night fighters. Major Porter formed and commanded a Marine carrier night detachment in late 1944, was transferred to VMF(N)-533 on Engebi in early 1945, and took command of VMF(N)-542, already deployed at Yontan Airfield, Okinawa, on May 23, 1945.*

In the three weeks after I took command, VMF(N)-542 pilots flying lone-wolf missions destroyed just three Japanese aircraft with the loss of its second (and last) pilot of the war. I flew my share of the lone-wolf missions, but I was never vectored against a target during that three-week period.

June 15, 1945, was not a particularly noteworthy day. I received a letter from my fiancee, but all she really had to say was that I was approaching my twenty-fifth birthday in August. That only got me to wondering if I would live that long.

Early in the day, my flight officer told me that I was slated to fly a night CAP from 2000 until midnight. This pleased me because half the squadron's kills had been scored during this active period.

The night was completely dark; there was no moonlight whatsoever and an extremely thick cloud cover. I checked my airplane in the darkness, just as I always did before a mission, but that was more customary than practical; I could not see very much. My plane captain helped me on with my harness and told me that my radar and radios were in top working order. He gave me a thumbs-up and yelled in my ear, "Good luck, Major!" just before jumping off the wing.

I ran up the engine to check the magnetos. Everything there was fine, so I released the brakes and taxied slowly to the pitch-black runway. I told the tower that I was ready to go, and I was given immediate clearance to take off. I pushed the throttle lever forward and took my feet off the brakes. Within seconds, I was rapidly gaining speed. My feet worked the rudder pedals to keep me on an even keel, and I slowly pulled back on the stick. I became airborne with plenty of room to spare. As I cleared the abyss at the seaward end of the east-west runway, I retracted *Black Death*'s landing gear and prepared to climb.

Shit! For no reason I could fathom, nervous antiaircraft gunners aboard several of the numerous transports and warships anchored beyond the cliffs opened up on my night fighter. I had been ready to ease off the power, but I kept the throttle on full power and jinked around to the right in a very tight turn, pulling heavy gees all the way. The tracers did not even come close to my tail as the gunners tried to follow the sound of my engine in the pitch darkness.

My heart was hammering in my chest. I thought that I was going to get to 25 the hard way if this nonsense kept up. When I had a moment to spare, I shook my fist at the fleet I was aloft to protect and reoriented myself toward my patrol station.

As I headed out over the empty sea, I listened intently to the sound of *Black Death*'s engine and felt for unusual vibrations through the seat of my pants. Everything sounded and felt fine. Then I fiddled with the instrument lights to set them where they would be most comfortable for my vision in this night's total darkness. I tested each of my radios, primary and spare. All okay there. My radar was perfect, too. I armed my four .50-cals and two 20mm cannon and test-fired them—first the machine guns with one trigger, then the cannon with the other trigger—just a squirt from each to reassure me that they would fire when I needed them. My fuel supply was normal.

As had become my habit, I said a little prayer of thanksgiving for the wonderful, dedicated people who had come into my care and who returned my good feelings and hopes by looking after me.

I reported my position to "Handyman," my Ground Control Intercept (GCI) officer on Ie Shima. (I learned many years later that he was Captain Bill Ballance.) Procedure dictated that Handyman not respond until he had read my IFF (Identification, Friend or Foe) signal, an automatic emission of changeable radio pulses that were keyed to his master radar set. Anything flying that did not emit a proper IFF signal was considered a bogey, an enemy contact.

"Hello, Topaz One from Handyman. Vector one-two-zero, angels ten, and begin CAP. Report when at altitude. Roger and out."

I was already in a climb and passing through 6,000 feet when the order arrived. I turned to the new course and continued to climb to my patrol altitude.

"Handyman from Topaz One. Angels ten. Starting CAP. How's business tonight?"

"Topaz One from Handyman. Pretty quiet. I bet it's black up there tonight."

I told him that it was indeed black. On clear nights, I had often been able to see signs of night battles between our ground forces and the island's remaining Japanese defenders. And I had once seen a distant fiery explosion in an adjacent sector when, I suppose, a night fighter from another squadron scored a kill. But on the night of June 15, there was solid cloud between me and the ground, though I was safely above the weather.

I flew lazy circles for the next 45 or 50 minutes. Without help from Handyman, there was little chance of my finding a target. I did remain vigilant in the event the Japanese sneaked one of their night fighters onto my tail.

Suddenly, my GCI officer called excitedly: "Hello, Topaz One from Handyman. I have an unidentified bogey for you. Target range thirty miles at 10 o'clock. Angels thirteen. He's indicated one-seven-zero knots. Handyman out."

Well, that started my adrenaline flowing. The intruder had 3,000 feet on me and was quickly closing. I dropped my belly tank and threw the throttle all the way forward, which added considerable power by engaging the water-injection system. This was good for an extra 15-knot burst of speed in emergencies. I also increased the engine RPM and nosed up into a steep climb. I made sure my guns were armed.

While one part of my mind was attending to putting *Black Death* in a position to score a kill, I reflected on something my old buddy, Major Jeff Poindexter, had observed aloud during a recent get-together. I had failed to note, during my first combat tour at Guadalcanal and the Russells, that I had scored a kill every time I had shared the sky with Japanese aircraft. I had protested to Jeff that the observation hardly rated a response since I had had the honor on only three days. Still, my mind went to Jeff's point as soon as the GCI officer announced the intruder. I found myself muttering, "Don't screw up now, Bruce."

Handyman reeled off the distances. Fifteen miles . . . ten miles . . . six miles.

"Hello, Topaz One from Handyman. Target range three miles at 11 o'clock. Bearing one-one-zero. Target crossing your screen. Go!"

I changed course and muttered aloud, "Steady, Bruce. This is it."

If Handyman had vectored me correctly, I would be turning right onto the bogey's tail. If not, I was going to be flying up nothing but empty sky.

I flipped on my finder as I came out of the turn. (The radar was on, but we kept the screen off to preserve night vision until we knew a target was out there.) My eyes became riveted to the orange scope on my instrument panel.

Nothing there yet. I was glad to note how cool I was. This was just like a textbook practice mission, of which I had flown hundreds. I was on full instruments and radar. All I needed to do was remain steady and do what my instruments and Handyman told me to do. If I trusted in the system, I would be coaxed into a perfect firing position. If the Hellcat could have flown itself, there would have been no need for me. I did precisely what I was told, totally without ego.

Bingo! My scope indicated a tiny orange blip at the very top. I was dead on target. The bogey was straight ahead. It had been a letter-perfect vector.

"Handyman from Topaz One. Contact!" I winced slightly when I heard my voice crack with excitement. I would rather have shown a better brand of professionalism.

I watched as the blip got larger and closer to the center of the radarscope, which represented my position. The bogey remained dead ahead, flying straight and level, as I crept up on its tail.

My ghost blip, which indicated the bogey's altitude relative to me, rapidly clarified itself. It appeared that the bogey was just a little higher than *Black Death*.

I flicked my eyes up to see if the target was as yet in sight. I thought I saw something so, after one more check of the scope, I peered at a slight ripple of movement dead ahead and slightly above my direct line of sight. A second or two later, I was staring at the bogey's exhaust flame.

My long training with similar practice approaches gave me ample reason to believe that the bogey was only about 350 feet ahead of me. He was within *Black Death's* boresighted firing cone. I flew in a little closer in order to positively identify him as an enemy warplane and to see precisely what I was facing. I was certain that he was an Imperial Army Kawasaki Ki-45 Nick twin-engine night fighter. Thus, there was an outside chance that he would be able to find me before I could open fire.

I climbed slightly to get right over him and then marginally increased my speed to close up. If he did not detect me and did not change course, this was going to be a sure kill.

As I nosed down slightly to bring all my guns to bear, I decided to fire everything in my armory. When I was in the best possible position and only 300 feet from the target, I gently squeezed both triggers. My .50-calibers roared and the 20mm cannon blew off rounds in a surprisingly slow, steady manner: *Bonk . . . Bonk . . . Bonk.*

My initial target was the right engine and right side of the fuselage, where some fuel was bound to be stored. *Black Death's* outpouring of lead had a literal buzzsaw effect upon the enemy airplane.

I eased off the 20mm because of a limited supply of ammunition, but I kept putting .50-caliber armor-piercing and armor-piercing incendiary rounds into the fuselage. I wanted him to burn so I would know beyond a doubt that I had scored a kill. Licks of flame showed up on the leading edge of the wing. Then a fiery orange tongue swept back over the fuselage. Suddenly, the twin-engine airplane stalled and lurched heavily to the right. My rounds poured into her vitals. I saw tracer strike the canopy. I doubt if the pilot ever knew what hit him.

It was over in about two seconds. When the Nick nosed over and fell away toward the sea, he was wrapped in flames from nose to tail.

Okay! My fourth confirmed kill!

"Hello, Topaz One from Handyman. He's off my scope at 2118. Great work."

I looked at my watch and thought I was taking it calmly.

Handyman brought me back to the center of my patrol sector and left me cutting lazy circles in the sky. I needed the time to collect myself. As soon as the thoughtful flying was over, as soon as I was parked in orbit, my heart leaped against my ribs. Oh, joy! I had been at bat four times and I had definitely downed four of the enemy. I paused a moment to dedicate this kill to my departed comrade, Major Jack Amende, who had not once scored in his many combat missions.

Without knowing quite what led me to it, I began thinking about the efficacy of the night-fighter program. I had been steadily training for the kill I had just scored for fourteen months. I knew that some of my fellow night stalkers in 542 and the other squadrons would never score, despite over a year of preparation. Given the resources we had committed to the night-fighter program, we had not scored all that many kills at night. I was not then (and am not now) certain that we had much effect on the outcome of the war. Certainly, we were not affecting the war as much as the very thin day squadrons composed mainly of tyros had in the latter half of 1942. The successful completion of all the missions flown by all the enemy planes we had thus far destroyed over or around Okinawa would not have had an overall negative effect on the outcome of the Okinawa campaign and, certainly, of the war. We had done good things, I knew, but I could not help musing on what it took to score even one night kill. Given the resources engaged in night work, with my first night kill I had just become a member of a minuscule fraternity. As far as I knew, the Marine Corps had yet to produce one exclusive night-fighter ace—that is, a pilot who scored five kills only during night missions. (The Marine Corps' only pure night ace, Captain Bob Baird, of VMF(N)-533, was exactly a week away from his fifth and sixth night kills.)

On the other hand, I also realized that the thrust of the night-fighter program was aimed at putting up 'round-the-clock protection during the projected invasion of Japan, which was set to begin, we were all certain, between late August and late September. Perhaps, I mused, the all-out, 24-hour air assaults we expected to meet in Japan were the justification. Perhaps all the operational night patrols leading to that climax were meant to shake us down, to prepare us for the ultimate confrontation. My own use of a mixed armory incorporating 20mm cannon was an experiment aimed at refining our killing capacity. It was, I realized, still too early to reach conclusions. Early? We were still really infants.

I played tag with my mind that way for about an hour without ever really lowering my vigilance, which was so ingrained that I swear I kept it up on the ground.

I heard from Handyman again almost exactly an hour after he had called out the first bogey: "Hello, Topaz One from Handyman. I've got another bogey for you."

Wow! A double night contact! As far as I knew, this was only the fourth such the squadron had encountered since deploying on Okinawa in mid-April. Two of the three double contacts had resulted in dead night stalkers.

"Handyman from Topaz One. Roger that. Out." Damn! My voice had again cracked under its burden of excitement.

"Topaz One from Handyman. Bogey at angels fourteen. Indicated one-eight-zero knots. Vector one-four-five at angels thirteen."

This guy was coming through high and fast. I would have to race him to the projected contact point.

"Handyman from Topaz One. On my way."

I pushed the throttle forward to get the water injection going, then I hauled back on the stick to rush to the required altitude. Even with luck, I was facing a difficult chase. I had the speed advantage, but it would take time to close on him because I had to use most of my power to climb.

As I climbed, I realized that I might face a problem with friendly antiaircraft. Our courses looked like they might converge right near the edge of the fleet's free-fire zone. Any airplane overhead was fair game for fleet gunners, except at rigidly designated times (such as during our night changeovers, I grumped, as I vividly recalled my hot reception over the fleet earlier that evening). It was clear from the vector that the bogey was going to try to strike the fleet. This led me to briefly consider that he might be a *kamikaze,* but that was doubtful because suicide missions were rarely launched at night, and even more rarely by lone aircraft. Most likely, he was a bomber, possibly a multi-engine bomber with a firm target.

I reached 13,000 feet and leveled off for my approach. Ahead, I could see fingers of light reaching into the black sky—searchlights. Farther on was Okinawa's west coast.

Suddenly, it seemed as if I would not overtake the bogey in time to set up an approach and a good shot before he reached the point where I would be forced to abort my run. Earlier in the month one of our pilots, 1st Lieutenant Bob Peterson, had locked onto a Nick but had been thrown around when a friendly antiaircraft round had burst beneath his Hellcat. Bob had not been able to reacquire the target; he had been lucky just to survive his encounter with the fleet. There was no way that I was going to fly into the fleet's antiaircraft pattern. No way!

But I was not out of the running yet. I flew up to 14,000 feet per Handyman's instructions (he must have thought at the outset that the bomber would drop down once it neared the fleet, but it did not). As I leveled off, I saw that my full-power setting had brought my speed up to 260 knots, or 300 miles per hour. As with all tail chases, it seemed to take an eternity to note any relative progress. Handyman kept reading off the closing distances, and I kept monitoring the rapidly approaching pillars of light from the anchorage ahead.

"Topaz One from Handyman. You're closing fast. Range about three quarters of a mile. Target at 1 o'clock and flying straight ahead. Go!"

I flipped on my finder for the second time that night. The scope flared orange. The bogey was right at the top of the scope and just a little way down toward the 1-o'clock position.

"Handyman from Topaz One. Contact!"

My closure rate was now too fast. If I kept it up, I would overshoot before being able to line up my gunsight. I eased back on the throttle, but the blip remained too large. Maybe he was throttling back, too.

Then I saw flames from the exhaust stacks. He was definitely a twin-engine airplane, but it was still too early to identify the type. The twin flickering exhaust flames seemed about to leap through my windscreen.

The real danger was that he was a bomber with a vigilant rear machine-gunner. If there was a stinger, I stood a good chance of being shot out of the sky.

I dropped down a little so the bogey would be silhouetted against the dark canopy overhead. As dark as the sky was, the solid airplane would still stand out against it.

My quarry was definitely a Betty medium bomber—a fast, maneuverable thoroughbred. It had a stinger, all right—a 20mm cannon quite capable of bringing me down as I stalked toward his tail. The Betty was also carrying an external load on its belly. I thought it might be a so-called Baka bomb, a manned rocket-propelled suicide missile typically hauled to the target by a mother plane—the Betty—and dropped. (The Japanese called it *Ohka,* which means cherry blossom, but we called it *Baka,* which means stupid.)

There was no time to dwell on the accuracy of my surmise. Someone might see me and the Betty might get away.

I drifted upward a bit to get a good belly shot. By the time I reached a comfortable height, I had closed to within 250 feet. I put the illuminated gunsight pipper right between the body of the aircraft—right beneath the flight deck—and the right engine. Then I slowly squeezed both triggers.

For the second time that night, *Black Death's* four .50-calibers roared, and the two 20mm cannon slowly spit their flaming popcorn-ball rounds. The tracer and the popcorn balls fell right into the target area.

After only a second or two, the wing fuel tanks ignited in a garish explosion, and the sky in front of my windscreen was filled with an expanding ball of flaming fuel. I instinctively ducked as pieces of the Betty scraped along *Black Death's* wings and fuselage. Then I dived away as the first fingers of friendly tracer reached up around me from the darkened fleet beneath *Black Death's* wings. I caught a momentary flash as the Betty's cargo—definitely a Baka bomb—blew up. I supposed that the flames had reached its volatile propellant.

Burning sections of the bomber and its volatile cargo floated down to the surface of the sea, where they were quenched.

"Handyman from Topaz One. Did you get the picture on your scope?"

"Topaz One from Handyman. Roger that. Congratulations. The time is 2226 on confirmation. It's a kill, Topaz One. Resume patrol."

He brought me back to my patrol sector and left me hanging for an hour, until my relief was on the way. I got a heading that would bring me back to Yontan, and a friendly "good night." It was then 2335. I would be on the ground by midnight.

I made a routine landing at Yontan, right on time, and taxied up to *Black Death*'s revetment. I was surprised to see that a crowd was gathered just off the flight line.

The first person to greet me was my plane captain. He shook my hand and patted me on the shoulder. Next up was our flight surgeon, Dr. John Ellis. "Congratulations, Skipper, on your double header. Why don't you come to my tent now? I have a surprise for you."

By then other pilots and the ground crewmen on duty that night had crowded around to shake my hand and offer their good wishes. It was all a bit overwhelming.

Once Doc Ellis got me alone and into his tent, he emptied numerous two-ounce medicinal brandy bottles into a pair of tumblers. We clanked glasses, offered one another good health, and swallowed it all down.

Before I got to sleep that night, I heard from the squadron armorers that I had fired a total of 500 rounds of .50-cal and 200 rounds of 20mm for both kills. Since the squadron average was 785 rounds per kill, I was the squadron champ for kills per rounds fired—less than half the average. I chalked that up to having the 20mm cannon on board.

What a night! Handyman and I had scored a rare double night kill, and I had fulfilled my fondest ambition as a fighter pilot. I was an ace!

*Bruce Porter never again shared the sky with a Japanese airplane, thus preserving his record of scoring at least one victory on every occasion he faced the enemy. As far as is known, he was one of only two Marine pilots to score multiple victories in both F4U Corsair and F6F Hellcat fighters.*

# EPILOGUE

## THE LAST DOGFIGHT

**Captain JOE LYNCH, USMC**
**VMF-224**
**Southwest Kyushu, July 2, 1945**

*At age twenty Joseph Paul Lynch entered the Naval Aviation Cadet program, in June 1941. He earned his wings and a Marine Corps commission in May 1942. His first combat tour was in the South Pacific, with VMF-112, for which he flew F4F Wildcats and transitioned into F4U Corsairs. Lieutenant Lynch was shot down once in the Solomons, but he ended his tour there with credits for 3½ Japanese fighters, all downed in January 1943. After spending over a year back in the States training pilots at Jacksonville, Florida, Captain Lynch returned to the Pacific with VMF-155, which defended the Marshall Islands. He was subsequently transferred to VMF-224 for combat duty as a Corsair division leader on and over Okinawa.*

Chimu fighter strip was on that portion of Okinawa closest to Japan. My squadron, VMF-224, had been sent to Chimu Airfield from Yontan Airfield for the purpose of early interception of aircraft in the event of enemy attack on Okinawa and for the purpose of mounting fighter sweeps over Japan itself. On July 2, 1945, we flew our Corsairs, equipped with auxiliary belly fuel tanks, from Chimu on a fighter sweep to Kyushu. Our goal was to try to draw the Japanese fighters into the air and engage them in a dogfight. I led one division of four planes from our squadron, and Major Mike Yunck of VMF-311 led a division of four from his squadron. The other three pilots in my division were 2d Lieutenant Lowell Truex, 2d Lieutenant Denver Smiddy, and 2d Lieutenant Schleicher.

It was a beautiful, bright-blue–sky kind of a day, and our flight to Kyushu was uneventful. When we were well up over the landmass of Kyushu, we began flying back and forth, generally on a north-south axis. We were at 20,000 to 21,000 feet altitude. On one of our southern legs, shortly after we had arrived on station and with Mike's flight off to my right, I was searching the sky in all directions. Suddenly I saw a tremendous group of Japanese fighters about 3,000 feet below our flight. They were streaming from dead ahead and back toward my 7- or 8-o'clock position. I had never seen so many Japanese fighters in one group since my days on Guadalcanal, and it was the *first* time that I ever had altitude advantage in the entire war. I identified those planes as Zeros as soon as I spotted them.

I "tallyhoed" and told everyone to drop their belly tanks. Just as I made my release, someone radioed, "You dropped your tanks, Joe." I rocked my wings—the attack signal— and rolled left almost into a split-S. Then all four of us made a nearly vertical dive right down into the formation.

Mike Yunck's division attacked this large fighter formation when we did, so our attack amounted to eight Corsairs engaging what we estimated later to be about eighty Japanese fighters. Maybe it was forty under my formation and forty under Yunck's, but, in any event, there was certainly a big group of them.

The Japanese fighters seemed to be very shiny, as if they were unpainted, still with the original aluminum showing. They were flying in just about perfect formation. As we dove on them, I couldn't perceive that they had spotted us as yet. Most of the formation had passed beneath us before I attacked with my division, and they had not made any move that would indicate that they had seen us.

I tried to get my sights on the leader, but doing so would

**328**

have caused me to pull flat in the midst of their whole group, so I settled on another plane. Its pilot may or may not have been an element leader. I managed to hit that plane in the engine from above as we dove through the formation. Immediately after going through the group, I pulled up through it again, trying to maintain my speed advantage. As I came up through what was now a breaking-up formation, I picked out another plane and fired. I hit it in the right wing and belly area. I flew almost straight up and past that plane and saw another one slightly off to my right. It was in a slight right turn. Finally, after I scored a great number of hits, this fighter caught fire. It showed cherry-red flames under the belly. I think the pilot might have left the right side of his cockpit and bailed out over the right wing. That plane had taken many hits in the fuselage before I saw flames. These fighters did not catch fire and explode as quickly as those we had encountered in the Guadalcanal area.

The dogfight raged on—and I mean raged. The sky seemed to be full of fighters flying and arcing up and down and in all directions. Tracers were streaming. It was spectacular. That's the only word I can use to describe the action. I had many more shots at many more planes and received credit for destroying 2. Lieutenants Smiddy and Truex got 1 each. Mike Yunck got 2 also, and two of his VMF-311 pilots scored 1 each. Mike and I both made ace in that fight.

The sky was full of planes. Then, as often happens in a dogfight, almost as if by magic, the sky was clear. Suddenly, the whole melee was over. I had just started to look for another Corsair to join up with when my right wing exploded before my eyes and a shell slammed into the armor plate behind my back. I never really saw who got me. All I saw was a glimpse of a plane in my rearview mirror, and I don't know if it was one plane or a flight of them.

The three .50-caliber machine guns in my right wing were blown right out of their mounts, the right aileron appeared to be shattered, and what ammunition I had left caught fire and began exploding. The wing became totally engulfed with flames, and I was choking from the cordite fumes that filled the cockpit and seeped right through my oxygen mask. The plane went into a 45-degree dive. I slipped the canopy back in order to bail out if I had to. I think the canopy had been partially shot off its tracks when I first got hit, so it was not difficult to get it open. I had very little control in the dive, which started at about 18,000 feet. As the plane fell, the flames subsided and the fire went out. I had a sense that I was dropping so fast that the flames sort of blew out. I kept doing everything I could to regain full control, and I finally hit on the right combination. I managed to level off at about 1,500 feet, luckily heading in the direction of Okinawa. I say "combination" because, when I finally got the plane flying straight and level, I had full right rudder on and had my left knee locked around the control stick. The plane wanted to roll over to the left, but, by being very careful on the controls and flying at full throttle, I was able to keep it in the air at about 110 knots airspeed.

After I leveled off, I noticed that the twisted metal in the right wing began to glow red. I thought, "How can the fire be starting up again?" Then it dawned on me that the metal had been white hot and that, as it was cooling, it went to red. The color eventually faded. It did give me a scare, though.

I was over water at this point and headed for Okinawa, which was over 300 miles away. I don't know why the Japanese fighters didn't follow me down and finish me off, but I imagine they saw me so engulfed in flames that they wrote me off.

The trip back was slow, uncomfortable, and uneventful until a Corsair joined with me as I neared Okinawa. He looked me over and radioed news that the plane was riddled with shell holes and he didn't know what was keeping it in the air. I didn't know either because, as I looked through the hole in my right wing, I could see the ocean below me. I figured that the hole was so large that a six footer could have dropped through it lengthwise, without touching head or toes on the jagged metal. The Corsair pilot told me that my belly tank was still attached to my plane. Evidently it had not released; the transmission I had heard at the start of the fight—"You dropped your tanks, Joe"—must have been directed at Lieutenant Joe Driscoll, who was flying in Mike Yunck's division. Talk about sitting on a time bomb! That tank was probably full of fumes. The way my Corsair had been blazing should have exploded that tank. My guardian angel was working overtime.

By the time I reached Okinawa, I had managed to climb to only 4,500 feet. I had the plane headed directly at a small mountain just beyond Chimu. I had been nicked by small particles of shrapnel on my right side, and my right leg was trembling from the sustained effort of pushing full right rudder for several hours. Attempting a landing was impossible. I happily bailed out. I dove out toward the trailing edge of the right wing and, as I fell clear of the plane, I saw how badly it had been shot up. Vought Aircraft came up with a good one when it designed the Corsair. The Corsair brought me home.

I landed hard in my chute a few hundred yards from the fighter strip at Chimu. By the time the flight surgeon got through treating my injuries, the story of our dogfight had already been told. I think it was at that point that the idea that we had engaged Tonys crept into the story. A combat correspondent had already gathered the salient facts and was writing them up for publication. Six of us were officially credited with shooting down 8 Tonys.

In the official report, I was quoted as saying that "the enemy pilots were aggressive and used very good tactics." I don't know what unit they belonged to, but I'll say this— they were among the very best fighter pilots that I ran into during the war, in my two combat tours overseas. I never ran into any "easy" Japanese fighter pilots. The Zero pilots at Guadalcanal were skilled, tough, and aggressive—at least, the ones I faced were. The pilots over Kyushu on July 2, 1945, were every bit as good. They were tough customers.

*Long after the war, aviation historian Henry Sakaida turned up evidence identifying the eight Japanese fighters destroyed over Kyushu on July 2, 1945, as being Kawanishi N1K2-J George interceptors flown by the Imperial Navy's crack 343d Air Group. It is not surprising that Captain Joe Lynch and his fellow pilots misidentified the Georges as Zeros or even Tonys, for the Georges, which had self-sealing gas tanks, were very rare birds indeed. Fewer than 500 were ever built.*

*Joe Lynch remained in the Marine Corps until 1956. In that year, following a helicopter crash, he was medically retired with the rank of lieutenant colonel.*

From July 2, 1945, to the end of the war, U.S. Marine pilots were credited with only 18 additional victories, and 11 of them were single bombers on night-heckler missions.

From December 9, 1941, when 2d Lieutenant David Kliewer and Technical Sergeant William Hamilton shared in the destruction of a Japanese twin-engine bomber over Wake Island, until 0308 on August 8, 1945, when 2d Lieutenant William Jennings downed a Ki-61 Tony fighter 11 miles off Okinawa, Marine pilots and gunners were credited with the destruction of 2,439 Japanese aircraft.

Two U.S. Army Air Corps pilots—2d Lieutenant Kenneth Taylor and 2d Lieutenant George Welch—are credited with the first three air-to-air victories of the war against Japan. They scored these victories over Pearl Harbor on December 7, 1941. The last of 5,214 Japanese aircraft claimed by U.S. Army pilots in the war was an Imperial Army Ki-84 Frank fighter downed at sea off Japan at 1215, August 14, 1945, by an unknown member of a flight of the 35th Fighter Squadron.

The first U.S. Navy aviator to down a Japanese airplane in World War II was Aviation Radioman 1st Class William Miller, a rear-seat gunner in an SBD dive-bomber from Scouting Squadron 6. Miller's plane had been launched from the *Enterprise*, off Oahu, just as the Japanese were starting the Pacific War. Miller downed a Zero over Barbers Point. The first U.S. Navy fighter pilot to score a victory in the war was Lieutenant (jg) Wilmer Rawie, of VF-6, who downed a Mitsubishi A5M Claude fighter over Roi Island, Kwajalein, during the raid on the Marshalls on February 1, 1942. Thereafter, Navy pilots and gunners scored 6,826 aerial victories in the war, including several handfuls in Europe and over North Africa.

The last U.S. aviation combat victory in World War II was scored by Ensign Clarence Moore of VF-31, who shot down a D4Y Judy dive-bomber at sea at 1400, August 15, 1945.

# GLOSSARY AND GUIDE TO ABBREVIATIONS

**A-20**  USAAF Douglas Havoc twin-engine light bomber
**A5M**  Imperial Navy Mitsubishi Claude fighter
**A6M**  Imperial Navy Mitsubishi Zero fighter (aka Zeke or Hamp)
**A6M2-N**  Imperial Navy Nakajima Rufe Zero-type float-plane fighter
**AA**  antiaircraft (gunfire)
**Abdul**  Imperial Army Nakajima Ki-27 fighter
**ack-ack**  antiaircraft gunfire
**Airacobra**  USAAF Bell P-39 or P-400 fighter
**AirSols**  Aircraft, Solomans
**Angels**  altitude in thousands of feet (e.g., Angels 12 = 12,000 feet)
**API**  Armor-Piercing Incendiary ammunition
**AT-6**  USAAF North American Texan advanced trainer (also USN/USMC SNJ)
**AvCad**  Aviation Cadet
**Avenger**  USN/USMC Grumman TBF or TBM torpedo-level bomber
**AVG**  American Volunteer Group (Flying Tigers)
**B-17**  USAAF Boeing Flying Fortress four-engine heavy bomber
**B-24**  USAAF Consolidated Liberator four-engine heavy bomber
**B-25**  USAAF North American Mitchell twin-engine medium bomber
**B-26**  USAAF Martin Marauder twin-engine medium bomber

**B5N**   Imperial Navy Nakajima Kate torpedo bomber

**B6N**   Imperial Navy Nakajima Jill torpedo bomber

**Baka**   Japanese Yokosuka MXY7 Ohka piloted bomb

**bandit**   enemy airplane

**Betty**   Imperial Navy Mitsubishi G4M twin-engine medium bomber

**bogey**   unidentified airplane

**buster**   emergency (speed)

**C-47**   USAAF Douglas Skytrain transport (also Navy R4D)

**C6N**   Imperial Navy Nakajima Myrt reconnaissance plane

**CAP**   Combat Air Patrol

**Catalina**   USN/USMC Consolidated PBY twin-engine amphibian patrol bomber

**CAVU**   Ceiling and Visibility Unlimited

**CIC**   Combat Information Center

**Claude**   Imperial Navy Mitsubishi A5M fighter

**Corsair**   USN/USMC Vought F4U fighter

**CV**   fleet carrier

**CVE**   escort carrier

**CVL**   light carrier

**D3A**   Imperial Navy Aichi Val dive-bomber

**D4Y**   Imperial Navy Yokosuka Judy dive-bomber

**Dauntless**   USN/USMC Douglas SBD dive-bomber

**deadstick**   powerless landing

**Devastator**   USN Douglas TBD torpedo bomber

**Dinah**   Imperial Army Mitsubishi Ki-46 twin-engine high-altitude reconnaissance plane

**division**   USN/USMC four-plane tactical fighter unit

**E13A**   Imperial Navy Aichi Jake long-range reconnaissance floatplane

**element**   USAAF two-plane tactical fighter unit

**exec**   executive officer

**F1M**   Imperial Navy Mitsubishi Pete two-seat reconnaissance float biplane

**F4F**   USN/USMC Grumman Wildcat fighter

**F4U**   USN/USMC Vought Corsair fighter

**F6F**   USN Grumman Hellcat fighter

**FDO**   Fighter direction officer

**flight**   USAAF four-plane tactical fighter unit

**Flying Fortress**  USAAF Boeing B-17 four-engine heavy bomber

**Flying Tigers**  American Volunteer Group, Chinese Air Force

**FM-2**  USN General Motors Wildcat fighter variant

**Frank**  Imperial Army Nakajima Ki-84 fighter-bomber

**G3M**  Imperial Navy Mitsubishi Nell twin-engine medium bomber

**G4M**  Imperial Navy Mitsubishi Betty twin-engine medium bomber

**GCI**  Ground Control Intercept

**gee**  force of gravity (times 1)

**George**  Imperial Navy Kawanishi N1K high-altitude interceptor

**Hamp**  Imperial Navy Mitsubishi A6M Zero variant

**Hap**  derivative nickname for Hamp

**Havoc**  USAAF Douglas A-20 twin-engine light attack bomber

**Hawk**  USAAF Curtiss P-36 fighter

**Helen**  Imperial Army Nakajima Ki-49 twin-engine heavy bomber

**Hellcat**  USN Grumman F6F fighter

**Helldiver**  USN Curtiss SB2C dive-bomber

**HVAR**  U.S. High-velocity Aerial Rockets

**IFF**  U.S. Identification Friend-or-Foe radio device

**J2M**  Imperial Navy Mitsubishi Jack high-altitude interceptor

**Jack**  Imperial Navy Mitsubishi J2M high-altitude interceptor

**Jake**  Imperial Navy Aichi E13A long-range reconnaissance floatplane

**jaygee**  Lieutenant junior grade

**jg**  junior grade

**Jill**  Imperial Navy Nakajima B6N torpedo bomber

**Judy**  Imperial Navy Yokosuka D4Y dive-bomber

**Kate**  Imperial Navy Nakajima B5N torpedo bomber

**Kingfisher**  USN Vought OS2U reconnaissance floatplane

**Ki-21**  Imperial Army Mitsubishi Sally twin-engine heavy bomber

**Ki-27**  Imperial Army Nakajima Abdul or Nate fighter

**Ki-43**  Imperial Army Nakajima Oscar fighter

**Ki-44**   Imperial Army Nakajima Tojo fighter
**Ki-46**   Imperial Army Mitsubishi Dinah twin-engine high-altitude reconnaissance aircraft
**Ki-48**   Imperial Army Kawasaki Lily twin-engine light dive-bomber
**Ki-49**   Imperial Army Nakajima Helen twin-engine heavy bomber
**Ki-57**   Imperial Army Mitsubishi Topsy twin-engine transport
**Ki-61**   Imperial Army Kawasaki Tony fighter
**Ki-84**   Imperial Army Nakajima Frank high-altitude interceptor
**KIA**   Killed in Action
**LDO**   Landing Deck Officer
**Liberator**   USAAF Consolidated B-24 four-engine heavy bomber
**Lightning**   USAAF Lockheed P-38 twin-engine fighter
**Lily**   Imperial Army Kawasaki Ki-48 twin-engine light/dive bomber
**LSO**   Landing Signal Officer
**LST**   Landing Ship, Tank
**Mae West**   Rubberized inflatable life jacket
**Marauder**   USAAF Martin B-26 twin-engine medium bomber
**Me-109**   German Air Force Messerschmitt fighter
**MIA**   Missing In Action
**MiG**   Soviet fighter manufacturer
**Mitchell**   USAAF North American B-25 twin-engine medium bomber
**Mustang**   USAAF North American P-51 fighter
**Myrt**   Imperial Navy Nakajima C6N Myrt reconnaissance plane
**N1K**   Imperial Navy Kawanishi George high-altitude interceptor
**NAP**   Naval Aviation Pilot (enlisted)
**Nate**   Imperial Army Nakajima Ki-27 fighter
**Nell**   Imperial Navy Mitsubishi G3M twin-engine medium bomber
**OS2U**   USN Vought Kingfisher reconnaissance floatplane
**Oscar**   Imperial Army Nakajima Ki-43 fighter
**P-26**   USAAF Boeing all-metal fighter

P-36   USAAF Curtiss Hawk fighter
P-38   USAAF Lockheed Lightning twin-engine fighter
P-39   USAAF Bell Airacobra fighter
P-40   USAAF Curtiss Warhawk fighter
P-47   USAAF Republic Thunderbolt fighter
P-51   USAAF North American Mustang fighter
P-400   USAAF Bell export-variant Airacobra fighter
PBY   USN/USMC Consolidated Catalina twin-engine amphibian patrol bomber
Pete   Imperial Navy Mitsubishi F1M two-seat reconnaissance float biplane
PSP   Pierced Steel Planking
RAAF   Royal Australian Air Force
RAF   Royal Air Force
ROTC   Reserve Officers' Training Corps
Rufe   Imperial Navy Nakajima A6M2-N Zero-type floatplane fighter variant
Sally   Imperial Army Mitsubishi Ki-21 twin-engine heavy bomber
SB2C   USN Curtiss Helldiver dive-bomber
SBD   USN/USMC Douglas Dauntless dive-bomber
Seagull   USN Curtiss SOC scout-observation floatplane
section   USN/USMC two-plane tactical fighter unit
SNJ   USN/USMC North American Texan advanced trainer (also USAAF AT-6)
SOC   USN Curtiss Seagull scout-observation floatplane
TBD   USN Douglas Devastator torpedo bomber
TBF   USN/USMC Grumman torpedo bomber
TBM   USN/USMC General Motors Avenger torpedo bomber (same as TBF)
Thunderbolt   USAAF Republic P-47 fighter
Tojo   Imperial Army Nakajima Ki-44 fighter
Tony   Imperial Army Kawasaki Ki-61 fighter
Topsy   Imperial Army Mitsubishi Ki-57 twin-engine transport
TWA   Trans-World Airlines
USAAF   U.S. Army Air Forces
USAFFE   U.S. Army Forces, Far East
USMC   U.S. Marine Corps
USN   U.S. Navy
USS   United States Ship

## GLOSSARY AND ABBREVIATIONS

**Val**  Imperial Navy Aichi D3A dive-bomber
**VB**  USN bombing squadron
**VBF**  USN fighter-bomber squadron
**VC**  USN composite squadron
**VF**  USN fighter squadron
**VF(N)**  USN night-fighter squadron
**VJ Day**  Victory over Japan Day
**VMF**  Marine Fighter Squadron
**VT**  USN torpedo-bomber squadron
**Warhawk**  USAAF Curtiss P-40 fighter
**WIA**  Wounded In Action
**Wildcat**  USN/USMC Grumman F4F or General Motors
FM fighter
**Wirraway**  RAAF fighter
**YE/ZB**  USN radio homing beacon
**Zeke**  Imperial Navy Mitsubishi A6M fighter variant
**Zero**  Imperial Navy Mitsubishi A6M fighter basic model

# BIBLIOGRAPHY

Belote, James H., and William M. Belote. *Titans of the Seas*. New York: Harper & Row, 1975.

De Blanc, Jefferson J. *Once They Lived by the Sword*. St. Martinsville, Louisiana: Jefferson J. De Blanc, 1988.

Galvin, John, with Frank Allnutt. *Salvation for a Doomed Zoomie*. Indian Hills, Colorado: Allnutt Publishing, 1983.

Hammel, Eric. *Guadalcanal: Starvation Island*. New York: Crown Publishers, 1987.

_____. *Guadalcanal: The Carrier Battles*. New York: Crown Publishers, 1987.

_____. *Munda Trail: Turning the Tide Against Japan in the South Pacific*. New York: Orion Books, 1989.

Hoyt, Edwin P. *McCampbell's Heroes*. New York: Van Nostrand Reinhold, 1983.

Lundstrom, John B. *The First Team: Pacific Naval Air Combat from Pearl Harbor to Midway*. Annapolis: Naval Institute Press, 1984.

Mondey, David. *Concise Guide to American Aircraft of World War II*. London: Temple Press, 1982.

_____. *Concise Guide to Axis Aircraft of World War II*. London: Temple Press, 1984.

Olynyk, Frank J. *Victory List No. 1: USMC Credits for the Destruction of Enemy Aircraft in Air-to-Air Combat, World War II*. Aurora, Ohio: Frank J. Olynyk, 1982.

_____. *Victory List No. 2: USN Credits for the Destruction of Enemy Aircraft in Air-to-Air Combat, World War II*. Aurora, Ohio: Frank J. Olynyk, 1982.

_____. *Victory List No. 3: USAAF (Pacific Theater) Credits for the Destruction of Enemy Aircraft in Air-to-Air Combat, World War II*. Aurora, Ohio: Frank J. Olynyk, 1985.

——————— *Victory List No. 4: AVG & USAAF (China-Burma-India Theater) Credits for the Destruction of Enemy Aircraft in Air-to-Air Combat, World War II.* Aurora, Ohio: Frank J. Olynyk, 1986.

Porter, R. Bruce, with Eric Hammel. *Ace!: A Marine Night-Fighter Pilot in World War II.* Pacifica, California: Pacifica Press, 1985.

Potter, E. B. *Nimitz.* Annapolis: Naval Institute Press, 1976.

Schuon, Karl. *U.S. Marine Corps Biographical Dictionary.* New York: Franklin Watts, 1963.

Sherrod, Robert. *History of Marine Corps Aviation in World War II.* Novato, California: Presidio Press, 1980.

Stanaway, John. *Peter Three Eight: The Pilots' Story.* Missoula, Montana: Pictorial Histories Publishing Company, 1986.

Tillman, Barrett. *Corsair: The F4U in World War II and Korea.* Annapolis: Naval Institute Press, 1979.

——————— *Hellcat: The F6F in World War II.* Annapolis: Naval Institute Press, 1979.

——————— *The Wildcat in WWII.* Annapolis: Nautical & Aviation Publishing, 1983.

Toland, John. *The Rising Sun: The Decline and Fall of the Japanese Empire, 1936–1945.* New York: Random House, 1970.

Toliver, Raymond F., and Trevor J. Constable. *Fighter Aces of the U.S.A.* Fallbrook, California: Aero Publishers, Inc., 1979.

Y'Blood, William T. *Red Sun Setting: The Battle of the Philippine Sea.* Annapolis: Naval Institute Press, 1981.

# INDEX

## INDEX